AF791697

पुरातत्त्व
PURĀTATTVA

Bulletin of the Indian Archaeological Society

No. 33 2002-03

Editors
K. N. Dikshit and K.S. Ramachandran

D.K. Printworld (P) Ltd.
New Delhi

Cataloging in Publication Data — DK

[Courtesy : D.K. Agencies (P) Ltd. <docinfo@dkagencies.com>]

Purātattva : bulletin of the Indian Archaeological Society, no. 33, 2002-03 / editors, K.N. Dikshit ; K.S. Ramachandran.

p. 29 cm.

Includes bibliographical references.

ISBN 8124603251

1. Archaeology — India — Periodicals. 2. India — Antiquities — Periodicals. 3. India — Civilization — Periodicals. I. Dikshit, K.N. II. Ramachandran, K.S. (Kattalai Sivasubramanium), 1939- III. Indian Archaeological Society.

First Published in 2003

First Reprinted in 2005

ISBN 81-246-0325-1

Price for volume 33 (2002-03): Rs. 1000 US $ 50

Reprint authorised by

Indian Archaeological Society

New Delhi - 110 016

© Indian Archaeological Society, New Delhi - 110 016

The Editors are not responsible for the opinions expressed by the Contributors.

Purātattva is published annually.

Manuscripts (whether in the form of articles or notes or book reviews) offered for publication should be sent to the Editor, Purātattva, Indian Archaeological Society, B-17, Qutab Institutional Area, New Delhi - 110 016.

Published and printed by:

D.K. Printworld (P) Ltd.

'*Srikunj*,' F-52, Bali Nagar

New Delhi – 110015

Phone : (011) 2545 3975, 2546 6019 Fax : (011) 2546 5926

E-mail : dkprintworld@vsnl.net

www. dkprintworld.com

PURĀTATTVA

CONTENTS

NOTES AND NEWS

MAJOR PROJECTS

BOOK REVIEWS

Obituaries

Dr. (Mrs.) Debala Mitra
14.12.1925 — 02.12.2003

Born on 14th December, 1925 at Ajagarah, District Khulna, now in Bangladesh, Dr. (Mrs.) Debala Mitra was educated at Khulna, Kolkata and later on in Paris. She had a brilliant academic career and was recipient of several scholarships, medals and prizes including the Griffith Memorial Prize from the University of Kolkata and B.C. Law gold medal from the Asiatic Society, Kolkata. She joined the Archaeological Survey of India in 1952, held different positions and retired as its Director General in 1983.

She was an archaeologist of international repute. She led a good number of expeditions in different parts of India and Nepal and of these the excavations carried out at Tilaurakot and Kodan in Nepal and Ratnagiri in Orissa are important. Though her specialised fields of research are Buddhist and Eastern Indian art, architecture and iconography, her contributions to Indian epigraphy, numismatics and history are also substantial. Her commitment to work was typical of her generation.

She is the author of the *(i) Buddhist Monuments, (ii) Excavations at Tilaurakot and Kodan and Explorations in the Nepalese Tarai, (iii) Telkupi – a submerged temple-site in West Bengal, (iv) Ajanta, (v) Sanchi, (vi) Bhubaneshwar, (vii) Konarak, (viii) Udayagiri & Khandagiri, (ix) Pandrethan, Avantipur & Martand, (x) Ratnagiri (1958-61) and (xi) Bronzes from Achutrajpur, Orissa, (xii) Bronzes from Bangladesh,* besides numerous other scholarly articles. Noted for meticulous details and objective assessment of facts, all her works stand out as models of archaeological research and investigation.

I called on her with Ms. Kapila Vatsyana and others on 10th Nov. 2003, that is the last image of her. She showed special warmth and affection. I have always admired her for this remarkable quality. She breathed her last on 2nd December, 2003 at her Kolkata residence and is survived by two daughters.

S.S. Biswas

K.V. Soundara Rajan
17.02.1925 — 08.05.2003

Born on the 17th February, 1925 at Cheyyur, Kanchipuram District, Tamil Nadu, to a family of traditionalists engrossed in *veda vritti,* and presiding pontiffs of the *Ahobila math,* K.V. Soundara Rajan, a versatile scholar, needs no introduction to scholars and academics in art, archaeology and architecture, in India and outside. K.V. Soundara Rajan graduated from the famous Madurai Draviyam Thayumanavar Hindu College and topped the Master's degree from the Allahabad University in Sanskrit with specialisation in Epigraphy and Ancient Indian Culture. He had a flair for English and was equally versed in Sanskrit and Tamil. Trained by Mortimer Wheeler and F.E. Zeuner in field archaeology and Prehistoric studies, Rajan in his career excavated several sites of varying nature in different parts of India.

Soundara Rajan started his career in the position of a Scholar in the Archaeological Survey of India in 1947. In the course of time, he became Pottery Assistant and Excavation Assistant in the Excavations Branch at Delhi, and was promoted as Superintendent in the Prehistory Branch, New Delhi in 1957–58. During 1964-68, he held the charge of the Temple Survey Branch, Southern Region, Madras. He rose to become Director at Delhi in 1975, Joint Director General in 1980 and retired as Additional Director General in 1983.

He made his mark in almost all the branches of Archaeology from excavations, prehistoric explorations, architectural studies, art history, epigraphy, iconography and numismatics to Muslim architecture.

His penchant for analytical perceptions of archaeological data and his belief that material remains cannot be studied in isolation without the total environment and ancillary frameworks of age is indeed commendable. His vast learning and knowledge of Sanskrit and Tamil texts enabled him to delve into the original sources and creditably interpret the data collected in the field of literature and art. His deep study of the *Silpa* Sastras and *Manasara* have enabled him to explain each metaphysical ideal behind an image, a culture, the human impulses and the longings of the human soul for connection with the cosmos.

The noteworthy lectures he delivered outside India are 'Megalithic Culture of South India', Department of Anthropology, Universtiy of Missouri, USA in 1971, 'Early Indian Art, An overview', Musee Guimet, Paris in 1971, 'Indian Art', University of Minnesota, USA in 1971, and five lectures on Archaeology, Classical Art and Islamic Architecture at Jerusalem Haifa Tel Aviv and Beersheva at the invitation from Israel Academy of Science and Humanities and Hebrew University.

Soundara Rajan has written more than four hundred articles and numerous books on Prehistory, Protohistory, Early history, Medieval history, Art, Architecture, Epigraphy, Numismatics and Relegion. His recent six volumes the 'Concise classified Dictionary of Hinduism' is perhaps the creation closest to his heart as the cardinal presentation of our cultural legacy.

Soundara Rajan along with his archaeological acumen had a passion in amateur drama, classical Carnatic music, sketching and trekking. His melodious voice, genial temperament, courtesy and kindness to all, his knowledge on varied subjects made him cherished in and outside the country.

His death on 8.5.2003 has indeed created a vaccum in the archaeological fraternity. The loss of such a versatile genius is inseprable to the nation. He is survived by three sons and his wife Mrs. Kumuda. We pray that the Lord grant peace to the departed soul and solace to the bereaved family.

K.S. Ramachandran

L.K. Srinivasan
15.12.1932 — 09.10.2003

Lakshmi Kumara Srinivasan, was born on 15th December, 1932 at Komaranapuram, a small village in district Mysore of the erstwhile Princely State of Mysore, now in Yelandur taluka of district Chamrajnagar, Karnataka State.

L.K. Srinivasan joined the fraternity of the Archaeological Survey of India as an Exploration Assistant on March 1957 in the South-Eastern Circle, Visakhapatanam, Andhra Pradesh and was posted at Chandrapur in Maharashtra between June 1957-September 1964. This was the beginning of his intimate association with the Survey which lasted for nearly thirty four long years till he relinquished his office in 1991 as Director. The age never came in his way and he kept himself busy in authoring research papers, bringing out felicitation volumes and more recently was the Associate Editor Encyclopedia of Hinduism, a joint venture of the Indian Heritage Research Foundation, Rishikesh and Columbia University, USA.

Among other branches of Archaeology, Srinivasan had a special fascination for the conservation and preservation of monuments. The inspection notes and guide lines drawn by him on restoration and conservation of monuments were comprehensive, scientific, precise and methodical.

Srinivasan was associated with the excavations in a number of sites like Harwan (1973-74), Pambarwan at Ambaran in Akhnoor (1973-74), Manda in Jammu & Kashmir; Mottur (1978-79) and T. Kallupatti (1976-77 and 1979-80) in Tamil Nadu; Hampi National Project, Hampi (1980-81, 1981-82 and 1982-83), Banahalli (1983-84), and Someswara Temple Complex, Bandalike in Karnataka.

The epigraphical studies and art history did not escape the attention of Srinivasan. He has critically studied and analyzed the art forms of the Gangas of Talkaad, the Hoysalas of Dwarasmudra, the Chalukyas of Badami and brought to light many interesting facets of the sculptural art of these schools.

As a Director, Srinivasan had long association with the Antiquity Branch of the Survey. This and his wide ranging experience made him a champion of antiquarian legislations. His interpretations and applications of these laws for the cause of archaeology were of the highest order and any archaeologist could hardly equal this achievement.

L.K. Srinivasan breathed his last on 9th October, 2003 after a brief illness at Bangalore and is survived by his wife and two sons.

C.B.Patil

PURĀTATTVA

Number 33 2002–2003

Editorial

The present number of *Puratattva* represents a panorama of Indian Archaeology. Among the articles included in this issue, one deals with the prehistory of Birbhum in West Bengal; others are Rigveda and the contribution of Rahul Sankrityayan, discussion on the veracity of Lothal being a port city, a never ending dispute among scholars, now joined by a Rear Admiral; salvage archaeology in Pune, besides full study of the inscription discovered at Ayodhya - completely deciphered and edited by an eminent epigraphist. Under the 'Notes and News' many new information has been gathered.

It is pertinent to mention about some of the major special projects sponsored by the Indian Council of Historical Research, New Delhi, and carried out by the Indian Archaeological Society such as "The Atlas of the Indus-Saraswati Civilization", "Growth of Cities in Ancient India" and "Salvaging and Conserving the damaged source material of history and archaeology in Gujarat". The final reports of the first two projects are under submission, whereas the last one on Gujarat has already been submitted.

Keeping in view the importance of Indian Ocean studies which have attracted much scholarly attention the Society also submitted a project 'History and Archaeology of Indian Ocean Trade' which was approved by ICHR in 2003. Excavations at Kamrej in district Surat, and Sanjan, district Valsad, both in Gujarat, were carried out by the Society; since so long only literary sources have been the main basis for historical reconstruction of the maritime history in India.

Dr. A.P. Khatri, a prominent prehistorian of our country has generously donated his palaeontological and prehistoric collections from the Narmada and Siwaliks regions to the Indraprastha Museum of Art and Archaeology managed by the Indian Archaeological Society. Presently he is preparing a catalogue of his collections.

It was suggested in the editorial of the last issue that excavated materials should also be displayed, besides organizing a photographic exhibition on the conservation works done by the Centre and State Departments of Archaeology on the occasion of the Central Advisory Board of Archaeology. This step was suggested so that the field-workers are acquainted with the excavated material of other regions and also the techniques involved in conservation.

It is with a heavy heart we are informing our readers the sad demise of Dr. Debala Mitra, former Director General, Shri K.V. Soundrarajan, former Additional Director General, Shri L.K. Srinivasan, former Director, all of the Archaeological Survey of India. In their death we have lost not only dedicated scholars but also good human beings. The archaeological fraternity will always remember the hard work and significant contribution made by them in the academic field.

The first "Dr. Y.D. Sharma Memorial Lecture" was delivered by Prof. B.B. Lal on 'Looking for the Authors of the Harappan Civilization' on 21st November, 2003 in the Conference Room of the National Museum, New Delhi. Shri M.N. Deshpande presided over the function which was arranged in collaboration with National Museum Institute.

The publication of this number of *Puratattva* has been possible due to financial support by the Archaeological Survey of India, Government of India and the Indian Council of Historical Research. However, these organizations are in no way responsible for the views expressed by the authors.

Thanks are due to Dr. S.P. Gupta for help and encouragement. The young colleagues from the Indian Archaeological Society deserve our appreciation. Ms. Gency Choudhury coordinated the printing of the journal with the press and Mahua Bhattacharyya extended all assistance in proof correction; Shri Manoj Harbola prepared the type-script and Ms. Rajrani provided references for the articles.

Thanks are due to Shrimati Anita Mehta of Aquarelle and members of her staff for bringing out this issue in such a short time.

K.N. Dikshit
K.S. Ramchandran

We mourn the sudden demise of Prof. Farzand Ali Durrani, a well-known archaeologist and the excavator of famous Early Harappan site of Rehman Dheri. He was the former Vice-Chancellor of the Peshawar University, Pakistan. He had visited India several times and given us the benefit of his erudite scholarship to all of us.

Farzand Durrani was a wonderful human being. His open-minded and forward-thinking ways will be sadly missed not only in Peshwar but across the world by all of those close to him.

Lothal: A Harappan Port Town Revisited

S.C. BINDRA*

Introduction

The discovery of the Harappan settlement of Lothal is one of the fascinating events of Indian archaeology. The most remarkable structure at Lothal is a burnt brick rectangular basin, measuring 219 X 37 m and connected to the acropolis by a large mud platform measuring 240 x 30 m, described by S.R. Rao. the excavator of the site, as a 'dock'. Rao has further argued that the structure proves that Lothal was a sea port.

Until the excavation of Lothal, direct evidence of Harappan maritime activity was limited to the depiction of boats on a seal and pottery from Mohenjodaro, and most likely, these represented riverine rather that sea going vessels. At the same time, it was an accepted fact that maritime shipping was a part of the Harappan trade and commerce. However, exploration by G.F. Dales (1962) and earlier excavations by Aurel Stein (1931), at Shakta-kah and Sutkagen-Dor along the Markan Coast, lent support to the possibility of sea-borne trade of the Harappans.

It was in this context of "strong presumption but lacking evidence that the discovery of a large basin, interpreted as a dock at Lothal assumed more than local interest" (Leshnik 1968:203). Indeed, Rao's discovery caused quite a stir. Not only did a number of statements expressing doubts on his interpretation of the structure as a dock appeared in print (Shah 1960; Leshnik 1968) but several Indian and European scholars expressed grave doubts in private on Rao's assertions (Leshnik 1968:211). A number of alternative usages of the structure were offered, which have been intensely debated but none of them has found universal acceptance.

The interpretation of Lothal as a sea port and the structure as a dock has already been accepted in the archaeological literature (Lal-1999-132-134; Chakrabarti-1995:99-102) but doubts still continue and the precise function of the structure and classification of Lothal as a sea port, still remain open question. The main reason, in our view, is that no exhaustive demonstration of the structure of its ship berthing role and of Lothal as a sea port has been offered so far.

With this background, we propose to have a fresh look on the various facts of the dock and port theories, with particular emphasis on the following issues:-

a) Operational efficacy of the structure as an 'inshore tidal basin' for berthing water transport.

b) Suitability of Lothal as a sea port, based on commonly accepted geographical, maritime and commercial attributes usually associated with ancient port towns.

*Rear Admiral S.C. Bindra (Retd.)P-8A, Hauz Khas Enclave, New Delhi.

Organisation of the Study

We will first define well-known marine concepts like 'harbour', 'port', 'dock', 'dockyard', 'open anchorage', etc. as we find that connotations of these terms are generally not correctly understood. Secondly, we shall examine the main controversial features of the dock, its environs, sea access from the mouth of the Gulf of Cambay, range and magnitude of the tidal activity in the area, and water transport requirements of Lothal.

Thirdly, the discovery and critical analysis of all the published views, both for and against on the subject will be examined. Attempt has also been made to marshal evidences from independent sources on disputed issues and offered views, based on my experience as a mariner.

Finally, in the 'Findings', all the hypothesis will be listed, which state that this structure served as a 'dock' and Lothal as a 'Port Town'.

Conceptual Connotations

A 'harbour' in marine parlance is understood as a 'stretch of water on the coast, which affords shelter to seagoing vessels' (Moore 1952:80) and a 'sea port' as a harbour with terminal facilities' (Mehta 1933:542-47). Similarly, 'entrepot' has been described as 'an intermediary centre of trade and trans-shipment' (Webster Dictionary 1993:387). An 'open anchorage', on the other hand, is a place suitable for anchoring vessels outside the confines of a harbour and a 'roadstead' is 'a place less confirmed than a harbour, where vessels can ride at anchor' (Webster 1993:1012).

A 'Dock' in general term can be described as an artificial basin or enclosure for the reception of ships with means of controlling the water height. The Webster Dictionary (1993:341) includes 'a waterway extending between two piers for the reception of ships' within the ambit of the definition of the word 'dock' H.P Oza however, describes it as 'an artificial enclosure having an entrance from a stream/sea for receiving shipping' (as quoted by Rao (1979:127)).

The term 'dockyard' denotes a yard, where ships are built and/or repaired. The expression 'dockyard' is also used in respect of Naval yards with facilities for berthing and repairing warships, underwater crafts and auxillary naval vessels. The usages of the term 'dockyard' as a synonym for the expression 'Dock' is a misnomer as the two words describe altogether different entities.

Harbours and Seaports

Some of the elementary requirements for the development of harbours in ancient times were, first, safe and sheltered anchorage and a quay or wharf from open sea; secondly, sufficient depth of water at anchorage/berth for vessels to stay afloat; and, finally, easy accessibility to and from the sea. On the other hand, availability of convenient landing and shipping ground and adequate foreland to accommodate cargos were considered basic facilities to upgrade a harbour to the status of a port.

A port owes its existence to a rich and fertile hinterland to supply cargo/passengers and easy access by way of routes and effective communication between the port and hinterland. Maritime transportation without a harbour and port without a harbour are imperfect entities. Seafaring activities, therefore, presuppose concomitant development of sea ports (Hariharan 1964:289-290).

Ancient ports can be divided in to 'littoral' and 'estuary' ports; those established at seafront ports being known as littoral and those on river mouths and estuaries as estuary ports. The littoral ports were generally exposed to the surf and sea breeze but the estuary ports were protected from these sea hazards, even though navigation was difficult due to lack of depth and because of dangers posed by shifting sand banks. Further, 'using moorings within the zone, where the alternating tides fetch and carry boats, these estuaries offered perfect shelter and facilitated linking of waterways with land routes or inland navigation' (Deloche 1983:442).

It is also to be noted that great forethought, planning and engineering skills to build harbours and ports on the seafront were required in the olden days, which could withstand the pounding and sucking effects of the ocean waves. The problem became more acute in case of harbours located at the junction of the sea and river, as these structures had to be erected in a sandy bed or mud with severe limitation of knowledge and tools. It seems that ancient Indians followed the line of least natural resistance and built most of their major harbours in the rivers, estuaries, away from the fretting and pounding of the sea, e.g. Tamrapalipti, Sopara, Bharuch, Goa, and Kaveripattanam. These establishments were built in small bays or coves, behind promontories, at the outlets of rivers and lagoons or below the tidal estuaries. The Dwaraka harbour provides the earliest clear evidence of modifying the natural rock to serve the needs of a harbour on the seafront (Rao 1998:107; Hariharan 1964:290; Deloche 1983:439-442).

Lothal and its Environs

Lothal is geographically situated at the northern end of the Gulf of Cambay in Saurashtra, Gujarat, 83 km. south of Ahmedabad. It was earlier approachable by a cart track, which used to be submerged under water four months in a year, but is now connected by an all weather motorable road. Lothal lies between two 'ranns' or salt wastes, the Rann of Cambay on the south and Little Rann of Kutch on the north, with Nal lake in the centre. The Rann is a long shallow dry estuary extending 52 km northwest from the mouth of the Sabarmati. Lothal is sandwiched between Bhogava and Sabarmati rivers. The bed of a river anciently flowing on the western margin of Lothal is still visible and is indicated by a natural depression in the north-south direction. At high tide, the sea water enters Bhogava river near Samani and overflows into the old river bed. The two channels are on the east and the other on the west; they were once connected by a nullah, the traces of which can still be seen along the northern edge of the mound of Lothal. 'The aerial photographs of the mound and its adjacent areas taken in 1958, before the dock was exposed, reveal a shallow river bed on the west, a nullah on the north and a bowl-like depression on the east' (Rao 1979:19).

Lothal has been explained as *Loth + thal*, meaning 'the mound of the dead' in Gujarat, whereas, according to Dhavlikar (1995:65), it denotes a place where boats are moored and repaired. The enclosed area of Lothal is relatively small (200 x 225 m) or around seven-and-a half hectares (Possehl 1980:72). However, Rao (1979:20) suggests that the town extended far beyond its boundaries. Whilst Harappa and Mohenjodaro are roughly three miles each in circuit, Lothal appears to be not more than one and quarter i.e. slightly less than half the size of Mohenjodaro'. The site is much smaller than Kalibangan but the excavated evidence indicates that 'it was more prosperous than Kalibangan, (Dhavalikar 1995:64).

Lothal was carefully planned and divided into segments, which led to economy of space. 'There appears to have been areas for a wide range of specialised or semi-specialised activities, each of which was performed in its own plan. The haphazardness associated with settlements, which grow by accretion is, if judged by the excavated areas, not a part of this plan. The order, which comes from an application of maxim 'a place for everything and everything in place' is far truer for Lothal than anything else' (Possehl 1980:72).

There is no unanimity among scholars on the status of Lothal as a city, town or village. Rao described it as a 'city' (1973:52, 61) as quoted by Possehl (1976, 212) but later called it a 'port town' (1979). Jansen (1979), Kenoyer (1989) and Chakrabarti (1979) call it a 'village'; whereas Possehl (1976:212), estimating the settlement's population from one to two thousand prefers it as a 'town'.

Recession by the Sea

The coastline of the Gulf of Cambay runs from the northeastern tip of the Saurashtra peninsula up to the estuary of the Tapti river. As the gulf is surrounded on the west, north and east by the mainland of Gujarat, it is generally safe from the distressing effects of the open sea but navigation is risky on account of the 'Bore Tide' peculiar to the gulf, and the rocks and shoals. But all the same, "this gulf on account of its sheltered position from the main sea and the broken nature of its coastline caused by the estuaries of its rivers, had provided since ancient times very favourable conditions for development of ports suitable to sailing vessels" (Hariharan 1964:312).

Lothal is presently land locked and the sea is located at a distance of 16-19 km. from it. But according to local traditions, it was much nearer in the ancient past and even at the beginning of the twentieth century and was approachable by boat at certain times of the year (Rao 1979:19; Chakrabarti 1999:172). Leshnik (1968:203) also concurs with this position and notes that "the siltation rate of Sabarmati is very rapid, so that in former times, the site might have been much nearer the sea." Rao (1973:50) has however estimated this distance "as not more than 5 kms" without offering any justification for this conclusion.

We may note in this regard that evidences for sea level changes have been observed at many places all along the western coast of India (Gaur 2000:152-159). George Dales (1966:9) believes that a number of sites on the Baluch-Makran coast have served as seaports during the third millennium BC but presently they are located as far as 40 km inland. A.V.N. Sarma (1971) has similarly taken note of the relationship between the successive phases of the Harappan civilization and variations in sea level.

The coastal region of Saurashtra also provides many indications of dried-up river beds and abandoned villages hinting at hydrographical changes, which may have occurred in the past (Gazetteer of the Bombay Presidency Vol. IV 1879:4-13). There is also evidence that the creeks of Dholera, Bavliari and Gogha have receded towards the sea due to silting, rendering the ports at their heads to shift from place to place (Gazetteer of Bombay Presidency Vol. IV 1879:13-15).

The environs of the modern port of Cambay also show evidence of silting causing the port site to shift from time to time towards the sea (Gazetteer of Bombay Presidency Vol. VIII Kathiawar:1884:54-60; Hariharan 1964:319-320).

In respect of Lothal, H.P. Oza, Director of Ports, Gujarat, after examination of the site in February 1960, reported that "In the Gulf of Cambay, there is enormous quantity of silt and also strong tidal current. But the main current is north-west. This has resulted in east-west narrowing of the sea from north and channels and creeks have silted up fast. Our experience of Bhavnagar creek, Sonai creek, and Dholera creek clearly shows that once the flow regime is altered, the siltation is very quick. .... It is, therefore, considered consistent to conclude on the basis of topo sheet and our experience, that a sea passage to Lothal approachable at high tide existed" (as quoted by Rao 1979:129).

Bhogava and Sabarmati Rivers

The Gulf of Cambay, in spite of its small size, receives the waters of a large number of rivers belonging to two groups, one flowing westward length, and the other, southward. The southward flowing main rivers are the Sabarmati and Mahi, while the westward flowing rivers are the Dadhor, Narmada, Kim, Tapti and Ambika.

Lothal lies between Bhogava and Sabarmati rivers. In the Bombay Presidency Gazeetter (BPG) Vol. VI (1879:7) on Kalhiawad, river Bhogava is described as thus "The river Bhogava or that broken portion of it, which flows through the Ahmedabad district, takes its rise in Dholka village of Bhingra and runs southward for about 10 miles, where it is joined by Omkar from the Limdi territory. Then it turns eastwards and after forming the boundary between Dholka and Dhandhuta for about eleven miles, empties itself into the sea by the mouth of Sabarmati....During the raining season, flood waters of the Nal also passes in the river. It is a brackish stream with few practical fords in its lower course". (As quoted by Shah 1960:314).

The name Sabarmati river is derived from the names of two rivers, namely 'Sabar' and 'Hatmati'. The Sabar rises in the south-western spurs of the Aravalli hills and takes a southerly turn before it is joined by the Hatmati. Thereafter it takes the name Sabarmati and flows for over 300 km through Dehgam, Diskri and Dholka taluakas before finally discharging itself into the Gulf. It is joined by the Khari, Katrak and Meshu rivers enroute and by the Bhogava at the mouth of the gulf (Rao:1979:8-9).

Hariharan (1964:320-321) informs us that "the rivers of the area are tidal to some distance. In the Sabarmati river, the tidal influence is felt even up to 12 miles from its mouth (BPG IV 1879:5). Presently, country boats sail up to Moti Baru about 4 miles from Lothal through the Sabarmati estuary (The Illustrated London News, 25 Feb 1961:303). The river Bhadar is navigable for small boats even up to 20 miles as far as Kutina (BPG VIII 1884:62). On the same river, at Bholad two miles from Lothal, even now (1964) a high tide of four to five feet can be seen. In early times, the high tide could have been more". (References as indicated by Hariharan 1964:320-321).

Rao states that both Sabarmati and Bhogava rivers were navigable during the protohistoric times. He writes "Trial pits sunk at several places within a radius of 20 kms from Lothal have yielded evidence of the frequent changes in the course of the river (Bhogava). Loam, sand and coarse gravel are found underlying the present surface soil. The stone anchors dug up from ancient river beds near the Nal lake bear testimony to the navigability of the rivers in the protohistoric times for more than 50 km inland". (Rao 1973:50)

Tidal Activity

The Gulf of Cambay is noted for the force of its tides; the earliest evidence of this phenomenon comes from the Greek text 'The Periplus of the Erythrean Sea' (59 AD or 83 AD – disputed). The anonymous writer of this text describing the tidal activity and its consequential navigational hazards in the Bay of Barygaza (Cambay) notes that, "Barygaza (Cambay) thus records native fishermen in the King's service stationed at the very entrance in well manned large boats called Trappaga and Cotymba, go up to the coast as far as Syrasterne, from which they pilot vessels to Barygaza, and they steer them straight from the mouth of the bay between the shoals with their crews; and they tow them to the fixed stations, going up with the beginning of the flood, and lying through the ebb at anchorages and in basins. These basins are deeper places in the river as far as Barygaza; which lies by the river three hundred stadia up from the mouth". The account continues, "Now the whole country of India has very many rivers, and very great ebb and flow of the tides: increasing at the new moon and at the full moon for three days and falling off during the intervening days of the moon. But at Barygaza it is much greater, so that the bottom is seen, and now parts of the dry land are sea, and now it is dry, where ships were sailing just before; and the rivers under the in-rush of the flood tide, when the whole force of the sea is directed against them, are driven up more strongly against their natural current, for many stadia". (Schoff 1992:40-41).

Graphically describing the tidal hazards, the text further notes "For this reason, entrance and departure of vessels is very dangerous for those, who are inexperienced or who come to this market town (Barygaza) for the first time, the rush of waters at the incoming tide is irresistible and the anchors cannot hold against it : so that large ships are caught up by the force of it, turned broadside on through the speed of the current, and so driven on the shoals and wrecked; and smaller boats are overturned; and those that have turned aside among the channels by the receding waters at the ebb, are left on their sides, and if not held on an even keel by props, the flood comes upon them suddenly and under the first head of the current they are filled with water. For there is so great force in the rush of the sea at the new moon, especially during the flood tide at night, that if you begin the entrance at the night at the moment, when the waters are still, on the instant there is borne on to you at the mouth of the river, a noise like the cries of an army heard from afar, and very soon the sea itself comes rushing in over the shoals with a hoarse roar" (Schoff 1992:41).

We also have reliable evidence of the force and violence of the tides in river Mahi during the nineteenth century from page 57 of the Bombay Presidency Gazetteer 1884 Vol. VIII, which reads as follows : "About a league southwards from Cambay glides the river Mahi, whose shores must be travelled at the low ebb of the sea, and not without great danger, because the sea rising flows up above five leagues and at low tide you are forced to wade through at the coming in of the tide, he would undoubted be swallowed by the sea, for when the water flows with great strength and higher than ordinary, it carries and washes away both horse and man, and often times with such force that an elephant cannot withstand the same, nor all his weight prevent him from being carried away" (as quoted by Shah 1960:319). By inference, we may reasonably assume that the tidal force in the Sabarmati was almost of the similar nature and magnitude during the same period.

The range of variations in the magnitude of the ebb and flow at the high tide are also one of the highest in the Gulf of Cambay. Tides Tables for the Indian Ocean for the year 1957 (p.298) records that the tide variation on the Baluchistan-Sing coast was about 2.25 meters. It rose to 2 to 6 meters in the Gulf of Kutch, then came down to 2.5 meters at Porbandar, only to rise again in the Gulf of Cambay and touch 8.5 meters at Bhavnagar. It further diminished progressively on the Konkan and Malabar coasts – 4 meters at Bombay, 1.50 meters at Mangalore, one meter at Cochin and 0.70 meter at Colombo. (Deloche 1983:442). We have no reliable information on tide variations during the protohistoric times. But keeping in view the observations made in "The Periplus" and tidal status in river Mahi as explained above, almost similar data for the period may be safely assumed.

The foregoing discussion, brings out that the sea tides at the mouth of the Gulf were strong and the rivers in its vicinity flowed with great strength in ancient times. Indeed, their fury, particularly during the spring tides, was so great that large ships at anchor, unless secured with great care, broke loose from their moorings and men, horses and even elephants at times, which came in their path, were swept away. The river banks were also not safe from the rising and receding flows and thus needed to be used with due caution during these periods.

It also follows that while strong force and wide variations in the tidal activity offered very favourable conditions for location of tidal ports and basins in the gulf's sheltered creeks, lagoons and sanctuaries; the shipping operations on the river banks and in the streams were prone to frequent disruptions due to the tidal phenomenon. But if the force of tides could be stemmed and slackened by placing obstructions in their path, the same adverse phenomenon became a natural boon in arranging sailing activities, even in comparatively shallow waters, by bringing ships/boats in and out along with the tides.

Water Transport Requirements of Lothal

It is now well recognized that the prosperity of Harappa, Mohenjodaro, Dholavira, Kalibagan, Rakhigarhi and Lothal, the six main centres of the Harappan Civilization depended to a large extent on trade. At Lothal "the agricultural products of the neighbourhood were exchanged here for metal tools and lithic implements, the manufacture of which depended on imported raw materials brought by land and sea routes from within and outside the (Indus) empire" (Rao 1973:114).

Possehl (1976:214), elaborating the economic role of Lothal, observes that "diverse and evidentially voluminous specialized craft activity produced much more in the way of finished products than the settlement itself could have consumed". We also know that Lothal was not situated in a location particularly suited to resource extraction. Its immediate environs in fact "produced almost none of the bulky, hard to transport raw materials" (stone, shell, ivory, copper and other ores). Copper came from Rajasthan as did steatite, agate was found on the Narmada, in Saurashtra and Kutch, and shell was found in the Arabian Sea and might have been ferried as far as the Straits of Manar (Possehl 1980:72).

It has also been generally accepted that Lothal acted as an important procurement centre for supply of different types of raw materials (e.g. steatite, carnelian, shell, ivory and copper) which were not available in the greater Indus valley. Possehl (1976:216) says that "much of this raw material must have passed through Lothal en route to the more central reaches of the civilization". He adds that both the direct overland route across the Rann of Kutch into south-eastern Sindh and "the sea route down the Gulf of Cambay to the Arabian Sea and then to the Indus river may have been used". (Possehl 1976:216).

We have no estimates of the volume of trade handled by Lothal. Rao (1973:73) however suggests that "the same can be judged from the size of the warehouse and the massiveness of the wharf, the latter being more than 240 meters in length". Be as it may, our discussion does indicate that 'a variety of bulky raw materials' and 'voluminous quantity of finished products' were transported to and from Lothal for 'manufacturing' and 'trading' activities and any disruption in their regular supply and dispatch would have been injurious to the economy of the settlement.

The transportation system, therefore, played a pivotal role in the smooth functioning of the commercial life of the settlement. This linkage in turn, "serves to accentuate the fact that the settlement must have had strong and reliable ties to a means of transportation. The dockyard and possible maritime transportation are certainly complementary to such a scheme. Overland movement through the Rann of Kutch by means of an already mobile pastoral nomadic group or others specialized in goods transportation must be considered. The latter groups are however suggested only on the basis of inference. There is no firm archaeological data to support them" (Possehl-1980: 76-77).

The Structure

Discovery

Lothal was excavated on a large scale for six seasons from 1955 to 1962 by S.R. Rao. A full report has been published in two volumes (Rao 1979;1985). Besides much information is available in various issues of "the Indian Archaeology" – A Review of the period and other writings of the excavator (see plates 1-9).

The entire eastern section of Lothal is taken up by a trapezoidal basin, measuring on average 214 X 36 m and closed by masonry walls of kiln fired bricks with two gaps, described by the excavator as 'inlet' and 'slipway' in the shorter sides on the north and south, respectively. The length of embankment walls in 212.4 m on the west, 209.3 m on the east, 34.7 m on the south and 36.4 meters on the north. The foundation is 1.78 m wide with two off-sets on the exterior, but the width of the walls above the ground is reduced to 1.04 m. The inner faces of the walls are strictly vertical with no access to the bottom. There is a 7.01 m gap on the eastern wall, which has been described by Rao as the 'Eastern Inlet'. This gap leads to a channel outside, also, of the same width and cut into natural soil. This channel linked the Eastern inlet with the second stage of the ancient river bed. Full details of the structure and changes made by the river Bhogava in its ancient bed are given in the Excavation Report. (Rao 1979:63-64;123-136).

The constructional features, which seem to mark this structure as a dock, are primarily five: (1) 'Northern Inlet'; (2) 'Southern Spillway'; (3) 'Eastern Inlet'; (4) strict verticality of the inner face of the 'Embankment Walls' and (5) Post holes in the embankment walls. Very briefly, Rao's dock concept is based on the premise that the vessels seeking entry in to the dock awaited their turn at anchor in river Bhogava as also in the Nullah located along the northern margin of the town and flowing in the ancient river bed. At high tide, they were sluiced into the basin through a 12.2 m wide specially built channel, connecting the nullah and the 'Dock', and entered the basin through the 12.2 m wide 'Northern Inlet' built in the embankment. At the opposite end, a 1 m wide, channel was constructed for allowing excess water to escape at high tide. It served not only as slipway (the Southern Slipway) but also could be used as 'water locking device'. "Its mouth could be closed by lowering the shutter in the vertical grooves provided therein, so that a minimum body of water was retained in the basin to allow flotation of vessels at low tide, when the water column in the basin would have been around 2 m, the maximum on high tide being approximately 3.5 m. This arrangement enabled ships of 20-25 m in length and 4-6 meters width (very roughly 75-100 DWT) to use the basin. The inlet channel was wide enough to allow two vessels to pass simultaneously as well as enough space for maneuverability once inside the basin. The easy flow of water at high tide ensured desilting of the basin automatically" (Rao 1970:86-87).

The Eastern inlet, according to Rao (1965:32), was created much later (Phase IV), when the flow channel at the river was silted up due to 'an unprecedented flood' leading to the shifting of the river to the eastern margin of the town instead of the west one. In the history of the Dock, this marks the second stage. Rao (1965:33) points out that "because of a comparatively narrow eastern inlet (7.1 meters against 12.2 meters and somewhat restricted depth (2 – 2.5 meters) of the connected channel, large ships could not have entered the dock in the second stage" (Chakrabarti 1995:101).

The strict verticality of the embankment walls indicates that the vessels could berth alongside the wharf without any obstructions protruding out. Rao notes that "the bricks are found worn out at uniform level at which the edges of the ships' anchored (berthed) in the basin touched the embankment wall" (Rao 1979:126). Post holes in the embankment suggest that some vessels were secured to wooden posts (Rao 1970:87).

Rao (1979:126) further states "the builders of the dock took care to provide a mud brick platform 800 feet long (243.84 m) and 64 to 72 feet (19.51 m to 21.95 m) wide adjoining the western bank for easy handling the cargo". He adds that they also built the largest warehouse of the Bronze Age so far known on a four meter podium of mud bricks in close proximity to the dockyard and a ramp was provided to transport goods in vehicles from the wharf to the warehouse. He also says that the dock was built not in the stream, but away from it to minimize the dangers from silting and floods. (Rao 1973:70).

To substantiate the general idea of marine environment in Lothal, the excavator has referred to the discovery of a few 'anchor stones', mostly large spheroid perforated stones, three miniature models of boats and pot sherd of Micareous Red ware painted with two boats and having multiple oars (Rao 1979:132) as well as the evidence of external maritime contacts of the settlement as a whole (1973:114-119). Rao has also cited the opinion of the then Port Commissioner Gujarat State, Shri H.P. Oza, professionally familiar with the Saurashtra Coast; in this regard as also the occurrence of estuarine shells in the basin, and the extraordinary salinity of the slit from the 'dock'; and the usage mechanism of a similar ancient dock at Gogha, in support of his thesis (Rao 1979:126-33). Finally, he has also produced ethnographic support in the form of a goddess, Vanuvatimata, worshipped by the local fishermen and sailors to make "the idea of a dock more plausible" (Chakrabarti 1995:101).

Discussion

The Water Storage Tank

U.P. Shah (1960:310-20) was the first scholar to question Rao's dockyard thesis. Emphasizing the present day scarcity of potable water in the region, he hypothesized that the structure was used as a water storage tank. L.S. Leshnik (1968:209) supporting Shah's conclusions, however, added that its primary function was to store water for irrigation. In a note appended to Leshnik's aforesaid paper, K.H. Janghans opined that the proposed irrigation tank was in fact meant to water a vegetable garden. He argued that the tank capacity was about 5000 cubic meters of water, and, if filled 3-4 times a year, it would have allowed a total capacity of 1500 – 2000 cubic m, which coupled with 700 – 800 mm rainfall, would have been sufficient to irrigate 10-12 acres of land.

Leshnik (1968:208) further argued that 'The Shadul System', a widely practiced traditional method of lifting water out of wells and irrigation reservoirs, was used for lifting water out of the tank. A shadul, consists of two poles, one of which is stationary and erect, while the other attached to it moves in a vertical plane. A bucket is suspended from the latter at one end and counter balancing weights are affixed at the other end. It is operated by a single person. Leshnik also suggested that the stones recovered from the bottom of the structure (described by Rao as anchor stones) were some of the counter-weights used in operating the shaduls.

This theory has been discussed widely and many serious questions have been raised on its validity. The main arguments against the theory are summarized as follows:-

a) The existence of water wells and river in the vicinity of the settlement would have met the drinking water needs. Discharge of a city drain in the basin further confirms that the tank was not used as drinking water tank (Lal 1997:132; Possehl 1976:213; Dhavalikar 1995:71).

b) There was no need for agricultural irrigation as seasonal inundation is sufficient for one crop grown in the region (Possehl 1976:213; Dhavalikar 1995:71).

c) The water lift system is not satisfactory. "The holes in the stone said to have been used for passing a rope are quite small; of the order of two or three inches in diameter. This is a size appropriate for a rope but not suspension as a counter weight on a branch two or three inches in diameter" (Possehl).

d) The fact that the tank is located on one side of the settlement limits its potential for irrigating all the areas around the settlement (Possehl).

e) Janghan's proposal for utilization of the structure for 10-12 acres of vegetable gardening is not cost effective. "I doubt if a wealthy landlord in the western world would today build such a large structure for such a purpose" (Dhavalikar).

f) Presence of estuarine shells in the silt of the basin and salinity in the silt as compared to outside soil are indicative of marine environment (Fairservis 1971:271; Rao 1979:127).

g) The absence of steps normally met in water tanks, precludes the possibility of usage of the tank for bathing and laundry as per traditional practice. (Lal; Possehl; Rao 1973:72).

h) There is no wide opening for water from the catchment area in the basin (Rao 1973:72).

i) The following discoveries on the site are indicative of ship berthing activity in the basin:

i) vertically of the inner side of the walls

ii) definite indication of a loading platform for cargoes and wearing out of bricks at various uniform levels on the embankment walls.

iii) discovery of three anchor stones – 22 to 26 inches in diameter and 100 to 150 kgs in weight.

j) Usage of precious kiln fired bricks for the embankment walls, when mud walls would have sufficed for a water tank, is indicative of a different usage. Harappans "were a very practical people, very parsimonious with pecuniary habits, which are reflected in their material equipment and they would not have wasted resources in building such a structure for drinking water and irrigation" (Dhavalikar).

R. Nigam conducted a 'Foraminifera test' by collecting four representative samples from the lowest sediments of the structure in 1986 to check as to whether the structure was filled in the ancient times with fresh or marine water. He reports that "study of sediments reveals a fairly well preserved assemblage of foraminifer ... can be considered in situ .... occurrence of well preserved assemblage of the foraminifera can be compared with present day beach, inner shelf and marine environment of Western India" (Nigam 1988:21). Nigam's evidence clearly indicates that the structure was filled with marine water and thus could not have been used for either drinking or growing cotton, wheat, barley or other crop as suggested by Leshnik.

It is further noted that since the appearance of the original writings of Shah (1960), Leshnik (1968) and Janghans (1968), a number of scholars like (Fairservis (1971) and Deloche (1983), have merely endorsed the thesis but none has come forward to counter the arguments against it. It would thus appear that this hypothesis has been gradually loosing steam over the decades. In fact, its chief proponent, Leshnik himself was not fully convinced of the validity of his hypothesis as is evident from his conducting remarks. "Admittedly, this view lacks the weight of decisive evidence, but it seems at least to be reasonably in keeping with the general rural character of the Lothal settlement as we know it" (Leshnik 1968:210).

We propose the hypothesis may now be permitted to rest in peace till some new evidence or arguments are adduced it its support.

Construction Features of the 'Dock'

The various construction features of the dock were commented by archaeologists, historians and scholars from various other disciplines spread over a period of more than 40 years. Similarly, the excavator has responded to these observations in a piece-meal manner in his many writings but others have merely endorsed or rejected a particular view without elaborating their argument. The net result has been a great deal of repetitive rhetoric and consequent confusion. To get a clear picture, we have clubbed the major observations for and against the 'dock' construction feature-wise and propose to discuss each item separately to establish its current status clearly.

Northern Inlet

It has been argued that the inlet on the northern embankment wall cannot be identified (Leshnik 1968:207). In fact, the wall is nearly complete and there is hardly any gap for an inlet (Pandya 1977:101). Rao (1979:126) clarifies in the excavation report that "This gap was not clear enough in the early stage of the excavation owing to limited digging. However, after excavating the entire basin, the original inlet is now traceable fairly accurately". Elsewhere he adds (Rao 1991:144) "Traces of brick constructions against erosion of the inlet can be seen in the robber's trench".

Eastern Inlet

It has been contended that the second stage (Phase IV) approach is very awkward involving first a turn in a narrow flow channel and second an entry (Eastern Inlet) into the basis for berthing alongside. Further, access over the peripheral wall to the interior of the facility is shallow. It appears to consist of seven brick courses of about two feet height, which is not good enough for entry of vessels having more than 3 feet draught (Possehl 1980:72; Leshnik 1968:206). We have already noted that Rao has conceded this reduction in the draught and consequent size of the vessels using the basin in the second stage and justifies it as the best of a bad situation after the destruction caused by the floods of 2000 BC. But this has apparently not satisfied many scholars, (Leshnik 1968:207; Possehl 1976:213; Dhavalikar 1995:70-71) and the controversy continues to persist.

It may be noted here that the Eastern inlet was exposed much earlier than the Northern inlet during the course of the excavations, and initially, the excavator had identified it as "the original entry" point into the basin instead of the Northern inlet. Oza, who visited the 'dock' in Feb., 1960, pointed out that the vessels entering the dock would have to take a 90 degree turn to berth and also opined that if the entry had been from the shorter arm

(Northern end), it would have permitted passage of longer vessels as also better maneuverability inside the dock. But in spite of the shortfall, the structure was operable as a berthing dock (Rao 1979:129). As it happened, an entry inlet with a proper approach connecting the river, from the north side was actually excavated after some time and the excavator gave a completely different operational profile of the basin, which was not well received in the scholastic circles and "a number of scholars both in India and abroad expressed doubts in private discussions about the dock interpretation" (Leshnik 1968:211 Note 3). In the words of Leshnik (1968:207). "The most recent interpretation is hard to reconcile with previous ones, for prior the report of Northern inlet, Rao wrote that the entrance of the seagoing vessels through the Eastern inlet had been 'established beyond doubt'. He does not tell us why he changed his mind, but one can guess the nature of Eastern inlet had something to do with it". Since then, the inlet controversy has dogged the structure.

Spillway and the Sluice gate

Leshnik has also questioned the concepts of spillway and the sluice gate in the Southern embankment. He writes (1968:207) "The conduit constructed of burnt bricks, has been traced in its length for several yards. The water passage is about one yard wide and contains at the lower end, near the basin, a stepped descent that serves to decrease the water velocity. The orientation of the steps and the gradient of the conduit as a whole are toward the basin. Obviously then, its purpose must have been just the reverse of an outlet." Rao's response is quite explicit. He says that "the spillway with steps falling towards the basin might have been an intake channel for recouping water which is not borne out by facts because the shutter resting towards the flanking walls would be thrown away by the water entering the basin. On the other hand, the grooves at the mouth are so designed as to hold the shutter in position by thrust of water from inside the basin. Hence the channel in the Southern embankment was more suitable as an outlet than as an inlet and was designed to facilitate automatic desilting and discharge of excess water" (Rao 1991:145). Clarifying the position further he says that, "The foundation of the channel walls is as deep as that of the embankment wall for a length of 15 feet. Beyond, it is very shallow. A horizontal row of six weep holes is provided both arms of the channel at regular intervals of one foot nine inches. In two such weep holes of the Western Wall, wooden channels were found inserted to serve as outlets for water seeping from behind the wall. The vertical recesses provided at the mouth of the channel were meant for inserting a wooden door to regulate the outflow of water through the channel which served as a spillway for the excess water entering the basin at high tide" (Rao 1979: 125; Pl.: CIVA).

Levels and Displacements

It has been opined by a number of scholars that the silt is too high to permit the passage of vessels entering the basin through both the Northern and Eastern inlets (Pandya 1977:101; Dhavalikar 1995:70-71). On the other hand, it could lock the water inside the basin during the ebb, which would have affected floatation of vessels and the 'Dock' would have faced siltation (Pandya 1977:101). Rao in defence, has quoted the various MS levels and draughts inside the basin, starting with the benchmark of the Government Trigonometrical Survey at Lothal to the river bed (first stage), where silt rock was encountered on the slope, to show that there would have been a 4.15 feet minimum draught available at low water, taking one foot water above the silt of the inlets. (Rao 1973:70, 1979:126, 132-133; 1991:145). This position has also been confirmed by N.K. Panikkar and T. M. Srinivasan, (1972: 269) two learned oceanographers, who state that" ships had to enter and leave the basin at high tide, when level was maintained sufficiently high above the inlet silt level – the easy flow of Water level. The easy flow of water at high tide ensured desilting of the basin".

Scouring Effects of the Tidal Waters

Leshnik (1968:207) has also opined that the Eastern Inlet should have had a sluice gate, "especially one to withstand an enormous internal water pressure at ebb tide". Pandya (1977:101) on the other hand, notes that there was not enough provision for protecting the wall from the scouring effects of the tidal activity. The excavator clarifies that the designing of the structure reveals that all problems relating to dockyard engineering, such as the rate of silting, the velocity of the current and thrust of water in the basin were, carefully considered. First class kiln fired bricks were used in the construction of the embankment walls, which are gradually reduced by stages from 1.78 meter to 1.04 m in width by providing offsets on the exterior to counteract the water thrust (Rao

1970:85). His reaction to Leshnik's aforesaid statement is, however, very sharp "He has confused the whole issue, when he says that the inlet of the second stage (22 feet wide) is too large to bear the pressure of tides. There was no direct tidal wave from the sea or creek to the dock at this stage. The boats entered the dock through a channel connected with the river, which was one mile away" (Rao 1979:134). Rao's position has been vindicated by Panikkar and Srinivasan (1972:269), who observe that "The scouting effects of the tidal water were arrested by construction of two buttress walls- one on either side of the inlet gap. To counteract the thrust of water inside the basin, the enclosure walls were buttressed on the outer surface with a 12 to 13 meter wide platform of mud bricks".

We thus find that the excavator has convincingly answered all the technical queries voiced so far on the construction features of the basin and one would have expected due acknowledgement of the same. But recent studies on the subject (Dhavalikar: 1995; Gaur: 2000) suggest that Rao has not fully succeeded in removing all the doubts of the archaeological fraternity and "several aspects in the subtle parameters of the structure need reasonable explanation to accept the (concept of) Dockyard" (Gaur 2000:47). Dhavalikar 1995:70 is more explicit in identifying the 'Eastern Inlet' as the core disputed issue and states "I doubt if the issue will be ever resolved unless the Archaeological Survey of India holds a site seminar, where all the records should be made available to specialists in Harappan studies and those from other disciplines".

We have no comments to offer on Dhavalikar's suggestion as, in our view, the dispute relates more to a credibility gap bided on archaeological techniques and ethos rather than on the operational viability of the various sub functions of the Dock. However, based on the published data of the Archaeological Survey of India on the subject (Rao 1979, 1985), we are of the view that there are no nautical impediments in the operational utilisation of the various individual functional features including the Eastern inlet of the berthing basin. This position has already been acknowledged by the then Gujarat Port Commissioner H.P. Oza in 1960 (Rao 1979:127) and later by Panikkar and Srinivasan (1972:269). These two reputed oceanographers have observed that "we may affirm, therefore on the basis of studies made regarding Lothal that this dock was purely tidal and the Lothal engineers had possessed a knowledge of the tidal effects, the amplitude, the erosion and thrust. From this knowledge, they developed a competence at Lothal for receiving ships at high tide and ensuring flotation of ships inside the dock at low tide". Additionally, a number of maritime historians have also expressed similar views on these matters. (Moti Chandra 1997:31-32; Sridharan 1982:13-14; Sahay 1996:15).

Analogies for comparison

Leshnik has noted that evidence for actual docks in the ancient world against which the Lothal basin can be measured is not available and lack of textual reference, particularly from Mesopotamia, perhaps points to the fact that none existed. On the other hand "the complex harbour at Pharos (modern Alexandria), which dates back to 2000 BC, was so skillfully constructed with break waters and jetties that an expert, Sir L.H. Sevile, has called it the work of a genius, equal to the standard of modern engineers. By contrast, the Lothal basin is a quite elementary structure, and, if meant to function as a dock, then it was very poorly designed. Yet the excavated remains of Harappa and Monenjodaro leave us in no doubt that the Harappan competence in civil engineering was the equal of any in the third millennium BC" (Leshnik 1968:205).

We agree with Leshnik that analogies for comparison for the Lothal basin during the protohistoric period are lacking. But the art of building and using estuarine ports and tidal basins has been practiced for a very long time and is still in operation on a number of sites on the western coast of India. Rao (1979:133) has cited the example of an ancient port at Gogha (near Hathab) with links to the Late Harappan period, where a tidal basin, though smaller in size but resembling the Lothal dock is still working.

For a more recent analogy, the working of the minor port of Panvel may be mentioned here. "The Panvel Bunder is situated inland about 10 miles away from Bombay harbour. The river Panvel, which empties into Bombay harbour, connects the port with the sea; as far us Ulva Bunder, five miles from entrance; the river is navigable for sailing vessels, thereafter the river, mostly dried, is tidal. Small sailing vessels proceed at high tide to Panvel Bunder, where they discharge" (Hariharan 1964:321-22). Similarly, Malat Bunder in Mumbai harbour, a large sized stone-built rectangular basin for sailing vessels, has been functional for more than 300 years now, if not longer.

Leshik's comparison between the Pharos port and Lothal basin is also ill founded. Pharos was situated adjoined to the sea and was subject to constant pounding and eroding effects of the waves and currents. To overcome this problem, the ancient Egyptians used carefully hewn large blocks of limestone in building the piers and other major structures of the harbour (Sevile 1941:210-15). On the other hand, Lothal was located well away from the sea coast and the 'Dock' was not subjected to the direct impact of the force of the tides; probably by the time they reached the basin, they would have lost most of the velocity and force. Accordingly, the Harappans built the structure in kiln fired bricks, using the appropriate technology for harnessing the tidal force. It has to be remembered that ports and berthing basins are built as determined by physical geography and sea conditions of the region concerned and comparisons between differing ground conditions, as in this case, are not only inappropriate but also misleading.

Ethnographic evidence

Marine Environment

Rao had opined that the presence of thin gravel and estuarine shells noticed underlying fine sand silt in the beds of flow channel and the basin indicated that the tidal waters reached the 'dock'. Leshnik has countered the suggestion by pointing out that "at one time, the Nal lake was connected with the sea; this entire area would have been subjected to flooding and deposits of the kind observed readily left in surface depression". (Leshnik 1968:207) keshnik's suggestion seems to get confirmation from a petrography study on Harappan pottery from Lothal conducted by Panjwani (1989) in which he has suggested presence of fragments of foraminifera; which in turn indicates that the Lothal settlement was under marine environment at one point of time. However, Nigam's (1988:21) foraminifera analysis, which has been discussed in some detail earlier, clearly shows "profuse" presence of gypsum and micro organism foraminifera 'in situ' in lower levels of the bottom of the basin", thereby indicating regular ingress of sea water in the basin. In our view, Nigam's evidence overshadows Leshnik's and Panjwani's suggestions, and certainly merits consideration.

Anchor Stones

Leshnik has also contested the identification of three stone objects, recovered from the floor of the basin, as anchors. He (1968:207) notes "the largest of the stones has a diameter of about sixteen inches, making it doubtful as heavy enough to have served as an anchor by itself, whilst a series of them would have been unwieldy". Pandya (101) has supported the suggestion by adding that "the gulf would require an anchor of two to three quintals as the current velocity of the Gulf is 10 km per hour". Psero Nicola Gargulla in his essay "Anchors of Antiquity" (1961:31-35) has identified at least eleven different primitive types of anchors in various sizes "from the monster block 1.72 meter long and 6.4 cm wide at ends, and weighing all 500 kilograms to a midget of 8 kilograms," The anchors found in the basin actually very in diameter from 22 to 26 inches (Rao 1979:134) and not 16 inches as stated by Leshnik, almost half of the largest parameters suggested by Gargulla. We, therefore, consider these stone pieces to be barge enough for usage aboard a variety of smaller vessels, which types might have been used for transportation of bulk raw materials and other cargos in and out of Lothal, (e.g. flat bottomed barges, shallow daughter vessels, riverine cum coastal vessels) and, may have belonged to anyone of these types. Limiting their usage to the larger types of vessels only which possibly used the basin, does not sound nautically wise to us.

Sea Goddess

Rao (1991:146) has cited the traditional worship of a local sea goddess Vanuvatimata to substantiate his case for a marine environment. He writes that "religious feelings were aroused, when the stones symbolizing the goddess were removed for excavating the warehouse. Subsequently a small shrine had to be built nearby to meet the demand for traditional worship". Pandya (1977:102) has disputed the claim by stating that "before excavation, there was a small shrine of Sikotrimata on the mound. Sikotrimata is a goddess of lower Hindu castes. Sikotrimata and Vahannvatimata (presumably Vanuvatimata as stated by (Rao) are different goddesses, even if any Vahanvatimata was known. Again, sea is always considered as male god e.g. Dairyalal amongst the Kharavas".

It is generally well recognized that a very large

majority amongst the ancient seafarers belonged to the lowest class viz. Shudra an they had been further pushed to the lowest fringes of the modern Hindu social structure over the centuries (Basham 1964:162-166; Larus 1979:62). Further, though it may sound strange it is yet true that many amongst the seafarers also actually practise their religions devotedly acquiring their favourite icons from the local deities of their homelands – to whom they always turn for divine help in times of need. As regards the specific questions of the identification of goddess Vanuvati mata, Rao (1973:118) notes that "The name Sikotrimata is an honorific of the sea goddess (Vanuvatimata) of Lothal, and is said to have been derived from the name of an island known as Sakotra, which lies on the East African coast."

Pandya's suggestion that the Hindu pantheon of gods and goddess Aditi has been worshipped by Indian seafarers since the Vedic time and this practice is still continuing by invoking her blessings at the launching ceremonies of all sea going vessels built in the Indian shipyards. Some parts of a Vedic hymn from Atharvaveda (VII.6(7). 1-4) recited on the occasion are reproduced below.

"Though art the heavens, O Aditi
And thou art the unfathomable
By thee we are measured and protected
And Thou art us, Thy Children
Thou art all the Gods in Heaven
Thou art the Five Nations
Thou art our present and future
Thou the Measure of Goodness
Thou the Mistress of Righteousness
To Thee we tender out offering
Far Flung are Thy domains
Ever whitening, Ever prospering
Happy OADITI and Blessed is
Thy Guidance
With thy blessing we embark on this ship
That rides well the waves
So broad in beam, and,
Spacious, comfortable, resplendent,
Blessed are her courses, her rudders strong
Faultless in construction, her bilges dry
So with these words of praise to thee
We embark on this venture"

The Vedic seers, further citing goddess Aditi in Rig Vedic verse x.63.10 advise that those wishing for a happy sea voyage must ensure that their vessel is well oared (properly manned), lets no water in (checked for water tight integrity prior to sailing) and is free from defects.

Sea level Fluctuation

Pandya (1977:100) has pointed out that the investigations carried out by S.K. Gupta (1973) have revealed 2 to 6 m higher sea level than at present during the Harappan times. As the dock is 12 m above the present sea level, even if the sea level was 3m higher, sea waters could not have reached the dock. A.S. Guar of NIO, Goa (2000-46) dismissing the suggestion counters "The recent work of the M.S. University Baroda, in Mahi river valley suggests that the area is rising very significantly. In the last 2000 years, the area has risen to 6 meters, which indicates that this area is very unstable and therefore no firm conclusions can be drawn from Dr. S.K. Gupta's study".

We have also already noticed that country boats used to reach up to Lothal from Moti Maru at high tide in the 1960s. "The tidal waves, which rise as much as 10 feet high in Bhogava river near Bholad, must have enabled the boats to sail up to Lothal" (Rao 1979:19).

Location of the Basin

Possehl (1980:71) has questioned the precise functions, necessity and location of the basin. He writes that "There can be a serious question as to whether a large dockyard would have been necessary. Today ships come into riverine ports on and adjacent to the Gulf of Cambay and anchor at night tide on mud flats, where they are loaded and unloaded without other facilities. It appears to be a simple and efficient system". Questioning the approach to the basin, he adds that "these ships would have had to come past the settlement and to have made at least one right angle turn in a narrow canal channel".

In the same vein, Deloche (1983:446) elaborating the

harbour installations during the ancient and medieval India, notes that "these structures are not extraordinary at all. They are all remnants of ghats (landing places) found in all the river towns on the Indian waterways. If there was no need for dockyards and sluice gates (even) in the seventeenth century, why should such an elaborate system have been necessary in, for example, the Harappan times".

Our earlier studies have shown that ports and berthing basins are built as determined by local geography and sea conditions of the region concerned. In this context, there has been wide silting of the rivers discharging in to the Gulf of Cambay and the sea has also receded by many kilometers over the millennia. Accordingly, the sea-cum- riverine scenario of Lothal is vastly different presently than four millennia ago, and therefore any analogies between the two are prima facie suspect. Perhaps a comparison between the conditions described in 'The Periplus' during the first century AD with the protohistoric period as known to us would be more apt.

Even at the risk of repetition, we would like to note on the authority of the graphic Greek account that the rush, force and velocity of the incoming gulf tides in this area was so great around the time Christ was born that anchors could not hold against them and vessels caught by their force were turned broadside on through. Now the question arises as to whether loading and unloading of vessels was feasible on a regular and continuing basis in such tidal conditions? Further, could the vessels in loading/ unloading process fend the pull of tides? Admittedly, there were short slack windows for working cargos in between the flooding and ebbing periods and at other times, but were they adequate to meet Lothal transportation needs, described as "voluminous" by Possehl himself? (1976:214). These are highly debatable questions and need an in-depth analysis.

In our view, the safest and logical method of meeting the situation at Lothal during the Harappan period was to harness the tides by stemming and slackening the tidal force, and, thus make them shipping friendly. For this purpose, the Harappan builders had two options viz. either build an artificial barrier in the path of the waves or divert a part of them to an adjoining flow channel and onto an enclosed basin, where they could support shipping operations. The Harappans obviously preferred the latter, making use of the existing Nullah. This arrangement not only ensured that by the time the Gulf waves reached the basin through the Sabarmati estuary, river Bhogava, the Nullah and the narrow flow channel, they were sufficiently slackened to have any damaging effect. Additionally, the distant location of the basi from the river bank also minimized the flooding and silting dangers and its proximity to a stacking jetty and the warehouse made the double handling of cargos an easy task.

The approach difficulties for the vessels being sluiced in the basin as described by Possehl are well appreciated but these are not considered insurmountable. Considering the small sizes and DWT of the vessels (max. 25 m length, 75-100 DWT), the ancients could have comfortably devised a suitable ship manoeuvre for turning vessels, if necessary, even by creating small turning bends in the flow channel.

Lothal: A port Town

We have already noted that Lothal has been described both as a village and a town but the evidence in favour of its being classified as a town is more weighty. Further, we have also discussed the commercial importance of the settlement, concluding that water transportation provided an important linkage with the outside world and its smooth functioning was essential for continuance of the commercial and manufacturing activities of the settlement.

We have also noted that for ensuring regular water transportation services, the excavator has proposed a two-tier port structure for Lothal viz. an anchorage in the river for larger sea going vessels and an inshore berthing complex with an adjoining wharf, a cargo handling area, a warehouse, a commercial complex for support facilities and a rich hinterland; with river Bhogava serving as a link between the settlement and the sea. Leshnik (1968:205) has objected to the port model on the ground that "apart from the basin, there is little upon which the claim to Lothal's being an international port rests".

We have already pointed out the elementary requirements for development of harbours in ancient times and the conditions required for their upgradation to the status of a 'port'. Additionally, busy and important sea ports catering to long distance trade were also expected to provide ship replenishment viz. victuals, water and ship stores, ship repair facilities, and harbour support crafts viz. pilot boats, lighters and barges. Besides, ancient port towns were also not merely manufacturing and trading centres, where merchandise was transferred to and from vessels but the centres of retail commercial activity as well. "Goods were sold and exchanged at the quay, for which purpose merchants built permanent establishments and tavern keepers were as familiar to the water front as they are even today" (Leshnik 1968:203).

Lothal, in comparison to the aforesaid requirements, in my opinion certainly possesses all the elementary features of a port, albeit in a very limited manner with a single basin to support the whole edifice; and practically none of the other desirable attributes, at least, as witnessed from the excavations so far. This position, however, suffers a setback in the second stage, where Rao envisages working of the larger vessels anchored in the river stream; which our earlier analysis has already indicated as a feasible but restricted solution.

We have, however, not considered the immediate socio-politico-economic environment of Lothal in determining its port status so far. We learn from Frank Broeze (1997:3) that it is this "environment of a port city or town", which makes it different from other 'cities' and 'towns'. He adds "the explicitly and conscious use of the term 'port city' (or town) entails far more than that. It specifically means that the economic, social, political and cultural life of the city is also determined by and has to be analysed in the light of the port functions". It, therefore, follows that the ports functions of a town cannot alone in isolation determine its 'port' status and the immediate socio-politico-economic development must also be taken into account to finalise the matter.

It was perhaps with such similar thoughts that H.D. Sankalia (1974:374) wrote that "Though Leshnik accepts the fact that some 4500 years ago the sea might have been very near Lothal, because he thinks that the place was at most a large village, it could not have been a port. This view is certainly wrong, from what we know of early towns and cities in India and outside, and from the various criteria that culture-historians have prescribed for an ancient site as a town or a city. A city in the strict sense, it was probably not, but a town it was with its three monumental buildings, three large streets, a bead factory, a separate cemetery and evidence of the knowledge of writing, besides rich and varied finds. One has yet to see such a well-laid out "literate" village in India or outside. Leshnik's outlook is internally vitiated and prejudiced and, therefore, he refuses to regard Lothal as a port, though he concedes proximity to the sea".

In view of the above discussion, we have no hesitation in referring to Lothal as a port town.

Findings

We had set ourselves two tasks at the beginning of this study – first to examine the efficacy of the trapezoidal structure as a 'tidal berthing basin' and secondly to examine the suitability of 'Lothal' as a seaport. We have accordingly analysed various aspects of both the subjects in depth; and as a result, a number of firm indications and suggestions have emerged on the various aspects of the subject, which, for ease of reference, are summarized as our findings in the succeeding paragraphs. We seek readers indulgence for some repetitive material in this section but the same has been considered necessary to present our views clearly and without any ambiguity.

Sea Access

The siltation rate of the Gulf of Cambay is very rapid and as a result, sea access to Lothal is presently landlocked. But there are sufficient reliable indications to suggest that the sea coast may have been much nearer to Lothal during the Harappan period. Rao has estimated this distance to be around five kilometers but no firm evidence to that effect is available.

The range of variations in the magnitude of the tidal ebb and flow on the Gulf of Cambay during the spring tides is the highest on the western coast of India, almost touching 8.5 m. Further, on account of the rush, force and velocity of the incoming tides in Harappan times, no human activity might have been feasible in their path or on the river banks. However, on the positive side, sailing vessels under experienced pilots could sail deeper in river estuaries, sailing along with the rising tide and similarly returning back to the Gulf and thereon to the open sea.

There are also clear suggestions that navigable sea

access existed in the ancient times between the Gulf and Lothal. The sailing vessels could use this stretch of water through the Sabarmati estuary and river Bhogava riding in with the high tide and sailing out at the beginning of the ebb.

Water transportation requirements of Lothal

Large quantities of raw materials and finished products were transported in and out of Lothal by water transport and their regular transportation seemed essential for smooth conduct of the manufacturing and commercial activities of the settlement. This need dependence on shipping activities in turn accentuates the vital requirement for supporting port structure and facilities for servicing the visiting ships and crafts in the vicinity or around the settlement. This analysis also leads us to believe that the river Bhogava's stream and banks were only available for 'restricted' usage for this purpose and the Harappan seafarers and engineers would have had to perforce look for innovative solutions further inland for regular working of the cargo shipped through the water routes.

The Controversy

To interpret the purpose of the structure, two different opinions have been advanced. The first school supports 'Dock Theory' or Inland Tidal Basin thesis and consists of Rao (1979, 1985), Wheeler (1973 VIII), Lal (1997) and Chakrabarti (1995, 1999), Shah (1960); Leshnik (1968) Fairservis (1971) and Deloche 1983) on the other hand support the 'Tank theory', and advocate that the basin was used as a tank for storing drinking water and probably for agriculture irrigation also.

A third school has also emerged since the nineteen seventies. It consists of Possehl (1976, 1980) Pandya (1977) Dhavalikar (1995) and Gaur (2000), who find fault with both the interpretations but have no alternative suggestions for usage of this largest ever Harappan structure discovered so far. These scholars except Possehl (1976) are also silent on the transportation model for ferrying goods in and out of Lothal, who has suggested use of the river bank for loading and unloading cargo in ships and boats anchored in river Bhogava, which at best can be described as 'a feasible but limited solution'.

The Tank theory had gained wide currency during the nineteen sixties and seventies but has been losing ground in the face of mounting criticism, most of which has remained unanswered. Nigam's findings (1988) of the presence of abundant gypsum crystals and marine organisms (foraminifera) in the basin silt and thus the water being unfit for drinking and agricultural usages seems to have finally sealed its fate.

A large number of questions have also been raised against the Dock theory over the decades, which have been logically and suitably answered by the excavator (Rao 1970, 1973, 1979, 1985, 1991). But the same does not seem to have fully satisfied the archaeological fraternity and doubts are still being cast on the approach and entry of vessels in the basin without assigning any specific shortfalls in the excavators' findings.

Assessment of the Dock Theory

We have carefully examined the broad contours of the approach, entry, exit, flotation and tidal management profiles as described by the excavator (Rao 1979, 1985) and various observations made on them by the scholars over the last four decades. After due examination, we affirm these profiles to be operationally viable propositions and capable of being put to use in actual practice under specified conditions. We may very briefly describe our reasons for the same as follows:

a) There are five specific constructional features, which distinguish this structure as a ship berthing basin from other similar structures viz. (i) the two inlets (northern and eastern); (ii) the spillway with its dwarf wall; (iii) verticality of the inner side of the walls with signs of uniform wearing of bricks at a uniform level on the wall and (iv) post holes in the enclosure walls suggesting tie posts for ships.

b) Access from sea to the river Bhogava up to the settlement and ship approaches from the river to the Nullah, onward to the flow channel and into the basin during both the stages are navigable. The difficulties described in ship handling both by Leshnik and Possehl due to right angle turns, while sluicing the vessels in the connecting channel, are not insurmountable.

c) The builders of the basin, taking due note of the

undue water pressure on the outer side of the brick walls, have provided offsets to serve as wave breakers. They also designed a greater thickness for the western wall, which experienced the maximum water thrust and it was further buttressed by a mud brick wall of 13-20 m width. Similarly, the northern margin of the township was protected from erosion by the approach channel by a colossal wall built of burnt bricks.

d) Vessels entered and left the basin during the high tide, when water level was maintained sufficiently high above the inlet channels during both the stages. The easy flow of water in turn ensured desilting of the basin.

e) The problem of ensuring flotation of vessels at low tide was resolved by closing the spillway and inserting the wooden shutter in the grooves. This unique water locking device introduced in the spillway could be kept open or closed according to necessity.

f) The various questions raised about the eastern and northern inlets, spillway, sluice gate and silt level by Leshnik, Possehl and Pandya have already been analysed earlier and, in our view, they have been appropriately replied to point-wise. But as noted earlier, while no specific shortfalls are mentioned, there seems to be a "credibility gap on the specific issue of the" two entry inlets viz. Eastern and Northern". We are not very familiar with the archaeological techniques and methodologies and hence are in no position to comment. But it does seem to us that if the design parameters of most of the main features of the basin, viz. the Nullah, the flow channel, spillway, sluice gate, and offsets to control water thrusts, are considered dock oriented, then we must also trust Harappans' ability to have overcome these "inlet" and other such minor difficulties. After all, the core issues of an inshore tidal basin design are tidal management, maintenance of flotation level at low tide and silt clearance and certainly not the height and depth of the inlet channels, which are only a part of the technical details of civil engineering. However, the final decision on this issue must rest with the archaeologists, as a mariner's opinion in such arhaeological matters can at best be treated as an aid to the decision making and certainly not the verdict by itself.

g) The ethnographic support adduced by the excavator, viz. salinity in the basin's silt as a compared to outside soil, discovery of anchor stones and worship of a local goddess, are very relevant and provide weighty evidences of the marine environment of the site.

h) Keeping the technical requirements of their respective disciples in view, a port management expert (H.P. Oza), two reputed oceanographers (N.K. Panikkar and T.M. Srinivasan) and a number of maritime historians (Moti Chandra, K. Sridharan and Baldeo Sahay) have supported the usage of the structure as a tidal berthing basin.

i) No better explanation has been offered for usage of the structure, even after an intense debate lasting almost four decades.

j) Lastly, this transport model meets the major water transportation requirements of the settlement, which were considered essential for its continuing economic prosperity.

Emergent Picture

Lothal possesses all the essential prerequisites for identification as an ancient sea port. There, is however, no evidence for some desirable facilities usually offered by ports catering to long distance trade, viz. ship replenishment, ship repairs, boat pens, river bank retail marts, and entertainment establishment usually linked with ancient port towns to classify the settlement as a 'port town'. But then, the port functions alone in isolation do not determine 'the port town' status of a place and its immediate socio-economic-political environment must also be taken into account. Viewing both these factors together, viz. the available port functions and the socio-economic structures, we find overwhelming evidence in favour of a port town status for this protohistoric settlement.

We therefore fully support the nomenclature "Lothal : A Harappan Port Town" and further opine that no other title would have perhaps better explained the commercial and maritime functions performed by this unique Harappan town.

Acknowledgments

The author wishes to express his sincere gratitude to

Shri K.N. Dikshit for his advice in the preparation of this article and to Dr. V.N. Misra for reading the draft and making useful suggestions for improving its content. The line drawings and plates are by the courtesy of the Archaeological Survey of India.

BIBLIOGRAPHY

Basham, A.L. 1964. Notes on Seafaring in Ancient India, in *Studies in Indian History and Culture* (A.L. Basham ed.), pp. 146-166. Calcutta.

Broeze, Frant. 1997. *Gateways of Asia*. London: Kegan Paul International.

Chakrabarti, *Dilip*. 1979. The size of the Harappan Settlements, in *Essays in Indian Proto-History* (D.P. Agrawal and D.K. Chakrabarti eds.). New Delhi: D.K. Publishers. Pp. 205-215.

Chakrabarti, Dilip. 1995. *The Archaeology of Ancient Indian Cities*, Reprint 1998. New Delhi: Oxford University Press.

Chakrabarti, Dilip. 1999. *India An Archaeological History*. New Delhi: Oxford University Press.

Dales, G.F. 1962. A search for Ancient Seaports Expedition, *the Bulletin of the University* Museum of Pennsylvania IV (2): 2-10.

Dales G.F. 1962. Harappan Out Posts on the Markan Coast, *Antiquity*. 36(142). Pp. 86-92.

Dales G.F. 1966. *The Decline of the Harappans, South Asian Archaeology* 241.5 92-100.

Deloche, Jean. 1983. Geographical considerations in the localization of the Ancient ports, *The Indian Economic and Social History* Review 20, pp. 439-448.

Dhavalikar, M.K. 1995. *Cultural Imperialism Indus Civilization in Western India*. New Delhi: Books and Books.

Fairservis, Jr., W.A. 1971. *The Roots of Ancient India The Archaeology of Early Indian Civilization*. New York.

Gargallo, Piero Nicalo 1961. *Anchors of Antiquity* as translated by Evelyn Prebesen Archaeology 14 (5): 31-35.

Gaur, A.S. 2000. *Harappan Maritime Legacies of Gujarat*. New Delhi: Asian Publication Services.

Gibson, E Charles 1958. *The story of the Ships from the Earliest days to the Present*. New York: Abelard – Sehuman.

Green, Charles 1961. East Anglian Coast-line Levels Since Roman Times, *Antiquity* 35 March 1961, pp. 21-28.

Gupta, S.K. 1973. *Stability of Saurashtra coast during the late quaternary and Silting of Rann of Kutch during Holocene*, Unpublished PH.D. Thesis, IIT, Bombay.

Hariharan, K.V. 1964. *Seafaring in the Proto-historic Period of the Indian History with special reference to the western coast of India*. Unpublished PhD Thesis presented to Bombay University.

Jansen, M. 1979. Architectural problems of the Harappan Culture, *South Asian Archaeology* 1977 Naples pp. 405-31.

Kenoyer, J.M. 1989. *Social-Economic Structures of the Indus Civilization as reflected in specialized crafts and the question of specialization, in Old Problems and New Perspective in the Archaeology of South Asia* (J.M. Kenoyer ed.), Archaeological Reports, Vol. 2, University of Wisconsin., pp.183-92

Lal, B.B. 1997. *Earliest Civilization of South Asia : Rise, Maturity and Demise*. New Delhi: Aryan Books International.

Lele, V.S. "Docks at Lothal", *Journal of Institution of Engineers Ltd.* Pune Centre (As quoted by Shri R.S. Rao 1973:78).

Leshnik, L.S. 1968. The Harappan "Port" at Lothal Another View, American Anthropologist, 70(5): 911-922 as Reprinted in G.L. Possehl (ed.) *Ancient cities India*. New Delhi: Vikas Publishing House, New Delhi 1976, pp. 202-211.

Mackay, Dorothy 1945. Ancient River Beds and Dead Cities, *Antiquity* 19: 135-144.

Majumdar, R.C. 1960. The *Classical Accounts of India*. Calcutta: Firma K.L. Mukitaopadhaya.

Mehta, G.L. 1933. Ports and Navigational Development, *The Modern Review*, Calcutta 542-547.

Moore, G. 1952. *A Dictionary of Geography*. London: Harmonds Worth.

Mookerji, Radha Kumud 1912. *Indian Shipping – A History of the Seaborne Trade and Maritime Activity of the Indians >From the earliest times*. New Delhi: Munshi Ram Manoharlal.

Moti Chandra 1977. *Trade and Trade Routes in Ancient India*. New Delhi: Abhinav Publications.

Nigam, R. 1988. Was the large Rectangular structure at Lothal (Harappan Settlement) a 'Dockyard' Or an Irrigation Tank? In *Marine Archeology* of Indian Ocean Countries (S.R. Rao ed.), pp. 20-21, Society for Marine Archaeology, Goa.

Pandya, Suman 1977. *Lothal Dockyard Hypothesis and Sealevel Changes, in Ecology and Archaeology of Western India* (D.P. Aggarwal, B.M. Pande eds.). Delhi: Concept Publishing Company, pp. 99-103.

Panjwani, P.A. 1989. Petrography of Harappan Pottery from Lothal, *Man and Environment* 83-86.Pannikar, N.K. and Srinivasan T.M. 1971. The Concept of Tides in Ancient India, *Indian journal of History Sciences 6(1)*.

Pannikar, N.K. and Srinivasan T.M. 1972. Early Concepts of Oceanographic Phenomena of the Indian Ocean, *Proceedings of Royal Society of Engineers*, London.

Possehl, Gregory L. 1976 Lothal : *A Gateway Settlement of the Harappan Civilization as in South Asian Pre-history, in Ancient Cities of the Indus* (G.L. Possehl ed.), pp. 118-131. New Delhi: Vikas Publishing House.

Possehl, Gregory L. 1980. *Indus Civilization in Saurashtra*. Delhi: BR Publishing Corporation.

Rao. S.R. 1963. A Persion Gulf Seal from Lothal, *Antiquity* 37: 96-99.

Rao, S.R. 1968. Contacts between Lothal and Susa, Proceedings of The *Twenty-sixth International Congress of Orientalists*: II: 35-37.

Rao. S.R. 1970. Shipping in Ancient India, in India's *Contribution to World Thought and Culture*. (Lokesh Chandra ed.) Madras: Vivekanand Memorial Committee, pp. 83-107.

Rao. S.R. 1973. *Lothal and the Indus Civilization*. New York: Asia Publishing House.

Rao. S.R. 1979. *Lothal A Port Town, Memoirs of the Archaeological Survey of India* No. 78 Vol. I. New Delhi.

Rao. S.R. 1985. *Lothal A Harappan Town Archaeological Survey of India*, Vol. II. New Delhi.

Rao. S.R. 1991. *Dawn and Development of the Indus Civilization*. New Delhi: Aditiya Prakashan.

Rao. S.R. 1998. *The Lost City of Dvaraka*. New Delhi: Aditiya Prakashan.

Sahay, Baldeo 1996. *Indian Shipping*—A Historical Survey, Publications Division. Ministry of Information and Broadcasting. New Delhi:

Sarma, AVN 1971. *Decline of Harappan Cultures A Re-look*, K.A. Nilkantha Sastri Felicitation Volume. Madras.

Savile, Leopold Holliday 1941. Ancient Harbours, *Antiquity* 15(59): 209-232.

Schoff, Wilfred H. (Tr) 1992. *The Periplus of the Erythraean Sea (Travel and Trade in the Indian Ocean by a merchant of the First Century)*. New Delhi: Orient Books Reprint Corporation.

Shah, U.P. 1960. Lothal – A Port, *'Journal of Oriental Institute*, Baroda IX (3): 310-320.

Sridharan, Rear Admiral K. 1982. *A Maritime History of India*, New Delhi, Publication Division: Ministry of Information and Broadcasting.

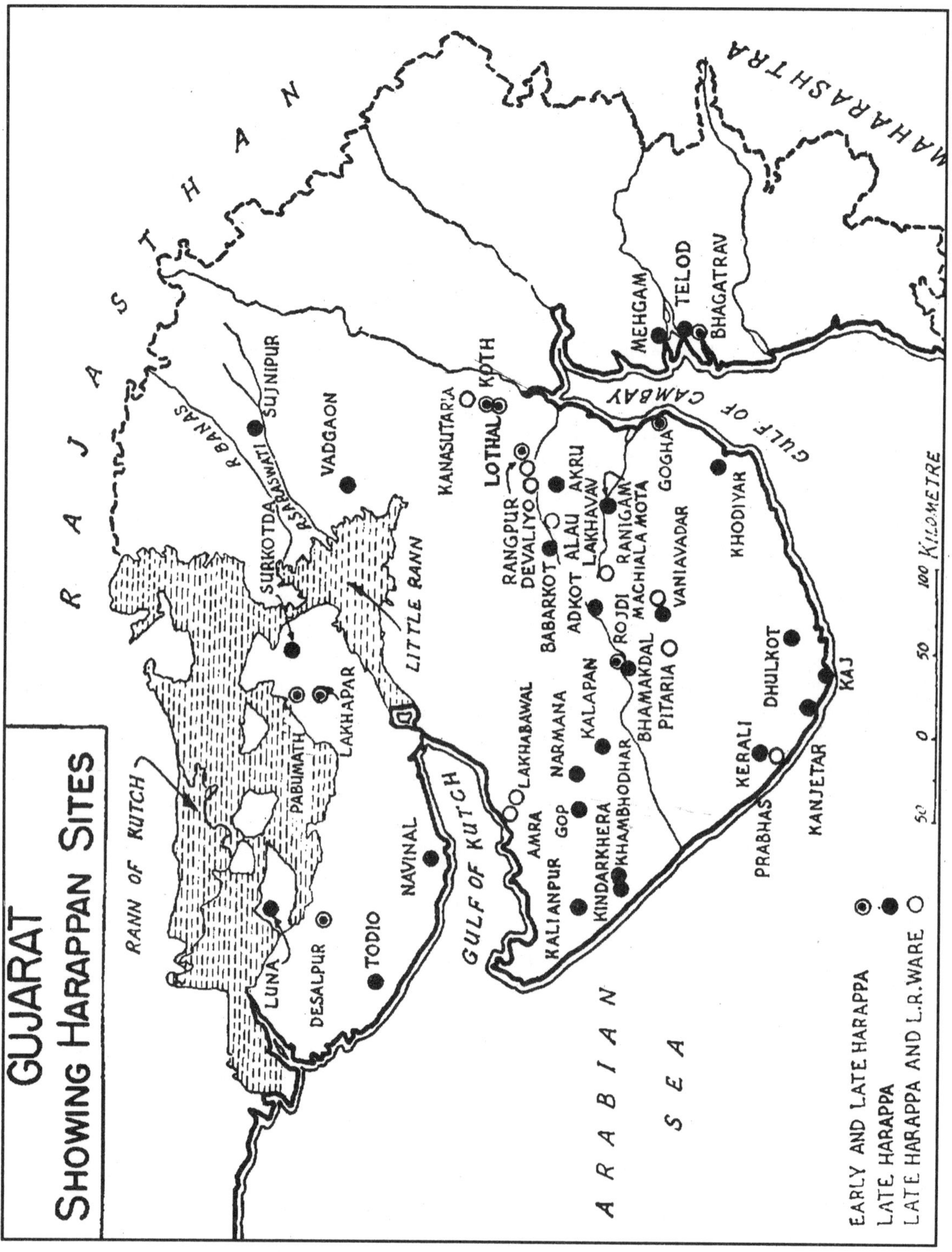
GUJARAT
SHOWING HARAPPAN SITES
RAJASTHAN
MAHARASHTRA
RANN OF KUTCH
LITTLE RANN
GULF OF KUTCH
GULF OF CAMBAY
ARABIAN SEA
BANAS
SARASWATI
SURKOTDA
SUJNIPUR
VADGAON
PABUMATH
LAKHAPAR
LUNA
DESALPUR
TODIO
NAVINAL
KANASUTARIA
KOTH
LOTHAL
RANGPUR
DEVALIYO
BABARKOT
ADKOT
ALAU
AKRU
LAKHAVAV
RANIGAM
MACHIALA MOTA
GOGHA
VANIAVADAR
KHODIYAR
ROJDI
BHAMAKDAL
PITARIA
LAKHABAWAL
NARMANA
KALAPAN
AMRA
GOP
KALIANPUR
KINDARKHERA
KHAMBHODHAR
DHULKOT
KERALI
KAJ
PRABHAS
KANJETAR
MEHGAM
TELOD
BHAGATRAV
EARLY AND LATE HARAPPA
LATE HARAPPA
LATE HARAPPA AND L.R.WARE
50 0 50 100 KILOMETRE

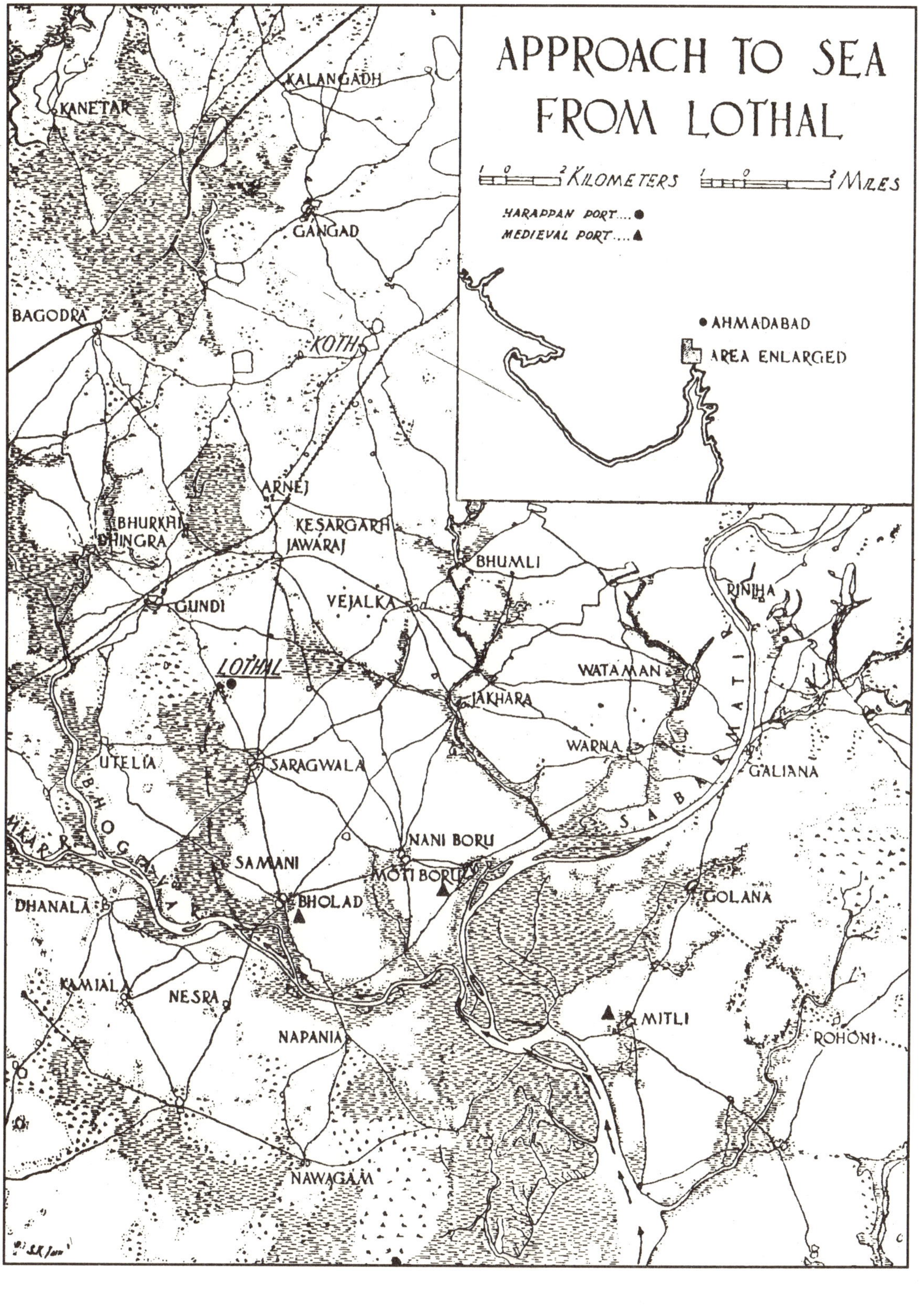
APPROACH TO SEA FROM LOTHAL
KILOMETERS
MILES
HARAPPAN PORT....
MEDIEVAL PORT....
AHMADABAD
AREA ENLARGED
KALANGADH
KANETAR
GANGAD
BAGODRA
KOTH
ARNEJ
BHURKHI
DHINGRA
KESARGARH
JAWARAJ
BHUMLI
VEJALKA
GUNDI
LOTHAL
WATAMAN
JAKHARA
WARNA
GALIANA
UTELIA
SARAGWALA
SABARMATI
BHOGAVA
NANI BORU
SAMANI
MOTI BORU
BHOLAD
DHANALA
GOLANA
NESRA
NAPANIA
MITLI
ROHONI
NAWAGAM

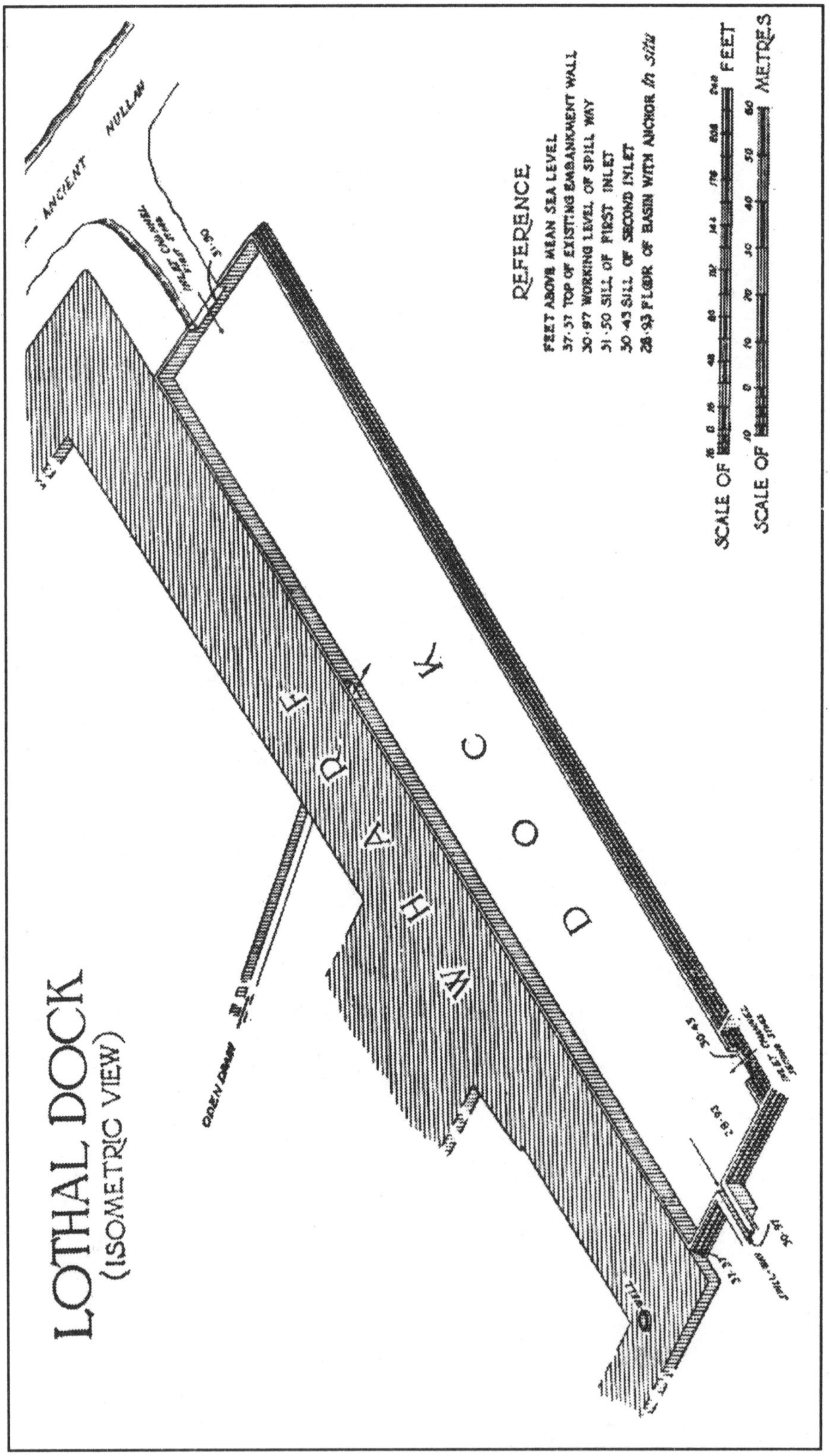
LOTHAL DOCK
(ISOMETRIC VIEW)
WHARF
DOCK
ANCIENT NULLAH
OPEN DRAIN
REFERENCE
FEET ABOVE MEAN SEA LEVEL
37.37 TOP OF EXISTING EMBANKMENT WALL
30.97 WORKING LEVEL OF SPILL WAY
31.50 SILL OF FIRST INLET
30.43 SILL OF SECOND INLET
28.93 FLOOR OF BASIN WITH ANCHOR In Situ
SCALE OF FEET
SCALE OF METRES

Archaeology of Birbhum: The Past Informs the Present

SUBRATA CHAKRABARTI*

Introduction

The district of Birbhum at 23° 32' 30" N and 24° 35' 00" N : 88° 02' 40" E and 81° 05' 25" E covers an area of about 4514 km sq with an average elevation of about 80 m above mean sea level, and could be viewed as a upside down funnel. At its southern border with Burdwan, the funnel mouth reaches a width of about 100 km in east-west direction, which is traversed by the river Ajay and forms the natural boundary between the districts of Birbhum and Burdwan. The tapering narrow end at the northern tip of the district, the width of the funnel has decreased to less than 10 km east-west and is appended to the body of the hills of the Santhal Parganas in the west and to the Gangetic plains in the east. The western part of the district is more rugged as it shares the geomorphology of the Bihar Plateau and is marked by a few inselbergs or isolated hillocks to the Rajmahal Highlands. The monotonous level plain of the deltaic Bengal is broken in the district by the undulating upland, which exerts an influence on the climate and thus effects the distribution of plants, animals, soils, water-courses and, above all, people.

Much of the area of the district is taken up by undulating lateritic outcrop. Aside from this topographical unit, the large and small rivers - the Ajay, Mayurakshi, Hingla, Bakreswar, Sal-Kopai, Singra, Dwarka, Brahmani, etc., structure the surface of the narrow valley corridors and narrow valley segments of Birbhum. The character of the plateau governs the drainage pattern of Birbhum and most of the rivers have west to east flow, the cross-section of the valley floor(s) being broader in the west, that is the upstream region. Most of the rivers of the district originate from the Santhal Pargana highlands and fall into the 'dead delta' zone below the higher land along the Ganga-Bhagirathi bank. It does not have in strict sense the lowland plains but does have several sub-units of large enough stretches of level land for human habitation.

Geology

Birbhum is an area of great geological complexity. At its geological base is the Precambrian landmass. The Gondwana sediments of continental origin are found in parts of the district. In sequential development of rock systems of the district, as that of the Eastern Plateau of India, there are unconformities, but the evidence of the Precambrian rocks followed by basalt flows of Upper Jurassic/ Lower Cretaceous and subsequent developments from Eocene through Miocene-Oligocene to Mio-Pliocene speaks volume about the geological antiquity of Birbhum, which has considerable bearing upon the Pleis-

* Visva Bharati Univeristy, Shantiniketan, West Bengal

tocene and Holocene geomorphology of the country in question.

Uncertainty exists between the Pliocene and Pleistocene boundary in Birbhum. Neverthless, the Quaternary stratigraphy of Bengal can be seen to have developed in a sequence beginning from, what has been designated by Ghosh and Majumder (1991) as, the Lalgarh Formation with its Lower and Upper Member units to Older Alluvium and Younger Alluvium series.

The Lower Lalgarh Formation consists of rounded pebbles, cobbles and boulders of quartzite, amphibolite, schist, granite, laterite, fossil wood and pellets of white shale and represents the primary laterite. The Upper Lalgarh Formation is re-worked and re-deposited sediments of the Lower Lalgarh Formation. Nowhere in the district of Birbhum, the Lower Lalgarh Formation could be associated with the Palaeolithic archaeology but the Upper Lalgarh Formation incorporates the lithic industries from the Lower Palaeolithic to the Upper Palaeolithic not only in Birbhum but also in Bengal, Bihar, Jharkhand and Orissa (Bose and Sen 1948; Bose, Sen and Ray 1958; Ghosh 1962, 1966; Chakrabarti 1999, 2000, 2001, 2002).

The alluvial and fluviatile fan sediments overlie the Lalgarh Formations and make up the post-Pleistocene geomorphology of the Upland Bengal including Birbhum, which have great bearing upon the growth and development of the Mesolithic cultures of the region.

A composite stratigraphy of Birbhum that can be worked out from exposures and erosions, either natural or geo-archaeological section cuttings, is as follows:

A thin veneer of humus

Yellowish brown to reddish brown silt and fine grained sand
with grits of quartz and chert (Slope wash material)

Yellowish red silt and medium grained sand with
iron-oxide granules and grits of rock fragments constituting
mainly of vein quartz and chert
(Slope wash material)
Holocene

Old surface built by alluvial and fluviatile fan Pleistocene sediments

Unconformity

Laterite Bed comprising of nodules, quartz pebbles,
fossil-woods in a clayey matrix

Plio-Pleistocene Boundary

Unconformity

Yellowish feldspathic mottled clayey Bed

Conglomerate Bed with pebbles of different rock types,
fossil-woods, agate in a clayey matrix

Yellowish-greyish mottled horizontally bedded sand and mud

Unconformity

Jurassic Volcanic rocks of the Rajmahal Traps

Subsurface basement ridge of Gondwana rocks

Basement granitoid Precambrian rocks, at places
intruded by dolerite dykes

Prehistoric Hunter-Gatherer Societies

The prehistoric hunter-gatherer societies evolved during the geological period called Quaternary. This geological period is subdivided into the Pleistocene and Holocene or Recent Epoch. The Pleistocene began approximately 3 million years ago and ended around 10,000 years before present. The Holocene began about 10,000 years ago and continues at present. The boundary between the Pleistocene and Holocene, like the boundaries between the various preceding glacials and interglacials, is not very well defined. Some authorities would not consider the Holocene as a separate series but just regard it as the most recent stage of the Pleistocene (Goudie 1983).

The cultural remains of the Pleistocene humans have not survived in its entirety. It is only the most durable objects that were preserved that gives us glimpses of the cultural activities of the past hunting-gathering soceities. Since tools made of bone or wood rarely were preserved, most of the evidence about human activities during the Pleistocene comes from stone artefacts. Therefore, this culture is designated as Palaeolithic or Old Stone Age Culture. The Palaeolithic is again subdivided into Lower, Middle, and Upper periods. These subdivisions are mainly based on the technology of stone tool manufacture.

Lower Palaeolithic

In Birbhum, the evidence for the presence of the Lower Palaeolithic cultural remains is associated with the Acheulian. The Acheulian has been sub-divided into early, middle, and late periods, but our advanced knowledge on the Acheulian culture suggests that it had only two subdivisions viz. early or lower and later or upper stages. In the Old World, the Acheulian first appeared approximately 1.5 million years ago. In India the oldest dated Acheulian is around 1.2 million years. There is a lack of well-dated Acheulian sites in Bengal. The *in situ* occurrence of Acheulian implements in the Upper Lalgarh Formation in Midnapur district (Ghosh 1966; Chakrabarti 2001) and on the Pleistocene beds from the area around the Susania hills in Bankura district (Sastry 1966) probably indicates their origin in Upper Pleistocene. At the Susania hill complex about thirty-five sites from which more than two thousand Acheulian tools were recovered (Dasgupta *et al.* 1973) but it is unfortunate that there is whatsoever no study on them that make scientific assessment difficult to define and designate this otherwise important assemblage or assemblages. It seems from Dasgupta *et al.'s* (1973) report that the Acheulian industry, as in other parts of Bankura and Midnapur districts, represents Lower Acheulian tradition. But the Acheulian appeared later in Birbhum and, as it stands today, has a very limited distribution, mainly in northwest Birbhum at Maluti Sadar Ghat on Chila, the rivulet that flows in Birbhum - Jharkhand borderland. It should be borne in mind that the report (Dasgupta *et al.* 1969) of 'Early Stone Age tools', comprising of stray finds described as handaxes, from Jibdharpur in Suri P.S. Birbhum has not been published either with documentation or description of the tools and, furthermore, subsequent explorations carried out there yielded negative results.

At Maluti Sadar Ghat site at 24° 7' N and 87° 40' E, the Acheulian finds, discovered from three locatities, one of them fossiliferous, include handaxes, cleavers, choppers, scrapers and unmodified wastes - flakes, cores and chips and are made of raw materials - traps, basalts, quartize, chert, jasper (Chakrabarti 1993, 1999, 2001, 2003). The assemblages at Maluti Sadar Ghat Acheulian sites show preponderance of various other tools, such as retouched flakes, side scrapers, end scrapers, points, borers and sundry light-duty tools over the diagnostic Acheulian artefacts - handaxes, cleavers and knives. It should be noted that such assemblage character is common with the Late or Upper Acheulian world over. However, the typo-technological traits of the assemblages at Maluti Sadar Ghat represent the Upper Acheulian tradition, the fossilised mammalian teeth and bones, belonging to *Bos* sp. and Cervus sp., associated with the assemblage at the fossil-bearing locality, and the geological horizon in which these are found indicated that the Acheulian here belonged to Late Upper Pleistocene.

Middle Palaeolithic

Traditionally the Middle Palaeolithic is characterised by artefacts mostly made on flakes. However, there are many Middle Palaeolithic assemblages that contain a great frequency of blades, which were produced from specially prepared cores. There is no sharp boundary between the beginning of the Middle Palaeolithic and the end of the Late or Upper Acheulian. And almost all Middle Palaeolithic tools had its antecedent in the Late Acheulian. Several Thermoluminescence and Uranium/Thorium decay series and radiocarban dates are available for the Middle Palaeolithic in India. These range in age between 150,000 and 10,000 B.P. The culture of the Middle Palaeolithic period thereby continued to exist for a long duration, covering the Terminal Middle Pleistocene to the end phase of the Upper Pleistocene. In Bengal, however, there is no radiocarbon dated Middle Palaeolithic site.

The first good evidence for the Middle Palaeolithic in Birbhum has come from the Chila Valley (Chakrabarti 1993, 1998, 1999, 2001). The Middle Palaeolithic sites, seven in number, lie in the Mid-reaches of the Chila river, extending over 4.4 km stretch of the Valley. Perhaps such a spread is by itself can be regarded as a remarkable feature of the industry. The shaped tools include scrapers, points, bores, notches, etc. The preponderance of unmodified waster over shaped tools characterised the Middle Palaeolithic industry from the Chila Valley, and it shows exclusive reliance on silicous rocks. These occur as surface finds as well as in the second fluvial gravel bed having, at places, sharp contact to the channel gravel (Lower Palaeolithic) but usually separated by a thin layer of alluvium.

Further south from the Chila Valley, about 17 km to the east of the Maluti Sadar Ghat Acheulian site and 12 km north from Suri, the district headquarters, in the vicinity of the basalt quarry, E/1 - 14 A (2), at Hatgacha Mouza, in the Mahammadbazar area, a Palaeolithic site has been recently discovered (Chakrabarti i.p. 1998-1999, 2001). The site is an open-air station and the artefacts found on the tertiary rock surface, which, by no means, could be their geological context. Nevertheless, the occurrence of Palaeolithic artefacts in this region is important from the viewpoint of the past hunter-gatherers' movement in Birbhum. The artefacts from this site, even though the collection is random and from a small portion of the site, incorporate scrapers, borers, notches, burins, flake-blades, blades and unmodified waste. Chert as raw material dominates over jasper and agate in this collection.

The Hatgacha Palaeolithic artefacts do not represent either morphologically or technologically the typical Middle Palaeolithic. It also does not qualify as belonging to an Upper Palaeolithic industry. But as it does share a similar trait from two of the assemblages from among the seven Middle Palaeolithic assemblages in the Chila valley, it may be placed as a Transitional Middle Palaeolithic- Upper Palaeolithic industry.

Upper Palaeolithic

The Upper Palaeolithic is that stage of Stone Age culture when humanity earned the denotation of *Homo sapiens sapiens* or wise human. Not only the Upper Palaeolithic industry is characterised as having more tools made on blades than the Middle Palaeolithic but also new types of stone tools, such as strangulated blades, gravetted points, truncated pieces, pressure-flak, leaf-shaped points appeared during this period. Art in various forms became important component of diurnal existence of humankind. As modern humans, *Homo sapiens sapiens* had appeared on earth approximately 100,000 years ago, their culture may have begun since the species arrived, but the evidence for the Upper Palaeolithic cultural remains all over the world is better known between the dates ranging from 40,000 to 10,000 years B.P. There is widespread evidence of the Upper Palaeolithic cultural remains in India but not of the makers of this culture. However, well-dated geomorphic data and rich fossil record of fauna and ostrich egg shells from several Upper Palaeolithic sites in India suggest that the culture may be placed in the time-range of 20,000 - 10,000 B.P.

In Bengal the Upper Palaeolithic industry is neither geographically very widespread nor culturally as varied as sites known from Central, Western and Southern India. The stone artefacts that have been designated as Flake-Blade industry, represents the first appearance of the Upper Palaeolithic in Bengal. It should be noted that the Upper Palaeolithic stone industry reported from the north Midnapur region is dominated by Flake elements than Blade tools (Datta 1991). However, a blade-based leptolithic industry discovered in 1999 from the Paruldanga area at 23° 42' 15" N: 87° 43' 20" E, represents the Upper Palaeolithic in Birbhum and reflects the gradual development of flake industry into blade industry (Chakrabarti 1999, 2001).

The Upper Palaeolithic artefacts at Paruldanga, which were found sealed in on an earlier geomorphic surface at a depth of 1.5 m at the southeast corner of the site by covered up slope wash material of yellowish red to yellowish brown silt of the recent geologic period, suggest their primary context. Over 300 artefacts have been recovered from the old surface, which conformably overlie the upper part of the zone of nodular laterite making up the Upper Lalgarh Formation.

The Upper Palaeolithic industry at Paruldanga includes a bone tool, possibly a hide-burnisher, and a varied stone artefacts: curved-backed knives/points, straight blades/ knives or points, tanged points, gravers or burins, beck-like boring tools, microlithic backed blades and debitage - cores, anvils, etc. Variously coloured cryptocrystalline rocks, chert, quatzite and fossil-wood were employed to fashion the artefacts. The assemblages of this type have not been found elsewhere in the region till now. The geologic context in which the Upper Palaeolithic artefacts lie suggests that these have unquestionable great antiquity, definetly greater than 12,000 years B.P.

Mesolithic

The Mesolithic hunter-gatherers were the most successful colonisers from among the past hunter-gatherers who preceded them. On the one hand, it is a cultural survival from the Palaeolithic, on the other hand technological changes are reflected in the Mesolithic. The Mesolithic stone industry is characterised by microlithic tools. The culture began around 10,000 years ago in Postglacial environment and survived well into the Neolithic-Chalcolithic and even much later when iron had been introduced.

The Mesolithic sites in Bengal are well distributed in space and time. We find the number of sites has increased during the Mesolithic period in Bankura, Purulia, Midnapur, Burdwan and Birbhum. The Mesolithic hunter-gatherers in Birbhum have shown greater mobility along the banks of the rivers Ajay, Bakreswar, and Kopai, and better adaptability, by occupying the laterite uplands. In the lateritic uplands in and around Santiniketan, there are at least five Mesolithic camp-sites Paruldanga, Syambati, Cheap-Kuthi, Deer Park, Ballabhpur - all located within a 15 km radius of the Ajay-Mayurakshi water divide in the Kopai-Bakreswar valley. Of the five camp-sites or open-air stations of the Mesolithic hunter-gatherers, the camp site at Paruldanga represents activities of longer duration and indicates that probably larger groups were occupying the site. Trial excavations at this open-air settlement have helped establish three phases of occupation (Fig. 1). The Mesolithic - 1 tools occur here at a depth between 0.26 m and 1.5 m in yellowish red silt and, above it, in the yellowish brown to reddish brown silt at a depth between 5 cm - 7 cm are found the Mesolithic - II tools (Chakrabarti 1993, 1998-1999, 1999-2000, 2001). In the assemblage composition, there is indication of lithic reduction sequence in the manufacture of artefacts consisting of flake-blade to blade and bladelet tools. In the Paruldanga collection the finished tools are outnumbered by debitage, possibly an indication of tool knapping at the site. The finished tools consist of blades, lunates, points, borers, burins, scrapers, notches and retouched flakes. A few pieces of triangles were found from the surface but none found in excavation. The debitage includes primary flakes, cores, unclassified lumps, and core-rejuvenated flakes. The chert is the dominant raw material followed by agate, quartz and fossilwoods employed for tool manufacture at Paruldanga. No radiometric dates are available for ascertaining the chronology of the Mesolithic assemblages at Paruldanga, nevertheless the occurrence of microlithic tools in a stratigraphical sequence over an old land surface sealed in by two sets of slope wash material suggests continuity ranging from Early Holocene to Late Holocene period.

Microlithic artefacts purportedly belonging to Mesolithic Period are reported from Sukhbazar, Tatarpur, Kondiapur, Dubrajpur, Hetampur, Nalhati, Suri, Bakreswar and many other places from the district of Birbhum. However, non-geometric types and, mostly waster products, represent the microlithic artefacts from these sites. The raw material used for manufacturing these tools is predominantly chert but quartz, agate and fossil woods are not uncommon. The stratigraphical horizons of artefacts from most of the sites are not known but it is been reported that the artefacts at Sukhbazar and Tatarpur lay over an old surface scattered with fossilwoods whereas at Kodaipur the upper layer of a bed of pisolithic laterite, which has a thickness of about 1.50 m incorporated the microlithic tools (Dasgupta *et at.* 1965: 43). It does seem that some of the sites may represent the Mesolithic - I and some the Mesolithic - II stages of culture as reflected in the Paruldanga assemblages.

Early Farming Communities

Transition to Neolithic in Bengal is more speculative than contextual. This is true in the case of archaeology of Birbhum also. The Neolithic is that time segment when band level societies first evolved into tribal societies with nomadic pastoral existence coupled with food production and lasting until the appearance of copper metallurgy, which marks the beginnings of the Chalcolitic. Archaeology has, however attested that even some of the early Neolithic societies knew cold hammering of native copper. The genesis of the Neolithic in the district of Birbhum is, nevertheless not only uncertain but even doubts exist as to whether the sites with polished and ground stone axes could be assigned the status of the Neolithic. On the contrary, our picture of the early settled farming communities of the Chalcolithic is far more comprehensive than the Neolithic in the district of Birbhum. The Chalcolithic cultures of the region are divisible into two or, more probably, three phases of development: Early Chalcolithic, Late Chalcolithic and Iron-using Later Chalcolithic. The Radiocarbon dates, now calibrated, place the Early Chalcolithic at 1690–1035 BC, Late Chalcolithic at 920–795 BC whereas in the last phases of the Late Chalcolithic, the first farmers became iron user and may have evolved into Iron Age at 820–595 BC (Possehl 1988; Agrawal and Yadava 1995).

The Chalcolithic villages are numerous in the district of Birbhum. These villages are located below 50 metre contour and stood on proximal reaches of the river valley built up by alluviums. On imagery the villages present a picture of 'chaotic agglomeration'. But their spatial distribution locates each other at a distance of 5 km (Nag 1987). The radius drawn around each village gives an idea of the catchments of the settlement, which usually spreads over an area not more than 4 to 6 acres. The general arrangment of settlements is Linear.

Excavations in half a dozen sites, e.g. Naur (23° 42' N : 87° 51' E), Mahisdal (23° 42' 49" N : 87° 41' 42" E), Haraipur (23° 52' N : 87° 45 E), Bahari (23° 38' 30" N : 87° 46' E), Hatikra (23° 49' N : 87° 35' E) and Kotasur (23° 52' N : 87° 45' E) have provided with settlement and cultural data based upon which life and time of the early farming communities of Birbhum can be reasonably reconstructed (Das 1967; Kar *et al.* 1969; Chakrabarti and Hasan 1982; Ghosh *et al.* 1988; Chakrabarti 1986; Ghosh and Chakrabarti 1990). The salient features of the Chalcolithic settlements and cultural remains in Birbhum are examined and presented below.

The earliest Chalcolithic villages in Birbhum are found in the southeastern part of the district. The settlement sites in Birbhum and adjacent parts of South Bengal, with the exception of Mangalkot (23° 32' N : 87° 54' E) on the Ajay river and to some extent Mahisdal on the Kopai river, do not take the form of *tells* or mounds made up of the debris of long occupation. Such *tells* or mound-sites occur in other parts of India. The accumulation of debris layer upon layer suggests longer duration of occupation of such settlements, which could have been possible due to easy access to water and availability of rich fertile soils thereby giving settlement stability. On the other hand, the Chalcolithic villages in general in Bengal and in Birbhum in particular reveal two or three sequential stages of development. The Chalcolithic habitation sites in Birbhum incorporate cultural deposit of 2 m at its maximum showing two stages of development. The first stage is distinctively Copper Age during which the early farmers of Birbhum variously used the softer metal whereas in the second stage in its late phases iron was adopted by the peoples who had been settled in this region for many centuries previously. Some authorities have applied the term 'Early Iron Age', despite notable absence of an appropriate high-temperature technology that would make iron smelting techniques seem plausible, but it would be premature to regard the case as proven and, therefore, until archaeology provides us with a better answer it would not be inappropriate to designate this cultural interlude as Iron-using Late Chalcolithic phase.

The origin of the early farming communities which settled on the terraces in river valleys in the uplands of south Bengal is decidedly unclear. They appeared on the scene with copper metallurgy but did not discontinue their stone technology. This certainly would not imply a generic relationship between the antecedent and continuing cultures. The point is that knowledge of copper-working is evident from the presence of copper celts, fish-books, bangles, rings, etc., and that native copper was available not at far distance away from the Chalcolithic settlements of the region but, despite this, none of the sites indicate prolific use of the soft metal. This may imply the Chalcolithic villages though maintained inter-village trading network, the inter-regional exchanges may have involved only high-value objects, which probably occurred vertically among the high-ranking individuals of different early farming communities.

It does seem from the location of Chalcolithic settlements that each settlement had its own farming territory. By setting up their villages along rivers, especially on low-lying terraces and floodplains, the Chalcolithic farmers were able to exploit the fertile soils. Perhaps the selection of the most productive territories along rivers for permanent settlements also suggests that these villagers ensure that continous growing of crops and cereals on the same plot of land would lead to soil exhaustion if the farming territories were not rejuvenated and made rich annually through floods. It is not known whether these farmers rotated cereals and legumes to prevent soil exhaustion but certainly they did cultivate rice, which is evident from the fully exposed barn, measuring 1.28 m in diameter with a depth of 1.25 m, from Mahisdal. Two such barns have been located in an excavated area of 40 m x 20 m = 800 m^2 at Mahisdal. Each ban could contain 900 kilogram of paddy and assuming that there existed twenty such barns at one time in this settlement. Ghosh (1986) noted that to produce 180 quintals of paddy at one time in a year these farmers would need atleast 72 acres of land to cultivate, which could hold a population size of about 250-300 people in a settlement of about 8000 m^2. It is highly unlikely that all the settlements of the Chalcolithic period were large settlements and existed in one time period.

Nevertheless considering the variations of sizes of

settlements and farming territories, if the average population size is estimated to 200 souls per village, then the total population of Bengal in the Early Farming stages of history should not exceed 10,000. In comparison to other parts of Bengal, if more number of sites indicates more population, the district of Birbhum could have hold substantial population of 6000-7000 souls.

Data from Mahisdal suggest that the main occupation of the Chalcolithic farmers was agriculture, which is evident from the presence of a large quantity of charred rice over the second floor-level of Period-I occupation at this site (Das 1967:60). The cultivated species was *Oryza sativa* but these farmers also exploited its wild progenitors. Furthermore, it is also evident from archaeological data that the agriculture based economy had to be supplemented by animal husbandry. This is testified by the presence of charred remains of wild and domesticated animals (Banerjee 1982). Humped cattle (*Bos Indicus*), buffalo, sheep, goat pig, domestic fowl and pariah dog were reared but the recovery of bones of swamp deer, spotted deer, barking deer, nilgai, sambar, chital, falconer, and even jungle cat and wolf, from excavations at several Chalcolithic sites clearly demonstrate that how hunting remained a substantial mode of economy in these village societies. Fish, turtle and snails had rooms in their larder, but fishing as an economy could have been relatively unimportant at this stage of cultural existence.

These villages contained mud houses, the traces of which are completely obliterated but in excavations floors of beaten earth with soiling of rammed terracotta nodules, reed-impressed clay daubs, burnt husk-impressed clay plasters and post-holes have been indentified. These give an idea about the houses the Chalcolithic villagers built albeit without any idea of house plans. The houses no doubt were simple and built of perishable materials and the presence of large quantities of ash in floors (Das 1967) suggests their vulnerability to fire. Probably the houses the early farmers constructed were small and occupied by single family units, and if the average population as estimated on the site size and availability of cultivable land is correct, the single units of family could have consisted of not less than 10 persons per house.

As craftsmen, these villagers could not have succeeded much in introducing sophisticated techniques of metalworking. Conditions essential for casting copper, such as a temperature of about 1100°C (Renfrew 1969), and a reducing atmosphere, the evidence of which have not been attested from any of the excavated sites. But as potter their inventory is much more impressive. Various pottery types included bowls, basins, dishes, vases, lids and jars, urns etc., which were used for storage, drinking, serving, cooking and ritualistic purposes. The shapes and sizes of pottery differed considerably. Both monochrome and polychrome pottery appeared that included different shades in black-and-red, red, black slipped and grey. Pottery ornamentation in white pigment on black surface, simple bands, dots, dashes, sigmas, solid triangles, *swastikas* and some other designs focuses upon characteristic attributes and levels of complexity of material culture of the Chalcolithic farmers. Likewise, terracotta discs with pin-holed petal motif in double-rows and cubes with enigmatic figures, such as the ones probably of human, recognised from Hatikara, and black ware depicting incise designs and pin-hole decoration may stand for attributes that could have association with these villagers socio-cultural or ritualistic status system or even social ties with people beyond their immediate vicinity. For instance, Sankalia (1974:312) has reminded us of the existence of a similar black ware with incised and pin-holed decoration from close at Chirand and distant Tekkalkota.

However, the evidence of items like beads, bangles, decorated combs, hairpins is not wanting in the archaeological record in this phase of culture. But the distribution of these materials is not uniform in all the Chalcolithic sites of Birbhum. For example, the preserved evidence of 1993 excavation at Mahisdal- I shows that, in addition to terracotta beads, agate, jasper, chalcedont, carnelian, coral and steatite were in circulation (Fig. 2 and 3) probably as prestige goods. The shapes of the beads are varied: disc, bi-cone, circular, crescent, spherical button, barrel, conical, tubular, pentagonal and hexagonal. In length, breadth and thickness a considerable variation is noticed, the maximum is 3.5 cm, 1.4 cm and 0.7 cm whereas the minimum is 0.2 cm (in the case of micro beads 0.1 cm only), 0.1 cm and 0.1 cm respectively. It is significant to note that some of the materials used in bead manufacture are not available in the vicinity of Mahisdal. Perhaps these items came from further northerly sites as exchanged prestige goods between high-status individuals on the basis of balanced reciprocity and passed on to other members of the community. It is not clear what products were exchanged between the Chalcolithic communities in return for these prestige goods but it is not necessary to assume that huge quantities of goods moved across the Ajay valley at this stage of culture.

The first farming settlers of this region did not discontinue the use and making of stone tools. This implies they did not neglect the non-domestic food resources available in the vicinity of their settlement. But all the same, it should not be overlooked that the stone inventory of these villagers comprised of scrapers and points. Lunates and short blades would also have gone well with the need for composite tools in reaping cereals and paddy from the field in a more efficient way. There is as yet, however, no evidence that would suggest freeing of a part of population from subsistence for fulltime craft specialisation that is copper smiths, potters, bead-makers, stone tool fabricators etc. in the early farming communities of this region.

Even though limitation exits in our knowledge of the total material culture inventory of the Chalcolithic communities of Birbhum, we do have records of mortuary practices of the communities. Three types of disposal of the dead can be archaeologically recorded. These are a) Extended Burial, b) Fractional or Secondary Burial, and c) Urn Burial. It is, however, not known whether the variations in burials are signs of status differences of related to the differences of burial treatment of the dead between the communities or within the groups in the community. The graves contain no goods, thereby making it impossible to locate the individual significance of the deceased thus buried. In the Ajay-Mayurakshi divide, there are only two sites that have yielded evidence of burials, and these sites even though are situated at a distance of about 30 km from each other, the deceased were subjected to extended burial at Pandurajar Dhipi show east-west orientation (Dasgupta 1965: 43) whereas the orientation of the dead is north-south at Haraipur burial (Kar, Pandey and Singh 1969: 46). Therefore, we may assume that in their extracorporal ideas and beliefs, the structure of the societies of the early farming communities is far from being monolithic.

The mortuary practices apart, there is evidence of a terracotta phallus as part of cultural inventory of the first farmers at Mahisdal. It is most likely that in these village societies, food and fecundity, the sustenance and reproduction in good numbers, writ larger than ceremonial propensities of life. We do not know what this realistic vulva in rough terracotta stood for. Nevertheless, human interest in generative organs, both male and female, is much deep rooted than a peevish children's covert obsession with libido. Analogous evidence of fertility symbols is not wanting in archaeological records of the contemporary societies. The pudenda and the penis, sometimes in enlarged form or in erect position respectively; loom large in village ritual.

The six or seven levels of continuous occupation in type-sites in southeast Birbhum do not show any appreciable break in material culture tradition. The society did evolve initially but at the end it was an evolution in retrograde material culture in Period- II of the Chalcolithic phase in Birbhum vis-à-vis Bengal. Despite the knowledge of iron, as it has been recorded from the top of the lower level, i.e., Layer - 5 of the Period - II at Hatikra, Mahisdal and other Chalcolithic sites, and proliferation of variety of shapes in different wares, notably the finesse in black-slipped ware, the overall craftsmanship shows sign of Chalcolithic genius deteriorating. The coming into contact of people with comparatively advanced iron technology was disadvantageous for the Chalcolithic village societies in this region. The apparent initial material boost up but lack of capacity to cope with challenges the black metal posed resulted in derailment in rank and file of the Copper Age specialists. The appearance of iron artefacts in the last phases of the Chalocolithic sites in Birbhum and contiguous regions did not have as great an ecological impact as did the diffusion of agricultural techniques in Early Chalcolithic. The introduction of iron technology affected the culture of the Chalcolithic population of the region more drastically. In their attempt to adapt to new technology, the iron-using Chalcolithic population presents a picture of a culture as if it was the last flicker before final extinction. From a dozen of radiocarbon dates, now available for the lowest, middle and top levels of occupations at three of these farming settlements, as seen earlier, it appears that the fluorescence in material cultural lasted for about seven hundred years, whereas despite of a supposedly new pottery type, the material culture of these settlers began to go downhill from about 900–800 B.C., and they wore a deserted look much before 700–600 B.C. None of the type site of the Chalcolithic in Birbhum could attract the population with real knowledge of iron metallurgy when they colonised the region in the second half of the third century B.C.

Early Historic Settlers

There is a hiatus of about two to three hundred years in the culture history of Birbhum prior to ushering of urban dimensions in settlements in the region. As compared to Chalcolithic villages, the early historical settlements are a negligible few. The only noteworthy settlement is Kotasur (23° 58' N : 87° 45' E), located on the northern bank of the Mayurakshi river, which now flows about 8 km down south from the settlement.

Excavations were carried out at this settlement site in 1985 and continued in 1986–1987 by N.C. Ghosh *et al.* (Ghosh 1993; Chakrabarti 1995). Two trenches, measuring respectively 3m x 5m and 3m x 3m, were dug to ascertain the cultural sequence at Kotasur. Five broad periods of cultural deposit have been identified at the site. Period - I is distinguished by NBP and other associated wares, indeterminate iron objects and beads of terracotta. The NBP appeared in excavation when the thickness of the initial deposit reached 30 cm above the natural soil. The quality of the NBP is inferior when compared with the ware found in the middle Ganga plains and their presence is limited in quantity as well. The evidence of structures is absent, except the occurrence of a couple of rammed floor levels of mud. In Period - II, there appears mainly the typical bowls and other types in plain red ware but more importantly fragments of moulded terracotta figurines, ascribable to Sunga craftsmanship, are located at this level. Mainly a few floor levels with post-holes represent the structural remains in this horizon. The diagnostic pottery in Period - III is red ware but often a thick bright red slip that characterise this red ware. The types inculed bowls, basins, pans, vases and jars. The pottery with ring-handle has also been recorded from this stratum. The noteworthy structural remain is a two baked brick walls of one and a half course in width even in a limited area of digging in this period.

The succeeding two archaeological horizons at Kotasur are in distrubed context. The deposits in Period - IV contain appreciable amount of sand and silt resulted from long lasting water logging, which might have been due to the vagaries of the Mayurakshi. Nevertheless, the pottery and antiquities recorded from this level, Ghosh (1993) suggested the period between fourth and eight century A.D. Period - IV has been badly vandalised by brick robbing that has totally disturbed this archaeological horizon. Thereby, it is a serious impediment in understanding the full circle of cultural development at the early historic Kotasur.

The site has also yielded a few punch-marked coins in disturbed horizon 30 cm below the surface in the trench dug on the northern face of the habitation mound atop which now lies the Madanesvar Siva temple. Two, if not more, of these coins bear representation of boat or ship and sun and six-armed symbols.

But more importantly, the Kotasur site is a fortified settlement (Fig. 4). It is evident that an impressive mud fortification wall, 1 km in circuit and about 10 m wide, with a canal-like ditch protecting the wall, encircled the settlement (Chakrabarti *et al.* 1981; Chattopadhyaya 1993-94). It is possible that the fortification of the settlement served the entire population, including domestic animals and arable lands. Perhaps it served a dual purpose: it could resist inroads of floods and the accumulated water in the canal-like ditch could have been conveniently used in irrigating fields. For Kotasur does not seem to be a hierarchical settlement nor does it reflect an increasingly complex socio-political organisation and an intensification of warfare.

It should be noted that fortification wall alone would not suffice to designate an urban character to a settlement. The nature of settlement organisation, population distribution and status differences, free space within the settlement, reflection of relative wealth of the homes of some members of different profession or between the homes of some members as compared to others practicing the same occupation, patron-client relationship, political levels of authority etc., are some of the issues, which are basic to understanding urban dimensions of the settlement of Kotasur and its like in the Ajay-Bhagirathi delta, that not only remain inconclusive, these issues even cannot be raised in early historic archaeology of Bengal. Even diagonostic artefacts fair poorly as culture markers at several early historic sites, including, Kotasur, in this region and to assign them a time bracket is not free from problems. For example, India entered into the historical age with the Northern Black Polished Ware culture but one cannot say with certainty when this ware entered in to the Ajay-Bhagirathi delta. Furthermore, there is properly speaking no NBPW culture sites in Bengal as we have in the Middle Ganga region. Could it be an early historic diaspora from time to time from the neighbouring *mahajanapadas*, notably Anga and Magadha, to this region in the 6th - 5th century B.C. acted as an important agent in introducing new material inventory, the reflection of which is manifested in the artefactual remains found in archaeological horizons in some sites and as surface scatters in many others. We should not lose sight of the observation of the iterant Jain monk, Vardhamana Mahavira as recorded in the *Acharangasutta*, that the land of the Ladhas (i.e., the Radhas) was a pathless and rugged country, habitations were few and far between, people cavalier but did not refer to settlements of any consequence that could be regarded as urban centres. Undoubtedly, this suggests the absence of urban centres in Birbhum and neighbouring areas in the 6th–5th centuries B.C.

BIBLIOGRAPHY

Agrawal, D.P. and M.G. Yadava. 1995. Dating the Past. Pune: *Indian Society for Prehistoric and Quaternary Studies.*

Banerjee, S. 1982. The Archaeological Material from West Bengal in the Zoological Survey of India, *Puratattva 11*: 162-164.

Bose, N.K. and D. Sen. 1948. *Excavations in Mayurbhanj.* Calcutta: University of Calcutta.

Bose, N.K., D. Sen and G.S. Ray. 1958. Geological and Cultural Evidence of the Stone Age in Mayurbhanj. *Man in India* 38 (1): 49-55.

Chakrabarti, D., A. Nag and Subrata Chakrabarti. 1981. An Archaeological Reconnaissance in Birbhum. *Puratattva* 10 (1978-79): 25-32.

Chakrabarti, D. and S. Jamal Hasan. 1982. The Sequence at Bahiri (Chandra Hazrar Danga), District Birbhum, West Bengal. *Man and Environment* 6: 111-149.

Chakrabarti, S. 1986. Kopai Valley Post-Palaeolithic Settlers, Birbhum, in *The Pleistocene Perspective*. Vol. 2, Section D, pp. 1-9. Southampton: The World Archaeology Congress.

Chakrabarti, S. 1993. Mesolithic Typology in Upland West Bengal. In *Proceedings of the XXI Conference of the Indian Society for Prehistoric and Quaternary Studies*. pp. 1-7.

Chakrabarti, S. 1995. Consolidated Report 1985– 1995 on archaeological explorations and excavations carried out by the Department of Ancient Indian History Culture and Archaeology, Visva-Bharati, Submitted to the Archaeological Survey of India.

Chakrabarti, S. i.p. Exploration in Birbhum. *Indian Archaeology 1998-99:* A Review.

Chakrabarti, S. i.p. Exploration in Birbhum, *Indian Archaeology 1999-2000:* A Review.

Chakrabarti, S. 1999. The Context, Character and Chronology of Microliths from Paruldanga. *Bulletin of the Deccan College Post-Graduate and Research Institute* 58-59 (1998-1999): 3-10.

Chakrabarti, S. 2000. Recent Advances in Prehistory of Mayurbhanj, in *Archaeology of Orissa* (K.K. Basa and P. Mohanty Eds.), pp. 77-101. Delhi: Prativa Prakashan.

Chakrabarti, S. 2001. *Prehistory in Bengal: Progres and Regress at the Close of the Twentieth Century (Professor Dharani Sen Memorial Lecture, 2001)*. Kolkata: The Anthropological Society of India.

Chakrabarti, S. 2002. Mesolithic Cultures in West Bengal, in *Mesolithic India* (V.D. Misra and J.N. Pal Eds.), pp. 332-346. Allahabad: Department of Ancient History, Culture and Archaeology, University of Allahabad.

Chakrabarti, S. 2003. Mesolithic Hunter-Gatherers: Bengal in Perspective, in *Anthropology in Eastern India (Silver Jubilee Volume 1979-2001)*, Kolkata: Eastern Regional Centre, Anthropological Survey of India.

Chattopadhyaya, B.D. 1994. Urban Centres in Early Bengal: Archaeological Perspectives. *Pratna Samiksha* 2-3 (1993-94): 169-192.

Das, R.. 1967. *Indian Archaeology 1963-64: A Review*. pp, 59-60 and p, 61.

Dasgupta, P.C. 1965. *Indian Archaeology 1962-63: A Review*. pp, 43-46.

Dasgupta, P.C., D.K. Chakrabarty and S. Mukherji. 1969. *Indian*

Archaeology 1964-65: A Review. pp, 46-48.

Dasgupta, P.C., D.K. Chakrabarty and S. Mukherji. 1973. *Indian Archaeology 1965-66: A Review.* pp, 55-57.

Datta, A. 1991. Upper Palaeolithic Culture in West Bengal - A Distinct Regional Development, in *Studies in Archaeology* (A. Datta Ed.), pp. 67-76. New Delhi: Books and Books.

Ghosh, A.K. 1962 Discovery of Prehistoric Stone Implements from North West Midnapore, West Bengal. *Science and Culture* 28: 338-339.

Ghosh, A.K. 1966. Implementiferous Laterite in Eastern India, in *Studies in Prehistory, Robert Bruce Foote Memorial Volume* (D. Sen and A.K. Ghosh Eds.), pp. 149-162. Calcutta: Frima K.L. Mukhopadhyay.

Ghosh, N.C. 1986. The Chalcolithic Background of West Bengal, in *Indian Studies* (Amita Ray, Hitesh Sanyal and Sunil Ray Eds.), pp. 15-19. New Delhi: Books and Books.

Ghosh, N.C. 1993. *Indian Archaeology 1987-88: A Review.* pp, 110-111.

Ghosh, N.C. and Subrata Chakrabarti. 1990. Protohistoric Investigations in the Western Fringe of the Bengal Delta, in *Adaptations and Other Essays* (N.C. Ghosh and Subrata Chakrabarti Eds.), pp. 207-213. Santiniketan: Research Publications, Visva-Bharati.

Ghosh, N.C., A. Nag and P.K. Chattopadhyay. 1988. The Archaeological Background and Archaeological Sample from Hatigra. *Puratattva* 18 (1987-88): 21-27.

Ghosh, R.N. and S. Majumder. 1991. Geological and Morphostratigraphy of West Bengal: A Database for Archaeological Exploration, in *Studies in Archaeology:* A. Datta Ed.), pp. 7-37. New Delhi: Books and Books.

Goudie, A. 1983. *Environmental Change.* Oxford: Clarendon Press.

Kar, R.C., R.G. Pandeya and A. Singh. 1969. *Indian Archaeology 1964-65: A Review.* p, 46.

Nag, A. 1987. Spatial Analysis of Pre-and-Proto-Historic Sites in Ajay-Damodar Valley, in *Archaeology and History: Essays in Memory of A. Ghosh* (B.M. Pande and B.D. Chattopadhyaya Eds.), pp. 265-280. Delhi: Agam Kala Prakashan.

Pissehl, G.L. 1988. Radiocarbon Dates from south Asia. *Man and Environment* 12:169-196.

Renfrew, C. 1969. The Autonomy of South-east European Copper Age. *Proceeding of the Prehistoric Society* 35: 12-47.

Sankalia, H.D. 1974. *The Prehistory and Protohistory of India and Pakistan.* Poona: Deccan College Sastry, M.V.A. 1996. Pleistocene Vertebrates from Susunia, Bankura District, West Bengal. *Indian Minerals* 20 (2): 195-197.

Ṛgveda: A Historical Outline and the Contribution of Rahul Sānkrityāyan

VARUN SINGH*

Abstract

The study of Rigveda has for best part of the last 200 years been the province of Europeans, in particular the Germans who have often made a dedicated study of Ṛgveda with their own origins in the fore front of their minds. By contrast very little has been written by Indians, the main reason for which being that most Vedic scholars do not speak or know English well and have little interest in history. There has been a major resurgence in debate and research on the origins of the Indo-Europeans and naturally by virtue of its antiquity and uniqueness, Ṛgveda has attracted enormous attention in the last two decades. This has in part resulted from the recent major advances that have been made in the Archaeology and Anthropology of Indus Valley Civilisation and notably the rejection of the Āryan invasion hypothesis.

Due to Western pre-occupation with the linguistic links between Sanskrit, Greek and Latin and the belief that the Āryans had originated in the West, Western scholars have attempted to try and fit the material in Ṛgveda into a pre-conceived framework, often with scant regard to the evidence available with in the Ṛgveda. The present study is based on Sanskirt-Hindi material and attempts to draw an outline of the salient historical aspects of Ṛgveda.

Ṛgveda holds a unique position in world literature not only for its antiquity but also for having been preserved unaltered for centuries, thanks to the oral tradition of the Āryans. A search for a common language, common ethnicity and homeland for the so called Indo-Europeans has continued ever since Sir William Jones suggested a similarity between Sanskrit, Greek and Latin and naturally Ṛgveda has been the focus of attention for such studies. Recent advances in the field of Indus Valley Civilisation have revived interest in Ṛgveda with regard to its historicity, temporal relationship with the Harappan Civilisation as well as the subsequent cultures of India.

Framework for the study of Ṛgveda: The present approach to the study of Ṛgveda has been immensely influenced by "Ṛgvedic Ārya" by Rahul Sānkrityāyan, considered by many as one of the most illustrious and brilliant scholars India has produced since Raja Ram Mohan Roy. Written in Hindi, this book approaches Ṛgveda from a historical perspective and shows the consummate command Rahulji had on languages particularly Sanskrit. This peerless command and deep knowledge of Sanskrit and Pali (Buddhist) literature resulted in his being honoured. The Buddhist Sangha in Sri lanka awarded him the title of Tripitakacharya and then that of Mahapandit by the Pandit-Sabha of Benares. He also spent a number of years in the USSR in his quest for the origin of

*Kent, CT94AN, England.

the Āryans. Rahulji takes note of the opinions current at the time of publication (1957), especially those of Childe and Wheeler, which in view of the recent advances in Indology may sound dated, but all the same his commentary is of phenomenal importance to any student of Ṛgveda. The first 250 pages of the book consist of an analytical essay on many aspects of Ṛgveda, the remaining 300 odd pages (appendix) contain perhaps the best translation of the verses ever made; alas he only translated the verses he refers to in his essay.

He points out that for a student coming from a background of classical Sanskrit, Ṛgveda poses enormous difficulties. Grammatical difficulties aside, the major problem as I see, is that a lot is not explicitly stated and what is implied has to be inferred, which with the passage of time has become very difficult and has led to difficulties in interpreting the text.

This study of Ṛgveda is based on three Sanskrit–Hindi Translations. Satvalekar's much admired translation is backed by the one from Ramgovind Trivedi which appeared in monthly instalments from 1933-35 and was highly regarded in its day. Unfortunately, Book I is missing from this set. Shriram Sharma's translation was also used to supplement the study. A relational database was used to store information. It is worth pointing out that a Ṛgveda authority in India must be able to recite the entire work and this puts the commentaries from India on a total different footing than those from overseas, who have to depend on transliterations of Sanskrit text in either German or English. Indian Sanskrit Scholars also would have been required by tradition to have mastered the Sanskrit grammar by the age of 10 or so. Rahul Sankrityayan's translation, when available has been given primacy. I have tried my best to transfer this information into English. For the sake of brevity initials RS would be used when referring to Rahul Sānkrityāyan.

Edwin Bryant's book "*The Quest for the Origins of Vedic Culture* " a timely seminal review of the subject has been used as a major source and reference..

Archaeologists, linguists and historians continue to express their theories and opinions regarding the Āryans and Indo-Europeans citing Ṛgveda and other Sanskrit texts as a source. However, considerable confusion and misunderstanding exists regarding some of the very elementary aspects of Ṛgveda. Although ethnicity of the Āryans is not the subject of this paper, some general comments may be in order. There is no mention in the entire Ṛgveda of the physical appearance of the Āryans, except for one instance-VII:33.1 when Ṛṣi Vasiṣtha says " White skinned wearing the knot (in the hair) to the right my sons (family) please me from all corners." (RS).

Indians even to this day remain obsessed with subtle changes in skin pigmentation, lighter the pigment the better. The Persians 2500 years ago seemed to have been proud of their complexion as exemplified by Darius who "when out of doors a parasol was held over his head to preserve his complexion" (Cook). Buddha is said to have been of good complexion (Suvarṇa) and had blue eyes (RS), but then prince Rāma, who antedates Buddha, is described as of Śyāma (swarthy) complexion. Both belonged to the family line of Ikṣvāku (Rāmāyaṇa-BK S:I.8, and RS), who is mentioned only once in Ṛgveda (X:60:4). Lord Krisṇa was dark (black), because that is what the word means in Sanskrit. More importantly there are three ṛṣi in Ṛgveda who were probably dark skinned. Krisṇa Āngirasa (author of VIII:74-76. X:42,43.), and mentioned by Kakśivāna twice (I:116:23, I:117:7). The name Asita Devala (author of IX:5-24) also suggests a dark complexion and the great Ṛṣi Kāṇva, who was also dark. Krisṇa Āngirasa could not have been very late as Kakśivāna talks of his lost grandson been united with his son Viśvaka, by the Aśvins.

The Compilation : Hymns recited to invoke the gods were collected into 10 books (Mandalas) at some stage but long after the hymns were composed. RS quotes Bate Krishna Ghosh with the opinion that the language of the first nine Books is older and similar, but both share the opinion that the language and in particular the content of parts of Book X is certainly later.Although the compilation has been attributed to Veda Vyāsa (Krishna Dwaipāyana), RS states that Krishna Dwaipāyana should not be confused with Parāśara, grandson of Vasiṣtha, as a great deal of confusion was created by later literary tradition. One can not see how a grandson of Vasiṣtha would have allowed a son of Viśvāmitra (the arch enemy) to be given the honour of opening this sacrosanct opus.

I am of the opinion that an attempt was made to gather all the surviving hymns of Ṛgveda perhaps for fear of being lost for ever. By the time this rescue effort was made, probably few generations (centuries), after the last hymns had been recited, the descendents of the åñis, although preserving the compositions of their famous ancestors, had become separated and spread over a large geographical area. This probably is the main reason for the patchy quality of the collection, as the arrangement lacks any order.

Tradition accords a position of primacy to seven ṛṣis, a tradition that was to persist until Rāmāyaṇa and also Buddhist literature. The seven Rishis were; Bhardvāja, Kasyapa, Gotama, Atri, Viśvāmitra, Jamadagni and Vasiṣtha. Of these only Bahradvāja (Book VI), Viśvāmitra, (Book III) and Vasiṣtha (Book VII) had sufficient hymns surviving to constitute a book. Gotama features in Book I along with a number of very important ṛṣis, including Agastya, Kaṇva and his two sons even when a large part of Book VIII contains hymns of the same family. Kaśyapa on the other hand features in Book IX mainly (64,67:5-7, 91,92,113,114, in a fragment of a hymn (I:99) and IX: 97. Jamadagni is the sole author on only 3 occasions, (VIII: 90, IX:62 and X:110), Hymn IX: 65 is shared with his father Bhrigu and III:62 -X:167 with Viśvāmitra. Book X which is thought to be of a later provenance contains hymns of some the most important names in Ṛgveda. The patchy nature of the collection therefore can only be explained in one way. That some of the ṛṣis had moved away from there family seats and established themselves in distant parts, hence Viśvāmitra's son Madhuchhandā and grand son Jetā and also Vasiṣtha's grandson Parāśara appear in Book I.

The responsibility of collecting the hymns in one book would have been entrusted to someone local. One can't help thinking that a lot of material has been lost for ever, as some of the very famous names are very poorly represented.

Period of composition : RS believed that the most crucial and core part of Ṛgveda that of the battle between Divodāsa (Atithigva) and Śambara and the wars between his son Sudāsa and other Āryan clans, was composed some 300 years after the arrival of Āryans to India. He chooses to stay with the date of 1500 BC for entry (invasion) of the Āryans into India, a practice which has lingered until today. The period of 300 years is based on the assumption that the authors of Ṛgveda were 14th or 15th generation descendants of the invaders. After a further lapse of some 300 years Yajurveda, Sāmaveda and Eitareya and Shatpatha Brāhmaṇs were composed. The authors of the Brāhmaṇs; Mahidāsa (Eitareya) and Yāgyavalkya (Shatapatha) lived at a time when Kuru-Pānchāla land (Western UP) was their domicile and not Saptasindhu. According to RS mention of Anga (Bengal) and Magadha renders Atharvaveda of even a later date. (C 800–700 BC).

The hypothesis that the Āryans came to India from outside runs in three often unrelated arms, all of which connect to a central core theme of an Āryan homeland from which different branches of people speaking a similar language emerged. This linguistic, shall we say, spine to the theory remains unsupported by Archaeological muscle. There seems to be little agreement amongst the linguists themselves as to when the Āryans are supposed to have filtered in a slow trickle, now that the idea of Āryan invasion has become a myth in itself. The first line of inquiry stems from the discovery of Mitanni seals in 15th C BC. This, it was percieved suggested to some scholars that the Sanskrit speaking Mitanni were the forefathers of Ṛgvedic Āryans who took this long route from Anatolia and Northern Mesopotamia to India, stopping on their way in Persia. No one has yet, to my knowledge stopped to think or proposed the timescale for this diaspora. In any event the Indian Āryans had forgotten this journey completely as their is not even a hint of memory of such a past in Ṛgveda. The absurdity of having to reconcile the dates of the Mitanni seals, the long travel and an arrival many centuries before the composition of Ṛgveda, will not be lost on an enquiring mind. The widely used date of 1500 BC is therefore no more than an expedient as no archaeological or literary basis for the arrival of the Āryans into India can be found. Max Müller was first to suggest a date of 1200 BC for the composition of Ṛgveda , long before the discovery of Mitanni Seals. For some strange reason despite criticisms of his method, the date remains in place[2]. The sudden and rapid spread of horse drawn chariots in various parts of the Near East around this time was perhaps the main reason this date was applied (Barbarian Tides, Wilhelm). Wilhelm, a foremost authority on the Mitanni has lucidly expressed his views on this West to East migration theory;

"A Hurrian related but nonetheless distinct proto-Urartian language appears to have been spoken around 2000 BC. This latter pattern (West to East migration- my

insertion) would be confirmed if Hurrian or proto-Urartian borrowings were found in India; so far, however, there has been no proof of this. The flow of influence would have been one way only, from Indo- Āryan into Hurrian".

We can with certain confidence lay to rest a Mitanni ancestry to Indian Āryans. Alternative directions in which this migration may have taken place have been reviewed in considerable detail by Bryant[3]. Despite a lack of convincing evidence for a single rout of passage, most western linguists continue to believe in this migration from West-East with, Persia forming a half way stop.

Paleo-incarnation- Sarasvatī or Harax^{v}aitī ? The second line of reasoning much fancied by a number of Western Scholars is the similarity in the names of Avestan Harax^{V}aitī and the Vedic Sarasvatī. This proximity of names is seen as a proof for a West to East transit, with the name Harax^{V}aitī signalling a river in Persia which led the Indian Āryans to rename a dried up river in Punjab. Note should be made of the fact that while the Indian Āryans seemed to have remembered the name correctly, the same name in Persian hands had undergone a change.

Before we proceed with the Sarasvatī of Ṛgveda, we must identify the Avestan Harax^{V}aitī first and establish its geographical location. According to Skjaervo, there are no geographical references in the old Avesta[4]. In the younger Avesta (in Vedēvdād chap. 1 and in Yasht 10 to Mithra) and the old Persian inscriptions, Harahwati is the name of a land/province = Greek Arachosia, the area of modern Kandahar[5] .

Skjaervo (1995) goes on to say[6]:

"*A very few georaphical names appear to be inherited from Indo-Iranian times. For instance:OPers. Harax-^{V}aitī, Av.(acc.) Harōiium and Opers. Harauvati-, Av. Harax^{V}aitī, both of which in the historical times are located in the area of Southern Afghanistan (Herat and Kandhahar), correspond to the two Vedic river names Sarayu and Sarasvatī. These correspondences are interesting, but tell us nothing about the early geography of Indo-Iranian tribes.*"

Mary Boyce[7], on the other hand feels that Harax^{V}aitī in Avesta is a mythical river. Her opinion, however rests on the evidence in Greater Bundahis, a commentary written many centuries later. A perceptive student of ancient history would notice that it is logically impossible for a name like Sarasvatī to have emerged from Harax^{V}aitī, the reverse is true as suggsted by Skjaervo, a point also emphasised by Burrows[8]. However both Burrows and Boyce due to a mindset of West-East transfer must yield to the idea that this name must have existed in Persia.

The discovery on Landsat images of a very large channel exactly in a place where the ancient Sarasvatī had flowed, has been a subject of much debate. New research suggests that this channel had dried up by 1900 BC (Lal[9]), and this has prompted Indian Scholars to have another look at the dating of Ṛgveda. The same discovery on the other hand, by putting the proposed time scale of the Āryan migration into question, has been unacceptable to many Western Indologists.

Bryant in his book has quoted Witzel as suggesting that by the time of Ṛgveda, Sarasvatī was extinct and that ṛṣis Bharadväj and Vasiṣtha were praising a mythical river which they seem to have remembered from their ancient past. If so then this would appear to be the only instance when a remote memory has surfaced in Ṛgveda. The assumption being that they had memories of another river during their sojourn in Persia and that this river was Harax^{V}aitī.

Having established that there is no major river in Persian history to match the large, life supporting river of Ṛgveda, we must turn our attention to the point of view taken by Bryant. In quoting Witzel, Bryant himself agrees that the Ṛgvedic Sarasvatī is no more than a figment of imagination. The evidence offered comes from Hymn 33 in Book III by Viśvāmitra. This according to Witzel is an 'older' work and offers evidence of a confluence of Śututdri (Sutluj) and Vipāś(Vyas). This, it is suggested, is hard geological evidence for a change in course of the Sutluj, a major tributary of Sarasvatī, as a result of which Sarasvatī probably was not an extant river by the time of the composition of hymn 33. By 'older' Witzel means prior to the hymns of Bharadvāja and Vasiṣtha, who have praised Sarasvatī in their hymns.

That Witzel has difficulties in grasping the fundamentals of the chronology in Ṛgveda is evident from his writings in which he seems to think that the ten books in Ṛgveda have been arranged in a chronological order, especially Books II-VIII. One does not need to have mastered Ṛgveda to work out that Divodāsa was the father of Sudāsa and Bharadvāja, who was the officiating ṛṣi for Divodāsa has written a hymn on Sarasvatī (VI:61). Sudāsa had Vasiṣtha officiating for him during the prolonged ten king war. Vasiṣtha was then replaced by Viśvāmitra, one assumes after Vasiṣtha's death. Vasiṣtha also wrote 2 hymns on Sarasvatī (VII:95,96). Thus, it should be patently obvious that Viśvāmitra was about 2 generations behind Bahradvāja and one generation behind Vasiṣtha. Hymn 33, a poetical masterpiece does suggest the two river flowing together (Verse 2) which was taken to mean a confluence by Sāyā. However verse 2, is the only occurrence in the entire Ṛgveda to suggest such an event.

In addition Gritsamada (II:41.16) speaks of Sarasvatī as "supreme in mothers and rivers, Sarasvatī." Gritsamada's father Shunhotra is listed in Book VI and was probably a pupil of Bharadvāja. The most crucial line of evidence, however, comes from Sindhukshita, a son of Priyamedha. Sindhukshita lists all the major rivers in the North-West India (X:75) and Sarasvatī is listed between Yamunā and Sutluj (see later). Once again placing Sindhukshita in time tells us that his father had received gifts from Indrota, son of Divodāsa (VIII:57.15-17). In other words, we can with some confidence extrapolate that both Gritsamada and Sindhukshita would have been either contemporaries of Viśvāmitra or followed him. Bryant suggests that this paleo-incarnation of Sarasvatī "can not be used to prove absolute contemporaneity of the Indus Valley residents and Vedic Āryans". Significantly, the Sindhukshita listing of most of the important rivers in North-Western India does not mention Vipāś although it mentions Sarasvatī between Yamuna and Sutluj. This in all probability suggests that at the time hymn 33 was composed and until the time of Sindhukshita, Vipāś had merged wirh Sutudri but that this merger had not affected Sarasvatī significantly.

Bryant also quotes French archaeology team's (Francourt 1992) findings of an old Holocene channel where Sarasvatī is supposed to have existed, much older than the date of Mature Harappan to be of historical importance. In this very technical article, the author has not been able to explain why Rākhigarhi had been built in between the flow (interfluve) of Ghaggar and Chautanga rivers. The French identified small canals which they believed supplied the cities with water. But they are unable to tell us where this intricate canal system arose from? In other words where did the water come from, especially if the large rivers had dried up. Perhaps the weakness of the study lies in its methods. Novel techniques for dating and mapping were used and unless it can be shown that other geologists have produced similar results in the same area using similar techniques, the French report can not be accepted as providing robust evidence.

Talking of mythology and re-inventing, there is very little by the way of paleo-incarnation in the whole of Ṛgveda, and nothing to suggest that the Ṛgvedic Ārya had the need to re-invent Sarasvatī with the fore knowledge that over 4000 years later people from the west would cast doubt on the existence of this river and in the process the very credibility of the text itself. Two eminent Archaeologists on the other hand have not been persuaded by the French team's work or by the concept of Paleo-incarnation. Kenoyer (1999) accepts that the high number of sites discovered along what is now the Ghaggar-Hakra channel would have been situated along the Vedic Sarasvatī. Possehl (2002) also affirms that Sarsavatī was very much in existence at the time of the mature Harappan:

"During the Mature Harappan, the Sarasvatī (Ghaggar-Hakra) river terminated in an inland delta near Fort Derawar. There are about 140 Mature Harappan sites in the vicinity of this delta, making it the most densely settled area of the time".

Possehl continues to point out that the occupation of this area starts with some 82 Hakra Wares sites which in Early Harappan drops to some 20 Kot Dijian settlements, the number increasing again during the Mature Harappan to 140. This Possehl believes suggests a fluctuating level of flow in Sarasvatī. The final phase of drying up being reflected by the progressive drop off in settlements during Post-urban (Cemetary H,40 sites) and Painted Grey Ware (14 sites). Rivers must have changed their courses many times during the period Ṛgvedic ṛṣi lived and perhaps the confluence, if that is what happened, of III:33 was one such transient event.

The study of Persians, a group very closely related to Indo-Āryans has also been prone to similar problems in terms of their origins and migration. The current consensus opinion amongst the experts in Persian history

(Dyson) suggests ongoing presence of Persians in north east Iran and argues for a probable local origin. Skjaervo also proposes north eastern Iran as the most probable locus for the composition of Avesta.

The above discussion therefore casts serious doubts on the proposal that the the Āryans arrived several centuries before the composition of Ṛgveda starting at around 1200 BC. The assumption that Sarasvatī, renamed after a similar river in Persia can now be rejected. Had a similar channel been found in Persia then the case for Harax^{V}aiti would have been much strengthened. Existence of a dried up river in the precise location where Sarasvatī has been described should, one hopes, temper further animated discussion on the subject.

The third string or line of enquiry relates to the discovery of Iron in India. This subject once again has been well discussed by Bryant. One view, which finds some favour is that Black Iron is mentioned in Atharvaveda. western view that Atharvaveda is the closest to Ṛgveda where language is concerned. Therefore dating of Iron between 1300-1000 BC, enables the pursuants of this view to conclude that Ṛgveda could only have been composed a handful of centuries earlier. The fundamentals behind this reasoning are flawed and result from poor reading and understanding of Sanskrit texts. Atharvaveda is not mentioned in any of the other two Vedas, the Yajurveda Saṃhitas and the two early Brahmaṇs, (Aitareya and Shatapath, see RS' views above). Besides, Iron has been documented as early as Mature Harappan phase. A detailed discussion on the subject can be found in Bryant and Possehl[11] .

Absence of any mention of origin outside of India in Ṛgveda is matched by a lack of evidence of a massive population movement or change in anthropological record in India, either before, during or at the decline of the Harappan period [10]. The possibility of Āryans arriving from Bactria and Margiana (BMAC), a fashionable proposition not so long ago (Hiebert), has been emphatically rejected by Possehl .

Lack of mention of large cities in Ṛgveda has also led some to conclude that the Āryans arrived in the country after the fall of Indus Valley civilisation. This view is also mirrored by Erdosy. He is at great pains to point out that there is no evidence that the Āryans were necessarily outsiders and even if they were they had been in Indian subcontinent for a long time. Thus in his excellent review of the subject, even Erdosy can not resolve this puzzle of the date of arrival of Āryans in India. Bryant while reviewing this very subject agrees that the absence of mention of the cities in Ṛgveda does not mean a lack of knowledge of them.

Cities (Pur) as a matter of fact are mentioned in Ṛgveda and also cities of some size. Ṛṣi Babhru Vaikhanasa in X:99.3 tells us [11] He (Indra) went by a good path to the battle, He brought the plan (lay out) of the 100 gated city (Nagari) . Unruffled he overpowered the Shiçnadevah with his brilliance (RS). In hymn VI:16.39, Agni (Indra) like a bull with sharp horns is said to have destroyed 3 cities. Verse-X:99.3 is doubly significant in this respect, as the vanquished are described as Shiśnadevah[12], which is in keeping with the Harappans and their religious practices (Lal[13]).

The word Pur meaning a city, town or citadel occurs 112 times in Ṛgveda (Puri on 3 occasions), and some 68 times the word is used in relation to the enemies. Of these 68 only 20 can be identified as specific instances when names are mentioned with Śambara featuring 13 times. Rest are invocations usually addressed to Indra but occasionally to Agni and Soma. On some 22 occasions Pur forms a part of a title for Indra such as Purandara or Purbihta/da (destroyer or penetrator of Purs). There are 14 instances, when the word is used in relation to the Āryans themselves as the following verses show;

In I:173.10. Ṛṣi Agastya gives Indra a title of Pūrpati. Horace Wilson's translation quoted by Griffith is chosen , Wilson bases the translation on Sāyān and which is similar to the translation by Sharma:"*Emulous in commendations (like those contending for the favour) of men, may Indra, the wielder of the thunderbolt, be equally (a friend) to us; like those who, desirous of his friendship (conciliate) the lord of the city, Purpati, (ruling) with good government, so do our intermediates propitiate (Indra) with sacrifices*" [14].

VI:2.7 : Bharadvāj:"Like an old man living in a Puri".

VIII:6.23: Vatsa Kāṇv :"(give us) Pur full of kine".

VIII:58.8: Priyamedha: "worship Indra, sons also worship Indra like people worship a strong pur, (RS). or as people praise their pur, praise Indra", (Satvalekar).

IX:107.10: SaptaṚṣi :"Soma enters the container as a man enters a Puri (Satvalekar) or Lives in a Puri" (Trivedi).

I:149.3 : Dīrghatamā: "the indestructible Ātmā (Soul), in the Pur of the body." (Satvalekar).

We are unable to identify who the enemy in X:99.3 is meant to be. If the rich traders called Paṇi of Ṛgveda are the subject then it is possible that some of the hostility was aimed at them. The evidence in Ṛgveda, however offers us little support for this assumption. The reason for this being that the Āryans were not socially in the same league as the Paṇi (see later) and given the Āryan attitude towards the Paṇi, it is hardly surprising that they do not extol their riches and possessions (cities), as nothing could have been further from an Āryan mind. From the evidence within Ṛgveda it is evident that the Āryans were to some extent dependent on their wealth, and with the passage of time will succeed in dislodging the Paṇi from their economic hegemony. The result would be an eastward expansion of the population and also due to a decline in overland trade routes, establishment of coastal cities such as Lothal and Dholavira. Very little of the highly structured Harappan culture, specially its high achievements would survive, instead this eastward expansion will consist of predominantly a village culture with remnants only of the past magnificence of the Mature Harappan[15] .

In RS's view the period of Divodāsa and Sudāsa signifies a change in their status from nomadism to feudalism. He also points out that the accounts in Ṛgveda tend to span four generations at the most, making the time frame rather compact. For instance Bharadvāja, who he considers the most important and the most senior of the triumvirate involved in the centre stage action (Bhradvāja, Vasiṣtha and Viśvāmitra) was the 4th generation descendent of Angirā: Angirā- Lokanāmā-Brihaspati-Bharadvāja. We know nothing of the leaders and ṛṣis who lived before Angirā and Manu.

Chronology of Chiefs and Ṛṣis in Ṛgveda: At the beginning of each hymn are listed the Gods or Deities being invoked, the ṛṣi/s and then the meter/s in which the hymn is to be sung, in that order. This information is crucial in establishing a chronology in Ṛgveda. One of the aims of this study has been to attempt a structured chronology by stratifying the names. Equally important is to establish 'who says what' as often that helps to determine the proximity of a certain ṛṣi to an event. For instance, if it can be established that a ṛṣi credits a prince or rājā for granting him wealth, then that establishes that the two were contemporaries. Śambara's name occurs most frequently in book VI and although there can be little doubt that Bharadvāja took part in the action, it is not Bharadvāja who receives part of the booty and wealth, (of Śambara) but his son Garga (VI:47.22) suggesting that may be by this time Bharadvāja had fallen out of Divodāsa's favour.

The distinction between priestly Brāhmaṇs and warrior Kshatriayas does not appear to have evolved in Ṛgveda and in this regard the Purusha Sūkta X:90[16] is totally out of line with the rest of the collection. The last hymn in Ṛgveda X:191 (Ṛṣi Samvanan) preaches a moral code diametrically opposite to the Purusha Sūkta. At least some of the ṛṣis were rājās or chiefs and the rājās or their family members themselves composed hymns:Sudāsa-X:133; Trasadasyu-IV:42,V:27, IX:110; Pratardana son of Divodāsa IX:96 and Parucchepa, a descendant, probably a grandson of Divodāsa-I:127-139. RS believes that some of the ṛṣis were rājās in their own right and others fought in battles as military leaders. Ghoshā the daughter of Kakśivāna calls herself the daughter of rājā (X:40.5). Interestingly Shaṁyu, brother of Bharadvāj was in all probability a craftsman in the employ of Bribu, a Paṇi (VI:45:31-33).

Manu and Angirā: Manu features as the earliest leader in Ṛgveda, who in later tradition was considered the father of all Āryans (mankind). Terms such as mānuṣa and amānuṣa, meaning human and inhuman came into use[17]. Hymn IX:101: gives us an insight into the genealogy of the Manu family. Yayāti composer of verses 4-6 was the son of Nahuṣa, Nahuṣa son of Manu (verses 7-9) and Manu son of Saṁvarna or Sārvana,(10-12). Angirā was another great leader whose progeny constitute the most important family of ṛṣis in Ṛgveda. From Hiraṇyastūp, probably one of the sons of Angirā, we learn that "Like Agni, Manu and Angirā used to come to Yayāti's yagya":I:31:17 (RS) suggesting that Manu and Angirā may have been contemporaries.

Only 5 hymns attributed to Hiraṇyastūp have survived and the content of these hymns in my opinion makes him one of the most senior ṛṣis. His treatment of the Vritra legend (I:32) is the most detailed and describes Vritra as an entity, if not a person. Vritra in later Ṛgveda was treated as a generic term for enemy. One senses that natural forces such as a glacier obstructing the flow of rivers are being described.

Hiraṇyastūp also mentions Nahuṣa "Nahuṣasya Vishpatim" (I:31.11); "Gods made Nahuṣa the master/ leader of the people" (RS). Parucchepa descendant of Divodāsa in I:139.9 says " The, ancestors, Dadhyada, Angirā, Priyamedha, Kāṇva, Manu knew of my birth"(RS).

One particular problem in interpreting the names of Manu and Nahuṣa should be pointed out. Sometimes the names are taken to mean leaders and sometimes in abstract form to suggest mankind or people. Even RS is prone to this as in the hymn I:31.11 he interprets the name Manu as mankind and Ilā as grain. If it is to be agreed that Manu and Angirā were contemporaries and that we are not talking of personalities from a remote past, but from only a few generations earlier, then the names Manu and Nahuṣa in Ṛgveda should be taken as individuals.

Attempt has been made to identify contemporaries as carefully as possible. From a historical perspective, hymns relating to Indra's exploits/victories are the most important. Unfortunately a large number of times such hymns are no more than a listing of Indra's achievements. Often a long list of names is recited without any indication that the author is speaking from personal experience, or if the list is merely part of a tradition. For example, Gritsamada (II:12.11) who mentions 40 year war with Śambara, would have been close enough to the action but only by a generation or so. His father Shunhotra features before Bharadvāja's sons Garga and Ṛjishvā in Book VI, and was probably a pupil of Bharadvāja and so may have had first hand knowledge of the battle.

From Viśvāmitra onwards we see a trend which suggests a settled existence as the battle hymns become less frequent and by the time hymns of Book X were composed, the milieu appears to have changed completely. Apart from hiding behind assumed names the ṛṣis are more concerned with mystical, philosophical thought as in the famous Nāsidéya Sükta (X:129).

Awareness of and great respect for Sindhu and Sarasvatī suggests that the Ṛgvedic Ārya were not only very familiar with North Western India, but that these rivers were central to their culture. Although a discussion of the hydrology in Ṛgveda is out of the scope of this paper, it is worth pointing out that the word Sindhu occurs some 194 times, of which 27 times specifically as the river but on as many as 139 occasions, as waters or river. On 24 occasions Sindhu is listed along side deities. Sarasvatī also appears as a river on some 16 occasions, but is invoked as a goddess 45 times, mostly as one of three goddesses who are invoked together, Sarasvatī, Ilā and Bhārati, occasionally Mahé. Ilā or Idā features only once, if it can be taken as a river (V:41;19) but Mahé, is not mentioned as a river although on two occasions a case can be made for a river being described (V:11.5 and V:41.15). We know that there is a river by that name in Gujarat not far from Lothal (Fig 4, Thapar). The position which Sindhu has been accorded suggests, that to the authors of Ṛgveda, Sindhu was so important as to be barely needed being mentioned as a river. For example, the rippling of soma juice is described by the use of the the word Sindhorūrmā (ripples or waves of Sindhu). Translators have often given different meaning to this word; stream or flood by Griffith and an ocean by Indian commentators, which is unnecessary as the word 'samudra' occurs frequently enough in Ṛgveda.

One would not be rash in assuming that leaders such as Manu, Nahuña and Angirā were the first leaders of farmer/pastoralists who began to assert themselves but it would not be until Sudās that the Āryans could claim to have established an empire. Ṛgveda gives us an image of a militant people who when not fighting, were praying for VĀJ; a word which means provisions as well as booty. The presence of such hostile bands would have affected the overland trade routes of the Harappans through Afghanistan and Eastern Iran adversely. So although there had never been an invasion, the presence of these Āryans in the North Western part of India would have been one, if not the sole factor in the decline of the peace loving non-warring Harappans. The heavy fortification, often double, at sites such as Dholavira, Lothal and Kalibangan has not been adequately explained by the archaeologists, although flood protection may have been one aim. None of the Indus- Sarasvatī valley sites show signs of damage or destruction as a result of warfare which in itself constitutes a very strong argument against an invasion.

Mention of Yamunā by Vasiñtha (VII:18.19) and listing of most of the important rivers in two groups, Eastern and Western, by Sindhukshita, son of Priyamedha (X:75.5-6)[18], establishes their familiarity with a considerable part of the subcontinent. It should be pointed out that rivers, Sarayu and Vipāś (Vyas) are not listed in this hymn.

Apart from the knowledge of the rivers, there are cultural traits in Ṛgveda which are unique to India, even to this day. Firstly, the use of ghrita (ghee-clarified butter) occurs frequently through out Ṛgveda and played a very important role in their religious ritual. In a hymn to god Savitā,(Sun-VI:71.1)"Ghriten Paṇi." meaning Savitā raises arms of Ghrita high above. Ghrit, in this instance probably symbolising the glitter or shine of the early morning Sun. Also in a hymn to Vāyu " Vāyo Ghritasnah, means pure as ghee Vāyu" VIII:46.28 indicates the importance given to this item by the Aryans.

Another feature unique to India is the six seasons (Kenoyer) or six 2 month divisions of the year and an extra month (13th) testifying to the use of a lunar calendar by the Āryans. The Indian Āryans also considered Kine as an important mark of wealth along with horses and gold as in VIII:32.9 (Medhatithi Kānva). They (the Āryans) were considered very conservative in their religious beliefs and so it is difficult to see how this group would have incorporated names of the rivers and a life style alien to them, into their religious system, even if we allow for a domicile of a few hundred years. Instead the evidence in Ṛgveda supports either a local origin of the Āryans or total assimilation into a superior material culture. There is no indication in Ṛgveda that they considered themselves 'subsumers'; a role frequently ascribed to them- a people who are supposed to have wiped out all trace of language and material culture preceding them.

The Paṇi and Harappans: Since the Harappan script remains un-deciphered and we have practically no description of the Harappan people other than what has been deduced from archaeological and anthropological finds, we will not know if the two groups did come in direct contact, friendly or hostile. The proposal by the modern archaeologists that Harappans were a non-warring people, and that they were mainly traders although measuring their wealth in kine (Shaffer and Lichtenstein) distinguishes them from the militant Āryans who describe their settlements as villages (grāma). The village living Āryans probably were the pastoralists/farmers living in Punjab, a large area as yet not fully explored archaeologically (Possehl 1993)..

Use of horse by the Āryans has been used as a mark of distinction from the Harappans who either did not know the horse or did not consider it important to their life style. The horse does not feature on the Harappan seals. Solid wheel carts, used by the Harappans is another feature which is said to set them apart. However both of these arguments have been challenged by Indian archaeologists. The identification of horse bones discovered at Surkotada has remained controversial despite been affirmed as of bones of *Equus Caballus* by Bōkōnyi, an authority on horses. Meadows a prominent zoo-archaeologist specialising in South-Asia has, on the other hand, remained unconvinced[19]. The absence of the Horse from Harappan seals also can not be taken as a evidence as a horse may not have been considered a suitable candidate. As far as the question of spoked wheels is concerned, Lal has shown images of wheels with spokes, evident in relief as well as in paint in the material discovered at Rakhigarhi and Banawali[20]. The distinction between the Harappans and the Āryans on the basis of the presence or absence of horse and spoked wheels, is not considered valid any longer. Horse remains may continue to evade further archaeological research, particularly if the horse was not used for sacrifices. Horse remains have proved difficult in many situations including the BMAC[21]. In Tarim basin, although the well preserved mummies were found to have horse hair sutures, no horse remains have as yet been identified.

Claims that the artefacts from Bactria Margiana Archaeological complex (BMAC), have some features common with the Āryans, especially iconography are untenable as comparisons have been made by using material from the Near East and not India. Most interesting is the depiction of solid wheel carts driven by oxen in the BMAC seals [22]. Ox driven carts with hints of a stratified society as is evident in these images would be a more appropriate fit for the Avestan society than the Ṛgvedic. In Boyce's opinion;[23]

"The main migrations must have been of whole people, led by their fighting men but bringing with them their chattels in cumbrous ox-drawn carts, above all their

herds, their source of livelihood and wealth;....The main body of the Indian peoples presumably moved first through these territories....whereas the Iranians following pressed on south-westerly through Margiana and Parthia, and so on to the Iranian plateau".

There is little mention of ox-carts in Ṛgveda. Rath (Chariot) driven by horses appears to have been the burden carrier (Vasiṣtha). Chariot carrying people is described in I:126.3 in which Ṛsi Kakśivān says "*And granted by Svanay black horsed carrying Vadhoos (female slaves/brides) 10 Raths I received. Later 1060 cows also came* (RS). Oxen were, however, used for farming.

We then have an image of the Āryans in Ṛgveda that does not quite match the picture we are able to construct of the Harappans. While accepting that this construct is the result of Archaeology and Anthropology, we are tempted to ask ourselves "Are there people in Ṛgveda who could be identified as Harappans?

In my opinion people called Paṇi in Ṛgveda fit the characteristics of traders and therefore the Harappans. RS has suggested that it is not a Sanskrit word and points out that from this word are derived: Pāṇan = to sell, Paṇya= saleable object and Āpaṇ = Market or Bazar. The word Vaṇik meaning a trader, which occurs in Ṛgveda on a few occasions is also a derivative. Vaṇik in modern Hindi has become Baniya or in Malawi and Rajasthani Vaṇiya. He says that the Paṇi most probably were the civilised and wealthy occupants of Sindhu valley. There has always been a very strong tradition in India of hereditary business people who are often called Baniyas, amongst these the Mārwāris (coming from Rajasthan) have been the most successful. Traders have played a very important role in India's wealth through out her history, a tradition which most certainly goes back to the Harappan times. Paëi of Ṛgveda, the wealth wielding powerful group could well have been the Harappans.

Paṇi were wealthy but at the same time miserly and ungenerous (aditsu=nongivers). Ṛgveda is full of derogatory and insulting jibes aimed at the Paṇi who were clearly hated by the Āryans. There is no evidence that the Paṇi fought the Āryans. The tenor of the language implies that Paëi were not considered a hostile adversary, rather a wealthy group who had annoyed the Āryans by the lack of their generosity. Neither are the Paṇi described as black, Dasa or Dasyu. This suggests that by the time of Bharadvāja the Āryans had not achieved ascendancy and what is significant is that most of the hostile verses have come from members of the Angirā family. The following examples reflect Āryan attitude towards the Paṇi and tell us that the position of the Āryans in Ṛgveda was not one of domination and mastery as has often been assumed.

"Amassing wealth hey Pravraddha (determined) Indra, do not become a Paṇi for us" (RS). Hiraṇyastūp; (I:33.3).

"Hey Indra, here in battle with Kavi Dashoni, in their hundreds, Paṇi (warriors) ran away."(RS). Bharadvāja; (VI:20.4).

"Hey wealth endowed Ushā awake the generous ones (but) may Paṇi not wake up and remain asleep for ever."(RS). Kakśivāna; (I:124.10).

"Strike the greedy Paṇi for the wolf (Vriko) he is". Ṛjiśvā son Bharadvāja.(VI:51.14).

"Hey Pūṣana (you) encourage the non-giver to give, soften the hearts of Paṇi, " Bharadvāja (VI:53.3).

"Hey kavi Pûshan, pierce the heart of Paṇi with a spoke and make them come under our domination" (RS). Bharadvāja VI:53.5;

"You (Sarasvatī) gave devotee Vadhraśva a son, fearsome and freer of all debt Divodâsa. You swallowed the non giver Paṇi, Hey Sarasvatī, your gift is great". (RS). Bharadvāja; (VI:61.1)

"Lacking duty, loose mouthed, foul tongued, irreverent, without devotion and yagya, Paṇi–Dasyus you drove east, those yagyaless you drove west".(RS).Vasiṣtha; (VII:6.3)[24]

From a historical point of view the two hymns by Ṛsi Ayāsya (X:67 and 68) are of immense importance. The Pañi with their leader Vala had secreted kine into a stronghold, often interpreted as a mountain, clearly with the intention of preventing the Ārya from stealing them. Unfortunately RS has only translated two verses from these hymns neither of which I consider crucial, historically speaking. The hymns are dedicated to Brihaspati, not the deity but to Brihaspati Āngiras. To me it appears that Ayāsya must have been close to Brihaspati as he says in X:68.12; " Brihaspati who has spoken many richas, and who now resides in Antariksha (firmament), we salute him". In X:68.2 " Brishapati of Angirā family" is how the text is translated. Brihaspati was Angirā's grandson and father of Bharadvāja. He was a man of considerable stature and a great scholar as is evident from his two surviving hymns (X:71 -72).

The importance of Ayāsya hymns lies in the graphic detail with which an expedition of cattle rustling is described, leaving me in no doubt that we are dealing with a real life event. I have tried to condense these two hymns into a story.

When the kine made noises in the cave (secret place), then Brihaspati realised that they were hidden there, 68.7. Like swans the helpers of Brihaspati started making a commotion and with their help Brihaspati opened the stony door, the kine held within started to bellow, 67.3. The cows had been hidden through one door below and 2 doors above, Brihaspati by opening all 3 doors released the kine, 67.4. Slipping quietly in the night the back part of the Pur (building) was breached and the three doors to the deep ocean like guha (cavern or secret place) opened, in the morning they saw the sun and the kine, 67.5. As winter takes the foliage of the forest, so at Brihaspati taking (stealing) the kine, Vala wept, 68.10(RS). Also; Indra with a roar rent Vala, protector of kine with his hands, desiring milk and with the help of Maruta(Indra) snatched the kine and made Paëi weep, 67.6 (RS).

This would appear to have been one of the early attempts by the Āryans to obtain wealth (Kine) per force. Repeated attempts like these would have been enough to disturb the stability of this large and highly advanced but peaceful civilisation. From the examples given above it is evident that even until the time of Vasiṣtha, the Paṇi had held on to their wealth but not without being harassed and challenged. The Āryans on the other hand seem to have lead a marginal existence as their grudge against the Paṇi for their lack of generosity and mention of their leaders being rescued or saved from perilous situations by Indra.

Other Enemies

The Paṇi therefore appear to have held the sway in terms of wealth and then there is another group of enemies who the Āryans go all out to destroy. Śambara was the main adversary of Divodās after whose defeat the foundation was laid for Divodāsa's son Sudāsa to expand and in the process fight his own people; other Āryans. Descriptions such as black skinned, speaking a hostile tongue-Mridhravāc,(which RS believes gave rise to the word Mlecch-unclean) occur in Ṛgveda. These enemies also lived in Purs or Puris. Most Indian commentators in contrast to Western scholars, do not translate Purs or Puris as forts but as cities/towns or at best citadels. The word for stronghold or fortification in Ṛgveda is Drilhā, which gave rise to Dridh, a word in use today meaning strong, hard or tough.

However, neither of the adjectives mentioned above can be used to describe a race or a pejorative insult thrown at some one despised. Some of the ṛṣis themselves were dark skinned and so the use of this term may not reflect different racial types but subtle changes in skin pigment which even to this day remains an obsession with South Asians. Similarly the use of the term Mridhravāc does not imply a backward or inferior people. The term having once been applied to none other than Purus, the largest clan of Āryans (VII:18.13). Uṣā (Dawn) and other Gods have been on a number of occasions described as Amridhra- meaning peaceful or non-hostile (V:37.1)

The group of whom Śambar was probably the main leader, would have been part of the Hararpan population, but unlike the Paṇi they decided to resist the Āryans attempt to become dominant. Escaping to the mountains from where to run guerrilla type warfare, was their aim. Some of the fortified cities of the Indus-Sarasvati Civilisation may well have been the Purs or Puris of Ṛgveda, but as none of the major sites have shown any signs of 'stresses of conflict' the Purs in Ṛgveda can not with confident be identified with the big cities such as Harappa. Fortified settlements in inaccessible hill tops probably were the scene of the fighting in Ṛgveda as we are told that Śambara died on a major mountain, we assume Himālaya, IV:30.14 and I:130.7. The tradition of a population under threat escaping to inaccessible mountains was alive even until Alexander's time who had to build a

100 foot tall bridge head to cross a ravine to reach Pir Sâr. RS says that there was a most inaccessible fort in the Kangra mountains which was destroyed by an earthquake some 100 years ago, (150 years ago now).

The use of terms dāṣa or dasyu has no specific meaning in Ṛgveda. In modern language dāsa means slave and dasyu bandit. Ṛṣi Vasiṣtha in VII:86.7 says "*I like a dāsa* (slave) *work to please the gods*". These names certainly do not suggest any specific ethnic group as has been frequently suggested (Parpola). The two names were used interchangeably as in VI:26.5 Śambara is called a dāsa and in VI:31.4 a Dasyu. We also find both names used in the same verse (X:22.8) "*All around us are dutyless, mantraless, riteless amanuṣ dasyu. Hey Amitrhantā (Indra) destroy these dāsa by killing them*" (RS)[25]. The Persians often called governors in foreign lands *Dasyupati* (Dahyu/n/paiti), much like the word Satrapy which derives from *Kshetrapati*-lord of a zone or territory (authors opinion).

The Āryan Clans: Five people or clans are mentioned in Ṛgveda and are identified as *Puru, Turvaśa, Yadu, Anu* and *Druhyu*. Practically nothing remains of 3 of these clans in later Sanskrit literature. *Yadus* seem to have survived, as Lord Kriṣṇa was a Yādava, as are several Maharajas in modern India (RS). More often than not this name has been assigned to people of lower status such as cowherds. *Puru* on the other hand feature very prominently in Ṛgveda. *Bhāratas* were a branch of the *Purus* as were the *Tritsus* (Sudās). *Turvaśa* and *Yadu* are usually listed together and one senses that there must have been a falling out between the *Purus* and the other four clans, after the Ten King War as in VIII:10.5 *Purus* are not mentioned by Pragātha brother of Kaṇva. In IX:61.2 Amhihyu says" (Soma) in this manner (destroyed) Śambara purs for Divodāsa and them Turvaśa and Yadu also (RS). Turvaśa and Yadu appear together most frequently in the hymns of the Kaṇva family.

Śaṁyu brother of Bharadvāja says in VI:45.1 " *Who with easy(beautiful) transport brought Turvaśa* and *Yadu from the west, That youthful Indra is out friend*"(RS). In VI:27.7 *Turvaśa* are supposed to have been brought by Indra from afar and presented to Srinjaya and Vricivāna presented to Devavāta as subjects, one presumes. Bharadvāja[26] (VI:20.12) informs us that *Turvaśa* and *Yadu* were aided in crossing a flood or ocean. This is given as evidence of a west to east migration of the Āryan race by some experts (Witzel). Kāṇva family appears to have been the official priests for these two clans. However by the time of Vasiṣtha it seems that all five clans were fighting the Tritsus who would in the end be victorious. In VII:18.6, Indra saves Sudāsa from the midst of *Turvaśa, Bhrigu* and *Druhyu* (RS) and in VII:19.8 Indra is asked to kill *Turvaśa* and *Yadu*. A ṛṣi calling himself Indra (X:49.8) says "*I destroyed 7 forts of Nahuṣa and made Turvaśa and Yadu famous.*"

Bharadvāja is telling us that (IV:27.7) that *Turvaśa* were 'presented to Devavāt's son Srinjaya of Bharata family. Devavāt we know was the maternal grandfather of Sudās[27]. The arrival of these two clans from afar (*Parāvatah*) which involved crossing an ocean or a flood was not in a remote past. In any event the grandson of Devavāt would succeed in annihilating these two tribes and perhaps expelling them.

The last survivor of the Puru is the king who fought Alexander and whom the Greeks have called Porus. To most Indians his name should either read *Puru* or *Paurav* the latter meaning '*of Puru people or family.*' The name of *Bhāratas* would survive as the name of the Indian nation.

Other Clans: There are many other people named in Ṛgveda especially during the Ten King War at the time of Sudāsa. We are not told who these ten kings are but some of the people who fought along side Sudāsa still exist. Vasiṣtha inVII:18.7 has listed; *Paktha, Bhalāna, Alina, Vishāni* and *Shiva* as having come to the aid of the *Tritsu* leaders (Sudāsa). *Paktha* are indeed the Pakhtoons or Pathāns of North Western Pakistan and Afghanistan, while the Bolan Pass in Baluchistan bears the name of the *Bhalāna* tribe (RS). Alina may be the Alingars mentioned in Alexander's campaign against the mountain tribes who lived on the right bank of Kabul River (Pierre Bryant). Most important is the mention of two people in Ṛgveda which has enormous historical significance. The name of *Prithu*[28] and *Parśu* occurs only on a few occasions in Ṛgveda. *Pārthav* as a people appear for the first time in the Behistun inscription of 520BC, (Encycl Brit), *Pārthav* also occurs in Ṛgveda meaning "*of Prithu birth or family.*" Similarly *Parśu* or *Parśav* (RS) is cognate with names given to Persians; *Parsuwa, Parsa, Parasu, Pars, Fars* (Cook, Skjaervo).

Parśu: This name occurs only on 3 occasions but has often being confused with *Paraśu* meaning an axe which occurs more frequently. Most important to us is Hymn X:86.23. This Hymn is of uncertain authorship, as the ṛṣi has given himself a fictitious name and verse 23 has been tagged on to the end of this hymn to which it bears no relationship and is obviously not from the same ṛṣi; "*Parśurh nāma Mānavi...*" translated (Trivedi and Satvalekar) as "*Daughter of Manu by the name of Parśu gave birth to 20 children.*" Griffith translates *Parśu* as a rib, but I do not see what relevance rib has here. No wonder this verse has been described as obscure (very old?) and consigned to an appendix by Grassman (Griffith). A pointless exercise as nothing in Ṛgveda should be considered insignificant. This important verse is the only surviving fragment of a hymn which has been lost and serves as a good example for my argument that the surviving hymns, verses and fragments were put together into one collection in their own location.

The second mention of equal importance is in VII:83.1: (Vasiṣtha) Translated by RS as "*Hey Indra, Varuṇa netas (leaders), Looking to you and your friendship, with the intention of looting kine* ***Prithu*** *and* ***Parśu*** *went east. You killed the Dāsa and Ārya enemies and with your protection saved Sudāsa.*"

However both Griffith and Satvalekar imply"they went with large (*Prithu*) axes (*Paraśu*)" but the text does not say *Paraśu*. In my opinion RS' translation is superior in that people not implements are implied, which makes this verse monumentally important as it suggests that both ***Parśu*** and ***Prithu*** took part in the Wars. RS himself suggests that the ***Parśu*** and ***Prithu*** in this verse are most probably the Persians and Parhians.

Tirindīra is mentioned by ṛṣi *Vatsa* son of Kaṇva in VIII:6:46. This name is most unlike any other in Ṛgveda and was thought to be a Persian name by Griffith. The verse is translated as *Tirindīra the king and son of or of the family of,* ***Parśu*** *and of Yadu clan gave us 1000 goods (wealth).* Also of interest is the mention of camel, which occurs mainly in Book VIII (Kaṇva family). This then suggests a westward movement of some of the members of the Kaṇva family who had allied themselves to Turvaśa and Yadu clans. One assumes that this movement would have started after their annihilation by Sudāsa in the ten king war.

I can see no evidence of Vasiṣtha having migrated from Iran, as suggested by Witzel[29]. He quotes verse VII:33.9 as evidence. It appears that this scholar has taken this verse out of context. Hymn (33.1-9) is attributed to the sons of Vasiṣtha and almost certainly relates to *his death. It should read " Vasiṣtha travelled through the world of 1000 stations. With the help of Yama he travelled to the motherly apasarā who was spinning four garments.*" (Sharma). Griffith translates it as the "vesture spun by Yama." Either way nothing could be further from the Avestan theology here, as *Yama* in this verse (God for the dead) is guiding Vasiṣtha to the 'Other World'. The name of *Yama* and *apasarā* recurs in verse 12. I shall return to this subject later.

Prithu : Apart from the verse VII:83.1 quoted above, the most notable mention of ***Prithu*** is by Bharadvāja VI:27.8 in which he reports having received gifts including Vadhoo (brides in modern Hindi but probably meaning female slaves), from *Abhyāvarti* son of *Chaymāna*, who is the *Samrāt* (Emperor) of the *Pārthava* people. One assumes that it is the same *Chāymān* Kavi who is felled like an animal on the banks of Paruṣṇi in the Ten King War (VII:18.8). *Prithushravā* is mentioned twice, I: 116.21 by Kakśivāna and in VIII:46.21 by Vasha, descendent of Kaṇva. Vasha has also mentioned camels. In X:93.14-15 Prithvāna and Parthvya as kings or chiefs appear.

Soma sacrifice is exactly the same in all sections of Ṛgveda, which I consider to be distinctly different from Avesta. Whether the findings of large ceramic containers in which remnants of Ephedra, Cannabis and Opium have been found (Sarianidi) has links with Zoroastrian tradition is difficult to say but I see no possible connection between the Ṛgveda and the BMAC. The subject of Soma is covered in another paper in which it is shown that Soma was extracted from the Cannabis plant, specially its flower bearing part. RS believed that Cannabis could be the only candidate for the intoxicating drink. Ephedra would certainly be a good candidate for Haoma in Avesta but once again there is no suggestion that Hoama was mixed with Opium or Cannabis, as the BMAC find suggests.

Synthesis: I started the study of Ṛgveda convinced that there had been an Āryan invasion and that they had come from the west, the language in the Mitanni seals being so close to Sanskrit. I was unable to find any suggestion of a large scale migration or a single invasion in Ṛgveda. That by the time the hymns of Ṛgveda were composed (200-300 years or 12-15 generation at least) Āryans had been in the area for some considerable time, seems established. This is evident from the importance given to Sindhu and Sarasvatī rivers. Both are described as major rivers and both arise in the mountains and end in the ocean. By the time of Sudāsa and Sindhukshita, Āryans were moving freely from what is now Afghanistan in the west to Gangā in the east. We have shown that Sarasvatī was a major river in Ṛgvedic times which according to the Sindhukshita was one of the easterly rivers. The myth of another river in Persia, supposed to be the original Sarasvati can now be laid to rest. There is no evidence in Avesta of such a river having ever existed.

Above all it is the reliance on cow products for rituals such as milk and ghee and ox hide on which Soma was extracted from the plant, confirm that the Ṛgvedic Āryans were well established in India. There is no evidence whatsoever of cultural, linguistic or religious borrowings from outside India. According to Shaffer and Lichtenstein dependence on cattle is unique to the Harappan culture and the fact that the Āryans in Ṛgveda also use kine as a marker of wealth could only have been possible in India and no where else.

How do the Āryans of Ṛgveda relate to the archaeological profile of the Harappans? That the Āryans seemed to have lived in Purs has been shown but the picture presented in Ṛgveda does not suggest city dwellers. They appear not to have been unfamiliar with the highly evolved sanitary facilities which the Harappans used. That women washed themselves in the open in the rivers is clear from 2 verses. In V:80.5 Ṛṣi Satyasravā Ātreya in beautiful poetical language speaks thus of Uṣā "bright in colour showing all her body parts like a woman who comes to bathe, Uṣā appears in view of all." Ṛṣikā Apālā the daughter of Atri says in VIII:80.1; "when walking to the river to bathe, in the path I found Soma and bringing it home (I) said (I) will prepare you for Indra." Men who wore woollen clothes are described as cleansing themselves in Paruṣṇi (Ravi) river (V:52.9).

A role of pastorlists/farmers, therefore can be more confidently assigned to the Āryans, who managed the land and livestock sharing the material culture of the Harappan Civilisation and yet were not the dominant figures in the City state culture. Grāma meaning village occurs 15 times in Ṛgveda and Maruta were often invoked to provide rain to assist in their agriculture. In Yajurveda Saṁhitas, by contrast, the word Pur virtually disappears. Had Purs in Ṛgveda been the makeshift structures as suggested by Rau, there is no reason, why the construction of such flimsy and makeshift structures would not have gone on into Yajurvedic times.

The evidence within Ṛgveda suggests the status and power of the Āryans was on the rise and not in decline as would happen to the Harappan civilisation. Had the Ṛgvedic Āryans been the leading members of the Indus Valley Cities themselves then it is difficult to see how the highly advanced technology of building large cities, of the writing system and other markers of Harappan Civilisation would have disappeared for ever. This change which would be permanent and be followed by an unbroken Sanskrit tradition can only be explained on the basis of a social upheaval within the Harappan society with a group hitherto not prominent asserting their dominance and control.

If these Āryans did play a role in destabilising the Harappan Civilisation then it has to be agreed that they were present in the area for some centuries before 2000 BC a date which seems quite secure if one takes into account the slow drying of Sarasvatī, a process which appears to have completed by 1900BC.

The theory that the Āryans came from the west can only be substantiated if evidence of similar beliefs and cultural traditions contemporary with or antedating Ṛgveda can be shown. No such evidence either linguistic or archaeological exists (see Wilhelm). Did the Āryans bring the horse with them when they moved to the Indian subcontinent? Again this can not be confirmed with certainty as it is equally possible that they acquired the skills needed to use the horse as a means of transport. Certainly the fact that amongst all the Āryan Gods only Indra is given horses to drive his chariot, while other gods are not, suggests that the horse as a means of transport may have been acquired. For example Maruta have spotted deer, Asvins-goat and Pūṣan a donkey. Several scholars have suggested that the horse was an import and a property of the elite[30]. I feel this would have been unthinkable in a society like the *Kurgans* for whom horse would have been common property (Anthony). Wilhelm says that the horse and chariot became a domain of the aristocrats amongst the Mitanni, because the upkeep of horse and maintenance of a chariot was expensive.

If any people are closely related to the Ṛgvedic Āryans it is the Zoroastrians (Persians), in terms of language, religious rituals and theology. Even then by the time of Zoroaster, radical changes had taken place in all these areas suggesting that Zoroastrian ideas represent an evolution of the Ṛgvedic theology rather than a parallel or earlier development. There is nothing in Ṛgveda that would suggest that the Āryans brought influences from Iran or Mesopotamia with them, as would have happened if they had marched across Iran and Afghanistan into India. In fact the story of Yima building a Vāra (confused with Vala, a person in Ṛgveda) in Avesta has parallels in the Mesopotamian legend of the great deluge and has been assigned to the Parthian period and considered a late introduction due to foreign influences[31]. In Ṛgveda there is no mention of a deluge, no story of the creatures of the earth having to be rescued. Occurrence of Vahishta in Avesta has confused some scholars who have overlooked the simple fact that in Avesta it is used as an appellation (greatest) and in an abstract form and does not denote a person. This word Vahiṣtha (load bearer) also occurs in Ṛgveda(IV:14.4, I:134.3). This senseless linking the name of this great ṛṣi and the occurrance of Yama in VII:33.12 with Avesta or Persia, reflects very poorly on the standards of scholarship. Vasiṣtha is thought to have been of uncertain parentage (RS), and hence the mention of a parentage from Varuṇa and Urvashi the apsarâ.

There are clear indications of a time gap between Old Avesta and Ṛgveda. Trita Āptya one of the prominent figures in Ṛgveda has become legendary hero in Avesta, the same applies to the status of Yima in Avesta who became the first Ruler of the earth.

The evidence therefore supports a westward movement of the Kāṇva family and their allies, *Turvaśa* and *Yadu*, who were defeated by Sudāsa. This, one could argue may have been the beginning of an ideological rift and separation, away from dominance by Indra, between the Indian Āryans and Persian (Parśu) Āryans but a clear distinction between the two would take a long time to materialise. Boyce dates the oldest part of Avesta to 14th-11th centuries BC.

Parśu and Prithu (Persians and Parthians) who became so dominant in the middle to late 1st millennium BC are mentioned in Ṛgveda suggesting that there was an east to west migration of Āryans and not from west to east as has been continually proposed by some western scholars. This is supported by the views of Wilhelm, Dyson and Skjaervo and this is how the evidence in Ṛgveda speaks for itself. One would have expected to find a direct borrowing from Avesta in Ṛgveda if Ṛgveda had chronologically followed Avesta but there is very little to support this. Varuṇa, Mitra and Aryamā are recited as a trinity but Varuṇa 's supreme position has been challenged by Indra in Ṛgveda. It is inconceivable that Indra a demon in Avesta would have been promoted to a position of supreme Āryan God in Ṛgveda, specially since the word ARYA is frequently used when praising Indra. It is Indra who gets the credit of consigning other people/races to a lower or inferior station as in IV:28.4; *You lowered the Dasyu below everyone else and made the populace of Dāsa worthy of vilification* (RS).

Matters relating to the links between Sanskrit and other European languages can not be addressed by a study of Ṛgveda. The possibility of the Āryan having arrived from outside can not be rejected outright but taking the present level of knowledge into account, it could not have been achieved by the middle of the IInd Millenium. A date of 1200 BC for the composition of Ṛgveda only fits a conviction held by those who propose a mass migration from west to east. Eagerness on part of some scholars to try and place Ṛgveda sometime after the date of the Mitanni seals, reflects poor understanding of the time scale over which it was composed and then eventually rescued. In my opinion assigning a particular date such as 1200 BC is absurd as it has been shown, based on the list of ṛṣis and their generations, that it was composed over a minimum of 300 years.

It is far more likely that the Āryans spoke the same language as the Harappans as had their been arrival of new people several centuries earlier, one would have expected a variable mix between two established languages, which has not been shown so far. On the other hand if Sanskrit is supposed to have replaced the local language then it is difficult to see how it would have come about if the Āryans are supposed to have arrived several hundred years before the composition of Ṛgveda. We have shown that the Āryans in Ṛgveda do not wield a position of dominance so as to have subsumed the pre-existing language and culture. Rather the evidence points to a gradual change from a position of a marginal existence to dominance.

I am grateful to Prof Shri Nivas Rath for his help with Sanskrit translations and my late father Shiv Mangal Singh 'Suman' for helping me through some of the very difficult passages of Hindi in these translations.

REFERENCES

[1]Bryant, Edwin. 2001. *"The Quest for the Origins of Vedic Culture".* Oxford University Press, New York. page 15.

[2]Bryant, Edwin 2001. *"The Quest for the Origins of ..".* Page 243-245, in which he discusses the objections of Buhler and Jacobi.

[3]Bryant Edwin, Ibid page 200-220.

[4]For those who have not come across Avesta the sacred book of the Zoroastrians, the hymns attributed to the Prophet Zarathustra and hence the Old Avesta are contained in the Gathas and Haptanghaiti. The language of these hymns and prose (Haptanghaiti) is archaic and homogeneous as opposed to all the other works which can be dated to a later and much wider period of Zoroastrianism. A considerable part of this sacred book therefore is very late. As the language of these yasnas (Old Avestan) is thought to be close to Ṛgvedic Sanskrit, one should expect to find a mention of this River here. The fact of the matter is that there is no mention of a HARAXVAIT_ in Old Avesta.

[5]Oktor Skjaervo-personal communication (July 2003).

[6]Oktor Skjaervo. 1995. "The Avesta as source for the early history of the Iranians". in *Indian Philology and South Asian Studies; in The Indo-Aryans of Ancient South Asia:*

[7]Boyce,M. 1996. *"History of Zoroastrianism"* (1996), page 72.

[8]Erdosy G. 1989; "Ethnicity in Rigveda and its bearing on the question of Indo-European Origins" *South Asian Studies.* Vol:5 Page-41.

[9]Bryant E. 2001. *"The Quest for the Origins of Vedic Culture".* page 247, Possehl 2002.

[10]Kennedy, KAR. 1992; *"Biological Anthropology of Human Skeletons from Harappa 1928-1988".*

[11]Possehl 2002; *"The Indus Civilisation"* page 232.

[12]This word without exception has been translated as meaning "Lingam or Phallus worshippers" by Indian Commentators.

[13]Lal, 2001; *"Sarasvati Flows On"* page 118.

[14]Satvalekar, translates"Püh Pati" differently and does not, Lord of a City.

[15]Lal, 2001. "Sarasvati Flows On" page 119.

[16]The concept of 4 castes originating from the body parts of Puruña (a deity) does not occur elsewhere in the Vedas, other than where this hymn is repeated.

[17]Äkhmänush, the ancestor of Cyrus the great.

[18](X:75). **Eastern:**-Gangä, Yamunä, Sarasvati, Çutudri [Sutluj], Paruñni [Ravi], Äsikni [Chenab], Marudvridhä, Vitastä [Jhelum], Suñomä and Arjikiyä.

Western: - Sindhu, Triçtamä, Suñ urtä, Rasä, Krumu, Gomati and Kubhä [Kabul] and Mehatnu.

[19]Bryant, Edwin; 2001. *"The Quest for the Origins of Vedic Culture".* page 172.

[20]Lal, 2001. *"Sarasvati Flows On"* page;74-75.

[21]Bryant, Edwin 2001. *"The Quest for the Origins of Vedic Culture":* p-207,210,214,215

[22]Francourt, Henry-Paul 1993. Figures 10.1b and d, Francourt).

[23]Boyce, M. *"Historyf Zoaroastrianism".* page 15 .

[24]This is perhaps the best example of the differences in the religious system of the two groups.

[25]Note the word amitra meaning non-friend used almost as a synonym of dâsa or dasyu.

[26]The same verse occurs again (I:174.9) in a Hymn by Agastya.

[27]VII:18.22 Sudäs is described as Naptru of Devvät. (RS).

[28]Witzel's suggestion, that Prithu means Pathans. shows a poor knowledge of Indian History. Also it is difficult to see how Prithu can be translated into Pathan, a word which was coined by the British and has no relationship with Sanskrit.

[29]Witzel agrees that the Äryans arrived in India many centuries earlier so as to have forgotten their past homeland, and yet to suggest Vasiñtha crossing Sindhu on his arrival from Iran defies logic.

[30]Bryant, E 2001. *"The Quest for the Origins of Vedic Culture".*

[31]Boyce, M. 1996; *"History of Zoaroastrianim"*. page 95.≥p

BIBLIOGRAPHY

Anthony, David. W. 1986. *The Kurgan Culture, Indo-Eurpean Origins, and the Domestication of the Horse. A Reconsideration.* Current Anthropology, 27(4) 291-313.

Boyce, Mary. 1996. *A History of Zoroastrianism*, E J Brill, Leiden.

Bryant, Edwin. 2001. *The Quest for the Origins of Vedic Culture:* Oxford University Press, New York

Bryant, Pierre. 1996. *Alexander the Great* 'The Heroic Ideal' NewHorizons. Thames and Hudson, New York.

Cook, JM. 2000. *The Persians*, Folio Society.

Darmesteter, James. 1883. *'The Sirozahs, Yasts and Nyayis.'* The Sacred Books of the East Ed Max Müller. Vol XXIII, Clarendon Press, Oxford.

Dyson, Robert H Jnr 1993. *Paradigm changes in the study of Indus Civilization.* Ed: Gregory L Possehl. 2nd Ed. New Delhi, Oxford University Press IBH New Delhi- page 577

Encyclopedian Britannica. 1989 *Parthians*, (Micropedia)

Erdosy, George. 1989. Ethnicity in Rigveda and its bearing on the question of Indo-European Origins. *South Asian Studies.* 5.35-47.

Francourt, Henry-Paul 1992. Evidence for Harappan irrigation System in Haryana and Rajasthan. *Eastern Anthropologist.* 45:87-103.

Francourt, Henry-Paul 1993. "Dungeons and Dragons": Reflections on the System of Iconography in Protohistoric Bactria and Margiana. *in South Asian Archeological Studies: ed;* Possehl G, International Science Publisher, New York.

Griffith, Ralph T.H. 1889. *Hymns of the Rgveda*, Munshiram Manoharlal. New Delhi. (1987).

Hiebert, Frederik T. 1995. "South Asia from a Central Asian Perspective." *Indian Philology and South Asian Studies, The Indo-Aryans of Ancient South Asia: Language, Material Culture and Ethnicity,* Ed; Erdosy G, Walter de Gruyter. Berlin

Kennedy, KAR. 1992. "Biological Anthropology of Human Skeletons from Harappa 1928-1988". *Eastern Anthropologist,* Vol 45(1-2):55-85.

Kenoyer, Jonathan Mark. 1999 *Ancient Cities of the Indus Valley Civilisation*, Oxford University Press. Karachi, Pakistan.

Lal, B.B. 2001. *The Sarasvati Flows on:* Aryan Books International, New Delhi.

Parpola, Asko. 1995. "The problems of the Aryans and the Soma:textual-Linguistic and archaeological evidence." *Indian Philology and South Asian Studies, The Indo-Aryans of Ancient South Asia: Language, Material Culture and Ethnicity, Ed;* Erdosy G, Walter de Gruyter. Berlin.

Posseh, l G. 1993. *Harappan Civilisation : A contemporary Perspective.* Harappan Civilisation. Ed: Gregory L Possehl. 2nd Ed. New Delhi, Oxford University Press.

Possehl, G. 2002. *"The Indus Civilisation:A contemporary perspective"*. Altamira Press.

Sankrityayan, Rahul. 1957. *Rigvedic Arya:* Kitab Mahal. Allahabad.

Satvalekar, S.D. 1993. *Rigveda:* Swadhyay Mandal, Pardi, Bombay.

Sarianidi, Victor. 1991. Recent Archeological Discoveries and the Aryan problem. *South Asian Archeology:* Ed. Adalbert J Gail. Franz Steiner, Stuttgart.

Shaffer Jim G, Lichtenstein Dianne A, 1995. Concepts of ' cultural tradition' and 'paleoethnicity' in South Asian Archeology". *Indian Philology and South Asian Studies, The Indo-Aryans of Ancient South Asia: Language, Material Culture and Ethnicity,* Ed; Erdosy G, Walter de Gruyter. Berlin.

Sharma, Sri Ram. 1996. *Rigved;* Sanskriti Sansthan. Bareli (UP).

Skjaervo, P Oktor. 1995. The Avesta as source for the early history of the Iranians. *in Indian Philology and South Asian Studies; in The Indo-Aryans of Ancient South Asia:Language, Material Culture and Ethnicity, Ed;* Erdosy G., Walter de Gruyter. Berlin.

Thapar, BK. 1993. *The Harappan Civilisation : Some Reflections on its Environments and Resources and their exploitation.* Harrapan Civilisation; Ed; Possehl G L, IBH New Delhi.

The Aggressive Empires. 1987. *Barabrian Tides* (1500-600BC),. Time Life Books. New York.

Trivedi, Ram Govind. 1933-35. *Rigved Samhita;* Vedic Pustak Mala, Sultanganj (E.I.R).

Wilhelm, Gernot. 1989. *The Hurrians.* Aris and Phillips, Warminster, England.

Witzel, Michael. 1995. *Ṛgvedic History: poets, chieftains and polities,* in The Indo-Aryans of Ancient South Asia. Language, Material Culture and Ethnicity: Ed; Erdosy G. Walter de Gruyter, Berlin.

New Light on the History of Pune City: Results of an Archaeological Rescue Excavation

*Vasant Shinde, S.N. Rajaguru, Shweta Sinha Deshpande, Sanjay Deshpande, Prabodh Shirvalkar, P. Balkawade, P.P. Joglekar, S. Deo, S. Salim, Neha Kothari

Introduction

The recent (November 2002) accidental archaeological discovery in the Kasba Peth locality in the central and oldest part of Pune city in Maharashtra, has significantly stretched back the antiquity of the city by one thousand years. Pune, one of the most modern and upcoming cosmopolitan city of Maharashtra, is located on the Deccan Plateau, 150 km slightly southeast of Mumbai, the financial capital of the country. S.N. Rajaguru, while working for his Ph.D. on the River Mutha in seventies, had discovered Lower Palaeolithic tools in the gravel bed of Mutha near Dattawadi (Rajguru, 1970). Subsequently, the renowned archaeologist Professor H.D. Sankalia, founder of the premier centre for archaeology in South Asia, the Deccan College Post-Graduate and Research Institute in Pune discovered the earliest evidence of human activity in Pune when he found Palaeolithic stone tools, cleavers and handaxes over 1,00,000 years in age in the campus of the institute itself in the 1980's. This sporadic evidence clearly demonstrates that the area around Pune attracted mankind right from the beginning even when he was in the hunting-gathering stage.

In spite of the evidence of Stone Age tools, the earliest evidence of settled life and the history of Pune known prior to this research was dated only to the 7th–8th century AD, in the form of a plain rock-cut caves at Pataleshwar in the heart of the city on Jangli Maharaj road. The accidental discovery of an archaeological site beneath the rubble of modern buildings in the Kasba Peth area, the supposed oldest part of the city, has however, significantly stretched back the antiquity of settled life by one thousand years at one stroke. The finds rescued from this settlement belong to the early to late Satvahana (200 BC to 200 AD) and Vakataka (4-5th century AD) periods.

The Site

The site was discovered by Mr. Pandurang Balkawde a local resident who has been actively studying the history of Pune and its surroundings for the last 20 odd years when he noticed ancient pottery being unearthed out of the foundation trenches of Ashtekar wada (22, Kasba Peth), being dug for the construction of a new building coming up in the area. Following this discovery a team from Deccan College comprising of Dr. S.N. Rajaguru (geo-archaeologist); archaeologists Dr. Vasant Shinde, Shweta Sinha Deshpande, Prabodh Shirvalkar, S. Salim and Neha Kothari as well as heritage consultant Sanjay Deshpande from INTACH, Pune visited the site with Mr. Balkawde. The animal bones recovered from the rescue excavation were studied by Dr. P.P. Joglekar, an archaeozoologists while Dr. Sushma Deo assisted Dr. Rajaguru in carrying out geomorphological observations of the Kasba Peth area along the right bank of the river Mutha.

*Deccan College Post-Graduate and Research Institute, Pune.

A detailed archaeological survey of the Kasba Peth locality conducted by the team revealed a number of sites yielding archaeological material like pottery, artefacts including shell beads and bangle fragments and terracotta objects. A number of building sites under construction were visited in the Kasba Peth by this team and five of the localities produced archaeological evidence belonging to the same cultural period. The localities include foundation trenches at 22 Kasba Peth (Ashtekar Wada - KSB-1), 1209 (Lavalekar Wada - KSB-2), 1206 (Tapare Wada - KSB-3), 892 (Kagadipura - KSB-4) and 945 (Near Sattoti, Kagdipura - KSB-5). All these localities are located on the right bank of the River Mutha (Fig. 1), on an ancient flood deposit river terrace. The stratigraphy of the latter four localities (KSB-2, KSB-3, KSB-4 and KSB-5) has been badly disturbed due to floods (nuisance type floods) as they are close and within the reach of normal flood level (about 500m), whereas the first locality (KSB-1) is relatively away from flood reaches (1 km) and therefore quite intact. All these different localities, however, form part of one habitation site that is roughly spread over an area of 10 ha. The presence of weathered basalt bedrock under the sites suggest that this ancient village contemporary to the Satvahanas and later Vakatakas was the earliest habitation in the area and thus can be identified as the earliest Pune. In addition to the present material, earlier construction activity in this area had yielded a beautiful Vishnu sculpture of Gupta style and a rotatry quern similar to that of the Indo-Roman period and dated to circa 4-5th century AD or earlier.

The localities in the Kasba Peth area and the material unearthed from the foundation pits were studied as part of the rescue efforts, and though these localities belonged to different owners, all of them extended full co-operation and slowed down their work considerably to facilitate collection of material. As the digging was carried out by construction workers we could only participate in rescuing the material from the dirt unearthed and hence had no control over the digging methodology, which was unsystematic. Usually this kind of rescue work is undertaken where no systematic excavation is possible and where there is hardly sufficient place and time available and this in the modern context is also called "Urban Excavation". The nature of the work at the site was more towards rescuing the archaeological material from the deposit being unearthed and corresponds towards the definition of 'Salvage Archaeology'. The term itself explains the nature of work, i.e. salvaging or rescuing material with as much precision as is possible from the available deposit since the application of systematic excavation techniques is not possible. This technique is applied when the scope of the work is limited in time and space, and if not saved within the stipulated frame of time and space would be lost for study forever. At the locality of Ashtekar Wada, the major aim of the work was to collect the material on the basis of the depth and layer as systematic excavation of the deposit was not possible; however, immense efforts were made to yield the maximum reliable results possible by following the stratigraphy that was uncovered during the digging process and the material uncovered was recorded accordingly.

Though the actual rescue excavation was carried out at Ashtekar Wada, the remains of an early habitation deposit were first identified at the foundation pits of Lavalekar Wada. Unfortunately, the contractor started concrete work immediately after our visit to the site and hence we could not get an opportunity to do any work there. Both the sites yielded pottery similar to that of the Satvahana Period, which has also been found at sites around Pune, like at Bhosari, (15 km from Pune city) though never before within the city limits. The detailed survey of the Kasba Peth area (18° 31' 16" N and 73° 51' 52" E) yielded similar ceramic types at all the five localities studied.

Geomorphological Background

River Mutha is an allocthonous bedrock stream, having its origin in the Western Ghats. The mean annual rainfall in the catchment area of the Mutha is around 2000 mm, while Pune's rainfall is only around 700 mm due to its location in the rain shadow zone of the summer monsoonal winds. Geologically the Mutha valley is covered by basalts of the Cretaceous-Eocene age and is dominated by pao-hoe types (GSI 2002). The Mutha and its two important southern tributaries the Ambil and Nagzari flow on a denudation surface at an average elevation of about 550 m MSL in the area under study (see Fig.1). The surficial regolith consists of 8-10 m thick colluvio-alluvial deposits, mainly occurring on the southern or right bank of the Mutha (Fig. 2) and range in age from the Middle Pleistocene to the Late Holocene (Rajaguru, 1970). Our discussion however is confined only to the Late Holocene alluvial fills in which antiquities of the Satvahana period have been discovered

There are two distinct cut and fill type alluvial terraces preserved in the confluence zone of the Mutha. The oldest terrace surface occurs about 8-10m above the present channel of the Mutha, which is at about 540m MSL. The younger inset surface is 3-4m above the channel level and is older than the 18th century historical monuments like Shaniwar wada, Amriteshwar temple and Omkareshwar temple. On the other hand, the Satvahana settlements occur at the base (545-546m MSL) of the higher surface terrace. Kasba Ganpati temple, Nageshwar temple (which are around 300 yrs old) are situated on the top level of the terrace (550m MSL).

Fig. 2, shows the composite stratigraphy of the Late Holocene alluvial fills. Briefly the basal layer is either basalt or the calcretised reddish brown alluvium (deposited by the Mutha) or the yellowish brown calcareous colluvio-alluvium, deposited by the southerly tributaries. These basal layers are disconformably capped by non-calcareous brownish silts and clays containing lenses of sand, ash and antiquities ranging in age from the Satvahana period to the Early Medieval or Yadava period. The thickness of this deposit varies from 1-3m. The brownish alluvium grades to stone rubble with an average thickness of about 1.5m. The stone rubble (locally known as Bharav) forms the foundation layer over which late Medieval temples and houses were constructed, mainly in late 17th and early 18th century.

Environmental Significance

Brownish silts containing antiquities of early Historical period have been deposited during monsoonal floods of the Mutha and its tributaries. Detailed flood discharge studies of the Mutha (Rajaguru, 1970) indicate that these sediments have been deposited when the discharge of the Mutha was at least 1500 M3/sec or even more. As the antiquities are fairly well preserved in flood silts, it appears that these floods were non-flashy and of 'nuisance type' as commonly observed in the deltaic plain of the Ganga in central Bengal basin (Panja, et al., 2003). This mode of flood hydrology may be in response to better rainfall and good vegetation cover in the Mutha basin during the early part of the late Holocene (approximately 2nd cen. BC to 4th cen. AD). Recent high-resolution scientific investigation of Gupta et al., (2003) on marine cores collected in the northern part of Arabian Sea indicates better monsoonal rainfall in India during this period. Further archaeological data interpreted in terms of Nile River flood silts originating in the Central African highland with monsoonal rainfall also supports this increased rainfall hypothesis (Dhavalikar, 2003).

The occurrence of most of the important Late Medieval monuments on the lower surface suggests the lowering of flood levels during this time (past 400 years) and the above quoted work suggests weakened summer monsoonal rainfall during this period. Our work is only suggestive of possible environmental changes during the late Holocene around Pune and needs future detailed archaeological and scientific studies.

Cultural and Stratigraphical Sequence

At Astekar Wada, two trenches were being dug in an area of 9m (east-west) by 8.10m (north-south) for the foundation of the new building of which, Pit 1 or Foundation Trench 1 is located almost in the centre of the area, measuring 5.75 m by 2.60 m. This pit revealed a maximum habitation deposit of 3.30 m of which lower 1.30 m belongs to the Satvahana-Vakataka period, dated from the 2nd century BC to the 4th and 5th century AD. This lower deposit is represented by a blackish soil mixed with flood silt. From the stratigraphy observed in the northern section (facing south) three layers were identified in this lower deposit, the bottom most layer (30cm) is lying on *murrum* (weathered bedrock), the middle layer is 25cm thick, and the top 75cm thick. They are blackish in colour, compact in nature and contain pottery, bones and other objects almost evenly distributed and separated by thin lenses of yellowish clay.

The upper deposit of 2 m contains the remains of the late period ranging from 7th century AD to the present times in ascending order. The upper later deposit is separated from the lower by a 30 cm thick (part of the upper 2 m deposit) layer of alternate layers of *murrum* and black clay (each being 5 cm thick). The *murrum* at the base is reddish in colour same as that found at the virgin layers at the bottom of the habitation. There are two more layers of murrum 5 cm thick separated by black clay. The upper part of the layer is made of burnt brickbats. This layer is compact and appears to be intentionally rammed hard and is present in the entire section facing the south and extends in the western section to a length of 75 cm. This 30 cm thick layer appears to be the foundation of a structure located in the northern side of the trench, which was not dug. In the eastern corner of the layer lies a thick storage jar with the extant height being 60 cm; the thickness of the sherd near the mouth portion is 3 cm while in the middle it is 5 cm.

The second Foundation Trench or Pit 2 measuring 2.75m east-west and 2.30 m north-south yielded a habitation deposit of 3.90 m, of which the upper 1.60 m is later debris consisting of stone rubble, brick-bats and clay, mixed together indicating a disturbed stratigraphy because of later construction activities. The lower deposit of 2.30 m, however, yielded a very clear stratigraphy of seven layers, where layers 1, 2 and 3 belong to the late historical period, while the lower three layers 4, 5, 6 and 7 belong to the early historic period (Fig. 3).

Layer 1, is yellowish brown in colour, homogeneous and compact in nature, containing charcoal bits and pottery fragments with an average thickness of 40 cm. The layer is relatively disturbed in the upper part due to the later construction activity.

Layer 2, blackish in colour, compact and homogeneous in nature is 30 cm thick and contains stones and pebbles at places.

Layer 3, 30 cm thick is loose, brownish black in colour with flood silt deposits and disturbances at places, and contains charcoal bits, pebbles and pottery fragments.

Layer 4, is light brownish yellow in colour, homogeneous, loose in composition and contains pebbles of chalcedony and pottery pieces. This layer is 25 cm thick.

Layer 5, blackish in colour, loose and disturbed at places with an average thickness of 45 cm with burnt brickbats, pottery pieces and pebbles.

Layer 6, is heterogeneous, blackish in colour with large amounts of pottery and bones with an average thickness of 10 cm.

Layer 7, overlying the bedrock (*murrum*) is perfectly horizontal, blackish in colour, uniform and homogeneous with a small patch of yellowish deposit in middle. The concentration of pottery is highest at the base with an average thickness of the layer being 40 cm and lies on the reddish bedrock or *murrum* deposit found at a depth of 3.90 m.

Structural remains

No significant structural remains were encountered from any of the sites in the Kasba Peth area. The only structural remains of 4th and 5th century AD located at Ashtekar wada include thick floor levels 20 cm thick, noticed at the depth of 2.50 m from the surface. This thick floor is made of mixed material including soft stone, lime and clay and runs in the entire northern section extending into the eastern section to a length of 1.82 m and probably belonged to a domestic/residential structure.

Ceramics

The most common ceramic findings from the sites include vessels of various types for domestic use such as cooking and storage. These vessels typically made of clay, glass, stone or metal and gives information regarding the technological development, food habits, artistic and aesthetic qualities, trade patterns and economic condition of the habitation. The most common or bulk utensils include those made of clay or ceramics. The absence of availability of large amounts of metal and its importance in other aspects of ancient lifestyle made it a rare commodity for the common man. Hence to suit his requirements of need, economic conditions and artistic aspirations, he made various types of pottery in the period from the early Christian era to the 5th century AD (the Satvahana-Vakataka Period). Ceramics found include: Red wares including various types of fabric, slipped, washed and unwashed types; grey ware; black and red ware and Red Polished ware.

The Satvahana period is predominantly characterized by the presence of Burnished Red-Slipped, which ranges between bright red to tan and drab red in colour and Burnished grey ware. The Red-and-Grey ware are the most common types at most sites and were used both for cooking and storage purposes. The Black-and-Red ware has its antiquity going back to the Chalcolithic period and continued throughout into the early historic cultures and the Megalithic cultures of the South. All the pottery types are made on fast wheel, but are brittle, coarse and plain without any painted or other decorative elements. The shapes are represented by varieties of globular pots with different rim forms like out-turned, beaded and constricted neck; carinated *handi*; shallow bowls; storage jars with heavy rounded or beaded rims; conical and dome-shaped lids with grooved rims. The Satvahana level also has yielded few pieces of Black-and-Red ware, represented by deep saucers and dishes. The Red Polished ware present is considered to be an import from the Roman Empire from where the technology originated.

Red wares (Pl. 1): The study of the predominant ware at the site revealed its ordinary utilitarian nature and included storage jars, water vessels or pots (*matka*) and cooking vessels (*handis*). The pottery is coarse and gritty with a lot of grass and sand tempering making the vessel very light and the fabric porous (not compact) but it is well-fired in most cases, as the core is burnt red. There are two basic varieties of red ware; the bright slipped red burnished ware in which the colour of the slip ranges from deep red to tan in some cases especially the *handis* and the unslipped unwashed red ware. The brightly slipped red ware has medium to thin walls with a very thick and highly burnished bright red slip probably to cover the coarseness of the pot. The slip continues either on the whole pot or is restricted to the shoulder depending on the required use on the exterior. The unslipped vessels have a thin wall except in case of huge storage jars where the thickness of the sherd ranges between 5 to 7 cm. The most common shape in this variety is the cup-*cum*-lid bowl.

1. The pots vary between wide mouth short vertical neck and large globular body with a flat base; short narrow concave neck and a globular body with a narrow flat base (conical or cup like); narrow mouth short vertical neck with a globular body; narrow mouth vertical neck spherical body with thick beaded or rounded grooved rims and grooves at the neck, shoulder or the edge of the rim.

2. The *handis* are the cooking and serving vessels in tan to shades of bright red with thick and highly burnished slip on the exterior and the inner sides of the rim and an unslipped interior. The fabric is finer than those of the cooking pots. The vessels have a short out-turned rim with either a blunt or a sharp carination and grooves on the shoulder. The rims on the *handis* serve as holding ledges.

3. The other variety of vessel in the Red ware include lids-cum-bowls. These are of two varieties; one is a wide mouth, conical, flat base cup of the unslipped variety while the other is a shallow dome shaped lid with prominent ledge and a short slightly incurved concave rim with a grooved inner side to fit and seal the mouth of the pot. The later is slipped in shades of red from the interior and exterior but has eroded away though traces can be seen.

4. The other important variety in the red ware are the large storage jars with wide mouth beaded and rounded rims, a globular body and a conical narrow base or a rounded or flat base to be embedded in the ground. In most cases the upper portion of the pot is slipped while the lower portion is devoid of any exterior slip.

Grey ware (Pl. 2): The Grey ware of this phase like all others seems to be of the utilitarian variety specially used for cooking and storage. The ware is coarse, gritty, ill fired and has a thick slip. There is no evidence of any decorative element in this variety though some of the vessels are burnished while others have a rusticated bottom. The only decorative element visible include single, double or multiple grooves either on the neck or shoulder portion. The typical shapes include:

1. Large pots for storing water with out-turned or out curved rims, beaded rims with wide mouth and wide globular body or a narrow mouth with short vertical neck. The rims here are wide enough to provide a working handle for holding the vessel.

2. Cooking vessels like *handis*, which have a thick micaceous, slip and burnish, which could have been used for cooking as well as serving purpose. The rims include short out-turned, short out-curved or bevelled types and the carination at the shoulder is in most cases sharp but in some cases they are bluntly executed just to give them a shape. In some cases like the red ware there are incised punctured or cut marks at the top edge of the rim.

3. Lids are similar to the Red ware variety with a prominent or flat domed top and a prominent ledge and a short slightly incurved or concave rim to fit and seal the pot.

4. Large bowls with sagger base and vertical but slightly flaring sides are also a common shape and seem to have been used for liquid food of the porridge variety.

Black-and-Red ware (Pl. 3): The Black-and-Red ware like the other ceramic types has its beginning around the 3rd millennium BC in the Chalcolithic cultures of Rajasthan and seems to have continued through the Megalithic into the Early Historic period. The inverted firing technique of manufacture seems to have continued providing the characteristic black interior and rim portion with a red exterior body. The red colour ranges from shades of bright red to brownish red, which is probably due to firing. The fabric is coarse to medium grained with a lot of grass or hay and sand tempering giving a porous texture to the pottery fabric, ill-fired and the sherds are of medium thickness generally belonging to small or medium size vessels and mostly bowls of various types. In most cases the wide-mouth bowls cum dish, which are the principal type in this ware are slipped and burnished on the exterior and the interior showing that these vessels were used for serving purposes or as tableware and not for cooking. The various types of bowls include

1. Tulip shaped vases or bowls with straight sides and rounded tapering base.

2. Wide mouth, dish-*cum*-bowl with short incurved sides and slightly saggered base.

A few fragments of Red Polished Ware were found during the excavation and are suggestive of the role of Pune in the Satvahana and Roman trade that flourished during the 2nd century BC and 1st century AD and encompassed the entire country as far as Taxila.

Potsherds from the Vakataka levels recovered from KSB-1 are similar to those found in the earlier levels (Satvahana). As a detailed analysis of pottery has not been carried out, it is rather difficult to pin point the similarities and differences between the Satvahana and Vakataka pottery at this stage. We have dated this level to 4-6 century AD on the basis of the recovery of a rotary quern of basalt and a Vishnu image made of green schist stone. Typologically and stylistically they belong to this time bracket, however, they were recovered from the same depth as the Vakataka here two years earlier during another building construction nearby.

Other Objects

The rescue work at the site yielded a number of other artefacts besides pottery and animal bones. These artefacts included fragments of plain and decorated (incised) shell bangles, a triangular shaped pendant, a round shell bead and some amount of debitage indicating shell working at the site itself. Two of the noteworthy finds include a beautifully carved shell bangle curvilinear piece with a piece of iron attached to it on the edge that was possibly a screw for joining the ends of the bangle and a lion claw pendent made in shell indicating the fine developments in craft activities (Pl. 4). Terracotta objects (Pl. 5) included a few arecanut-shaped terracotta beads, a skin rubber, a conical funnel-shaped cup with a hole at the bottom in the centre, which has been identified as a head scratcher and an unidentified figurine. The pottery and the objects found in the lower levels are similar to those found in the Satvahana levels at Nevasa, Ter and Nasik.

Interesting evidence has also come forth as a result of earlier chance findings of a rotary quern and a green schist standing Vishnu sculpture. Both these were found at different places within the region of Kasba Peth during the work of digging foundations for buildings. The rotary quern (Pl. 6) belongs to the early 5th century AD as is clear from its style and typology. It consists of two circular stone slabs 35 cm in diameter; the one at the base is 9 cm in height with a circular hole 3.5 cms wide at the centre. The upper slab is dome or stupa shaped 13 cm in height and the same diameter as the base. It has a ring top 2.5 cm in height with a diameter of 18 cm above it. The centre perforation goes right through from the top to the bottom and is 9 cm in diameter and was used to pour whole grain inside the rotary grinder. There is also a horizontal perforation on the top ring for fixing a wooden 'T' shaped handle that would hold the two parts together and was used by two people sitting across each other to rotate the quern in a horizontal forward-backward motion for grinding grains etc. The modified version of this is used in the rural households even today. The stone used for making it is the locally available amygdaloidal basalt.

The standing Vishnu (Pl. 7) is made of green schist which is not found locally but in the region of Gujarat and Rajasthan, and the style of sculpting also belongs to the north Indian Gandhara style of the Gupta period with the intricacies of the drapery, jewellery and the features very carefully articulated. The standing Vishnu image is approximately 1.10m in height and is depicted with his four arms and his adornments the *chakra, gada, sankha* and lotus held in each hand and a crown adorning his head. At his feet are two gandharva figures carrying pitchers of water. The figure is identified as belonging to the 5th century AD of the Gupta period and probably came to the region as a result of trade along the Uttarapatha.

Subsistence related evidence

The amount of faunal material collected from the salvage excavation in the Kasba Peth of Pune City is small (only 441 g). Although this collection is not suitable to talk about quantitative dimension of the animal based economy, it is sufficient enough to comment on the use of animals by ancient inhabitants of Pune. Out of 21 fragments, except one small fragment (weight 1 g) all others could be identified (NISP). This small faunal assemblage revealed presence of 2 domestic and 2 wild species that were used as food (Table 1).

Table 1: Animal species found at Pune

Sr. No.	Taxonomic Unit	NISP	Weight (g)
1	*Bos indicus* (cattle)	7	308
2	*Capra hircus* (goat)	8	26
3	*Boselaphus tragocamelus* (nilgai)	2	98
4	*Antilope cervicapra* (blackbuck)	1	6
5	*Rattus rattus* (Rat)	2	2
	Total	20	440

The remains of *Bos indicus* (cattle) include fragments of cervical vertebrae (Pl. 8), rib, humerus, radius and femur. Two proximal femora, both from right side (PUN01 and PUN04) were found that were cut at the same location (just below the head). Thus it is interesting to note that even such a small assemblage revealed utilization of two adult animals for food purpose. The radius bone is along with the distal end of ulna (PUN07) and it is a tool. This tool shows marks of prolonged use, perhaps for digging or as a borer. Another domestic species used at Pune is goat (*Capra hircus*), which is represented by fragments of cranium (frontal and maxilla), rib, pelvis, femur and tibia. The epiphyseal fusion state reveals that these 8 fragments are derived from at least three individuals: young between 3-4 months, 1-2 years and an adult over 2.5 years of age.

The faunal material is well preserved, except the maxilla (PUN12) (Pl. 9) of *Boselaphus tragocamelus* (nilgai) that is very fragile in condition. The condition of the teeth and the absence of second-third molar indicate that this maxilla belongs to a young animal. Besides this maxilla, proximal portion of left femur (PUN11) of this species is found. This belongs to an animal of age less than 1 year. Perhaps the maxilla and the femur were derived from a single young individual. The blackbuck (*Antilope cervicapra*) is represented by a single maxillary fragment (right side) that belongs to an animal of age less than one year. Two small ribs of common house rat (*Rattus rattus*) were found. These are devoid of any marks and perhaps are later intrusions. It is obvious that they were not part of food economy and were derived from rat burrows that are commonly found at an archaeological site.

The bone analysis clearly indicates the use of animals like cattle and goat for meat products, which must have formed part of their daily diet including cereals like jowar, bajra and other millets like the present. Hence agriculture and animal husbandry was the mainstay their subsistence along with the increasing trade that was becoming important with the Roman contact.

Trade links with Gujarat and Rome

The period between 1st century BC and 2nd century AD with the Kushans in north India, Kshatrapas in Gujarat, Satvahanas in the Deccan and Cholas and Pandyas in the South, witnessed a very strong trade economy based on Roman trade and contacts with China via the silk route. There was a large inflow of gold and silver bullion into the country from the Roman empire in return for luxury goods like ivory, silk, precious stones, perfume, pearl, indigo etc. Roman glass and Roman wine was much appreciated in the Indian courts. It was a sea trade from a number of ports on the western and eastern coast and the Satvahanas and Kshatrapas being the powerful rulers in this region, to a great extent seemed to have controlled this foreign trade traffic and ports like Bharuch, Sopara, Kalyan on the western coast, Tamralipti, Masulipatnam etc on the east coast all testify to the archaeological evidence of this Roman trade. A large number of sites like Paithan, Ter, Nasik, Kaundinyapur, in the Satvahana territory have given evidence of Roman contact with the presence of Roman amphorae, Red Polished Ware, a Roman fine Red slipped ware which was later copied at many sites, fine coloured glass vessels, Roman type lamps etc. The excavations at Kasba Peth has yielded evidence of a Roman amphorae sherd and a Red Polished ware sherd, and a few sprinkler spouts, all of which are suggestive of Roman trade contact. Also a large number of shell artefacts include shell bangles, beads and debitage were found indicating local manufacture with the raw material being imported from the Saurashtra region of Gujarat which is one of the few coastal regions where conch shell is available. This contact is even more important in light of the fact that Bharuch in Gujarat and Kalyan in Maharashtra were two of the largest ports from where the external trade was conducted between India and Rome. Goods moved both towards the north via Ujjain, Mathura into the east to Patliputra and north to Taxila; and the south from Kalyan to Bhaja on the western Ghats into Paithan which was the Satvahana capital and other regions of the Deccan. And it seems that the contact with Pune must have been established via this route as Pune is close to Bhaja. This external trade gave a boost to the internal crafts, trading organisations as middlemen and led to a flourishing economy with social stability. This economic and social stability is reflected in the large religious donations that were made by trading families and craftsmen to the religious organisations as is seen from the inscriptions at cave sites like Karla, Bhaja, Nasik etc.

Conclusion

On the basis of the above data the history of Pune, long thought to begin around the 8th Century AD with the construction of Pataleshwar temple was pushed back to the 3rd - 2nd century BC with the discovery of the ruins of a village under the Kasba Peth region of the old city. This discovery confirms an ancient legend about the origins of Pune, which says that Pune once constituted of three villages *Kasarli, Kumbharli* and *Punewadi* located possibly at Kasar Ali, Kumbharwada and Kasba Peth respectively. The temples of Kedareshwar, Puneshwar, Narayaneshwar and Kasba Ganpati were said to mark these boundaries. The area was said to be sacred as it was near the confluence of the Mula and Mutha Rivers. The area under Kasba Peth long suspected of being the original site of Pune is on a high terrace level and would have been an ideal location for people to settle down, as the villages would have been protected from the floods of the Mutha River. The discovery of this site at the depth of 3-5 meters below the modern surface confirms this theory and suggests that the village of Punewadi lost in legends was once very much a real village. Perhaps in the years to come similar work will reveal the exact location of the other two villages and confirm the legend in its entirety.

BIBLIOGRAPHY

Gupta, A.K., D.M. Anderson and J.T. Overpeck 2003; Abrupt changes in the Asian Southwest monsoon during the Holocene and their links to the North Antlantic Ocean, *Nature* 421: 354-357.

GSI 2002; District Resource Map- Pune District, Maharashtra.

Panja, S., B. Basak, S. Chakraborty, S. Roychowdhary and S.N. Rajguru 2002; Preliminary Geoarchaeological studies in West Bengal, *Man and Environment* XXVII (2):45-60.

Rajguru, S.N. 1970; Studies in the Late Pleistocene of the Mula-Mutha valley, *Unpublished Ph.D Thesis*, Deccan College, Pune .

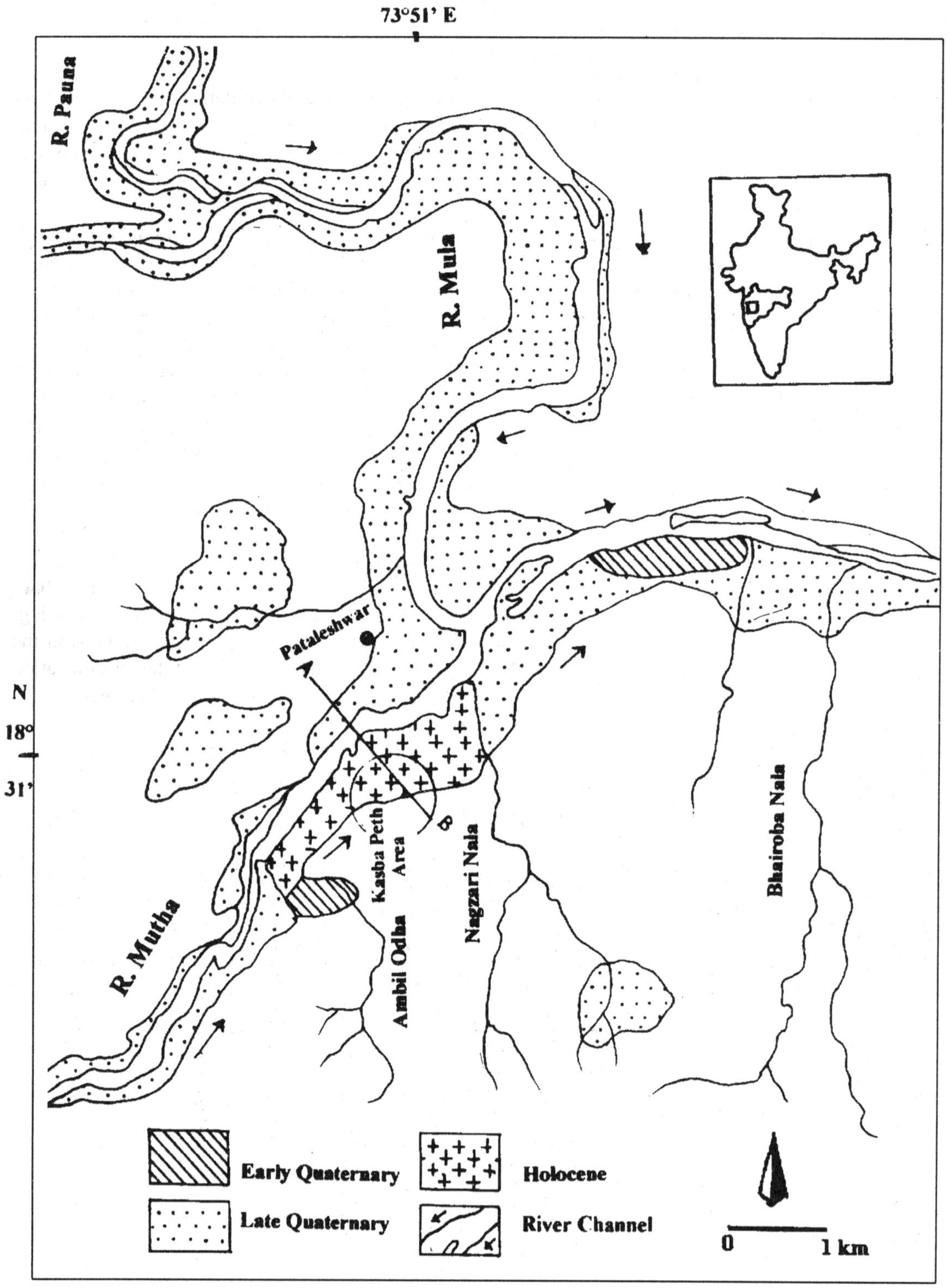

Fig. 1. Geological and archaeological map of the confluence zone of the Mula-Mutha rivers, Pune city

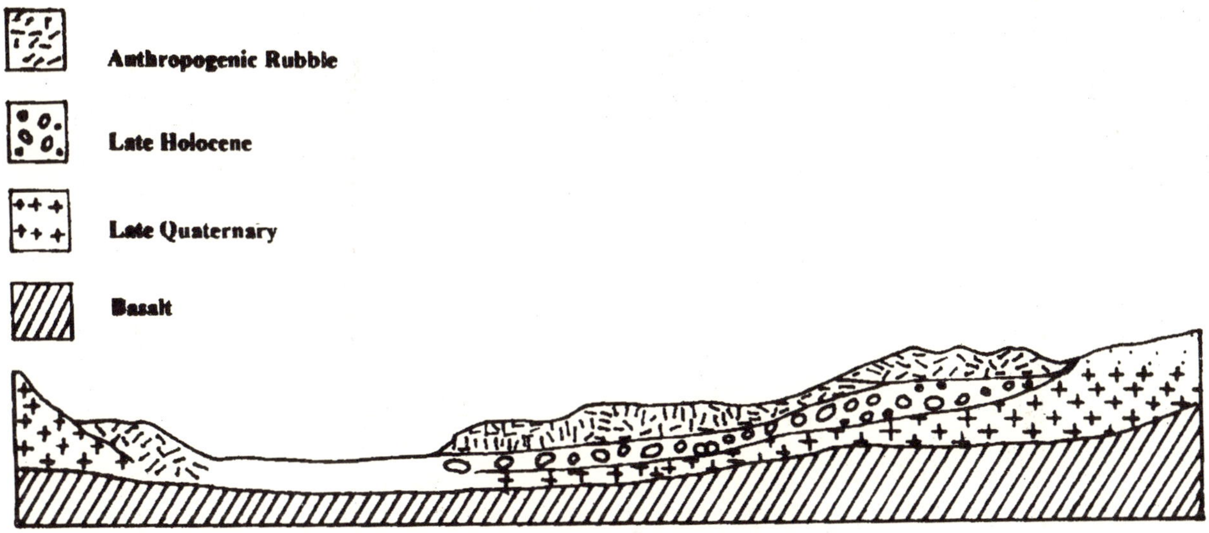

Composite Stratigraphy

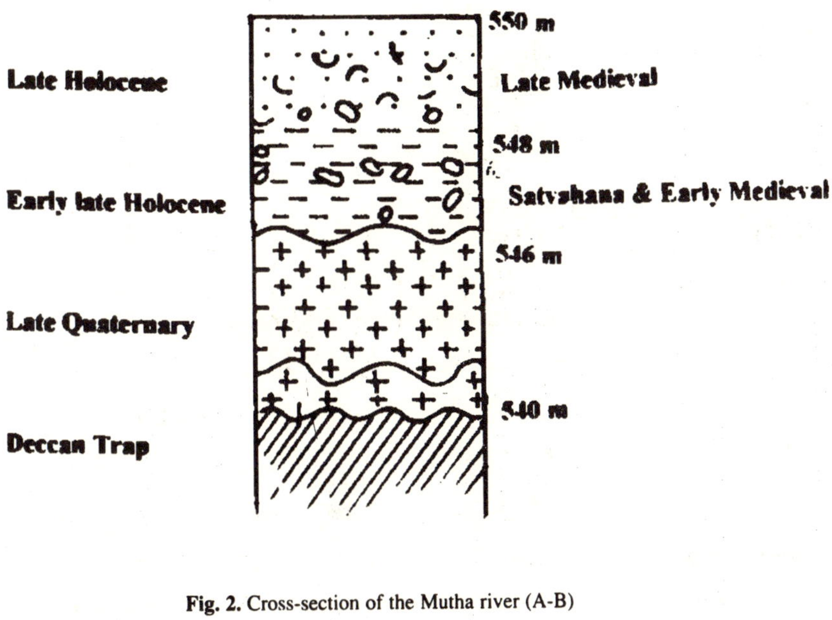

Fig. 2. Cross-section of the Mutha river (A-B)

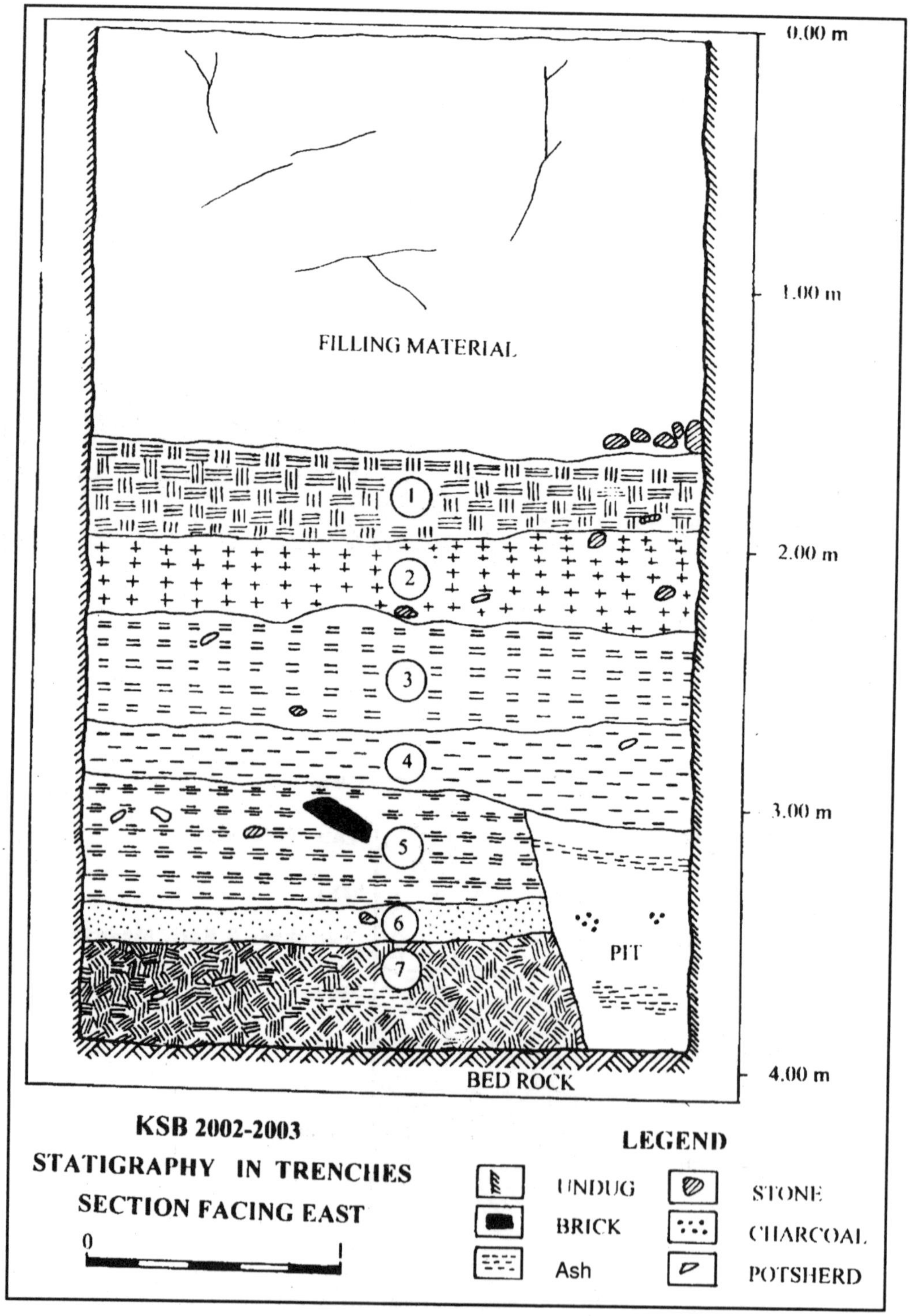

Fig. 3. Archaeological stratigraphy in trenches

The First Neolith in India – A Review with Special Reference to Karnataka

C.B. Patil*

The inventions, discoveries and results of the researches are reckoned from the day they are revealed before the scholarly world. This tradition holds equally good for the archaeological discoveries made across the world. In India, the archaeological investigations in its true sense began with the establishment of the Asiatic Society in 1784, in Calcutta. Since then, the archaeologists, geologists, amateur indologists, scholors, civilians and army officers and research institutions are publishing a variety of archaeological findings, interpretations and results regularly. Likewise, in Karnataka many prehistoric and protohistoric sites and early historic settlements have been discovered, reported and results of the investigations are disseminated from time to time since the beginning of the nineteenth century.

Unfortunately, many scholars of the recent times bestow the credit of discovering the first Neolith - ground or polished stone axe in India-Karnataka to Captain Meadows Taylor, having found it from Lingsugur in 1842 and some refer to it as a chance discovery for obvious reasons. These various claims/ discoveries and their authors are far from the truth. In fact, H.P. Le Mesurier was among the first to discover the Neolithic artifacts in 1860 from the Tonse valley in Uttar Pradesh. The present paper, therefore, seeks to examine and revive such various citations and acknowledge the due credit to the discoveries and their authors and place them in the order of merit in the historiography of archaeology of Karnataka in particular and India in general.

To begin with, the discovery of ash mounds in the Bellary, Chitradurga region of the Tungabadhara valley and the Mysore area in the Kaveri valley by Colonel Colin Mackenzie, the Commanding Engineer of Madras Presidency and later Surveyor General of India, who surveyed the antiquarian remains some time between 1796-1907 marks the beginning of the archaeological researches in Karnataka (Chhakrabarti 1988). During the last one hundred and fifty years, many Neolithic sites and artifacts have been discovered and reported from time to time in the region of Karnataka between the valleys of the Manjra and Karanja in the north to the Kaveri in the south. However, scholars like H.D. Sankalia quoting F.R. Allchin has mentioned in his tome, *The Prehistory and Protohistory of India and Pakistan* that 'the first Neolithic tool-ground or polished stone axe was found by Meadows Talyor at Lingsugur in 1842' (Sankalia 1974). Authors like V. Rami Reddy while discussing the origins of Neolithic cultures in his publication, *Neolithic and Post-Neolithic Cultures* has recorded that 'in the South, the first ground or polished stone axe was found by Captain Meadows Taylor at Lingsugur Raichur district in 1842' (Rami Reddy 1991). On the other, scholars like K.

*Assistant Superintending Archaeologist, Archaeological Survey of India, Bangalore Circle, Bangalore.

Paddayya in delineating the faunal background of the Neolithic culture of south India, refer to the first find of a Neolith as a chance discovery from Lingsugur taluka, district Raichur in 1842 (Paddayya 1979).

Early Discoveries of Neoliths in India

It is a well-established and accepted fact that the first Neolith in India was discovered in early January 1860 by H.P Le Mesurier, Chief Engineer, Jubbulpore (Jabalpur) Line, East Indian Railway. Le Mesurier reported the discovery of five polished stone celts of various sizes kept under a Pipal tree at village Mahadeo a worshiping place, from the Neehee village in the ghats westward of the Chachye Falls on the river Tonse (Le Mesurier 1861). Encouraged by this find, Le Mesurier and his colleagues discovered immediately a number of celts during the months of January, February and March in the same river valley. Le Mesurier announced these findings in a letter dated Allahabad 14th January 1861, addressed to the Asiatic Society, Calcutta. In this communication he drew attention to the fact that 'the celts were found invariably at village Mahadeo which abound in and near every village' and the discovery of celts from Manickpore, Surreaon, Khoh, Kirwee and Nagode etc., in the Tonse valley. All these details have appeared in the *Journal of the Asiatic Society of Bengal*, Volume XXX, for the year 1861 published in 1862. In the Kashmir Valley, the first recognization of Neolithic artifacts was by De Terra and Patterson during their Yale and Cambridge Expedition in 1935, when they encountred hoes, pestles and polished celts in the exploration and excavation at Burzhoam in district Srinagar.

Likewise, it was Robert Bruce Foote who discovered the first Neolith in the south India. Bruce Foote discovered a well polished half of an oval 'ringstone' or 'mace head' made of basalt in a rain-gully between Sattavedu and Roshanuggur in district Chingleput in 1864 and soon followed it with another find of a well-made celt found on the surface on the north side of the Corteliar opposite Takkoll, 8 km south-east by east of Arkonam Railway Junction in Korttalayar basin (Foote 1916). Again, it was R.B. Foote who sighted the first Neolithic artifact in Andhra Pradesh. Ir 1865, he found a small, but well made celt about 17 km south of Nellore, a district headquarters of the same name (Foote 1887). Bruce Foote in his learned article 'Notes on some recent Neolithic and Paleolithic finds in south India' published in the *Journal of the Asiatic Society of Bengal*, Volume LVI (2) has discussed in detail the earliest finds on the Neolithic sites and artifacts from the various regions of the peninsular India and has convincingly established that his discoveries of Neolithic artifacts found in 1864 are the earliest findings not only in Tamil Nadu but also in south India (Foote 1887).

Discussions

In view of these findings, the obvious reasons for sighting the first find of a Neolithic hand axe from Lingsugur in 1842 needs to be examined. Firstly, as early as 1842, one Dr. Primrose chanced to discover a few stone artifacts while clearing his garden at Lingsusgur in district Raichur (Allchin 1961). This cache consisted of knives and arrowheads made on jasper, agate and chalcedony. No doubt, this is the earliest find of stone implements in India. But these artifacts evidently cannot be accepted as neoliths in view of the raw material used for fashioning them and the types of artifacts manufactured. Hence, the earliest discovery of the Neolithic hand axe from the Lingsugur made in 1842 does not arise.

Bestowing the credit of discovering the first Neolithic ground or polished stone axe in India or Karnataka by Meadows Talyor also needs to be ascertained. It is too well known that Captain Talyor was among the first to study the Megalithic remains in the region of Karnataka while he was stationed as Political Agent of the then Colonial Rule in the erstwhile Shorapur Principality between 1842-53 and later as Administrator in 1858-61. It was in the year 1850 that he was attracted for the first time towards the Megalithic monuments at Rajankolur (Taylor 1873). Thereafter, he studied them at Hegaratgi (Hagaratgi), Belsettihal (Balsettihal), Chikanhalli (Chikkanahalli), Shahpur hills (Bheemarayanagudi-Vibhutihalli), Ijeri, Mandewalli (Mandewal), Jewarji (Jewargi), Andola, Gurmatkal all in district Gulbarga; Yemmigudda and Mallapur, district Raichur now in district Koppal in the region of Karnataka and few more in and around Hyderabad in Andhra Pradesh (Taylor 1851; 1852). Captain Talyor immediately published the results of his investigation one after another captioning them as 'The Ancient Remains at the Village of Jiwarji near Ferozabad on the Bhima' and 'Notices of Cromlechs, Cairns and Other Ancient Sychto-Druidical Remains in the Principality of Shorapur' in the *Journal of the Bombay Branch of the Royal Asiatic Society*, Volumes III and IV for the years 1851 and 1852 respectively. It is, thus, evident that M. Talyor undertook the investigations of the Megaliths between 1950-52. It was also a time when not even a single Neolithic artifact or site was discovered and reported in India save Karnataka. Moreover, all his publications on the Megaliths that appeared first in 1851, 1852 and the one later presented before the Royal Irish Academy on 12th May, 1862, do not have any kind of information or reference on either the Neolithic sites or artifacts having been discovered them in India. Further, the Neolithic traits have been found very recently at Yemmigudda and Ijeri and Mandewal (Ahmad 1942; Sundara 1968; Paddayya 1973) where Captain Talyor noticed the Megaliths. Thus, it is evident that Captain Talyor having come across any kind of Neolithic sites or artifacts in Karnataka or discovered and reported elsewhere in India

First Neolith in Karnataka

Having examined the various claims on the first discoveries of Neolithic implements from different regions in India now a question arises from where and when and who found the first Neolithic artifact in Karnataka. In the region of Karnataka, the first find of a Neolithic celt was made by one H.A. Mangles in the Cauvery (Kaveri) valley. Mangles found a fragment of a stone hatchet (celt) on the crest of a hill, 10 km north of Mercara (Madakeri) in district Coorg (Kodagu) (Mangles 1868). He communicated his discovery to the Asiatic Society of Bengal, Calcutta. It was announced in the Monthly General Meeting of the Society on 5th February 1868, which was subsequently published in the *Proceedings of the Asiatic Society of Bengal* for the year 1868. Later on, this artifact found its way as a present to the Indian Museum, Calcutta. J. Coggin Brown who catalogued the pre-historic collection in the Indian Museum, documented this implement with accession No.994 as a celt with upper part missing having a sharp crescentic edge fashioned on a smoothed diorite (Brown 1917) and the details have appeared in *The Catalogue Raisonne of the Prehistoric Antiquities in the Indian Museum at Calcutta.*

For the benefit of the scholars, it may not be out of the context to mention about the discovery of the first Neolithic habitation site/settlement in Karnataka although there is no controversy about its finding, date and the author. It was William Fraser, a District Engineer stationed at Bellary who discovered the first Neolithic habitation site in 1872 at the North or Face hill at Bellary, a district headquarters of the same name in the Tungabadhara valley. The merits of this find were commended by none other than Robert Bruce Foote, the father of Indian prehistory who wrote in 1916: 'Fraser.... had discovered that the North or 'Face' hill had been tènanted by neolithic man, and similarly also the Peacock hill or 'Kapgallu,' 4 miles to the north-east, and had made a small but choice collection of celts and chisels and other domestic implements of stone and to him belongs most certainly the credit of the first recognition of the settlement of neolithic man in the Deccan' (Foote 1916).

The foregoing analysis prove beyond doubt that the first neolithc artifact-hand axe in India was found in 1860 by H. P. Le Mesurier from Neehee village, Tonse valley, Uttar Pradesh; Robert Bruce Foote having sighted the first Neolithic implement in 1864 from a rain-gully between Sattavedu and Roshanuggur in district Chingleput in Tamilnadu and in 1865 near Nellore in Andhra Pradesh; the discovery of a celt on the crest of a hill near Madkeri in district Kodagu in the Kaveri valley by H.A. Mangles in 1868 as the earliest Neolithic artifact in Karnataka and; the North or Face hill at Bellary, brought to light by William Fraser in 1872 as the first Neolithic habitation site/settlement in Karnataka. On the other, the discussions also establish that bestowing the credit of finding the first neolith in India to Captain Taylor in 1842 at Lingsugur or referring to it, as a chance discovery being unaware of the early findings is not justified.

BIBLIOGRAPHY

Allchin, F.R. 1961. 'Ideas of History in Indian Archaeological Writing: *A Preliminary Study*' in Philips, C.H. (ed.), *Historians of India, Pakistan and Ceylon*, London, Oxford University Press: 250.

Ahmad, K.M. 1942 in *Annual Report of the Archaeological Department of His Exalted Highness the Nizam's Dominion 1347 – 49 F (1937-40 AC)*: 26-27, 31-32.

Brown, J.C. 1917. *Catalogue Raisonne of the Prehistoric Antiquities in the Indian Museum at Calcutta*, Shimla, Government Central Press: 70.

Chakrabarti, D.K. 1988. *A History of Indian Archaeology*: From the Beginning to 1947, New Delhi, Munshiram Manoharlal Publishers Pvt. Ltd.: 29-30.

De Terra, H. and Patterson, T.T. 1935. *Studies on the Ice Age in India and Associated Human Cultures*, Washington D.C., Carniegie Institution of Washington: 233-234.

Foote, R.B. 1916. *The Foote Collection of Indian Prehistoric and Protohistoric Antiquities: Notes on Their Ages and Distribution*, Madras, Superintendent, Government Press: 4; 78.

————, 1887. 'Notes on some recent Neolithic and Paleolithic finds in south India, *Journal of the Asiatic Society of Bengal (=JASB)*, LVI (2): 261.

Le Mesurier, H.P. 1861 in *JASB*, XXX (IV): 81-85.

Mangles, H.A. 1968. in *Proceedings of the Asiatic Society of Bengal*, February: 59-60.

Paddayya, K. 1973. *Investigations into the Neolithic Culture of the Shorapur Doab, South India*, Leiden, E.J. Brill: 11.

————, 1979. 'The faunal background of the neolithic culture of south India', in Allchin, F. R. and Chakrabarti, D.K. (eds.), *A Source-Book of Indian Archaeology*, Vol. I: Backgound, Early Methods, Geography, Climate and Early Man, Domestication of Plants and Animals, New Delhi, Munshiram Manoharlal: 347.

Rami Reddy, V. 1991. *Neolothic and Post- Neolithic Cultures*, New Delhi, Mittal Publications: 28.

Sankalia, H.D. 1974. *The Prehistory and Protohistory of India and Pakistan* (New Edition), Poona, Deccan College Post Graduate and Research Institute: 12, 279.

Sundara, A.1968. 'Protohistoric Sites in Bijapur District,' *Journal of Karnataka University*, Social Sciences, IV: 199.

Taylor, Meadows 1851. 'The Ancient Remains at the Village of Jiwarji near Ferozabad on the Bima' *Journal of the Bombay Branch of the Royal Asiatic Society JBBRAS*, III: 179-193.

————, 1852. 'Notices of Cromlechs, Cairns and Other Ancient Scytho-Druidical Remains in the Principality of Shorapur', *JBBRAS*, IV: 380-429.

————,. 1873. 'Description of Cairns, Cromlechs, Kistvaens, and Other Celtic, Druidical, or Scythian Monuments in the Dekhan' *Transactions of the Royal Irish Academy*, XXIV, (III): 329.

Karakambadi: A Late Early Historic Glass Production Centre

ALOK KUMAR KANUNGO*

South-east India has been the cradle of Indo-Pacific beads[1], which travelled to far off places from Africa to Japan both in quantity of material and its technological skill (with man power) at least for 2000 years (Francis 1990, 1991a, 1991b, 1996, 2002, n.d.; Gupta 1999; Kanungo 2000-01; Katsuhiko and Gupta 2000). Looking at the number of sites with evidence of glass and more particularly of its by-products in south India (Kanungo 2002), it is highly likely that glass workers of this part of the country were producing their own glass.

However, it is unfortunate that we know nothing about the place and technology of glass production at these places as the archaeological evidence at sites like Arikamedu and Karaikadu have been limited to slags and waste pieces rather than concrete evidence like that of furnace and crucibles. Here came the suggestion of Prof. Jayaraj Jacob of Sri Venketeswara University, Tirupati, who had located one such site, near Karkambadi tank, 15 km from Tirupati, which was to be developed by estate agents. A quick survey around the site not only yielded evidence of glass making but also evidences of this being of the late early historic period. Thus a small exposure of the site became more imminent. As the land was to be sold within a week, the owner, rather the watchman reluctantly permitted to work there only for three days. This made matters worse, but whatever little could be recorded is given below.

Karakambadi

The site is 15 km south of Tirupati near the Karakambadi tank. It is in the form of a bund about 150 m long and 3 to 4 m wide. Its height is 1.5 m adjoining to which the farmers have made their field boundaries. This bund is about 700 m north of the Karakambadi tank and 300 m east of a rail track (Fig. 1). There glittering evidence of glass manufacture in the form of numerous broken crucibles, slags and glass pieces all around the bund and in the nearby cultivated lands (Pl. 1). What is unusual about the find was that crucibles were unusually small, indicating the quantity of glass produced and number of crucibles put in the furnace. This size of the crucibles is not that surprising while considering that Somapalaiem glass furnace used to accommodate as many as 320 pots (crucibles) till early 20th century (Narayan Rao 1929, cited in Dikshit 1969)[2]. Enquiry revealed that the remains of this site and its by-products were spread over a large area towards Karakambadi tank. They must have been washed off with water, which comes next to the bund and stays there for months during the rainy season.

For verifying the existence of any furnace one trial trench of 2x2 m at the centre of the bund and two small

*Deccan College Post-Graduate & Research Institute.Pune.

scraping sections of about one metre width with step trenches were carried out at two of the most wide and raised points of the bund. They are numbered as trench 1, 2 and 3 (Fig. 1).

Trench 2

The area was selected for the trial trench because of the occurrence of a large concentration of crucibles and slags. At the centre of the bund four pegs were placed at the four corners and a grid of 2x2 m was made with the help of threads (Pl. 2). One peg was placed at the highest point on the western side of the trench as datum point. Cleaning the area inside the grid gave a number of broken crucibles, burnt clay and bricks, glass pieces and a few potsherds. Uppermost 5 cm soil was removed from surface while retaining crucible pieces *in situ* to see the alignment. Crucible pieces were found to be haphazardly scattered (Pl. 3). A dig of 10 cm was then called as the layer 1. From this layer, a number of broken crucibles, comparatively more glass pieces (mostly green in colour), slags, and some pottery pieces were noticed (Pl. 4). Their concentration was less towards the northern side. This area looked more like the piling of debitage rather than (anything to do with) furnace area as most of the crucible pieces were of broken tops and body parts (probably broken intentionally to remove the frit/glass), without any alignment. The soils were loose, not hard as it should be in a furnace. Besides this, potsherds were found inside. For confirmation another dig of 10 cm (layer 2) was taken and the evidence consists of only few pieces of broken crucibles in the centre in north-south direction. A test pit of 25 cm depth was then dug at the one corner. It revealed only loose soils which confirmed that it was not a furnace area (Pl. 5).

Trench 1 and 3

Due to constraints of time, two section scrapping of 1 m width from the top were attempted at the two most bulging and raised point of the bund. Debitage at these points was less but concentration of the crucible pieces was fairly high. However, at both places after scraping of about 5-8 cm, the soil was so hard that it was difficult to scrape. It gave evidence of the furnace of glass making. As neither time nor resources at hand would have permitted to expose the full furnace, it was decided to expose the section fully. It confirmed the existence of furnace at both places with the exposure of a thick layer of slag along with *in situ* crucibles and bellow pipes (Pl. 6).

As the scraping progressed, the soil became more and more hard and after scraping of about 30 cm of hard soil at both the places, an arrangement of crucibles was located (Pl. 7). At trench 3, the crucibles were found arranged in two layers and a cluster of slags below them. At the lower portion on both sides, a thick hard burnt clay section was visible and it was harder than any other soil. Perhaps that was a part of the furnace wall. The upper parts were evidently broken. The evidence of a bellow pipe attached to the wall confirmed that this was in fact part of the furnace wall. Also a blowpipe was found in the upper level of trench 1, which indicated that the bellow pipes were not always fixed at the lowest level (Fig. 1). The inclination of wall indicates that the furnace was of conical shape and also of smaller size.

Crucibles

There were hundreds of broken crucibles scattered on the surface and in the trenches, and *in situ* findings of crucibles with silica and pieces of flint stones inside them (Pl. 8). One crucible in trench 1 has given the evidence of frits in it.

Both the crucibles and the bellow pipes were made of clay. Crucibles were of pointed U shape (Fig. 2). The pointed base shows that the crucibles were kept in a small tripod over fire. From the appearance of the crucibles it appears that they were coated with quartz, which would have served to keep them hot for longer periods. There was an opening at the top of the crucible. There is a possibility that the glassmaker might be closing the opening of the crucible with a layer of quartz after inserting the raw materials into it. After the frit/glass was made it was removed by breaking the upper portion of crucible; this resulted in a debitage of plenty of crucible rims with quartz incrustation and smaller body parts. After taking out the frit/glass from the crucible, they were flaked from all sides of the soils and impurity. One such green coloured frit piece was found from Trench 1 (Pl. 9).

Size of the crucible

Length:	17 cm
Diameter of the opening:	21 cm

Pottery and Probable Date

Most of the associated pottery from the trench was simple coarse red ware. It appears to belong to the later part of the early historic period i.e., *c.* 4th-5th A.D. (personal communication Dr. Vasant Shinde, Deccan College). There are four potsherds with rims, with a thin layer of glass inside the potsherds indicating their association with glass making rather than deliberate glazing (Pl. 10 and 11). This layer of glass was uneven in its thickness and in no case were they found on the outer side. However, one piece of potsherd, was covered with a layer of glass all around, even on the broken borders. This confirmed that this pottery was associated with glass making.

Out of these glassy layered potsherds, three are globular pots with beaded rim (Fig. 3A) and one is a small basin with internal thickness and undercut rim from inside (Fig. 3B). Rest all are nondescript. Some give an impression of a bluish colour but that is due only to a thick layer of glass.

Some potsherds without any glassy layer are also noticed with one exception that has a rim (globular pot with beaded rim). All of them are nondescript.

Raw Materials

Fifty metres north-west of the bund there lay a silica deposit forming a bund of about 300 m spilling towards the north. It is evident that this silica was transported to this area from some nearby source.

The area is rich in palaeolithic deposits, one can see a number of palaeolithic tools (hand-axe, cleavers, scrapers etc.) in the dug out area 200 m north from the bund. At both the west and east corners of the dug out area, there was exposure of ancient brick structures and floors. A few pieces of glass were also seen on these floors. There are two old wells with brick lining, one towards the east of the bund and another towards the south.

Acknowledgements

The author is grateful to the Indian Council of Historical Research, for financial support; to Prof. Jayaraj Jacob and Mr. Munaf Abdul for their co-operation during field work; to Mr. Dvadatta Phule for help with line drawings; to Prof. V.N. Misra for his invaluable comments on the findings; to Prof. V.D. Gogte and Dr. P.P. Joglekar for thoughtfully going through the earlier version of this paper; and to Ms. Shubhangi Kardile and Dr. Shahida Ansari for their valuable comments.

REFERENCES

1. Indo-Pacific beads are made of glass using drawing technique, and are generally three to five millimetres in diameter (Kanungo 2000-2001: 339). In cross section they are usually round, but their profiles differ so much that they may be oblate, discoidal, tubular, or other shapes (Kanungo 2002: 167). This type of beads have been named variously by scholars as Trade Wind Beads (Van der Sleen 1956: 27), Trade Wind Beads Chemical Group (Davision cited in Francis 1990: 1), and Indo-Pacific Monochrome Drawn Glass Beads (Francis 1985: 44). Today this bead is produced with traditional technique only at Papanaidupet in Chittor district of Andhra Pradesh (Francis 1985, 1990, 1991b, 1994, 2002, e.d.; Kanungo 2000-2001, 2002; Stern 1987a, 1987b).

2. In a report on indigenous glass industry submitted to the Madras Government in 1927-29, D. Narayana Rao cites 15 centres in Chittor district itself viz., 1) Maddiledu, 2) Somapalaiem, 3) Kalahasti, 4) Jangarapalli, 5) Chintayapalle, 6) Upparapalle, 7) Bhimavaram, 8) Pillemedu, 9) Seetharampet, 10) Merelapaka, 11) Parapalle, 12) Kothapalayam, 13) Kanjiniputtur, 14) Kurukkamputtur and 15) Gundipedu, where glass was being worked. The industry was said to be flourishing in these at one time or the other. The method of preparing glass was practically identical with that in the North. It was made by levigating the alkaline earth, allowing the salts to crystallize out in the sun and by heating them in a mud crucible for several hours with bits of broken bangles. The vitreous mass produced is solidified into block glass which is removed by breaking the receptacle. Occasionally flint stones called Kanikiroy are used as an additional material.

   The most extensive remains were at Somapalaiem where twelve huge furnaces, some of them large enough as to accommodate 320 pots have been noticed; the production stopped due to competition by the year 1929.

BIBLIOGRAPHY

Dikshit, M.G., 1969, *History of Indian Glass*, Bombay: University of Bombay.

Francis, P., 1985, Bead report XVI, the Asian bead study tour II, Thailand: revolution and ruin, tradition and change, *Ornament* 9(2): 43-48.

————, 1990, Glass Beads in Asia, part II, Indo-Pacific beads, *Asian Perspectives* 29(1): 1-23.

————, 1991a, Glass Beads in Malaya: a reassessment, *Journal of the Malayasian Branch of the Royal Asiatic Society* 64(1): 97-118.

————, 1991b, Bead making at Arikamedu and beyond, *World Archaeology* 23(1): 28-43.

————., 1994, Towards a social history of beadmakers, *Beads* 6: 61-80.

————, 1996, Bead, the bead trade and state development in southeast Asia, in *Ancient Trades and Cultural Contacts in Southeast Asia*, pp.139-60, Bangkok: The National Office of the National Culture Commission.

————, 2002, *Asia's Maritime Bead Trade 300 B.C. to the Present*, Hawai: University of Hawai'I Press, Honolulu.

————, n.d., The beads and other small finds, in *The Ancient Port of Arikamedu: New Excavations and Researches 1989-1992*, Vol. II. (Vimala Begley Ed.), Paris: Memoires Archeologiques, Ecole Francaise d'Extreme-Orient.

Gupta, S., 1999, Indo-Pacific beads in Japan, *Beads Study Trust Newsletter* 24: 11-14.

Kanungo, A.K., 2000-01, Glass beads in Indian archaeology - an ethnoarchaeological approach, *Bulletin of the Deccan College Post-Graduate and Research Institute* 60-61: 337-53.

————, 2002, *Glass Beads in Ancient India: An Ethnoarchaeological Approach*, Unpublished Ph.D. thesis, Pune: Deccan College Post-Graduate & Research Institute.

Katsuhiko, O. and S. Gupta, 2000, The far east, southeast and south Asia: Indo-Pacific beads from Yayoi tombs as indicators of early maritime exchange, *South Asian Studies* 16: 73-88.

Narayan Rao, D., 1929, *Preliminary Report of the Survey of Cottage Industries. Chingleput (1929); Chittoor (1929); Coimbatore (1929); East Godavari (1929); Guntur (1929); Kistna and West Godavari district (1929); Nellore (1929); Tanjore and South Arcot (1929); Vizagapatnam (1929)*, (cited in Dikshit 1969).

Sleen, W.G.N. van der., 1956, Trade-wind beads, *Man* 56(art no 27): 27-28.

Stern, E.M., 1987a, On the glass industry of Arikamedu (Ancient Podouke), in *Archaeometry of Glass* (H.C. Bhardwaj Ed.), pp. 26-36, Calcutta: Indian Ceramic Society.

Stern, E.M., 1987b, The secret of Papanaidupet, *Glastechnische Berichte* 60: 346-51.

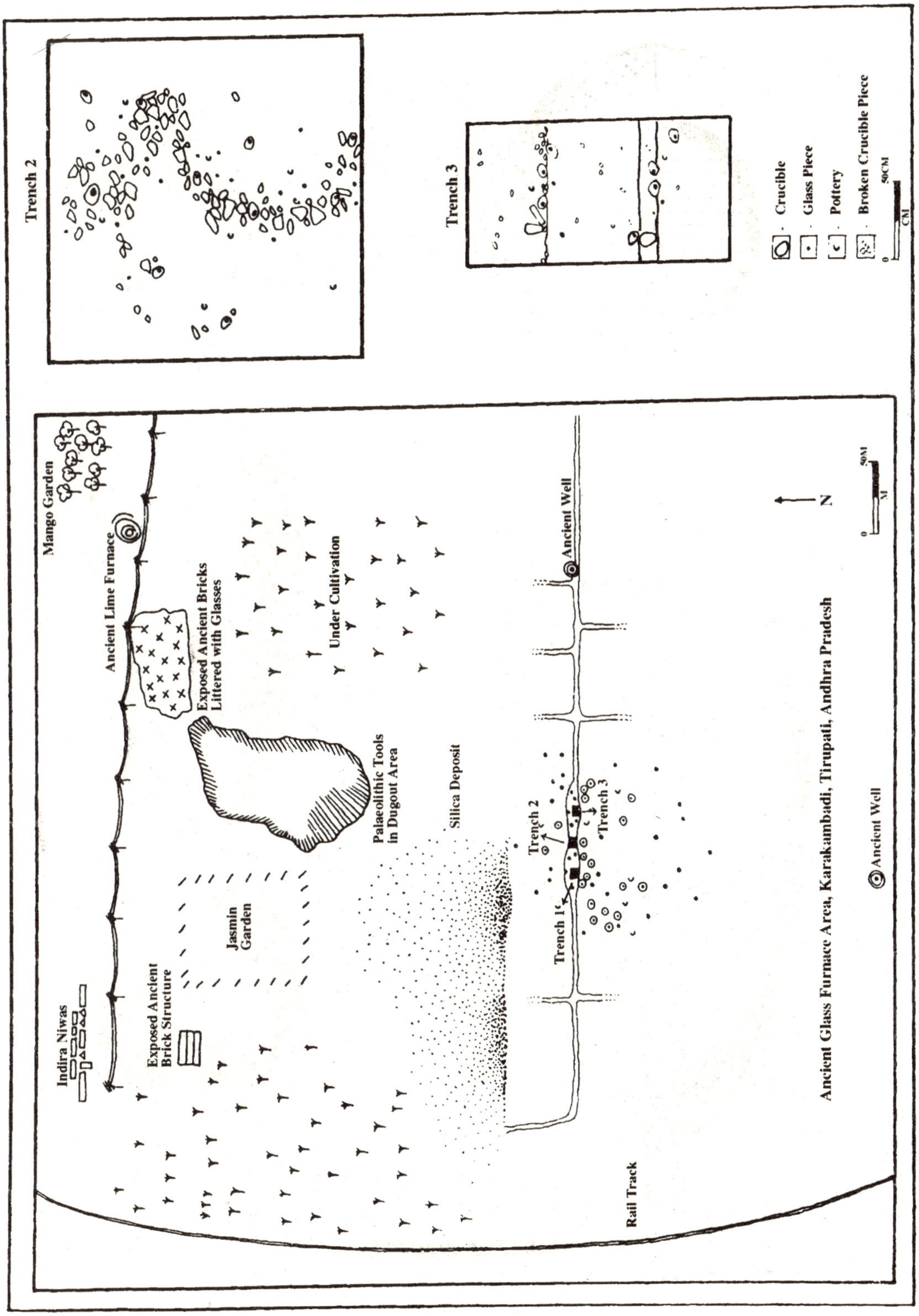

Fig. 1. Site map of Karkambadi

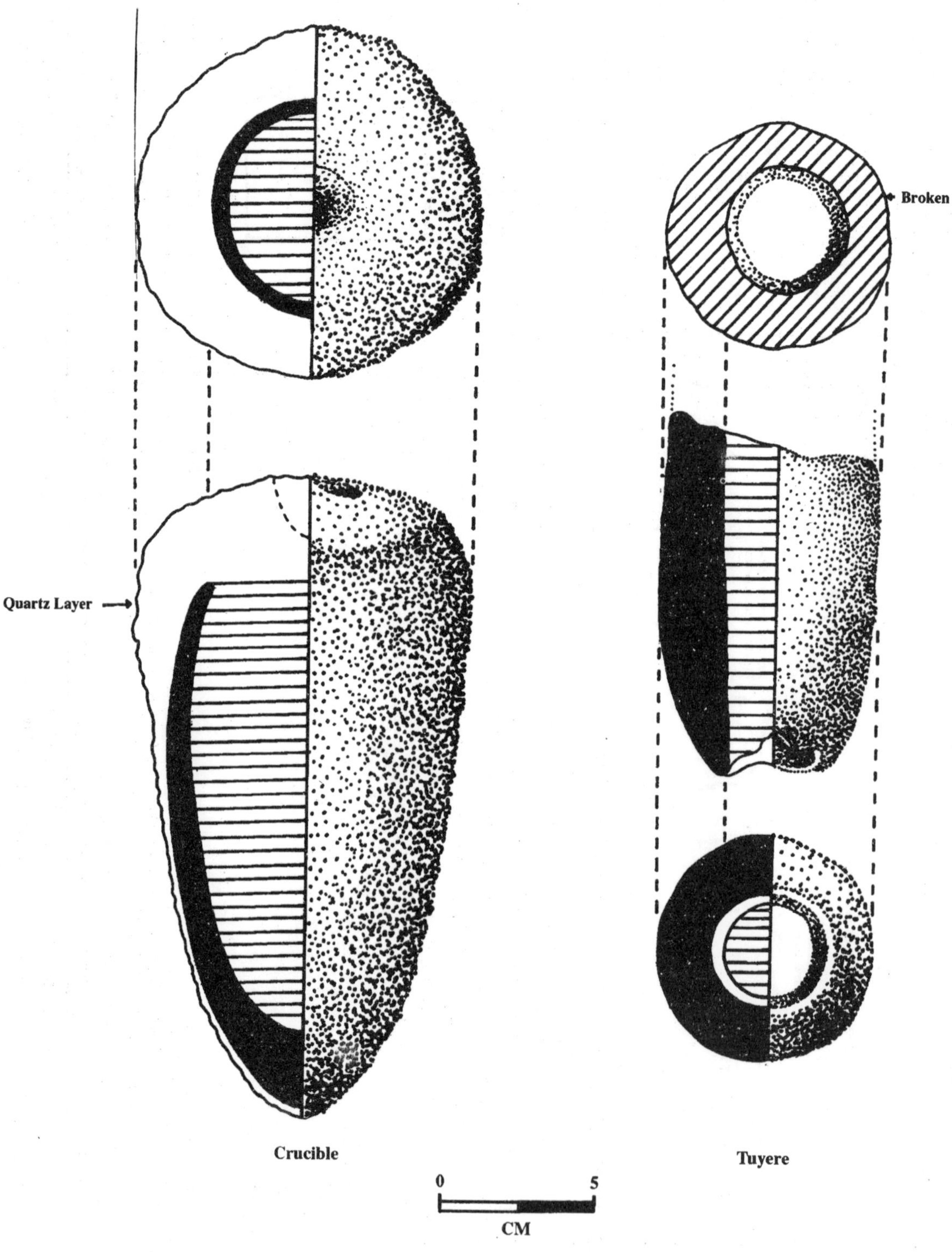

Fig. 2. Reconstructed crucible and Tuyere

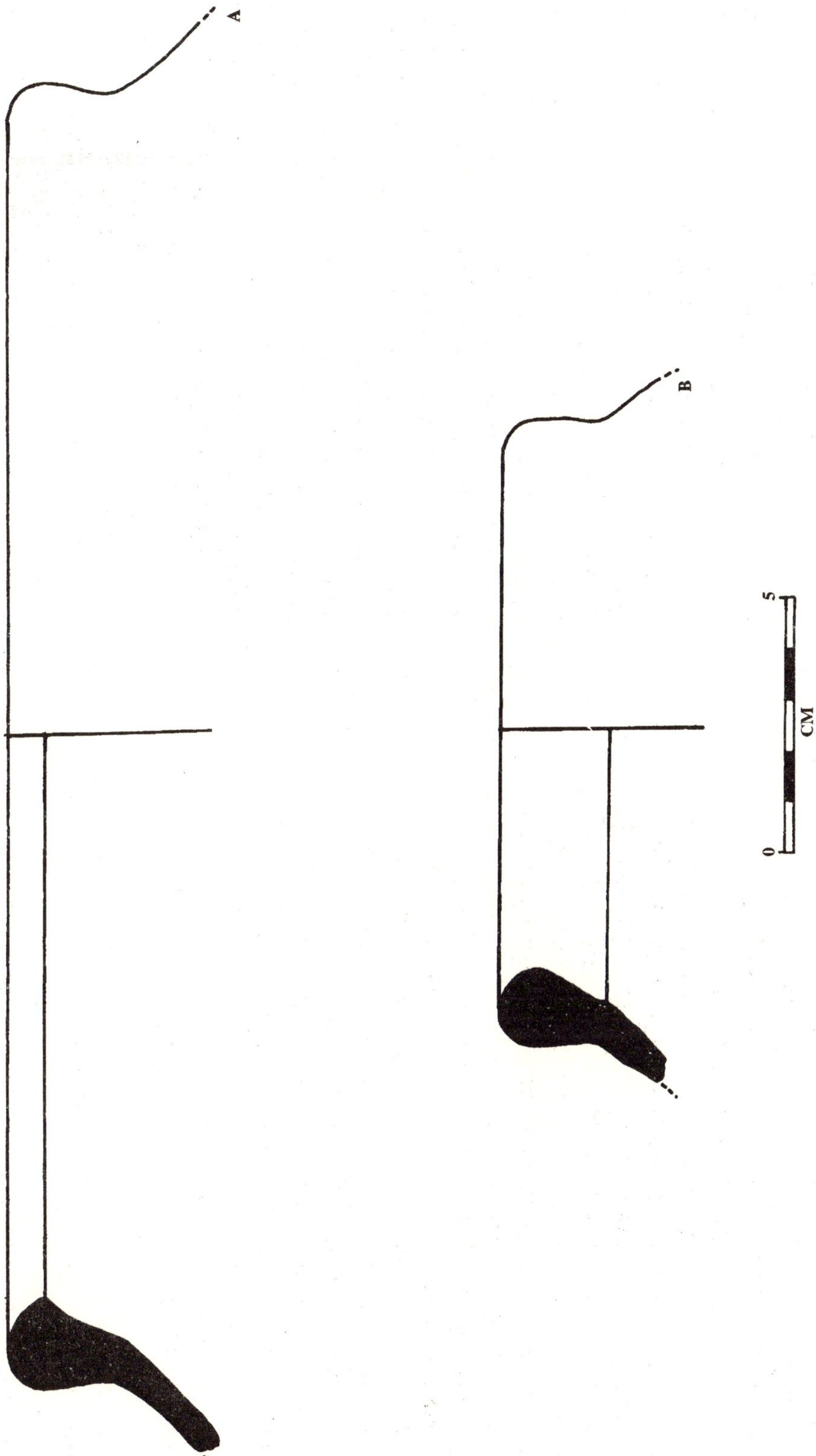

Fig. 3. Rim sections

Skeletal Remains from the Kudatini-sarcophagus burial

VEENA MUSHRIF[1], NICOLE BOIVIN[2], RAVI KORISETTAR[3] & S.R. WALIMBE[1]*

Introduction

In March of 2002, while carrying out geoarchaeological analysis of the well known Kudatini ashmound in Bellary District of mid-eastern Karnataka, a joint Cambridge University-Karnatak University archaeological team led by Boivin and Korisettar (see Boivin *et al.*2002) discovered three late prehistoric pots in the section of a Public Works Department trench adjacent to the ashmound (Fig.1). Though two of the pots were slightly damaged, one was fully intact, and it was clear that the pots had been deliberately buried intact. Given the risk of further unrecorded destruction of the locality, the team decided to carefully excavate a small test trench adjacent to the pot find location, in order to obtain contextual information which might help ascertain the significance of the three buried pots (with Biovin *et al.* forthcoming). This pit revealed the existence of a sarcophagus burial of Late Neolithic / Early Iron Age date. The 87 cm long, bathtub shaped terracotta sarcophagus with six legs (Fig.2), was oriented precisely along a north-south axis (see Fig.3). It contained the disarticulated remains of a human child (see Fig.4), as well as animal bones and a red chert blade. The sarcophagus was surrounded by at least 13 pots of Black-and-Red Ware and red ware, some of which also contained skeletal material.

Although the burial did not appear to possess a stone element, it may nonetheless be classed as a 'Megalithic' burial, in accordance with the common usage of this term in the south Indian context (Mohanty and Selvakumar 2001; Moorti 1994). Burials attributed to the so-called Megalithic tradition in south India are actually extremely varied, and some do not even involve stone constructions or markers. Nonetheless, these various burial forms may be grouped together on the basis of a number of shared traits, not all of which are found in any given burial. These include, for example, the presence of black-and-red ware pottery, iron and burial furnishings such as platforms (in rocks and caves.) urns of sarcophagi; orientation relative to the cardinal directions; graffiti marks on pottery and secondary burial vs. inhumation of skeletal remains. The Kudatini burial possessed some, but not all, of these traits, and displayed certain characteristics that link it also with the Neolithic period (Boivin *et al.* Forthcoming), suggesting that it may be a very early example of a Megalithic style burial.

Relative to many south Indian Megalithic burials, the majority of which contain a few poorly preserved skeletal elements or lack a skeletal component entirely (McIntosh 1985; Mohanty and Selvakumar 2001), the Kudatini skeletal remains displayed good preservation. In addition,

*[1]Department of Archaeology, Deccan College Post-graduate and Research Institute, Pune 411006, India.
[2]McDonald Institute for Archaeological Research, University of Cambridge, Downing Street, Cambridge, CB2 3ER, UK
[3]Department of History and Archaeology, Karnatak University, Dharwad, Karnataka 580003, India.

Table 1: Inventory and preservation of human skeletal elements found with the sarcophagus and pots

Skull	Dentition	Thoracic cage	Upper extremity	Lower extremity
Frontal: L side is better preserved than the R side;	**Maxilla:** maxillary fragment with RLII, L12 and RPm1 in crypt and Rdc, Rdm 1 and Rdm2 in situ. LC, RPm2, RM1, RLM2 (L is preserved in 2 crown fragments)	**Ribs:** there are 33 small to medium sized rib fragments, of which 25 are mid portion and 8 from the proximal (head-vertebral) ends.	**Scapula:** For R side, glenoid cavity, part of coracoid process, part of spine, acromoion; axilary border and body part. For L, side two fragments, from axillary border and part of spine.	**Femur:** L proximal extremity with greater and lesser tronchanter.
Parietal: R side is more complete than the L side				**Tibia:** R almost complete but distal end is missing and proximal end is damaged.
L temporal fragment including mastoid process and petrous portion;	**Mandible:** almost complete except R coronoid process and L Condylar portion. LPm 1 RC and RM2 are in crypt. R12 is isolated. RLdm 1 (R crown is half broken), RL dm2, RM1, LM2 (isolated).	**Vertebrae:** three cervical vertebrae including axis, 3rd and 5th.		
Occipital is preserved in small to medium-sized fragments; R and L occipital condylar portion.		One damaged thoracic vertebral body.	**Clavicle:** R almost complete.	**Fibula:** R shift portions. L complete.
		Posterior portion of lumber vertebra including superior articular facets and spinous process.	**Radius:** R almost complete, head is missing; L shaft fragment, both extremities are missing.	There are 9 small long bone fragments.
				Two damaged **epiphyseal caps.**
		11 fragments of vertebral column (individual identification is not possible)	**Ulna:** R complete	**6 phalanges,** individual identification is not possible.
			One **metacarpal.**	

skeletal remains were discovered in some of the pots that accompanied the burial, while in the vast majority of excavated Megalithic graves in south India, the multiple pots that are often found as burial furnishings are devoid of biological of cultural material (Mohanty and Selvakumar 2001). It was therefore recognised that the Kudatini burial provided an excellent opportunity to gain some unique insights into Megalithic burial practices, and to shed new light on the handling of human skeletal remains by the people who created these graves. The human skeletal material from the Kudatini burial was therefore transferred to the Department of Archaeology, Deccan College, Pune, for detailed recording and analysis by Mushrif and Walimbe. This report addresses the observations and findings that emerged from this analysis, and their implications. More detailed discussion of the Kudatini burial can be found in Boivin *et al.* (forthcoming), and colour photographs of the burial appear on the Bellary District Archaeological Project website.

Results

A. Skeletal inventory and preservation

After excavation, the total contents of the sarcophagus were dry sieved through a 2.5 mm sieve, while those from the pots were sieved through a 1mm to recover small finds. All skeletal material was collected and sent to Deccan College for identification and analysis. The total skeletal inventory is summarised in Table 1. Most of the Kudatini burial skeletal remains were located within the sarcophagus itself, where they were concentrated in a pile approximately half-way between the two ends (Figs.4 and 5). Some skeletal elements were also found distributed into some of the pots that surrounded the sarcophagus, however (Fig. 5 and Table 2). The skeletal elements within the sarcophagus and the pots are identical in both size and general morphological appearance. In addition, some of the remains from the pots articulate perfectly with skeletal remains found within the sarcophagus or in other pots (Table 3). For example, Pot F contained a near complete mandible, the left ascending ramus of which was found in the sarcophagus. In Pot D, two cervical vertebrae (the 3rd and the 5th) were found that were consistent in size with the axis vertebra found in Pot J. Also, no skeletal elements from the pots appear to be duplicated in the sarcophagus or in other pots. It is thus very likely that the skeletal remains from the sarcophagus and the pots all belong to a single individual.

Table 2: Inventory and preservation of skeletal elements found within the individual pots

Pot*	Type	Graffiti marks	Skeletal material
1	Black-and-Red Wate (large)	double curved/straight lines	n/a‡
2	Red Ware (med.)	double curved/straight lines	none
3	Red Ware (med.)	double curved/straight lines	1 epiphyseal cap, unidentified, but human; and 2 small-sized unidentifiable (1-1.5 cm; longbone?) fragments, some of which show signs of discoloration, possibly resulting from exposure to fire
A	Red Ware (med.)	arrow marks; base of inside also contains sets of double lines crossed by double lines	1 human vetebra (missing); broken shaft of left radius, 10.3 cm long and preserved in 2 pieces (only mid-shaft portion; extremities not preserved); and 2 tiny unidentifiable bone fragments
B	Black-andRed Ware (small)	double curved/straight lines	none
C	Red Ware (med.)	arrow marks	none
D	Red Ware (med.)	double curved/straight lines	2 human cervical vertebrae, 3rd and 5th, complete but lightly damaged on the body (3rd) an foramina transversarium (5th); and 1 small-sized unidentfiable bone fragment
E	Black-and-Red Ware (med.)	fish-shaped mark, variants of arrow mark (?), etc.	none
F	Red Ware (med.)	double curved/straight lines	1 near complete human mandible, with single tooth in crypt; and 1 broken body of human thoracic vertebra
G	Black-and-Red Ware (med.)	double curved/straight lines	none
H	Black-and-Red Ware (med.)	double curved/straight lines	1 small, unidentifiable bone
I	Red Ware (med.)	double curved/straight lines	none
J	Red Ware (med.)	double curved/straight lines	I human axis vertebra, 2 unidentifiable long bone fragments

*Pots 1-3 were discovered in an exposed section prior to excavation, Pots A-J during the excavation itself.

‡This pot was broken, and the sediment with in had thus been disturbed.

Table 3: Skeletal elements in pots that share strong morphological similarities to those in other pot or within the sarcophagus

Skeletal element in pot	Location of matching skeletal element
Brokent shaft of left radius in Pot A	Right radius in sarcophagus
3rd and 5th cervical vertebrae in Pot D	Axis vertebra in Pot J
Nearly complete mandible in Pot F	Left ascending ramus of mandible in sarcophagus

The representation of skeletal elements for this individual is incomplete (Fig. 5). Many of the bones missing from the skeletal assemblage are the smaller bones (eg. Metacarpals and phalanges) and finer ones (eg. The facial bones). However, larger bones like the right femur, the humeri, and the pelvic blades are also missing. There do not seem to be any clear patterns in terms of the representation of skeletal elements in the sarcophagus versus the pots, except that the pots seem to some degree to be dominated by vertebral elements. Rib bones, meanwhile, cluster in the sarcophagus.

While the Kudatini skeletal remains are well preserved relative to those in other Iron Age megalithic contexts in south India, they have nonetheless suffered substantial weathering effects. Bones are dry and brittle, with a chalky consistency when outer surfaces are scraped away with a scalpel. Protein preservation is poor, thus preventing radiocarbon dating of either the bones or teeth from the burial. A single bone fragment (in Pot 3) displayed discoloration possibly resulting from exposure to fire. Preservation of external bone morphology nonetheless permitted morphological identification and analysis.

B. Observations

i. Age estimation

The individual represented by this skeletal collection is sub-adult. Age has been estimated on the basis of the four long bones and twenty-two teeth found in the burial.

For long bones like the ulna, radius, femur and tibia, epiphyseal fusion is not seen. Three bones are measurable and the diaphyseal lengths of these bones are as follows:

Right Ulna: 17.3 cm
Right Radius: 15.8 cm (estimate)
Left Fibula: 24.0 cm

Walimbe-Gambhir (1994) provide charts for diaphyseal lengths of long bones for the age group '0-60 months'. They also observe that proto-historic children in this region exhibit a standard growth rate of approximately 80% of the normal growth rate (ibid.). Accordingly, the age of this individual at the time of death can be inferred to have been greater than 60 months, and probably around 6 years.

The second and more reliable indication of age comes from the dental evidence. The 22 teeth preserved for this individual exhibit various degrees of crown calcification and eruption.

All deciduous teeth were erupted and in use at the time of the individual's death. The deciduous second molar dm 2 is the last tooth to erupt in this category, around 30-32 months. This tooth exhibits a considerable amount of wear, and the occlusal morphology is obliterated to a great extent. The wear pattern suggests an age of more than 5.5 years.

Two permanent molars, URMI and LRMI, were fully erupted and in use at the time of death. Eruption of these molars is usually complete at around 6.5 years, provided there are no major nutritional insults.

Crown calcification for the second premolar is usually complete around 6 to 7 years. For this child, the maxillary RPm2 is preserved and exhibits almost completely calcified crown. Mandibular LPm2 is seen in its crypt. For this tooth also, crown calcification is probably complete. These observations suggest an age of around 6 to 6.5 years.

Crown calcifications for the maxillary first permanent incisors RLIIs, which usually finishes at the age of 5 years, are also complete. For URII, root formation has also commenced, and is approximately one third complete.

The Maxillary left canine, ULC, also has a completely calcified crown, a stage that is usually achieved at the age of 6 to 7 years.

Union of the two halves of the neural arch and the fusion of arch and body is complete.

On the basis of these various lines of evidence, the age of the individual buried in the Kudatini sarcophagus, at the time of death, may be estimated at around 6-7 years.

ii. Sex determination

Sex determination for this individual was not possible because this is a sub-adult specimen.

iii. Cranial morphology

Neurocranial elements are preserved in the form of disarticulated small to medium sized fragments and no bone is complete. No facial bones are represented in the collection, except the jaw-bones (Pl. and 2). The bones are delicately built because of the young age of the specimen. No distinct morphological assessment is possible on the preserved bones.

iv. Dentition

a) Dental measurements

Amongst the skeletal remains was a total of 22 teeth. Of these, 12 are from the maxilla (3 deciduous and 9 permanent) and 10 derive from the mandible (5 deciduous and 5 permanent). Of these, only 14 teeth are measurable; the remaining are either broken, or not fully developed and still inside the crypt.

Following Moorrees' technique (1957a, 1957b), two basic measurements have been carried out for each tooth: 1) maximum crown length (mesio-distal diameter); and 2) maximum crown breadth (ducco-lingual diameter). The mesio-distal diameter (MD) is the maximum dimension on the tooth crown in the mesio-distal direction, parallel to the occlusal and the labial surface. The bucco-lingual crown diameter (BL) is the greatest distance between the duccal and the lingual surface of tooth crown in a plane perpendicular to that of the mesio-distal diameter.

The primary comparative standard in the analysis of tooth size is the crown area (CA) or the cross-sectional area of the tooth. Crown area reflects the adaptive strategies of the population in response to subsistence patterns and level of technology. Since the dentition preserved for this individual is incomplete, no such analysis was possible however. The crown index (CI), a measure of crown shape, is the ratio of mesio-distal and bucco-lingual diameter expressed in terms of a percentage, as discussed by Wolpoff (1971). The measure of crown bulk, termed crown module (CM), is the average of the mesio-distal and bucco-lingual values.

The formulae for calculating crown area, crown index and crown module are given below:

Table 4: Dental crown dimensions and indices.

Tooth	Side	Crown Dimentions		Crown Indices		
		MD	BL	CA	CI	CM
Maxillary						
dc	R	7.91	7.12	56.31	111.09	7.51
dm1	R	7.90	8.73	68.96	90.49	8.31
dm2	R	9.74	10.19	99.25	95.58	9.96
I1	R	(8.91)	--			
	L	9.28	(7.09)	65.79	130.88	8.18
I2	L	7.52	7.17	53.91	104.88	7.34
C	L	9.52	7.67	71.71	121.90	8.51
Pm2	R	8.29	9.75	80.82	85.02	9.02
M1	R	11.95	11.87	141.84	100.67	11.91
M2	R	10.81	12.04	130.15	89.78	11.42
Mandibular						
dm1	L	8.85	7.02	62.12	126.06	7.93
dm2	R	10.96	9.51	104.22	113.24	10.23
	L	(10.87)	9.42	102.39	115.39	10.14
I2	R	7.43	5.65	41.97	131.50	6.54
M1	R	12.51	11.54	14.36	108.40	12.02

CA = MD X BL
CI = ND X 100˜BL
CM = (MD+BL) ˜2

Odontometric data is given in Table.4

b) Dental morphology

Occlusal morphology of the deciduous molars is obliterated, thus precluding any morphological assessment. Limited morphological observations are possible on four permanent teeth, ULC, URMI, URM2, and LLMI. The Arizona State University anthropology Scoring System (Turner *et al.* 1991) is followed.

In the maxillary canines, the mesiolingual marginal ridge is normally similar in size to the distolingual marginal ridge. Occasionally, the mesial ridge is larger than the distal ridge and is moderately attached to the tuberculum dentale as seen in the ULC of this individual (Pl. 3). The expression of this feature can be rated as 'grade 2' (ASU grading system). The extreme form of this morphological feature is frequent in Africans (especially Bushmen) and has been described ad *'Bushman canine'* (Morrees 1975, quoted in Turner *et al.* 1991).

The distolingual (cusp 4), hypocone of large sized 'grade 4' is seen on URMI, while the expression is very faint for URM2, which is graded as 'I'. An additional small cusp is seen on the distobuccal surface of URMI.

For mandibula LMI, a Y-5 cusp groove pattern is seen. The expression of cusp 5, hypoconulid is of medium size (grade 3) (Pl. 4).

v. Pathological lesions and anomalies

Important pathologies seen on this specimen include dental enamel development disturbances, attrition of occlusal surface, and lesions on one vertebra.

a) Vertebral pathology

Three cervical vertebrae (axis, 3rd and 5th) are preserved for this individual, of which the axis and the 5th do not show any signs of bone change. However, the body and the right transverse process of the 3rd cervical vertebra shows some bone remodelling. The extent of the lesion is about 1.5 cm on the anterior part, destroying the border of the vertebral body inferior to the right side. The bone is thin along the right transverse foramina border, as compared to the left side (Pl. 5). Even the inferior articular facets (more to the right side) also exhibit some bone remodelling (Pl. 6).

It is difficult to diagnose the etiology of this lesion at this stage. It could be traumatic in origin, but it was definitely not the immediate cause of death. There are definite signs of secondary bone formation at the site, and the edges of the lesion are rounded. Unfortunately, the 4th cervical vertebra is not included in the collection, as this element could have confirmed traumatic origin of the lesion. The other possible cause of this pathology is a non-specific infection. A wide range of pathogens are known to have influence in remodelling bones of the thoracic cage. However, since this specimen is coming from the cervical region, specific diagnosis of the pathology, if any, is difficult.

b) Enamel hypoplasia

Enamel hypoplasias are deficiencies in enamel thickness resulting from physiological disruptions during enamel formation (Pindborg 1970). The developing tooth responds to environmental stresses encountered during its growth. Disturbances in the formative phase result in lack of enamel production, and the resulting defect may occur localized within a single tooth or tooth class, or may be evident throughout the dental arcade of an individual as pits, lines, or bands of hypomineralization.

For this individual, enamel hypoplastic lines are seen on the maxillary LI1 (2 lines?), LC (1line), and RM2 (1 line) (Pl. 7). It is interesting to note that all the hypoplasic lines are seen only on the permanent teeth, which were still developing and were inside their respective crypts at the time of death of this individual. In several Neolithic-Chalcolithic period sites of the Deccan region, defective enamel formation in deciduous teeth has been taken to indicate possible nutritional or pathological stress in the womb (Lukacs *et. al.* 2001). This kind of abnormality is not observed in the deciduous teeth of the individual buried at Kudatini, however.

The hypoplastic lines are very faint, making it difficult to measure their distance from the cemento-enamel junction. In addition, all of these teeth were still being formed at the time of the individual's death, and bear some post-mortem damage. The approximate distances of the centre of the lesion from the cemento-enamel junction are; LI1:4.9 mm (crown height 13.2 mm), LC: 3.4 (estimated crown height 11.1 mm), and RM2: 2.5 mm (estimated crown height 7.6 mm). On the basis of these measurements, it can be inferred that this individual must have experienced at least two episodes of stress, either nutritional or pathological. The hypoplastic line on the incisor is indicative of a stress which probably occurred around the age of 3 years, whereas the lines on LC and RM2 reflect a second episode of stress which took place when this individual was around 5 years old (Mushrif 2002).

c) Attrition

Dental attrition is a normal reaction of teeth to mastication of food and other uses of teeth. The degree of attrition is based on the quality of food in the diet, as well as the techniques used to prepare it. Coarse food increases attrition rates. Rates of attrition are higher in hunting-gathering (Mesolithic) populations due to the consumption of unprocessed food (Brace 1978' Walimbe and Kulkarni 1993). In contrast, they are lower amongst farming (Neolithic/Chalcolithic) communities, in which cooked food was the dominant ingested form.

Moderate dental attrition is seen on the mandibular RLdm1s and RLdm2s. The crown of Rdm 1 is half broken, and complete gradation of attrition is not possible. According to *Standards for Data Collection from Human Skeletal Remains* (Buikstra and Ubelaker 1998), the wear pattern on Ldm1 may be scored as 'grade 2' (in which wear facets are large but large cuspe still present; see Scott 1979). For RLdm2, the pattern is 'grade 6', meaning that dentine exposed dentine is almost 3.5 mm deep (Fig. 9). This type of attrition is rather difficult to explain and may be attributed to possible caries infection, though confirmation of this pathology is not possible. The corresponding teeth in the upper jaw URdm1 and URdm2 of the maxilla, which would be expected to be affected also, are unworn and almost completely devoid of any enamel loss. Therefore, caries infection or the presence of a patch of deficient enamel on the occlusal surface appear to be the most likely etiological causes behind this unusual type of wear pattern (Fig. 7).

Discussion

The disarticulated nature of the skeletal remains in the Kudatini burial, and their deposition not only in the sarcophagus, but also in some of the burial pots that surrounded the sarcophagus, indicate this to be a secondary burial. Analysis of the skeletal elements from the sarcophagus and pots has led to the conclusion that the remains derive from a single individual, who probably died at the age of six or seven years. There is no clear indication of the cause of death, though enamel hypoplasia patterns suggest at least two episodes of nutritional or pathological stress during the child's short life, and analysis of the vertebrae revealed a lesion on the third cervical vertebra that was possibly traumatic in origin, though may also have derived from a non-traumatic cause. Even if traumatic, however, the latter was not the immediate cause of death, which remains unknown.

Although the skeletal remains from the Kudatini burial display taphonomic effects and little preservation of protein, they are nonetheless in excellent condition relative to the remains found in many South Megalithic burials. While the fact that we are dealing only with a single individual renders it difficult to make any reliable interpretations about economic and subsistence practices on the basis of the skeletal remains, it is possible to make some tentative suggestions concerning the burial process that led to the deposition of the bones within the sarcophagus and pots at Kudatini. As indicated, it seems likely that the Kudatini burial represents a reburial of skeletal remains that were initially buried or exposed elsewhere (although the possibility that the primary burial/exposure also took place at Kudatini, and indeed within the same pit, cannot be ruled out.) The absence of many of the smaller skeletal elements (like the metacarpals that it may not have been considered necessary to gather all the skeletal elements from the primary burial site (Dulanot 2002: 110; though taphonomic effects cannot of course be ruled out). Certain elements do appear to have been important, however. For example, the pot contents display a clear preference for vertebral elements (and possibly long bones as well), while numerous rib bone fragments occur in the sarcophagus. Analysis of Table 2 did not reveal any clear pattern of association of skeletal elements with particular pot type or graffiti form.

What emerges then is picture of a primary burial (or

exposure) at time of death, followed by subsequent exhumation, manipulation and reburial of some, but perhaps not all, of the skeletal remains. Ethnographic studies of secondary rites suggest that there was likely to have been a long intermediary period between the primary burial/exposure and secondary burial, during which time the body was transformed from corpse to defleshed nones (Hertz 1960; Huntington and Metcalfe 1979; Parker Pearson 1999). As in many societies that practice secondary reburial, primary and secondary rites may also have been spatially segregated (Barrett 1996; Parker Pearson 1999), such that exhumation of the bones was followed by their transfer from the original burial or exposure ground (perhaps located at or near a settlement site) to Kudatini for final burial. The entire process, from initial burial/exposure to final burial, may have been understood, as it is in a number of contemporary societies, as representing, enabling or assisting the transition of the person's 'soul' from the world of the living to the world of the dead (Hertz 1960; Huntington and Metcalfe 1979).

It seems clear, based on the structured placement of the remains and burial furnishings within the grave, that the secondary reburial at Kudatini was an event of ritual significance during which the skeletal remains were manipulated in particular, no doubt meaningful ways. In societies that practice secondary burial, manipulation of the exhumed bones in the context of secondary rites is a common practice: bones may be scraped clean, washed, wrapped, laid out in a particular arrangement or grouped with the bones of other individuals , for example (Huntington and Metcalf 1979; Parker Pearson 1999). In Neolithic Britain, it has been hypothesised that disarticulated bones were continually shifted around, within and sometimes even between different megalithic tombs, for the purpose of asserting a particular collective ethic (Barret *et al.* 1991; Shanks and Tilley 1982, 1987).

In a similar way, the selection or exclusion of particular skeletal elements at the final burial of the Kudatini remains, and their deposition within either the raised, north-south oriented central sarcophagus, or lower, peripheral pots must certainly have had some sort of meaningful aim. It may be that this arrangement drew upon structural oppositions between high and low, and inside and outside, for example, and/or upon symbolic meanings associated with particular cardinal directions. Ethnographically, cardinal directions and other structural oppositions are often linked to fundamental social and symbolic distinctions between the sacred and the profane, male and female and life and death, for example. These kinds of associations may have been played upon during the course of the reburial ritual to reaffirm cosmological understandings that may perhaps have been particularly challenged by the death of a young member of society. It is likely that by organising the child's skeletal remains in the way that they did, the graveside mourners at Kudatini drew upon wider structural principles and symbolic associations to comment upon the death that had occurred and to comprehend its place in their overall cosmological understanding of the world, its renewal and the place of the ephemeral individual within this continuous scheme (Bloch and Parry 1982).

The discovery of well-preserved skeletal remains in a Megalithic burial context is an important find for the archaeology of south India. In particular, the identification of skeletal remains in burial pots is exciting, since such pots are usually found to be empty in Megalithic graves. However, it is important to bear in mind that the Kudatini burial cannot be taken as representative of south Indian Megalithic practices in general, which have shown abundant evidence for variation both across space and through time (McIntosh 1985; Mohanty and Selvakumar 2001). The particular manipulation of skeletal remains practiced at Kudatini in the case of the present burial made sense within local strategies and cosmologies which need not necessarily have held wide currency across south India. Regardless of how wide-ranging the practices suggested by the Kudatini skeletal remains may or may not have been, however, their investigation in the present paper constitutes an important contribution to archaeological understanding of the Megalithic phenomenon in south India.

Acknowledgements

Bolvin and Korisettar would like to express their gratitude to those who participated in the 2002 field season, including P.C. Venkatasubbaian, Helen Lewis, Deepak Havanur, Kalyan Malagyannavar, S.K. Melakar and Subhas Chincholi. Funding for the 2002 Sanganakallu-Kupgal project was provided by the British Academy, with additional aid coming from the Society for South Asian Studies, the Prehistoric Society and Karnatak University. We are grateful to Jenny Doole for creating the three-dimensional image of the sarcophagus, and to John Robb and Jay Stock for providing critical feed-back on a draft version of the manuscript. All errors remain our own responsibility.

BIBLIOGRAPHY

Barrett, J.C. 1996 The living, the dead and the ancestors: Neolithic and Early Bronze Age mortuary practices, in *Contemporary Archaeological Theory* (I. Hodder Ed.), pp. 394-412. Oxford: Blackwell.

Barrett, J.C., R. Bradley and M. Green 1991. *Landscape, Monuments and Society*. Cambridge: Cambridge University Press.

Bloch, M. and J. Parry (Eds.) 1982. *Death and the Regeneration of Life*. Cambridge: Cambridge University Press.

Boivin, N., R. Korisettar, P.C. Venkatasubbaiah, 2003. Megalithic markings in context: graffiti marks on burial pots from Kudatini, Karnataka. *South Asian Studies* 19:1-12

Boivin, N., R. Korisettar and P. C. Venkatasubbaiah D. Havanur, K. Malagyannavar and S. Chincholi forthcoming. *Sarcophagus Burial a Kudatini*. Karnataka.

Boivin, N., R. Korisettar, P.C. Venkatasubbaiah, H. Lewis, D. Havanur, K. Malagyannavar and S. Chincholi 2002. Exploring Neolithic and Megalithic South India: the Bellary District Archaeological Project, *Antiquity* 76:937-8.

Brace, C. L. 1978. Tooth Reduction in the Orient, *Asian Perspectives* 19:203-219.

Buikstra, J. E. and D.H. Ubelaker. 1994. Standards For Data Collection From Human Skeletal Remains. Arkansas: *Arkansas Archaeological Survey Research Series*, No. 44.

Dulanto, J. 2002. The archaeological study of ancestor cult practices: the case of Pampa Chica, a Late Initial Period and Early Horizon site on the central coast of Peru, in *The Space and Place of Death* (H. Silverman and D. B. Small Eds.), pp. 97-117. Archaeological Papers of the American Anthropological Association No. 11.

Hertz, R, 1960. *Death and the right Hand*. Translated by R. Needham and C. Needham. New York: Free Press.

Huntington, R. and P. Metcalf 1979, Celebrations of Death: *The Anthropology of Mortuary Ritual*. Cambridge: Cambridge University Press.

Lukacs, J. R., Nelson G. C. And S.R. Walimbe 2001. Enamel Hypoplasia and childhood stress in prehistory: New data from India and Southwest Asia, *Journal of Archaeological Science* 28: 1159-1169.

McIntosh, J.R. 1985. Dating the South Indian megaliths, in *South Asian Archaeology 1983* (J. Schotsmans and M. Taddei Eds.), pp. 467-93. Naples: Istituto Universitario Orientale.

Mohanty, R.K. and V. Selvakumar 2001. The archaeology of the megaliths in India: *1947-1997, in Indian Archaeology in Retrospect, Volume I:Prehistory Archaeology of South Asia* (S. Settar and R. Korisettar Eds.), pp. 313-481. New Delhi: Manohar.

Moorrees, C.F.A. 1957a. *The Aleut Dentition*. Cambridge, Massachusetts: Harvard University Press.

Moorrees, C.F.A. 1957b. Mesiodistal Crown Diameters of the Deciduous and Permanent Teeth in Individuals, *Journal of Dental Research* 36: 39-47.

Moorti, U.S. 1994. Megalithic Culture of South India: *Socio-Economic Perspectives*. Varanasi: Ganga Kaveri.

Mushrif, Veena 2001. *Biological Anthropology of the Deccan Chalcolithic Population: A case Study on the Nevasa Human Skeletal Series*. Unpublished Ph.D. thesis, Deccan College, Pune.

Parker Pearson, M. 1999. *The Archaeology of Death and Burial*. Stroud: Sutton.

Pindborg, J.J 1970. *Pathology of the Dental Hard Tissues*. Copenhagen: Munksgaard.

Scott, E.C. 1979. Dental wear scoring technique, *American Journal of Physical Anthropology* 51:213-218

Shanks, M. and C. Tilley 1982. Ideology, symbolic power and ritual communication: a reinterpretation of Neolithic mortuary practices, in *Symbolic and Structural Archaeology* (I. Hodder Ed.), pp. 129-54. Cambridge: Cambridge University Press.

Shanks, M. and C. Tilley 1987. *Re-constructing Archaeology*. Cambridge University Press.

Walimbe, S.R. and P.B. Gambhir 1994. *Long Bone Growth in Infants and children: Assessment of the Nutritional Status*. Mangalore: Mujumdar Publications.

Walimbe, S.R. and S.S. Kulkarni. 1993. *Biological Adaptations in Human Dentition: an Odontometric Study on Living and Archaeological Populations in India*. Pune: Deccan College Research Institute.

Wolpoff, M.H. 1971. *Metric Trends in Hominid Dental Evolution:* Studies in Anthropology, Case Western Reserve University.

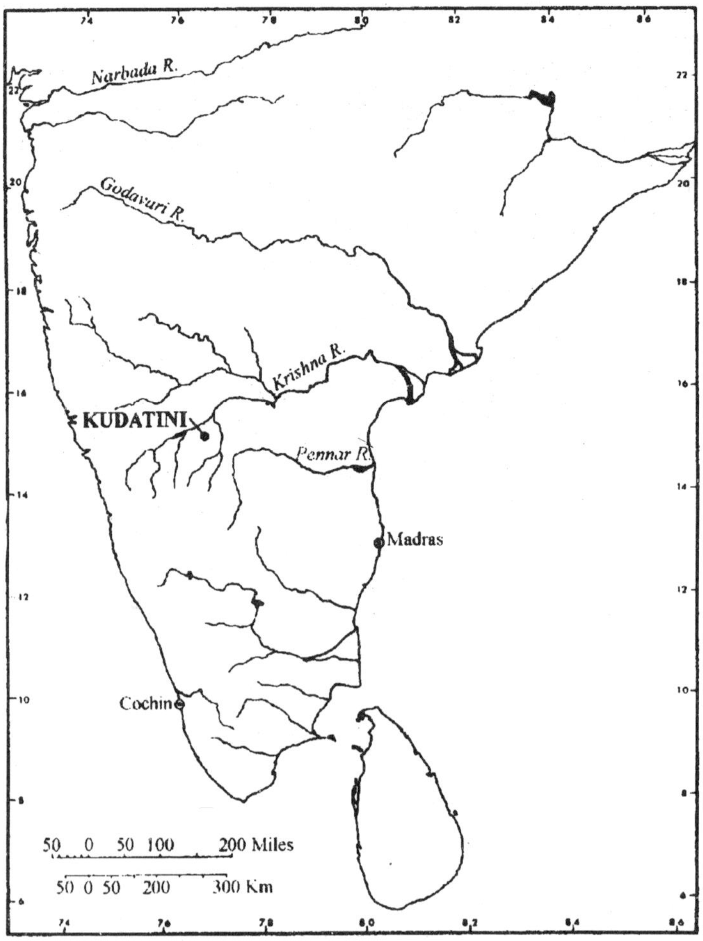

Fig. 1. Map showing location of Kudatini in South India.

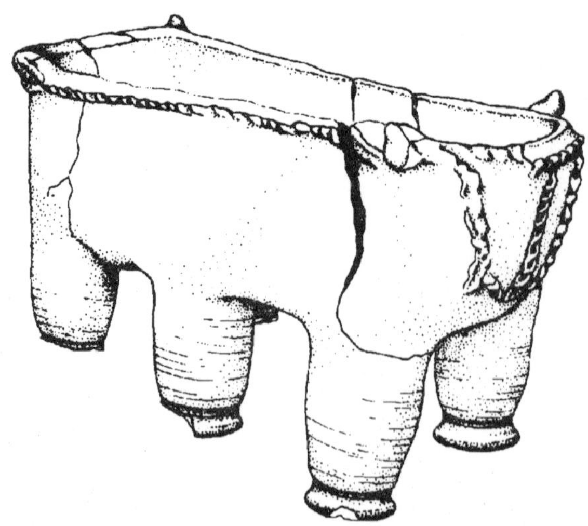

Fig. 2. Sarcophagus discovered at Kudatini (length is approximately 87 cm). Drawing by Jenny Doole.

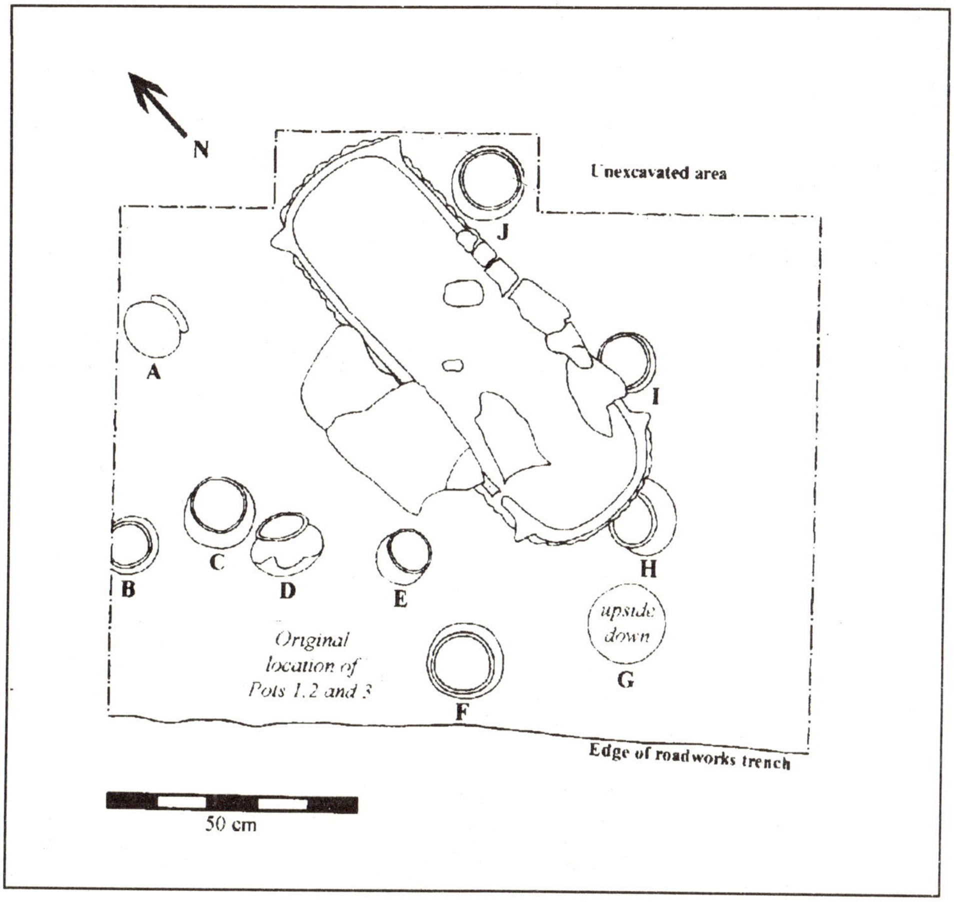

Fig. 3. Plan of Kudatini burial excavation, showing the location of the sarcophagus and burial pots.

Fig. 4. Sarcophagus interior showing disarticulated skeletal remains unerarthed during excavation.

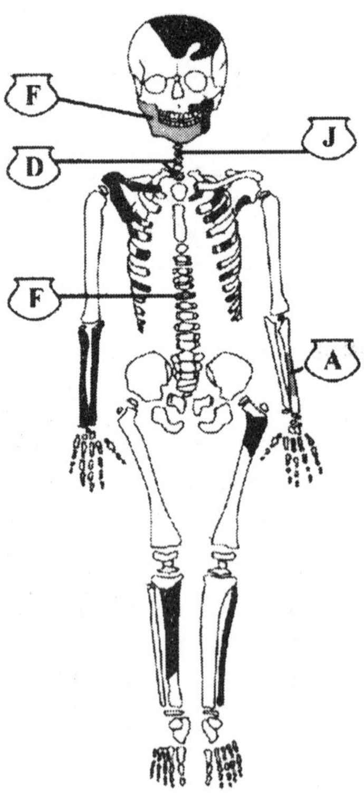

Fig. 5. Diagram indicating skeletal elements preserved and location within burial. The diagram is an approximation, and not all elements are indicated.

Buddhist Stupas in Haryana: New Evidence

ARUN KESARWANI* & S.K. VASHIST**

Introduction

Haryana (Fig. 1) has been the cradle land of civilizations. This was the most fertile land of India as it was watered by the mightly river Saraswati and its tributaries. The alluvial plain between the Saraswati and the Sindhu has also been referred to in the ***Rigveda*** as the region of ***Sapta Sindhu*** as here flows seven rivers such as the Sindhu, the Jhelum, the Ravi, the Chenab, the Beas, the Satluj and the Saraswati. These rivers here deposited very rich and extremely fertile soil which served as a meeting ground of various cultures appearing and disappearing during the last four millennia. Among all, the Saraswati was the most mighty and sacred river highly euoligised in the *Rigveda* as ***ambitame***, ***devitame*** and ***naditame***. It is interesting to note that the bank of this river was also inhabited earlier than the other river basins for the first time during the Protohistoric period by the people using Hakra ware pottery, which is pre-Early Harappan or pre-Kot-Diji type, and living in shallow pit-dwellings dated to between 3500-3000 B.C. From this period upto the rise of Buddhism the land was occupied by the Early Harappans, the Matrure Harappans, the Late Harappans, the Painted Grey Ware and the Northern Black Polished Ware people. The last mentioned belonged to the 6th century B.C. and it is likely that Buddha received alms in this pottery.

In the 6th century B.C. the centre of political activity shifted from this region to the mid Ganga valley and Magadha (Bihar) emerged as the most powerful state but still Kuru was one of the sixteen *Mahajanapadas* and it has been referred to in the Buddhist literature several times. According to *Mahasutasoma Jataka* the extent of Kuru Kingdom was 300 leagues and included parts of Western U.P. and Delhi (*Indapatta or Indapattana or Indraprashtha*). According to *Somanassa Jataka* the Kuru kingdom extended upto Uttarpancala, a town in *Kuruattha* ruled over by the King Renu. *Hatthinapura* was also a part of the Kuru region and Buddha is said to have visited the city. The place names such as *Indapatta* (Indraprastha), *Hatthinipura* (Hastinapur), *Thullakotthita* (Thanesar or twin village Thol-Kurri), *Kammasadamma* (Kaithal), *Kundi* or *Kundal* (presently located in Distt. Sonipat Near Delhi Border) and *Varnavata* are mentioned in the *Mahavastu*. Kundi was another village of the Kurus near which there was a forest where lived Anganika-Bharadwaja and close by was the Uggarama.

Buddhism which originated in the *madhyadesa* was brought to Haryana by Buddha himself. According to *Mahavastu* and *Digha Nikaya*, Buddha himself converted the people of the Kuru tribe. According to the *Vinaya* of the *Mulasarvastivadins* Buddha visited *Hatthinapur* (Hastinapur), Mahanagar (Indraprastha), *Srughna* (Sugh),

*Professor, Deptt. of Ancient Indian History, Culture & Archaeology, Kurukshetra University. Kurukshetra.
**Research Assistant, Dept. of Ancient Indian History, Culture & Archaeology, Kurukshetra University, Kurukshetra.

Brahmanagrama (modern village Tohana), *Kalanagar* (modern Kalanaur near Rohtak) and *Rohitaka* (Rohtak). Moreover, according to *Dipavamsa,* Buddha received alms on the banks of the *anotatta* lake which is identified with the lake *anyatah plaksha,* located in Kurukshetra and referred to in the *Satapatha Brahmana.*

According to the Buddhist literature, *Thullakotthita* and *Kammaṣadamma* were the two place where Buddha visited many times. At *Thullakotthita* or *Sthulakosthaka* Buddha converted Rastapala (a local saint of Vaisya family) to Buddhism and in turn Ratthapala is described to have converted the Kuru King Kauravya and his parents to Buddhism as well as contributed some verses to *Theragatha.* According to the *Madhuratthavilasini* two other Brahmanas Bhadrasala and Vijitamitra were initiated to Buddhism at this place.

The second place where Buddha visited was *Kammasadamma* or *Mahakammasaddama.* According to *Divyavadana* and *Buddhacarita* this was the famous trade centre and a town bigger than *Cullakammasadamma* or Kampilla. At this place Buddha delivered many discourses like *Satipatthana Sutta, Magandiya Sutta, Ananjasappaya Sutta, Mahanidana Sutta, Mahasatipatthana Sutta,* etc. One discourse each on *Samyutta-Nikaya* and *Anguttara-Nikaya* was also delivered here. The famous nuns Nanduttara and Mittakalika also belonged to this place. The town has been identified with Kamaspur or Kumaspur (in District Meerut), Kaithal (50 Km. southwest of Thanesar) and Kamoda (about 15 Km. from Thanesar) on road to Pehowa. There is another place Kamaspur in Distt. Sonipat which has yielded the remains of stone Buddha image and Plain Grey Ware, Early Historical and Medieval Pottery and which can be identified with *Kammasadamma.*

Buddhist texts also mention a town *Anguttarapa* which has been equated with *Aggalapura* or *Agrodaka* (modern Agroha) where Buddha is said to have stayed during his journey from *Bhaddiyanagara* (modern Sialkot) to *Savatthi* (Sravasti). During the historical period Agroha was an important Buddhist centre.

According to the *Vinaya* of the *Mulasarvastivadins* and *Divyavadana,* Buddha also visited *Rohitaka* and *Srughna. Rohitaka* was a great and prosperous city and at *Srughna,* Buddha won over the Brahamana Indra who boasts of having no equal in beauty, youth and learning.

The Stupas

Haryana was also visited by several Buddhist monk and *Sthaviras.* The above evidence indicate that Buddhism flourished in Haryana due to the efforts of Buddha and other monks but according to Buddhaghosha not a single monastery was built in the Kuru country during the lifetime of Buddha who was obliged to stay in the hermitage of a *Brahamana* or in the forest outside *Kammasadamma.* Moreover, no monastery or stupa were constructed by the time of the Early Mauryas in Haryana.

Thanesar: After the *parinibana* of Buddha ten stupas were erected - eight over the mortal remains, one over the urn in which the relics were collected and divided and one over the charcoal collected from the funeral pyre at Kusinagara. Ashoka is said to have collected relics from seven of these *Saririka* stupas and redistributed them into 84,000 Stupas throughout his empire. During the Gupta period Chinese traveller Fahien visited India and has refered to the existence of Buddhist establishment, possibly of Ashoka, on both the sides of the river Yamuna. During Harsha's time another Chinese visitor Hiuen-Tsang came to India and saw a Ashokan stupa at Thanesar:

> To the north-west of the city, 4 or 5 li is a stupa about 300 feet high which was built by Asoka-raja. The bricks are all of a yellow red colour, very bright and shining ; within is a peck-measure of the relics of Buddha. From the Stupa is frequently emitted a brilliant light and many spiritual prodigies exhibit themselves.

The above stupa described by Hiuen-Tsang is nowhere found today in the north-west of Thanesar. From the account of Hiuen Tsang it appears that the stupa was located towards the *Aujasa ghat* near the Saraswati bed where still a few mounds are seen thickly covered with large broken bricks 'of a reddish yellow, or yellowish red colour, exactly like that of a Gosain's freshly-dyed clothes'. In the absence of archaeological excavation, it is not possible to say anything more on it. Cunningham also stated:

> It is probable that the smaller mound may be the remains of the stupa from which all the large pieces of the bricks have been carried away, and the larger mound may be the ruins of an extensive monastery.

But there appears to be a remains of brick-stupa and monastery in the north-east of the Kurukshetra University, near the Brahmasarovar. Presently this stupa is in a dilapidated condition. Kushana and later wares have been discovered near it. Bricks of various sizes : 45 x 45 x 7.5, 45 x 35 x 7.5, 22.5 x 22.5 x 7.5, 12.5 x 10 x 7.5 cms. were used in its construction, which indicate that it must have been renovated time and again. During the renovation work of the Brahamasarovar by Kurukshetra Development Board the monastery was completely wiped out but the remains of a stupa still exist today. Only the excavation of a site can bring true results.

Sugh: After Thanesar the Chinese Pilgrim visited *su-lo-kin-na* situated 400 li to the north-east and identified as Srughna or modern Sugh near Jagadhari on the west bank of the Yamuna. Hiuen-Tsang's has described the presence of Buddhist remains found here:

> To the south-east of the capital and in the west side of the Jumna outside the east gate of a large monastery was an Asoka tope at a place where the julai had preached and admired men into his church. Besides this tope was one which has had hair and nail-relics of the ju-lai and round about were some tens of topes with similar relics of Sariputra, Mudgalputra and other great arhats.

It is also interesting to note that Sariputra and Maudgalyayana had died before Buddha and the stupas are said to have been built over their mortal remains. The stupas were also said to have been built over the hair and nail-pairings of Buddha by his followers during his very lifetime. Handa questions "Do these stupas of Sugh then provide the corroboratory evidence of the existence of stupas in the sixth century B.C.? It is probable that Buddha reached and converted considerably large portion of the population of Sugh to Buddhism." Panini has mentioned that this was a flourishing centre in the 6th century B.C. But the site was excavated twice but no remains of stupa has been encountered. More diggings are still required to find out its existence. However, *prima facie* it appears that Buddhism disappeared after the Nirvana of Buddha and resurfaced during the time of Ashoka and became an important centre of Buddhism. According to Hiuen Tsang the Ashokan stupa and monastery outside the eastern gate of the city seems to have been washed away by the Yamuna.

However, remains of a Kusana monastery have been dug out in the south-west of Sugh Village and not in the actual Sugh mound. It is a rectangular enclosure measuring approximately 130 x 70 meters, the longer axis being east-west. It had massive walls, 75cm in width. One of the walls, when exposed measured about 6 meters in height. This monastery may have been one of the five referred to by Hiuen Tsang at Sugh.

Chaneti: Moreover, it is interesting to note that an Asokan stupa has been located and can still be seen at a site named Chaneti, about 3 kms north-west of Sugh. Handa thinks that perhaps it was a suburb of Sugh which was 20 *li* or about 5 km. in circumference. The height of the mound is nearly 8 mts. and its diameter is about 20 mts. The original height may have been more than what it is at present. The brick (30x30x7 and 30x15x7 cms) used are well-burnt and yellowish-red.

The general shape of the brick-mound corresponds to the Shahpur and *Dharmarajika* stupas at Taxila. While laying down the rules of construction of stupa, Rhys Davids said "the first step was probably merely to build the cairn ... The next step was to build the cairn of concentric layers of huge bricks in use at the time to surround the whole with a wooden railing." In this case also the same method of laying the concentric layers of huge brick has been followed. This was a convenient method of constructing a stupa. No trace of the railing surrounding the stupa has been found. Possibly it was made of wood. The core of the mound is also made of burnt-bricks. There was a podium all around for circumbulation half a century ago. At the top of the structure, there is roughly a square of about 1.5 metres which is filled up not with bricks but with earth. This was the *harmika* of the stupa which bore the umbrella or the *chattravali*. It may have been one of those tens of stupas referred to by Yuan Chwang.

Agroha (District Hisar)

The ancient town of Agroha is located on the ancient trade route between Multan & Mathura in the semi-arid part of South Haryana. The township grew in the process of second urbanisation around the 4th century B.C. as is evident from the literary and archeological record. This site was referred to for the first time in the Panini's work and continues to be mentioned in the literary works till the Post-Mughal times. The site was excavated by H.L. Srivastava in 1938-39 and again by the Deptt. of Archaeology & Museums, Govt. of Haryana in 1978-82.

A Tibetan version of the *Vinaya* of *Mula-Sarvastivadina* records the travels of Buddha from Bhaddiya (Bhadrankara or Sialkot in Punjab) to *Savatthi* (Sarasvati in eastern U.P.). It states that on the way Buddha lived at *'Bab-Chu-rab-tu-bzan-moi-gramdu'*. According to Przylaski the Tibetan translator had the word *Agrodaka* before him while translating the expression *'A-Kia-lou-t'o*. The reference to *Ariguttarapa* and Aggalapura in the Vinaya as places visited by Mendhaka and Revata also indicate *Agrodaka* be the place. According to Przyluski, Ptolemy also mentions *Agra*. This may also refer to the Agra people of *Agrodaka*.

Chullavagga also mentions *Aggalapura* along with the capital of Audumbaras, a tribe of Indo-Gangatic divide as a strong hold of Buddhism. It is believed that Ashoka constructed a pillar edict at this place which was perhaps removed during the time of Firoz-Shah-Tughlaq and erected at Hisar and Fatehabad. In the latest excavation seven periods have been encountered i.e., beginning from the 4th century B.C. to the 14th century. Only period -V (A.D. 7th century to 9th century A.D.) has yielded the remains of a stupa. This period has been divided in sub-Phase A and B. In Phase-A massive circular structure of baked bricks having a diametre of 12.90 mts has been partially exposed. The bricks used in the construction are 30x20x5 cms. in size. It belongs to 6th-7th century A.D. on the basis of the style of the structure and may be a Stupa. However, the possibility of its being an apsidal temple could not be ruled out.

The second phase of construction was marked by the use of dressed bricks in the shrine area. A solid rectangular structure with a circumambulatory path, identified as a stupa was exposed and had an extent height at 3.5 m. The structure measures 16x10x15 mts. in area. The width of the circumabulatory path is between 2.50 mts. and 1.85 mts. The structure was made of baked bricks measuring 38x24x7cms. 22x15x6cms, 25x15x6cm and 25x20x7cm, 22x20xv5cm, in size. Two phases of construction activity have been noticed in the floor. Baked bricks have been used in the construction of the first phase. The bricks measure $23^{1}/_{2}$x17x6 cms. $26^{1}/_{2}$x23x5 cms. 36x25x7 cms. 39x24x7cms, 36x24x7cm 32x22x6 cms, 30x19x$5^{1}/_{2}$ cms, in size. The second phase of construction was characterised by the use of old bricks. Stratigraphically it can be placed between 3rd-4th century A.D. and 9th-10th century A.D.

Among the notable antiquities in phase-B mention may be made of a terracotta disc representing in the centre the base of a votive stupa enclosed within a circle. The disc is having a diam. of 8.5 cms. It is oval in shape and two cms. in height with rows of 27 dots in circle on the top of a wavy line all around. The occurrence of this disc is very significant since a circular structure which could be identified provisionally with some stupa has already been exposed from this period. Besides a few copper coins have also been found.

Asandh

The site is identified with ancient *Asandivat* which was the capital of Janamejaya II, Asandh is situated about 45 Km. south-west of Karnal on Karnal-Jind road. The huge mound is partly covered by the modern town and has yielded Painted Grey Ware, Early Historical pottery, Kushana coins and bricks, Yaudheya coins and Medieval relics. The remains of a Kushana stupa have been also discovered at the place (Fig. 2). The stupa whose remains are locally known as *Jarasandha ka Kila*, must have originally been a very gigantic structure as it still rises to a height of more than 25 metres. It shows a circular drum with an elongated dome. The core was filled up with earth and brick-bats between the walls which formed the spokes. At one place in an exposed section, as many as 44 courses of a circular wall were noticed. In shape, it may have been similar to the *Dhamekh* stupa of Sarnath, like which it may have originally been adorned with Buddhist images in shallow sunken niches on the cardinal directions. The bricks used are approximately 13.5x14x8.5 to 9x2.0x2.5 inches in size. Kushana coins, pottery and other relics have been found from near the stupa.

Railing Pillars of the stupas

Besides the actual remains of the stupas there are other evidences of their presence. The railing pillars from Hathin and Bhadas of the Sunga period indicate the existence of Bhuddhist monuments in Haryana. The Sunga pillars depicting Yaksa have been found from Palwal and Amin.

Hathin

It is a small village in Distt. Faridabad situated 16 kms. south-west of Palwal, on Palwal-Hathin road. The ancient mound is surrounded by the three sacred tanks, shrines in the east, south and west. There are many loose and mutilated art pieces near the site but the most important and interesting piece is the railing pillar of the Sunga period which is fixed in the wall of a tank and is worshipped as a *Khera-devata.* (Fig. 3) It is possible that a Kushana stupa might have existed here.

Bhuna

It is a very large mound, more than 25 metres in height, and is located in the present District of Fatehabad. A Kushana stupa might have existed at this site. A railing pillar of spotted red stone measuring 96x23 cms. has been found at the site. (Fig. 3)

Bhadas

The site is situated in Distt. Gurgaon 17 kms. north of Firozpur-Jhirka and 19 Kms. south of Nuh on Delhi-Alwar road. The name *Bhadas* is derived from *Bhagdanta*, a last ruler of Pandava dynasty. Besides other art objects it has yielded large sized Kushana bricks and a railing pillar of Sunga period. (Fig. 4)

Lalpura

The site is situated in District Rohtak and is a continuation of the Khokhrakot mound. A white spotted red sandstone cross-bar measuring 24x15 cms. and dated 1st-2nd A.D. has been found at the site.[1] (Fig. 4).

Amin

This village is situated 8 Km. to the south-east of Thanesar in Distt. Kurukshetra and 1.5 Km. west of Amin Railway Station on Delhi-Ambala Section. The place is known as the site of *Chakra-Vyuha*, a strategic arrangement of the army of the Kauravas, planned by Guru Dronacharya to trap the forces of Pandavas led by Arjuna's son Abhimanyu. The site known as *Abhimanyu Khera* is one of the highest mound in the region. It was here that two inscribed red stone rectangular pillars of the Sunga period were discovered and are said to have been preserved in a temple located inside the village. This was probably a part of a stupa which existed here in the past. (Fig. 4).

OTHER FINDS : NEW EVIDENCE

Khokharakot (Rohtak)

A very intersting find has been reported from this site which is unique its kind. Two large size stone *Danpatra* has been found at Khokharakot are made of red sandstone from Mathura. Both are preserved in the Deptt. of History, M.D. University, Rhotak. The inscription has been decipherid by Manmohan Kumar of the same Deptt. The two *Danpatras* are complete and on their rim inscriptions are found in Kushana Brahmi script. It is likely that the two were possibly placed near the entrance of the main stupa which reads as follows:

कमेयकम .... कवियेकस .... यय
धर्मशस्य कणिकस्य कनि कस्यद्ध दानमं

It means (that this danpatra) was donated by Kanishka whose real *dharma (Baudha Dharma)* is *danam* or charity. Another name Kaviyaka has also been mentioned in the aforesaid inscription.

The second *Danpatra* bears the following inscription

यह कस दानम संघ चतुर्द्विदशो
रूहं माता पिता धर्म राजो क कणिकस्यद्ध

The above inscription refers to the donation made by him alongwith his father and mother to the *samga* which was possibly given to the 14th stupa or on the 14th day.

STUPA AND MONASTERY NEW EVIDENCE: ADI BADRI

Adi Badri in District Yamuna Nagar has also yielded the remains of Bhuddhist stupa and monastery. Archaeological Survey of India, Chandigarh Circle is excavating this site in a large scale from Nov. 2002 which is likely to continue upto June 2003. The site is being excavated under the overall supervision of Shri Indu Dhar Dwivedi, Deputy Superintending Archaeologist and Incharge of a newly created Shimla Circle. While digging for the Project "Archaeology of Saraswati" sponsored by the

[1]Lalpura is a suburb of Rohtak and a continuation of the Khokrakot mound separated from it by the Rohtak-Jind road, (Devendra Handa, 1996).

Ministry of Culture & Tourism, Govt. of India the excavators have unearthed a stupa and a monastery. Its presence has also proved the existence of the river Saraswati and its importance in the 1st-2nd century A.D.

During the last ten years I visited the site many times looking for the source of the origin of the river Saraswati. It was extremely difficult to reach the site. There was no road then and it was difficult to reach the temple (Vishnu and Shiva) situated on a high hillock. After the construction of road by Haryana Govt. upto the temple site there is a slight change in the geomorphology of the region. The site is situated on the Haryana-Himachal border at a place where the Shivalik hills ends and plains begin. A deep and picturseque valley is surrounded by grey coloured sandstone hills with thin laminated carbonaceous clay within the sandstone of the late Miocence or Early Pliocene period. There are several very high and steep mounds made of fragile rocks alluvail soils, pebbles, baked bricks and potsherds.

This beautiful valley was inhabited by Buddhist monks in the 1st-2nd century A.D. The excavators have divided the site into 3 parts, viz., ABR-I, ABR-II and ABR-III. At present the excavation is continuing in ABR-III situated on the left side of the river Sombh, previously a tributary of the river Saraswati. Two phases of structural activity have been noticed. During phase-A burnt-brick stupa was constructed during the Kushana period which has been uncovered during the excavations. At present the diameter of the stupa is about 10 metres and the future excavations will give the clear picture. However, it appears that the original stupa might be larger in size. The typical Kushan burnt-bricks were arranged in a tapering circular fashion similar to the other Stupas. The size of the burnt bricks are 35x20x6 cms., 33x20x5 cms., 30x22x6 cms. and 23x26x6 cms. The lowest 23 courses of the burnt bricks were traced out uptill now.

There is a stratigraphical gap between Phase-A and Phase-B. It appears that the site was abondoned for a couple of centuries. In Phase-B square or rectangular monastery was built over some part of the earlier stupa. Here dressed greyish sandstone-bricks were used in the construction.

Large number of stone-bricks can be seen scattered on the site. About 10 to 12 courses of stone-bricks were noticed. The size of the brick is 30x20x9 cms. In the southern wall of the monastery a Buddha image can still be seen fixed in a shallow niche. The size of this image is 50x35x5 cms. The image is found seated in *Padmasana* and both hands are in *Dharma Chakrapravartan Mudra*. The image is found defaced. Below this image a pit filled with ash and charcoal has been traced out. It is likely that this pit might have been used for some ritualistic purpose.

Some other niches have also been traced out on the periphery wall of the monastery which do not have any images in it. It is likely that they might have Buddha images in it. One decorated stone slab has been found near the niche without Buddha image. This decorated stone slab might have been used in the door frame of the monastery. Besides these there are several other Buddha images-large and small, some defaced have been discovered at the site which are very important from our point of view. The site has also uncovered stamped pottery of the Kushana period. More excavations will throw adequate light on the Buddhist remains at Adi Badri.

Acknowledgement

We are extermly grateful to Sh. I.D. Dwivedi, Deputy Superintending Archaeologist, A.S.I. and Incharge of Shimla Circle/Adi Badri Excavation for providing us several photographs, line drawings and all necessary information regarding the excavation. We are also thankful to Prof. Phadke, Sh. D.K. Handa, Dr. Man Mohan Kumar, Dr. Sat Dev, Dr. Rajinder Kumar and Sh. Sanjay Kumar for their scholarly work on the aforesaid topic and from where we have gathered all relevant and necessary data for this work.

BIBLIOGRAPHY

Agrawala, R.C., 'Early History and Archaeology of Haryana', *Haryana Studies in History and Culture* ed: K.C. Yadav, K.U. 1968 p. 21-22.

Ahir, D.C., *Buddhism in the Punjab, Haryana and Himachal Pradesh, New Delhi,* 1971, pp-13-14

Bharadwaj, O.P., *Studies in the Historical Geography of Ancient India,* Delhi, 1986, P.150.

Bharat Singh Upadhyaya, *Buddha-Kalina Bharatiya Bhugola* (Hindi), Prayaga, V.S. 2018, p.-69

Buddhacarita, XX1.27

Cf. L.M. Joshi and Fauja Singh (Ed.) *History of the Punjab,* Vol. I, Patiala, 1976, p.-277.

Cunningham op.cit, pp26-27. *The Ancient Geography of India,* Varanasi, 1963 (reprint) pp 290-91.

————, Vol. II, p. 123 Pl. VIII.

Cunningham, A., *Archaeological Survey Report,* Vol.-II, pp 220-21.

Devendra Handa, 'Kushan stupa at Asandh', *Haryana Review, Chandigarh,* July 1982, p.133. Also "Discovery of a Buddhist Stupa at Asandh "*Vishveshvaranand Indological Journal* Vol. XXII (1984) pp. 218-20

Devendra Handa, 1996, *op.cit,* p.-4

Dipavamsa (Ed. H. Oldenberg, Landon, 1879) P- 43-44

Divyavadaan, pp.-47ff also see Handa (1970), Loc. cit.

Dutta, V.N. & H.A. Phadke, *History of Kurukshetra,* Kurukshetra 1984, p-39.

Fausboll, V., *The Jatakas,* No. 537, 1963, London.

Giles, H.A., *Record of Buddhist Kingdoms,* Cambridge 1923, pp 19-20.

Gupta, S.P., *The Indus-Saraswati Civilizations : Origins, Problems and Issues,* 1996, Pratibha Prakashan, Delhi.

Handa, Devendra, 'Heritage Haryana : An Introduction to the Buddhist Remains in the region', *J.H.S.* K.U.K. Vol XXVII-XXVIII, 1995-96. P-2 and Heritage of *Haryana-II Buddhist Remains* 1989.

Kumar, Manmohan, 'A note on two Danpatra Inscription from Khokhrakot', *Epigraphy of Indica* (under publication) & Sat Dev, *Ancient Rohtak, Historical and Culture Study (from Earliest times to 1206 A.D.)* unpublished Ph-D Thesis, Nov. 2000, K.U.K., p-26.

Kumar, Rajinder, *History and Archaeology of Haryana* (for C. 200 B.C. to C.A.D. 300) unpublished Ph-D Thesis 1996, K.U.K. p-57.

Kumar, Sanjay, *op.cit,* p. 29-30.

Law B.C., *Tribes in Ancient India 2nd ed. Poona,* 1973, p.22; *Majjnima Nikaya* (Ed. Jagdish Kashyap-Nalanda 1952), Vol.-II PP. 281 tt.

Mahavastu Digha Nikaya.

Marshal, John, *A guide to Taxila,* Combridge, 1960, Pl. IX).

Mitra, Debala, *Buddhist and Architecture-A Study:* Key note address in Art & Architecture section, First International conference on Buddhism & National Cultures, New Delhi, Oct 10-15, 1984 (Cyclostyled copy) p.3.

Prazyluski, J., *Ancient people of the Punjab* (translated into English by Chitrabhanu Sen, p-11

————, *Ancient people of the Panjab* (translated into English by Chitrabhanu Sen), p-9.

Rhys Davids, T.W., *Buddhist India* (Reprint), Calcutta, 1960, Pl. IX).

Samuel Beal, Si, Yu-Ki; *Buddhist Records of the Western World,* Vol. I, London, 1906 p. 186. See also Thomas Watters, on *Yuang Chwang's Travels in India,* Delhi 1961 (First Indian ed.) p. 316.

Srivastava, H.L., *Excavation at Agroha, Panjab* No. 61, *Memoris of the Archaeological Survey of India.* 1951. Sanjay Kumar, *Archaeology and Early History of Agroha and its Adjoining Area.* M-Phil dissertation, 1989, K.U.K., P. 22-23.

The Jatakas, No. 444. Also see G.P.

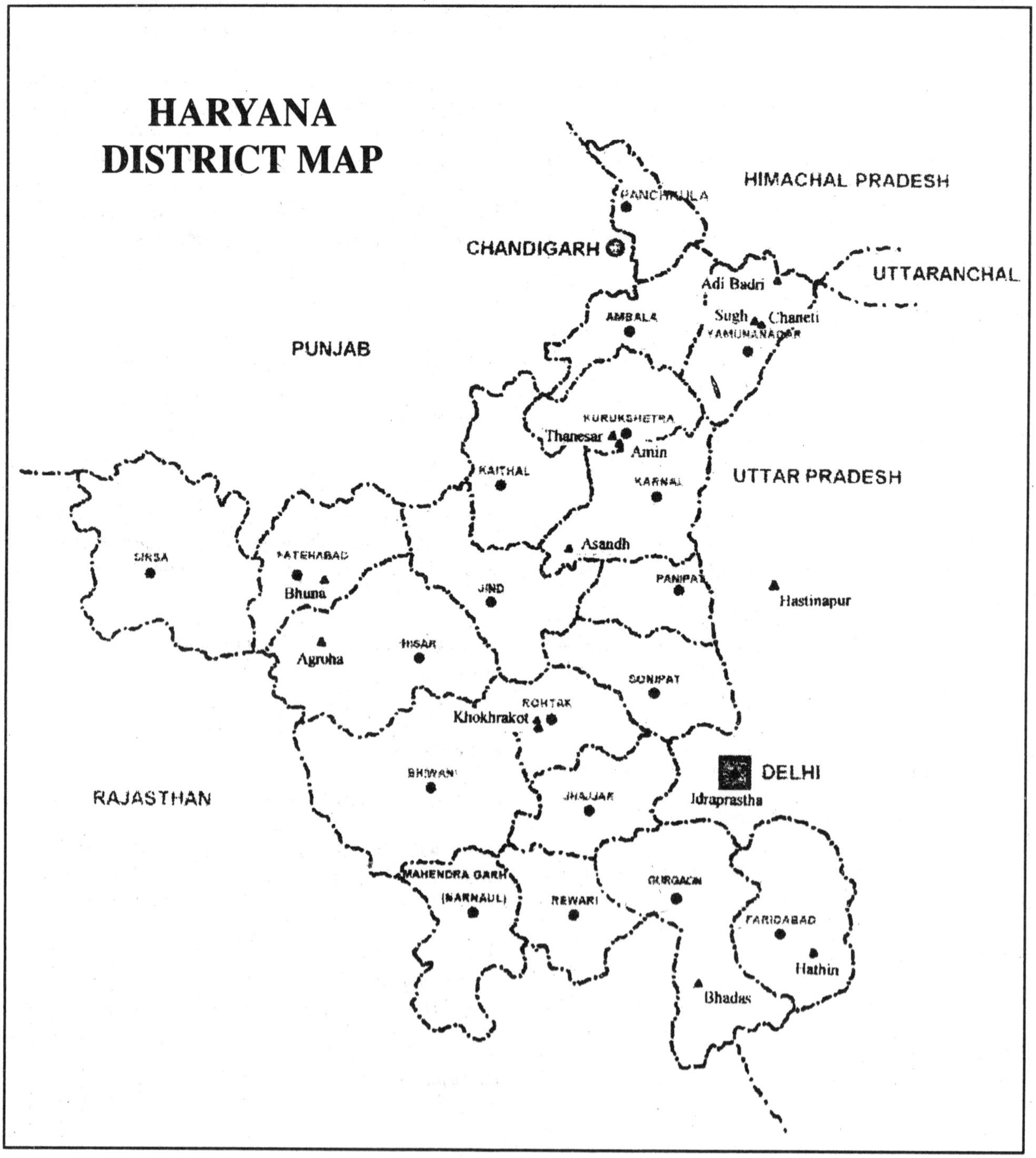
HARYANA
DISTRICT MAP
HIMACHAL PRADESH
CHANDIGARH
UTTARANCHAL
Adi Badri
Sugh
Chaneti
YAMUNANAGAR
PUNJAB
AMBALA
KURUKSHETRA
Thanesar
Amin
KAITHAL
KARNAL
UTTAR PRADESH
Asandh
SIRSA
FATEHABAD
Bhuna
JIND
PANIPAT
Hastinapur
Agroha
HISAR
SONIPAT
ROHTAK
Khokhrakot
DELHI
Idraprastha
BHIWANI
JHAJJAR
RAJASTHAN
MAHENDRA GARH
(NARNAUL)
REWARI
GURGAON
FARIDABAD
Hathin
Bhadas

Fig. 1

Stupa at Asandh: Kusana period

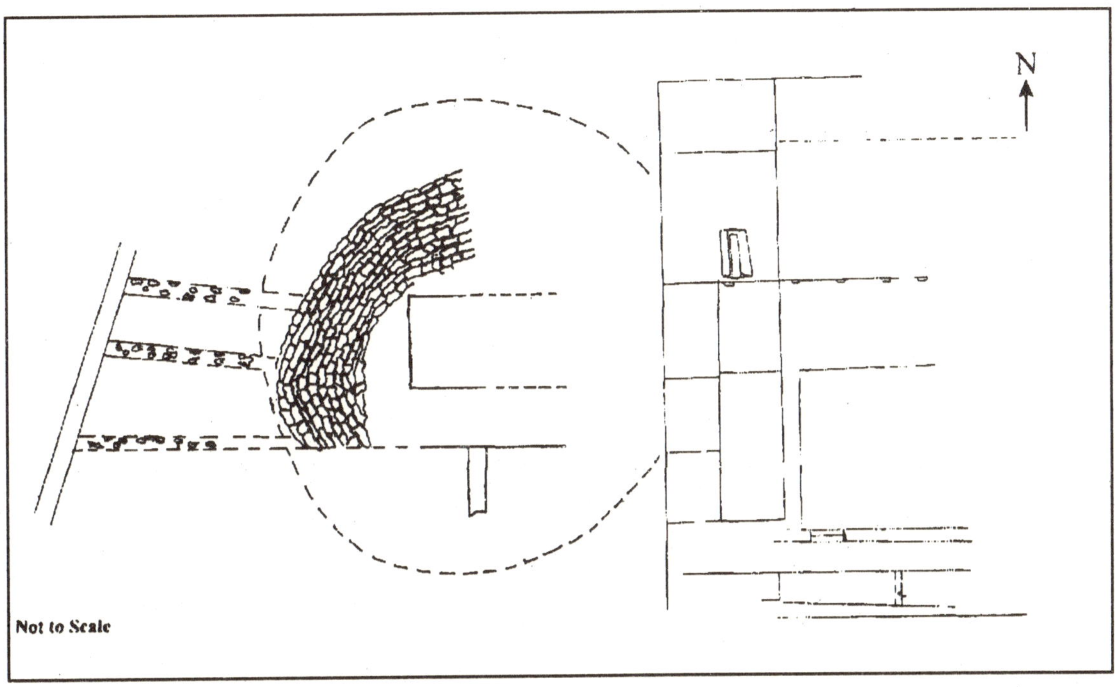

Plan of a Monastry overlying the earlier Kushan brick stupa

Courtesy: ASI, Mini Circle, Shimla

Fig. 2

Vertical Railing Pillar from Hathin | Railing Pillar from Bhuna | Other side of Railing Pillar Bhuna

Fig. 3

Cross-Bar Depicting a Stupa from Lalpura.

Vertical Railing Pillar from Bhadas

Two Railing Pillar from Amin.

Fig. 4

Ayodhyā Viṣṇu-Hari Temple Inscription

K.V. RAMESH*

The subjoined stone inscription is engraved on a rectangle stone slab, the written portion roughly covering an area of 115 X 55 cm. The slab, at present extant, is diagonally broken in two resulting in the loss of a couple of letters in almost every line. Besides, the first and last two lines have suffered heavy damage, and many letters consequently were lost. All in all, the loss of letters have proved a handicap to epigraphists and Sanskritists in fully interpreting the content of the text. Nevertheless, the over all purport and the crux of its import are clear beyond doubt. In the first instance a hurriedly prepared estampage, and in recent times, a high quality estampage as well as some photographs were all provided by Dr. S.P. Gupta, Chairman, Archaeological Society of India, New Delhi for which I am highly thankful to him.

The text of the inscription is written in fairly chaste Sanskrit, the orthographical features being regular for the period to which the inscription belongs. The inscription is not in any way dated, but may be assigned, with confidence, to the middle of the 12th Century on palaeographical grounds as well as the internal evidence provided by the inscriptional text in question.

But for the opening salutation to Śiva at the very beginning, the entire text of the inscription is composed in Sanskrit verse of fairly high literary excellence. As has been stated above, the palaeographical and orthographical features are normal for the period to which the inscription belongs, as this was an important period of transition from classical Sanskrit to the north Indian vernaculars. This can be easily identified in contemporary inscriptions, including the present one, in the use of class nasals and *anusvāra*, and in the employment of the sibilants and palatals.

As for the contents of the text, it is fully reflective of medieval vanity as far as the eulogies of the heroes mentioned in the inscription are concerned. The most important internal historical information we get from this epigraph is the mention of Govindachandra, obviously of the Gahadavala dynasty, who ruled over a fairly vast empire from 1114 to 1155 A.D.

Verse 1 is entirely lost. Verse 2, which is badly mutilated, refers to Trivikrama and, hence, may have been composed in praise of Lord Viṣṇu. Verse 3, which is also badly damaged, seems to allude to the near-total decimation of the warrior clans by Bhārgava Paraśurāma. Verse 4 refers to the emergence of a Kṣatriya family, in which the heroes born successfully resurrected the decadent warrior clans. According to Verse 5, in that noble family was born the beloved of the people, Māmé. Verse 7 speaks of his detachment from mundane things, while Verse 8 informs us that he bequeathed his realm and wealth to his son Sallakṣaṇa. Verse 9 to 14 contain con-

*Retired Joint Director General, Archaeological Survey of India, Mysore.

ventional praises showered on this Sallakṣaṇa in which the poet has displayed a high level of poetic imagination. Verse 15 refers to the birth of his son whose stunning resemblance to his father was the talk among the people. Verse 16 refers to this son as Alhaṇa and credits him with retrieving the past power and glory of his family. While the next two (17 and 18) contain his conventional praise, verses 19 gives the information that his nephew, Meghasuta by name, as superseding a certain Anayacandra and obtaining the Lordship of Sāketa-maṇḍala through the grace of the senior Lord of the earth, Govindacandra. While verse 20 lauds the military might of this hero, verse 21 gives the important information that, in order to ensure his easy passage into the heavens, Meghasuta built a lofty stone temple for the god Viṣṇu-Hari. From verse 22 we learn that he, who was responsible for the stability of Govindacandra's empire, was succeeded by the younger Āyuṣacandra as the Lord of Sāketa-maṇḍala. Verse 23 contains his conventional praise. According to verse 24, he set up residence in the city of Ayodhya, which was adorned with lofty abodes, intellectuals and temples, and added to the entire Sāketa-maṇḍala thousands of small and big water reservoirs. Verse 25 and 26 contain more conventional praise of Āyuṣyacandra. Verse 27, which is partly damaged, alludes to the well-known episodes of Viṣṇu's incarnations as Narasiṃha, Kṛṣna, Vāmana and Rāma. The badly damaged verse 28 refers to a king (probably Āyuṣacandra) as warding off the danger of invasion from the west (i.e., from the invading Muslim forces). Verse 29, which is incomplete, mentions the king Āyuṣyacandra.

The reference to Sāketa-maṇḍala is interesting. It is well known that North India, just as in the case of the South, was divided into administrative divisons called *maṇḍalas* (see the word *maṇḍala* in the indices to H.C. Ray's monumental two-volume work *The Dynastic History of Northern India*, II edn., 1973, Delhi.).

Text

[Metres: verses 1(?), 2, 3, 4, 10, 13, 20, 21, 27. Śārdūlavīkrīḍitam; verses 5, 6, 7, 17, 19, 24, 25, 28, Vasantatilakā; verse 8, Śikhariṇī; verses 9, 22, 23, 29 Upajāti; verses 11, 18, 26, Anuṣṭubh; verses 12, Hariṇī; Verse 14, Śālinī; verse 16, Rathoddhatā; verse 15, Mālini]

१.. नमः शिवा[या] [II*] - - - U U - U-U U U - - - U - - U - - - UU-U-UUU- - -U- -U- [I*] - - - UU - U - UUU- - - U - - U - - - UU - U - UUU - - - U - - U - - - - UU - U- UUU - - - U - - U - [II* 1] - - - UU -
स्-त्रिविक्रम-तनो र्-आ U - - U प्रांशुत्वे कृन निखेर्व्व-षो -

२. डश-समुद्दे शांदधानस्तनुं [I]

संवर्त्त-प्रमद्-ओ द्धत्तःकुलगिरि-ग्राव-प्रहार-क्कणद्-ब्रह्माण्डं करसंपुटे न

विधुवन्-मध्यो ह - - U -[II*2] - - द्धार्ग्गव वि U - U U U -द्वंसो (शो ऽ) वतंसो भुवः I यस्मिन्-रा-

३. U U - ल-संक्लिमिर्-इव स्थायिन्य्-उदंचद्-भुज - - श्च्-ओ पचिते परार्थ-घटना वंध्य्-आननं जज्ञिरे ॥ [3*] ते चंडीपति-चंड-तांडव-चलच्-चूडा (U - - U -
ब्रह्मांड्-ओ च्च-कपाल-रंध्र-सरणी-प्रस्थायि-सत्कीर्त्तयः I वीरास्-तत्र कुले जनिं जगृहि-

४. रे ये भार्ग्गवीय्-आहव-क्षीण-क्षत्रिय-शे ष-रक्षण-विधौ (ब)द्धो ऽभियो गग्रहः ॥ [4*] वंश्यन्-तद्-एव

कुलम्-आकुलता-निवृति-निर्व्यूढम्-अप्रतिम-[विक्रम]-जन्मभूमिः I यत्र्-आतिसाहस-सहश्र(स्र)-समिद्ध-धामा मामे ऽजनिष्ट जगद्-इष्टतम्-ओ त्त-

५. मश्रीः ॥ [5*] मा मे दयास्तु वपुषि द्रविणेषु तृष्णा

निष्णातिर्-अप्य्-अविरसा सरसेंद्रिय्-आर्थे I इत्युद्धृणन्न-अनुदिनं स दिने शवत्सो मामे प - U जगदे जगदे क [वीरः]॥ [6*] तद्-युद्धके लि-दलित्-आखिल-मे द-भिल्ल-पल्ली-सहस्र-वनितासु निकुंजगासु I उत्कंट-

६. का विटपिनो विट-विष्टितानि ते स्वस्तनेषु जघने षु मुहुर-लिखंतः ॥ [7*] पुरा कीर्त्त्यां न्यस्तन्-तदनु तनुन्-आध्यासितुमना मनस्वी स्वलोकं परिणतिम्-उपे [त्य्-आति] शयिनीं (I*) स सर्व्वस्वं क्षत्रं क इव भुवि सल्लक्षण-सुते श्रिया सार्द्धन्-दध्रे हुतभुजि विव-

७. श्वा(स्वा)न्-इव महः ॥

[8*] तद्-धाम-निस्सीमम्-अमह्यम्-अन्यैर्-अन्य-ऐ व सा काचन दान-शक्तेः I अमानुषं पौरुषम्-आविरासीत्-सल्लक्षणे विश्व-विलक्षणन्-तत् ॥ [9*] खड्गः श्रीकर [वालत्-आ]धिकं (क)रणं वा(बा)हुर्-महावाहिनी कीर्त्तिः

संभृत-[सू]पकार-विधये पाच्यं सदा दं-

८. शनं I राज्ये न्-आपि विना निजो पकरणान्य्-एतानि निःकंटकं यत्-सां(सा)म्राज्य-परिच्छदं विरचिरे चिंता-वितान्-ओ ज्झितं(तम्)॥ [10*] समर्-आजिर-भाजो ऽस्य चिरं निस्त्रिंश एव सः I [खड्गश्-च्-आ] पि धृतो मूर्ध्न यो जहार्-आसु(शु) जीवितं (तम्) ॥ [11*](मलय-)वलयस्य्-आन्ते शांते

९. वियत्तटिनी तटे हिमगिरि-गुहागे ह-द्वारे दरीम्-अधिनैषधीं I प्रथम-लिखितां सिद्धैर्-यस्य प्रशस्ति-पदावलीं पठति निपुणं स्त्रैणं मो दान्-नभस्थलचारिणां(णाम्)॥ [12*] कैलास्-आचल-मे खलासु मलय-स्वच्छे षु मे रो :शिरो भागे स्वर्गतरंगिणी-तटभुवि-

१०. स्थाने षु च्-आन्ये ष्व-अपि I कृत्वा तर्प्पण-शिल्पजां प्रतिकृतिं वृद्ध-ओपदे शात्-पति-प्राप्त्यै खेचरकन्यकाभिर्-अनिशं यद्-बाहुर्-अभ्यर्च्यते ॥ [13*] एज्यग्व सः पेशलैर्-इष्ट-सिद्धि-प्रा - - पह्नरं स्वं जगद्भिः I. गे हे यस्ह श्री-विलास्-आभिरामे व्या-

११. गाद्वै तं गीयते चारण्-औघैः॥ [14*] अमरपुर-पुरंध्री-वं(बं) धुताम्-अव्यलीकां भजति सुकृत-रासौ (शौ) तत्र सल्लक्षण्-आख्ये I प्रतिवपुर्-इव तस्य प्राप्य सद्यो ऽनवद्यं सुतम्-उदित-विवे कं लो क-कौतुहलं तत् ॥ [15*] अल्हणः प्रणय-पे शलः सतां गर्ज्जतां क्रकच-

१२. को टिर्-उत्कटः I आनिनाय नय-निन्हवे न यः प्रह्वतां प्रकृति-चंचलां श्रियं(यम्)॥ [16*] लो क्-ओ त्तरः स खलु को ऽपि यदा' भिमुख्ये ऽहंकार-राशिर्-अगलच्-चिर-संभृतो ऽपि II संसारि-पाश-भिदु- U द्दशैव यस्य जाताश्लथाः सुकृत दुःकृत कंचुकाश्च ॥ [17*]

१३. पौरुष-प्रतिरंध्र-ईति पुरंध-ईति च बिभ्यतां I ये न लो क्-आनुरुद्ध-आपि प्रतिषिद्धा नग्-ओ न्नतिः॥ [18*] तद्-भ्रातृजो जगति मे घसुतः श्रुताढ्यः श्रीमान्-अमूद्-अनयचंद्र-पद्-आभिलंघ्यः I गो विंदचंद्र-धरणींद्र गुरु-प्रसादात्-मंडल पतित्वम्-अ-

१४. लंभि ये न॥ [19*] स(श) श्वत्संगर-रंग-नर्तित-रिपु-स्कंधेन युद्ध-ओ द्धुरा वीरास्-ते न न के वलं बलवता ये दुर्म्मदा मो चिताः I अप्य्-उद्दाम-चमु-प्रदान-निरत-स्वान्ते न च्-ऐ कान्ततो दूर्-आरूढ-वयस्यता-मदम्-असौ कल्पद्रुमस्य्-आजितः ॥ [20*] टंक्-ओ त्खात-वि-

१५. शाल-शैल-शिखर-श्रे णी-शिला-संहति-व्यूहैर्-विष्णुहरे र्-हिरण्य-कलश-श्री-सुन्दरं मन्दिरं I पूर्व्वैर-अप्प्-अकृतं नृपतिभिर्-ये न्-एदम्-इत्य्-अद्भुतं

संसार-आर्णव-शीघ्र-लंघन-लघ्-ऊपायन्-धिया ध्यायता ॥ [21*] गो विन्दचंद्र-क्षितिपाल-राज्य-

१६. स्थैर्याय निस्तंद्र-भुज्-आर्गलस्य I अथ प्रपे दे ऽस्य पदं कनीयान्-आयुष्यचंद्रो ऽल्हण-सूनुर्-एव ॥ [22*] न साहसांके न न शूद्रके ण तस्य्-ओ पमानं विदधुः कवींद्राः I कृतं भिया यस्य पुरो न कामाद्-अन्ये न मन्ये धनुर्-आततज्यं (ज्यम्)॥ [23*]

१७. उद्दाम-सौध-विबुध्-आलयनीम्-अयो ध्याम्-अध्यास्य ते न नय-निन्हुत-वैशसे न I साके त-मंडलम्-अखंडम्-अकारि कूप-वापी-प्रतिश्रय-तडाग-सहश्र(स्र)-मिश्रं ॥ [24*]
निद्रा-निरो ध-विधये निजवल्लभानां
हे माचल्-आमल-शिलातल-तल्प-

१८. लीनाः I कस्तूरिक्-एण-तरुणी-श्रवण-ओ पयीग्य-योग्यं जगुः सरस-मगं-रसो यशो ऽस्य ॥ [24*] अविमुक्त-विशालाक्षी ललित्-आनंदिता सदा I कासी (श्-ई)व यस्य दे हश्रीः सतां निर्व्वाण-कारणं (णम्)॥ [26*] अस्थिभ्यो वितरन्-हिरण्यक-

१९. सिपुं संयम्य वा(बा)णं रणे कुर्व्वाणो व(ब)लिराज-वा(बा)हु-दलनं कृत्वा व(ब)हून्-विक्रमान् I कुर्व्व न्-दुष्ट दशाननस्य हनन - - U- -U कः को ऽप्य्-अन्यः स दश्-आधिको UUU – – – U पुण्यो तता [27*] अद्ये ह -U नृपते UU

२०. तो निहन्ति पाश्चात्यभीतिमपि भीषणबाहु दंडः I ते जः प्रभावमहतां महसीयमे व पूर्व्वापरा UUU-UU-U--[28*] पुण्यैः प्रजानां परिणामवद्भिः ख्याते क्षितौ राज U-U-श्री [I*] आयुष्य[चंद्र] UU-

Transiliteration

1.. nama: śivā[ya] (there is space enough in the erased portion for accomodationg a verse in a lengthy metre like Śārdūlavikrīḍitam). - - - U U - s - Trivikrama-tanor-ā - U - - U - prāṃśutvena nikharva-ṣo-

2. ḍaśa-samuddeśāṃ-dadhānas-tanuṃ saṃvartta-pramad-oddhataJ-Kulagiri-grāva-prahāra-kvaṇad-bra hmāṇḍam kara-sampuṭena vivu(bu)dhān-madhyo ha - - U -11[2*] [śrīmad]-Bhārggava vi U - U U U - dvaṃso(śo')vataṃso bhuva I yasmin-rā

3. U U - la-saṅklimir-iva sthāyiny-udañcad-bhuja - - ś-c-opacite parārtha-ghaṭanā vandhy-ānanaṃ jajñire 11[3*] te Caṇḍīpati-caṇḍa-tāṇḍava-calac-cūḍā U - - U - brahmāṇḍ-occa-kapāla-randhra-saraṇī-prasthāyi-

santkīrttaya: I vīrāa-tatra kule janiṃ jagṛhi-

4. re ye

Bhārggavīy-āhava-kṣīṇa-kṣatriya-śeṣa–rakṣaṇa-vidhau-(ba)ddho' bhiyogagraha: 11[4*] vaṃśyan-tad-eva-kulam-ākulatā- nivṛtti-nirvyūḍham-apratima-[vikrama]-janmabhūmi: I yatr-ātisāhasa-sahaśra(sra)-samiddha-dhāmā Māmé janiṣṭa jagad-iṣṭatam-otta-

5. maśrī: 11[5•] mā me dayāstu vapuṣi draviṇeṣu tṛṣṇā niṣṇātir-apy-avirasā sarasendriy-ārthe l ity-udgṛṇann-anudinaṃ sa Dineśavatso mā me pa - U jagade jagadeka[vīra] 11[6*] tad-yuddha-keli dalit-ākhila-Meda-Bhilla-pallī sahasra-vanitāsu. nikuñjagāsu I utkaṇṭa-

6. kā viṭapino viṭa-viṣṭitāni te sva-staneṣu jaghaneṣu muhur-likhanta: 11[7*] purā kīrttyā nyastan-tadanu tanun-ādhyāsitumanā manasvī svarlokaṃ pariṇatim-upe[ty-āti]śayinīṃ sa sarvvasvaṃ kṣatraṃ ka iva bhuvi Sallakṣaṇa-sute śriyā s-ārddhan-dadhre Hutabhuji viva-

7. śvā(svā)n-iva maha: 11[8*]

tad-dhāma-nissīmam-amahyam-anyair-any-aiva sākācana dāna-śakte: I amānuṣaṃ pauruṣama-āvirāsīt-Sallakṣaṇe viśva-vilakṣaṇan-tat 11[9*] khaḍga; śrīkara[vālat-ā]dhikaṃ(ka)raṇaṃ vā(bā)hur-mahāvāhinī kīrtti sambhṛta-[sū]pakāra-vidhaya pācyaṃ sadā daṃ-

8. śanàṃ I rājyen-āpi vinā nijopakaraṇāny-etāni ni:kaṇṭakaṃ yat-sāmrājya-paricchadaṃ viracire cintā-vitān ojjhitaṃ(tam) 11[10*] samar-ājira-bhājo'sya ciraṃ nistriṃśa eva sa: 1[khaḍgaś-c-ā]pi dhṛto mūrdhnā yo jahār-āsu(śu) jīvitam(tam) 11[11*]

[malaya]-valayasy-ānte śānte

9. Viyattaṭinī taṭe Himagiri-guhā-geha-dvāre darīm-adhinaiṣadhīṃ I prathama-likhitāṃ siddhair-yasya praśasti-padāvalīṃ paṭhati nipuṇaṃ straiṇaṃ modān-nab-cala-mekhalāsu Malaya-svaccheṣu mero:śirobhāge svargga-taraṅgiṇī-taṭabhuvi

10. sthāneṣu c-ānyeṣv-api I kṛtvā tarppaṇa-śilpajāṃ pratikṛtiṃ vṛddh-opadeśāt-pati-prāptyai khecarakanya-kābhir-aniśaṃ yad-bāhur-abhyarcyate 11[13*] ejya-gva sa: peśalair-iṣṭasiddhi-prā- - -pahnaraṃ svaṃ jagadbhi: I gehe yasya śrī-vilās-ābhirāme vyā-

11. gād-vai taṃ gīyate cāraṇ-aughai: 11[14*] Amara-pura-purandhrī-vandhutāmavyalīkāṃ bhajati sukṛtarāsau tatra sallakṣaṇākhye I prativapuriva tasya prāpya sadyo 'navadyaṃ sutamuditavivekaṃ lokakautūhalaṃ tat 11[15*] Alhaṇa: praṇaya-peśala: satāṃ garjjatāṃ krakaca-

12. koṭirutkaṭa: I āninkāya nayaninhavena ya: prahṛtāṃ prakṛticañcalāṃ śriyaṃ (yam) 11[16*] lokottara: sa khalu ko'pi yadābhimukhye'haṅkārarāsiragalacci-rasambhṛto'pi I saṃsāripāśabhidu - udṛśaiva yasya jātāślathā: sukṛta du:kṛta kañcukāśca 11[17*]

13. pauruṣapratirandhrīti purandhrīti ca bibhyatāṃ I yena lokānuruddhāpi pratiṣiddhā nagonnati: 11[18*] tadbhrātṛjo jagati meghasuta: śrutāḍhya: śrīmānabhūdanayacandrapadābhilaṅghya: I govindacandrara dharaṇīndra guruprasādātsāketamaṇḍalapatitvama-

14. lambhi yena 11[19*] saśvatsaṅgararaṅganartitari-puskandhena yuddhoddhurā vīrāstena na kevalaṃ balavatā ye durmmadā mocita: I apyuddāmacamupradānani-ratasvāntena caikāntato dūrārūḍhavayasyatāmadamasau kalpadrumasyājita: 11[20*] ṭaṅkotkhātavi-

15. śālaśailaśikharaśreṇīśilāsaṃhativyūhairviṣṇuhar-erhiraṇyakalaśaśrī sundaraṃ mandiraṃ I pūrvvairapyakṛtaṃ kṛtaṃ nṛpatibhiryenedamityadbhutaṃ sāṃsārārṇava-śīghra-laṅghana-laghūpāyan-dhiyā dhyāyatā 11[21*] govindacandra-kṣtipāla-rājya-

16. sthairyāya-nistandra-bhujārgalasya I atha prapede'sya padaṃ kanīyān-Āyuṣyacandro'Ihaṇa-sūnur-eva 11[22*] na Sāhasāṅkena na Śūdrakeṇa tasy-opamānaṃ vidadhu: kavīndrā: I kṛtaṃ bhiyā yasya puro na kāmād-anyena manye dhanur-ātataiyaṃ (m) 11[23*]

17. uddāma-saudha-vibudh-ālayanīm-Ayodhyām-adhyāsya tena naya-ninhuta-vaiśayena I Sāketa-maṇḍalam-akhaṇḍam-akāri kūpa-vāpī-pratiśraya-taḍāga-sahaśra(sra)-miśraṃ(śram) 11[24•] nidrā-nirodha-vidhaye nija-vallabhānāṃ Hemācala-āmala-śilātala-talpa-

18. līnā:kastūrik-eṇa-taruṇī-śravaṇ-opabhogya-yogyaṃ jagu sarasa-magna-raso yaśo'syo 11[25*] avimukta-viśālākṣī lalit-ānanditā sadā I kāsīva yasya dehaśrī: satāṃ nirvvāṇa-kāraṇaṃ(ṇam) 11[26*] asthib-hyo vitaran-Hiraṇyaka-

19. sipuṃ saṃyamya Vā(Bā)ṇaṃ raṇe kurvvāṇo Va(Ba)lirāja-vā(bā)hu-dalanaṃ kṛtvā va(ba)hūn-vikramān I kuwan-duṣṭa-Daśānanasya hanana - - U - - U ka; ko'py-anya: sa daś-ādhiko U U U - - - U puṇyo tatā 11[27*] ady-eha - U nṛpate U U

20. to nihanti pāścāṃ Pāscātya-bhītim-api bhīṣaṇa-bāhu-daṇḍaṃ: (m) teja: prabhāva-mahatām mahas-īyam-eva pūrvv-āparā U U U - U U - U -- [28*] [puṇyai]: prajānāṃ pariṇāmavadbhi: khyāte kṣitau rāja. . . . . . śrī Āyuṣyaca. ....

TRANSLATION

Line 1... Obeisance to [Lord*] Śiva. . . . . .

Lines 1-2, verse 1. [This line is nearly totally erased. But there is enough space for a verse in a lengthy metre such as Śardūlavīkriḍitam].

Lines 1-2, verse 2. . . . Of the physique of [Lord] Trivikrama. . . . . by His height containing within His body the sixteen doctrines (or mahā-vidyās) . . . . in Whose palm He holds the universe like (holding) the Moon, whose *kulagiri* (in the case of Bharata-varsa, one of the seven great mountain ranges, *viz.*, Mahendra, Malaya, Sahya, Śuktīmat, Ṛkṣa, Vindhya and Pāriyātra) whose falling rocks (while striking one another) create noise had, out of wanton arrogance . . . .

Lines 2-3, Verse 3. The illustraions Bhārgava (i.e., Parasurāma). . . . an ornament of the earth . . . . like insects . . . . With firm hands upraised . . . . having increased, events brought into existence, barren faces . . . .

Lines 3-4, verse 4, during the violent dance of the Lord of (the goddess) Caṇḍī (i.e., Lord Śiva), from the rocking head-jewel . . . . Genuine reputations which emanated from the opening in the skull-shaped spherical half of the universe.. In that family heroes took their birth, who were determined to resurrect the warrior clan which had been rendered weak by the wars waged by Bhargava (Paraśurāma) (against them).

Lines 4-5, verse 5. Noble was that very family which was the birth-place of valour which had successfully removed the sufferings of the other (Kṣatriya clans) in which Māmé, the abode of thousands of perfect and extremely valorous deeds and who was the utmost favourite of the world.

Line 5, verse 6. That very Son of the Sun (i.e., Karṇa), Māmé the unequalled hero of the world, uttered everday the words "may I have no mercy on (my) body, may I not hanker for material wealth, may I be diligently disinterested in sensual temptations . . . .

Line 5-6, verse 7. The thorny trees, like the sensous villains, repeatedly wrote (i.e., scratched) on the skins of the breasts and hips and loins of the womenfolk of the tribal villages of the plains and hills who had taken refuge in the thickets as a result of the destruction of their abodes in sportive wars waged by him.

Line 6-7, verse 8. His fame along having pervaded till then the heavens, the high-minded [Māmé], wishing to go to the heavens in person and reside there in that wonderful world, he bequeathed his entire realm along with all the wealth to his sone Sallakṣaṇa just as the Sun-god had bequeathed all his luster to the Fire-god.

Line 7, verse 9. As a result of some unknown power of the gift of that realm, which had no bounds and was other-worldly, a super-human valour manifested itself in Sallakṣaṇa; it was indeed an earthly exception.

Line 7-8, verse 10. The sword was at the tip of his fingers, his hand was verily the great army, his fame, like sumptuously cooked delicacies, were ever palatable; even without a kingdom to rule, these personal instruments enabled him to spread extensively an empire *sans* worries.

Line 8, verse 11. He who was for long intervals enjoying himself on battle-fields, bore on his head his ruthless sword, which was quick to end the lives (of his enemies).

Lines 8-9, verse 12. Within the serene surroundings of the Malaya mountain, on the banks of the heavenly Gaṅgā, at the entrances of the cave-dwellings of the Himālayas, in the caverns in which the hunter-tribes dwell, the accomplished womenfolk gaily sing (literally, read) the strings of his eulogy composed for the first time by the semi-divine beings moving about in the skies.

Lines 10-11, verse 13. On the advice tendered by the elders, in the terrians of the Himālayas, in the pristine pure regions of the Malaya (mountains), in the lands along the banks of the heavenly Gaṅgā as well as in other regions the semi-divine unmarried girls, with intent to gain husbands, ever offer worship to the hands of the satiating images sculpted in his (i.e., Sallakṣaṇa's) likeness.

Lines 10-11, verse 14. He who is to be offered oblations by the beautiful for the realization of their desires . . . himself by the worlds . . . . . in whose abode, which is pleasing with wealth and happiness, he is sung about by multitudes of celestial singers.

Lines 11-12, verse 15. The people look upon as a phenomenon the fact that, Sallakṣaṇa, who was, through good fortune, enjoying the genuine company of the damsels of the heavens, had happily begotten a son who, by appearance, was no different from his father.

Lines 11-12, verse 16. [That son] Alhaṇa, who was the beloved of the good people, is like a pointed saw to the war-mongers. He retrieved the splendour of the habitually fickle-minded Goddess of wealth by means of fair and persuasive means.

Line 12, verse 17. He was indeed extraordinary and whenever he confronted (his foes the heap of their) arrogance, accumulated over a protracted period, melted away. The garb of good deeds and bad deeds (worn by them) slipped away by his mere looks.

Line 13, verse 18. He was the destroyer of (his enemies) manliness, and made those who were afraid effeminate; as against the belief among the people, his eminence far dwarfed that of the lofty mountains.

Lines 13-14, verse 19. His nephew (literally brother's son), the widely celebrated Meghasuta, the illustrious one, who superceded Anayacandra; he earned the lordship of Sāketa-maṇḍala through the grace of his elder, the Lord of the earth, Govindacandra.

Line 14, verse 20. Not only did he, who was powerful, put an end to the arrogant warriors who were dancing in unrestrained frenzy in the battles constantly fought by him, but he also gave (to his people) an excellent army which was replete with (soldiers comparable to) the wish-fulfilling trees.

Lines 14-15, verse 21. By him, who was meditating in his mind on the earliest means of quickly jumping across the ocean of worldly attachments, was erected this beautiful temple of [The god] Viṣṇu-Hari, [on a scale] never before done by the preceding kings, compactly formed [i.e., built] with rows of large and lofty stones which had been sculpted out.

Lines 15-16, verse 22. The position of Alhaṇa, whose tireless shoulders were like safety latches for the stability of the king Govindacandra's empire, was subsequently occupied by his younger (son?) Āyuṣyacandra.

Line 16, verse 23. Great poets dared not compare him with Sāhasāṅka and Śūdraka; out of sheer fear none save the God of Love dared draw the bow-string in his presence.

Line 17, verse 24. By him, who was of good conduct, and abhorred strife, while residing at Ayodhyā, which had towering abodes, intellectuals and temples, Sāketa-Maṇḍala was endowed with thousands of wells, reservoirs, alms-houses, tanks.

Lines 17-18, verse 25. The young damsels, who were as attractive as the female musk-deer and does, while they rested on the cool surfaces of the Himalayan rocks, sang about his (i.e., Āyuṣyacandra's) fame.

Line 18, verse 26. Whose bodily splendour, which was ever characterized by glowing eyes, was at all times pleasant with gentle feelings, was a source of salvation for the good just as (the holy pilgrimage centre) Kāśī is.

Lines 18-19, verse 27. Separating [the flesh and blood of the demon] Hiraṇyakaśipu from his skeleton, subduing [the demon] Bāṇa in battle, tearing asunder the arms of the [demon-] king Bali, and performing many valorous deeds, having killed the evil ten-headed [demon Rāvaṇa] . . . .

Lines 19-20, verse 28. And now, the fierce arms of the ruler annihilates even the fear caused by the western (i.e., the Islamic invaders from the west). The brilliance of the mighty great ones . . . . east and west . . . .

Line 20, verse 29. Because of the subject's effective acts of merit, the king being famous in the world . . . . the illustrious Āyuṣyacandra . . . .

The Genre of Circular Temples in North India

B.R. Mani*

The classical Sanskrit literature on Indian temple architecture contains details of various styles including types of circular temples besides those which are apsidal or semi-circular on plan at their *sanctum-sanctorum*. The apsidal chaityas are generally believed to have their Buddhist origin and archaeological evidence suggest their existence from at least the second-third century B.C. They are well represented in the western rock-cut caves at several places in Maharashtra and clearly indicate their prototype in timber architecture of earlier date. In Kondvite cave near Pune the circular enclosure within the hall represents the developed form of basically apsidal nature of the structure. However, the earliest brick-built circular temple was made during the Mauryan period (300 B.C.) at Bairat, near Jaipur in Rajasthan.

The Gupta age in the history of art and architecture brought about a revolution in the proliferation of various architectural styles under the framework of canonical treatises prescribing their classical form and dimensions. Varahamihira in his *Brihatsaṁhita* has described twenty types of temples in the chapter on *Prāsāda - lakshaṇa* (ed. R. Bhatt, 1981) in which besides *Kuñjara* and *Guhāraja* types, which are apsidal in nature, circular temples such as *Samudga, Padma, Vrisha, Ghaṭa* and *Vritta* have been mentioned. Though *Padma* is shaped like a lotus with eight petals and *Ghaṭa* is shaped like a pot, the other three types, i.e., *Samudga, Vrisha* and *Vritta* are clearly circular ones. These temples are said to be '*eka-bhūmishriṅga*' or having only one storey and dome, being circular all round. The *vritta* or circular temple is called '*añjanarūpa*' or dark inside. Bhattotpala, commenting upon them, states that these "dark temples do not have external light entering the interior. Close to the temple, walls should be constructed all round and the entrance should be on the western side. The walls should be so constructed with openings in the upper parts that they appear to be rising from temple structure itself and not away from it. People should enter by the outer gate in the west, go towards the north and coming to the eastern part of the temple, enter it by the door in the east." The idea is that the temple will have only one door in the east, but the outer gate will be in the west. The idol inside the *sanctum sanctorum* being made of gems, would illumine the interior by means of its effulgence. Such temples are called *'sāndhakārah'*, *'bhūmikaikāḥ'* and *'ekāṇḍarūpitāḥ'* by Kāshyapa.

In the description of 64 types of temples, *Aparājitaprichchhā* differentiates the circular shrines (*Vritta*) with the apsidal ones (*Vrittāyata*) (ed. P.A. Mankad, 1950). The text also mentions about the water-chute (praṇāla) in the description of the *Piṭhikālakshaṇa* (chapter 207) in a Śiva temple that it should be made on the northern side which invariably we find in the Indian temples, particularly in Śiva temples. Regarding *pīṭha* or *pīṭhikā*, the *Mānasāra-Śilpaśastra* mentions that it must match the phallus of which it forms the lower part. The *pīṭhas* are divided into three types, the *Nāgara* being squre, the *Drāvida* being octagonal, and the *vesara* being circular or round (P.K. Acharya, 2001). The circular temples are described along with similar ones in the 59th chapter of *Samarāṅganasūtradhāra* clearly mentioning

*Superintending Archaeologist, Archaeological Survey of India, Janpath, New Delhi.

their circular super-structure raised over a circular plan (ed. V.S. Agrawala, 1966).

The earliest circular type of temple, the Maniyār Math in Rajgir, supposed to be either *Ghaṭa* type of *Brihatsaṁhitā* or *lingākāra* of *Vishṇudharmottarapurāṇa*, is a brick-and-stucco structure of unique plan and design with delicately and sensitively modelled beautiful stucco figures. "The temple is cylindrical, with *bhadra* - projections at the cardinal points and a circular interior (of c. 11 ft. diameter). The temple stands on a *vedībandha* of tall *kuṁbha*, well-formed *kalaśa*, and plain *paṭṭikā* The temple also was embellished with at least 13 niches, framed by pilasters that show *ghaṭa*-bases on lotus-pedestals and shafts with both square and octagonal sections. The upper part of the square section was embellished with a large *ardhapadma* on some pilasters. The niches once contained stucco images which have disintegrated; vestiges remain of a seated figure of Gaṇeśa on the south *bhadra*. Old photographs as well as descriptions attest to the existence of nine other images: a Śivaliṅga, four-armed Viṣṇu (east bhadra), nāginī, five figures of nāgas, and six-armed Naṭēśa.

"Built on the ruins of previous structures, this temple underwent restorations and alterations. The upper portions of the niches are replaced by a plain circular wall of large bricks; this constituted the first restoration. The wall shows a neck-like constriction toward the top, with simple ornaments of compressed pilasters, floral pattern, and stylized *chandraśālikā*; these indicate a date not earlier than the beginning of the sixth century. At a later point, the temple was blocked on the north and an entrance pierced through the wall to give access to its well-like interior. Concrete pavements indicate successive floor levels. The monument was later surrounded by a large oblong structure approached on the north by an imposing stairway. The most recent restoration was a circular construction concentric with the original temple". (Fig. 1) (M.A. Dhaky, ed. 1988).

The Magadhan style of circular temples became popular in brick architecture, the growth of which was encouraged by the alluvial nature of soil of the Gangetic valley. Very few of such buildings have survived the frequent marches of invading armies of the Muslims and the ravages of man and nature. While Maniyar Math at Rajgir is datable to c.500 A.D., other brick temples of circular type have not been precisely dated so far. The Chandrehe Śiva temple in Sidhi district of Madhya Pradesh, which is a stone structure of circular type of temple, has been dated to c.950 A.D. on epigraphical evidence. The Chandrehe stone inscription mentions the construction of a Śaiva maṭha close to the temple earlier constructed by Praśāntaśiva, the āchārya of Mattamayūra clan of the Śaivite sect. The maṭha was constructed by Śaiva pontiff, Prabodhaśiva in A.D. 973 whose preceptor was Praśāntaśiva and thus the circular stone temple at Chandrehe has been considered to have taken its shape a generation earlier, around A.D. 950 (Krishna Deva, 1995, 1998). Mainly on stylistic grounds having similarity with Chandrehe example of Kalachuri temple, other circular temples of the region such as at Masaon in district Rewa (Madhya Pradesh) and at Tinduli and Kurari in district Fatehpur (Uttar Pradesh) which are all stone temples, have been dated to about tenth century A.D. V.V. Mirashi (1955) believed that temples having circular *garbhagriha* were a speciality of the Chedi country and were built for the first time by the āchāryas of the Mattamayūra clan. This belief is unacceptable in view of the evidence of circular temples as contemplated by Varāhamihira and one in existence in Rajgir. The Rajgir example in brick masonry followed by evidence at Siddharthnagar, Sravasti, Kashipur and other places in Uttar Pradesh suggest that circular temples in brick masonry must have been quite in vogue before tenth century A.D. and particularly in the ninth century A.D. in the Ganga-Yamuna plains.This style was adopted by the Kalachuris or Haihayas of Tripuri who were lords of Chedi or Dahala country and who assumed the imperial status in the ninth century. Kalachuris were perhaps the first to build large circular stone temples of earlier smaller prototypes in brick masonry.

The Kalachuris of Sarayūpār region in U.P. (V. Pathak, 1973) who had established at least two kingdoms in Gorakhpur – Deoria area after conquering Ayomukha and Svetapada and whose one dynasty ruled from Kasaya near Kushinagar seems to have established themselves there in the eighth century A.D. They became the feudatories of the Gurjara-Pratihāras and after their downfall they allied themselves with the Kalachuris of the main branch of Dahala who had their sway upto Kashi in the beginning of the eleventh century in the time of Gāṅgeyadeva. With the rise of power of the Gāhadavālas, the Kalachuri feudatories also vanished as confirmed from their last known Kahal inscription of 1077 A.D.

belonging to Sodhadeva. The constant touch of the Kalachuris of Sarayūpār with their main branch might have been responsible for the development of circular temple architecture from brick to stone masonry in the Kalachuri area of Central India.

A circular brick temple has been noticed recently at Sikhara Kohanda in Siddharthnagar district, about 6 km from Domariyaganj where eight brick structures – four circular and four square have been noticed with the vestiges of plain and decorated bricks having the motifs of scrolls and āmalaka, etc. They have been associated with a simple *antarāla* or *kapilī*, in plan and have been roughly dated to approximately eleventh century A.D. (Personal Comm. R. Tiwari and R.K. Srivastava)

Another prominent circular brick temple has been excavated at Chirenath in Sravasti whose *śikhara* is missing but on plan the temple upto its jaṅghā portion is circular from exterior having a circumference of 14.70 m. with three niches in all the three cardinal directions and entrance in the west. The *garbhagriha* is roughly square, measuring 2.10 x 2.10 m with a 1.70 m high Sivalinga of red sandstone in the middle (Fig. 2) (I.A.R. 1997–98).

Krishna Deva has described the circular temples in stone attributed to the Kalachuris and their counterparts in brick in the districts of Fatehpur and Kanpur in Uttar Pradesh. He writes, "The Kalachuri temples of the tenth century A.D. generally are available on square-orthogonal plan, the exception being the Chandrehe and Masaon temple. They have a *vṛtta-saṁsthānaka* or circular plan with 16 *bhadras*, the type having a limited vogue both spatially and temporally which was more popular in the brick medium in the adjoining districts of Fatehpur and Kanpur in Uttar Pradesh, forming part of the ancient Vatsadeśa. Further, the hypaethral and circular plan and the elementary design of the Chausaṭha Yōginī temple is exceptional and obviously was dictated by religious compulsion". (Krishna Deva 1998).

Describing the Chandrehe temple he writes, "This temple adjoins the Śiva monastery, in a forest-village now known as Chandrehe situated on the right bank of the river Son, about 50 kms southeast of Rewa in Madhya Pradesh. It is a west-facing *nirandhāra* temple with a circular *garbhagṛha* preceded by an *antarāla* and a *mukhamaṇḍapa*, the whole resting on a lofty *jagatī*, measuring 46.5 ft. x 28 ft., with flights of steps attached to the *jagatī* and the *mukhamaṇḍapa*. The *jagatī* has *bhadra*-projections on the west, north and south, co-axial with the cardinals of the *garbhagṛha*, and originally had moulded courses showing *puṣpapaṭṭī* and bands with *vallī*, *tamālapattras*, and broad chequers; however, the surviving courses were haphazardly rearranged in a later restoration. (Fig. 3).

'The temple stands on a common conspicuous pīṭha composed of *khura-kumbha*, *jāḍyakumbha*, *karnikā*, *kapōta*, and *vasantapaṭṭikā*. The *garbhagṛha* and the *kapilī* carry above the pīṭha a bold and ornate *vēdībandha* with an *antarapaṭṭa* carved with *ratnapaṭṭī*, and *kapōtapālī* underscored by triangular frills while the *mukhamaṇḍapa* has, in lieu of the *vēdībandha*, a *mattavāraṇa* complex composed of *rājasēna*, *vēdikā*, *āsanapaṭṭa*, and *kakṣāsana*.

'The *garbhagṛha* is circular both internally and externally and is composed of 16 curved *bhadras* which are carried over the entire elevation from the *vēdībandha* to the tip of the *śikhara*. Of these *bhadras*, only 11 are actually represented while the remaining five have been omitted on account of the presence of *kapilī* at that segmental point.

'The *jaṅghā* divided into lower and upper registers by a *paṭṭikā* of *tamālapattra* design surmounted by a *karṇikā*, is composed of plain pilasters, one for each *bhadra*; this is supervened by a *grāsapaṭṭi* and a bistriated *varaṇḍikā* of two ornate *kapōtapālis*. The handsome *latā* of the *śikhara* terminates in a tongue of *udgama*. Though the *vēṇukōśa* is conspicuous by absence, the *śikhara* is noteworthy for its subtle, elegant curvature and the filigree-like fine carving of the *gavākṣa-jāla* on the *latās* of which all 16 are present above the *śukanāsa* level. The *śikhara* is crowned with an *āmalasāraka*, *chandrikā*, *āmalaka*, and *ghaṭa*-finial.

'The *kapilī* shares with the *garbhagṛha* a plain *jaṅghā* and a *dvistara-varaṇḍikā*, above which occur a succession of ornate zones carved with *gajapīṭha*, *kakṣāsana* mouldings, *ratnapaṭṭī* and a pair of *phāṁsākāra* aedicules harbouring sculptures of a divinity flanked by attendants. These are surmounted by the lateral face of the *śukanāsa* ornamented with registers of *vallī*, chequers and *tilakas*. The front of the *sukanāsa* repeats some of these registers which are crowned with a *śūrasēnaka* harbouring a head of *Mahēśamūrtī*.

"The mukhamaṇḍapa is partly enclosed by a *vēdikā, āsanapaṭṭa,* and *kakṣāsana* and its roof is supported on two pairs of pillars and a pair of pilasters, all intercepted by the *āsanapaṭṭa*. The pillars and pilasters are of the plain *Bhadraka* order surmounted by a ribbed capital and brackets of plain curved profile. The *mukhamaṇḍapa* has a large *Padmaśilā*-ceiling carved in low relief, fringed around by *vallī* and *grāsamukhas*.

"The *mukhamandapa*-doorframe is plain *triśākhā* but relieved by a *vallī* on the *udumbara* and by a row of *tamalapattras* on the architrave. The *aṁtarāla* is a small chamber and leads through a narrow entrance flanked by a pair of plain pilasters into the interior of the *garbhagrha* which centrally enshrines a large Sivaliṅga on a *pīthikā*.

"The adjoining Śaiva matha bears an inscription proclaiming the building of the matha by the Śaiva pontiff Prabōdhaśiva in A.D. 973 and close to the temple earlier constructed by his preceptor Praśāntaśiva. As the two structures are situated within a few yards of each other and have striking stylistic affinities, there is no doubt that this Śiva temple was built a generation earlier, in c.950 A.D.".

The other Kalachuri stone circular temple is located in Masaon, about 20 km. due east of Rewa. With slight variation, it resembles in general with the Chandrehe temple. It "lacks a *jagatī* and has a less pretentious *pīṭha* but a *vedībaṁdha* very similar to that at Candrehe. Its *jaṅghā* too, is composed of plain pilasters of ashlars but has three registers in place of two, the top row capped by a *haṁsapaṭṭikā*, a new feature. The *varaṇḍkā* is likewise *dvistara* and is surmounted by the *latās* of the *śikhara* numbering 16, as indicated by the surviving fragments. Of the *śukanāsa* only the basal *rathikās* are intact containing figures of a divine *mithuna*, and *vyāla*, besides conspicuous designs of lotus and diamonds". The temple is constituted of an *ardhamaṇḍapa, antarāla* and a circular *garbhagriha* enshrining a Śivaliṅga. The structures are larger than Chandrehe temple. The outer diameter of the *garbhagriha* is 5.17 m which is 33 cm larger than that of Chandrehe. (Fig. 4).

The circular brick temples at Kurari and Tinduli in Fatehpur district of Uttar Pradesh are in the style of the Kalachuri temples and can be roughly dated to the mid-tenth century A.D. They have plain square interior and a circular exterior with 8 to 16 *bhadra*-facets uniformly carved with decorative brick-work over the *jaṅghā* and the *śikhara* gradually tapering upwards. The temple 1 at Kurari has a simplified version of the domical ceiling like that of the Vishṇu temple at Thithaura, another site in Fatehpur district. Some such temples of circular type had been reported earlier, like one at Parauli in Fatehpur district, but most of these have since been vanished due to vandalism.

A group of four temples have been located at Kurari, about 24 km. south-west of Fatehpur in Uttar Pradesh on the bank of a tank. Out of these, one temple has become only a heap of mound, while three of them stand in varying stages of decay. They have circular exterior with 16 facets of decorative brickwork and a square plain interior.

The temple 1 at Kurari is locally called *Dēvarā* which is best preserved temple of the complex. It measures 1.55 m. square internally while its exterior diameter is 8.10 m.

"The temple stands on a plain *jagatī* and originally had a low moulded *upapīṭha* which has crumbled. The *vēdībaṁdha* consists of tall *kuṁbha, kalaśa/vasantapaṭṭikā* on alternate facets, *antarapaṭṭa, kapōtapālī* embellished with scrolls on the main moulding and underscored by festoons and *vasantapaṭṭikā*. The *jaṅghā* and the curvilinear *śikhara* bear identical design of integrated scrolls and the two are separated by a *varaṇḍikā*-recess containing an ornament of festoons seemingly made of cut bricks. The *jaṅghā* shows three *bhadras* marked by small niches, one at the back and two on the lateral sides. Each niche is a sham oblong window of latticed design framed by a pair of pilasters and an architrave, all bearing the identical scroll ornament that monotonously covers the façade of the *jaṅghā* and the *śikhara*. Since the circular façade comprises 16 facets, every fourth facet has a *bhadra*-niche. Bereft though of any other ornament and even when it has lost its *grīvā* and the crowning members, the *śikhara* has an elegant curvature of *Latina* type. (Fig. 5).

"The *garbhagṛha* interior has severely plain walls with a corbelled domical ceiling of a small size with a course of carved lotus petals at the base. The *śikhara* is internally a hollow chamber with gradually contracting sides. Like other known brick temples, it had a stone doorway of which jamb fragments exist at the site together with fragments of Gaṇeśa and Viṣṇu images.

The *garbhagṛha* perhaps enshrined the Viṣṇu image of which a portion of the *parikara* is available depicting some of the Vaiṣṇava incarnations. The images and the structure together with the stone jambs are stylistically assignable to c. mid tenth century".

The temple 2 at Kurari is similar to temple 1 in plan situated towards west, but smaller than it as its *sanctum sanctorum* internally is 1.25 m. square. The *vedībandha* of the temple is composed of tall *kumbha, kalaśa, antarapaṭṭa* and *kapotapālī*, while the *varaṇḍika* has only one *kapotapālī*. The brick ornamentation on the façade is bolder and more varied, but there are no indications of *bhadras* on the *jaṅghā*. The temple 3 is situated towards north-west of temple 1 and is of the same size as of temple 1, but its entire face of the decorative brick-work has been damaged. (Fig. 6).

The other important circular temple in brick in Fatehpur district is the temple at Tinduli village situated along the bank of the Rind rivulet, about 3 km north of Bindki in district Fatehpur which has been considerably repaired in past. (Fig. 7).

"The temple's interior is square (side 6 ft. 8 in.) and the exterior is circular-stellate having 16 *bhadra*-facets and 16 *karṇa*-projections. Of the *bhadras* four are sham and four are real, each separated from the other by an acute-angled projection produced by turning the square. The doorway which, originally was preceded by a *prāggrīva*, faces north, while the three *bhadras* face the remaining cardinal directions.

"The *vedibandha* is composed of tall kumbha, *kalaśa, antarapatta* relieved with chequers, *kapotapālī*, and *vasantapaṭṭikā*. Except for the *kumbha* all other mouldings are embellished with scrolls and some additional designs. Thus the *kalaśa* moulding has its shoulder adorned with lotus petals while the *kapotapālī* is underscored by festoon design.

"The *jaṅghā* has three *bhadra*-niches, each with frames, architraves, and pilasters in addition to thin and wide *udgama*-pediments; but in the absence of proper spacing, with plain surface around, they all merge with the decorative brickwork of the other parts of the *jaṅghā* which are monotonously covered with scrolls.

"The *jaṅghā* is capped by a conspicuous band of chequers and a plain *kaṇṭha* of the *varaṇḍikā* relieved by vandanamālikā, above which rises the high ponderous *Latina śikhara*.

The *śikhara*, too, is covered with identical design of scrolls, and is well integrated, but monotonous, and probably had seven *bhūmis* of which only four are clearly indicated by the surviving *bhūmi*-divisions. The *grīvā* and the crowning members of the *sikhara* are lost.

"Of the *pañcaśākhā*-doorframe of the *garbhagṛha*, only a fragment of jamb remains carved with multiple śākhās of gods such as Viṣṇu and the demigods including apsaras.

"The *garbhagṛha* has plain brick walls but an ornate stone ceiling of two intersecting squares supported on *bhadraka* pilasters showing *ghaṭapallavas* at the base while the upper part is linked by a vertical panel of finely delineated *patravallī* design. The pilasters have ribbed *bharaṇī* and plain curved brackets. The *garbhagṛha* enshrines a standing image of Sūrya (head broken) with an elaborately carved *parikara* showing a large number of female archers in graceful postures.

"Stylistically, this brick temple together with its image and pilaster of stone, is assignable to the mid tenth century".

The hypaethral and circular temples of *yoginis* are well known in north and Central India. They have been mentioned by Krishna Deva as at Dudhai in Jhansi district, Mitaoli in Morena district, Bheraghat in Jabalpur district, Ranipur Jharial in Bolangir district and Surada near Kalahandi and Hirapur near Bhubaneswar in Orissa. They range from 16.72 m to 39.52 m in outer diameter, with 65 to 81 peripheral chapels and a principal shrine, normally in the centre of the courtyard. Inscribed *yogini* images from Central India suggest more such temples and one such shrine has been excavated and identified as Golakimatha in Jabalpur district (Krishna Deva 1999). The proliferation of circular temples with their identification with the types mentioned in classical treatises require further investigative studies of their origin and developmental process.

BIBLIOGRAPHY

Aparājitapṛcchā of Bhuvanadeva, ed. by P.A. Mankad, Baroda 1950, pp.461–463.

"वृत्तो वृत्तायतश्चैत्य: किड़िकणी लयनस्तथा ।
पट्टिशो विभवश्चैव तथा तारागणो मत: ॥" 179.15
"वृत्तो वृत्तायतश्चैव चैत्यो वै वेद्यलड़कृत: ।
सुभद्रो भद्रश्रृङ्गेषु किड़िकणी नाम प्रोच्चते ॥" 179.55

"प्रमाणारधिकं कार्यं प्रणालं चोत्तरे तथा ।
पृथुपीठ त्रिभागेन निष्काशं तस्य कारयेत् ॥ " 207.23

Encyclopaedia of Indian Temple Architecture, ed. By M.A. Dhaky, Vol.II, Part 1 : Text, Delhi 1988, p.103, Fig. 41.

Indian Archaeology 1997-98-A Review, Archaeological Survey of India, New Delhi 2003, pp.193-95, pl.136.

Krishna Deva, Encyclopaedia of Indian Temple Architecture, vol.II, Part 3, Text op. cit., p.40, 1998.

————, *Temples of India* Vol.1: Text, New Delhi 1995, p.159; *Encyclopaedia of Indian Temple Architecdture* op.cit., Vol.II, part 3 : Text, New Delhi 1998, p.43.

————, *Temples of Khajuraho*, Vol.I, New Delhi 1999, p.26.

P.K. Acharya, *An Encyclopaedia of Hindu Architecture*, Delhi(Reprinted) 2001, p.307.

R. Tewari and R.K. Srivastava, Explorations along the Ami river and in its Nearby areas in districts Siddhartha Nagar, Basti & Gorakhpur', *Pragdhara*, NO.4, pp.32-33.

Samarāngaṇa-sūtradhāra of Mahārājadhirājā Bhoja, revised and edited by V.S. Agrawala, Baroda 1966, p.455.

"वृत्तस्तत्र तलन्यासचतुरस्रो ंडशपञ्चकम् (?) ।
वृत्ताद्यमूर्ध्वतो वृत्तं यकाशोभं समुत्थितम् ॥ " 59.233

Varāhamihiraís Bṛhatsamhitā, ed. and trans. By M. Ramakrishna Bhat, Part I, Delhi 1981, P.541.

"मेरुमन्दर कैलास विमानच्छन्दनन्दना:।
समुद्गपद्मगरूड़नन्दिवर्धनकुञ्जरा:॥
गुहराजो वृषो हंस: सर्वतोभद्रकोघट:।
सिंहोवृत्रश्चतुष्कोण: षोडशाष्टाश्रयस्तथा ॥
इत्येते विंशति: श्रोक्ता: प्रसादा: संज्ञया नया ।
यथोक्तानुक्रमेणैव लक्षणानि वदाम्यत: ॥" 56.17-19

"वृत्तो वृत्ताकृति: कार्या संज्ञातुल्यास्तधायरे ।
सान्धकारास्तु सर्वे ते भूमिकैका: समावृता: ॥
एकाण्डरूपिता: सर्वे पञ्चभिश्चतुरस्रक: ॥ "

V.V. Mirashi, *Inscriptions of the Kalachuri-Chedi Era (Corpus Inscsriptionum Indicarum*, Vol.4) Ootakamund, 1955..

Vishuddhanand Pathak, *Uttar Bharat Ka Rajnitika Itihas* (in Hindi), Lucknow 1973, pp.609-10.

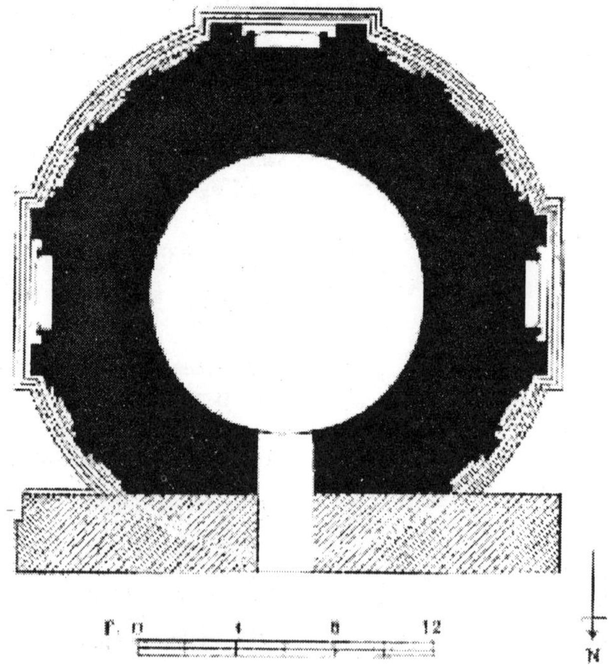

Fig. 1. Maniyār Maṭh, Rājgir

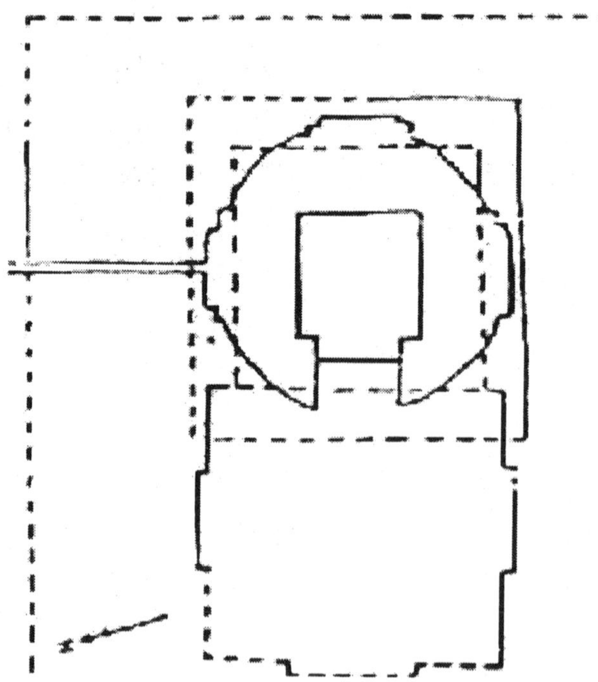

(NOT TO SCALE)

Fig. 2. Plan, Chirenath Temple, Sravasti

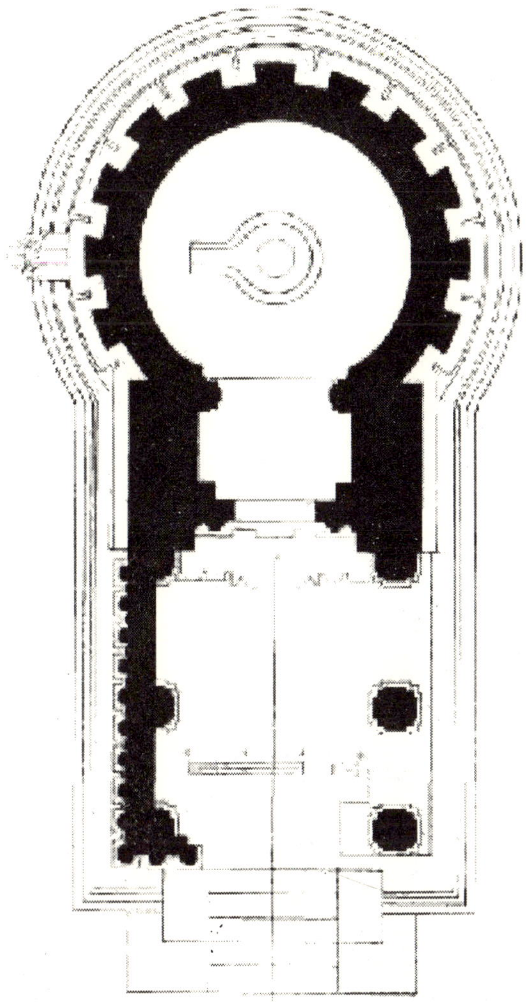

Fig. 3. Plan. Śiva Temple, Chandrehe

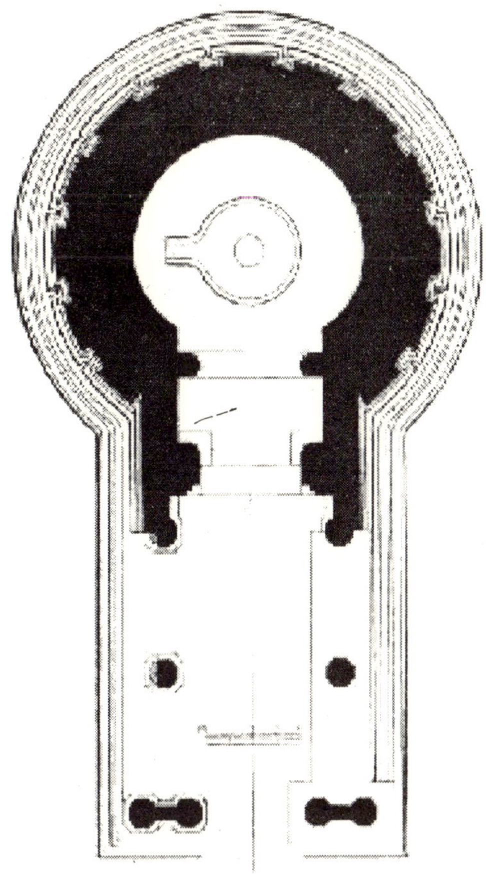

Fig. 4. Plan. Śiva Temple, Masāon

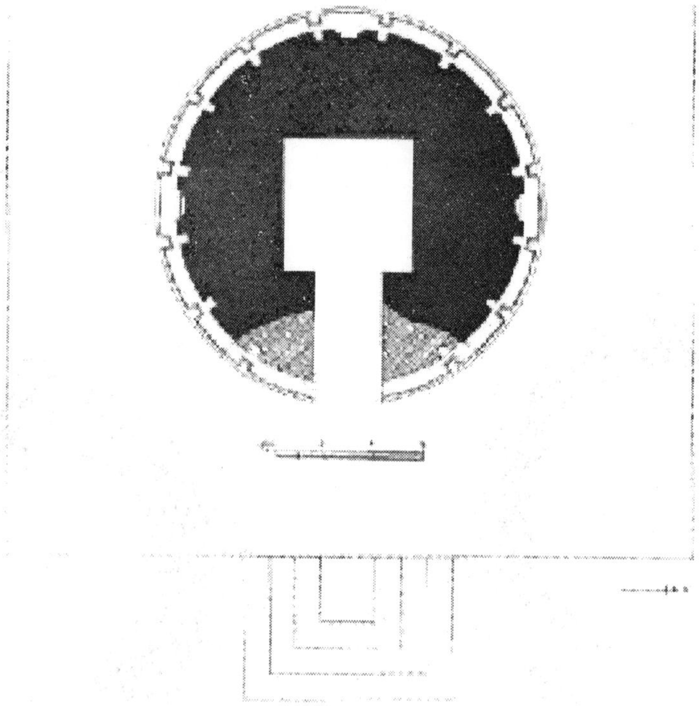

Fig. 5. Plan. Temple 1, Kurārī

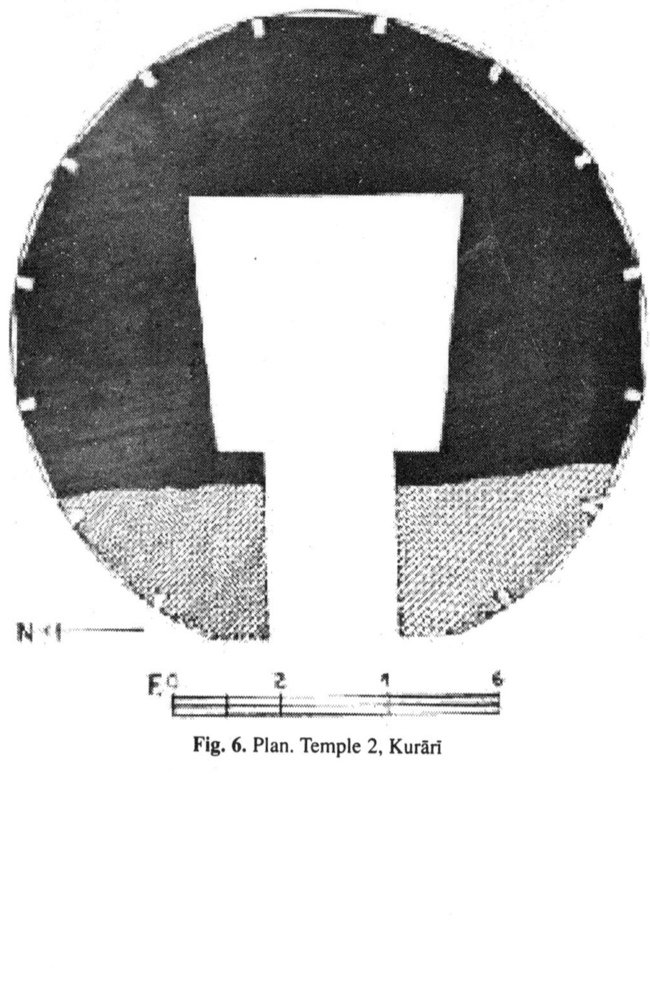

Fig. 6. Plan. Temple 2, Kurārī

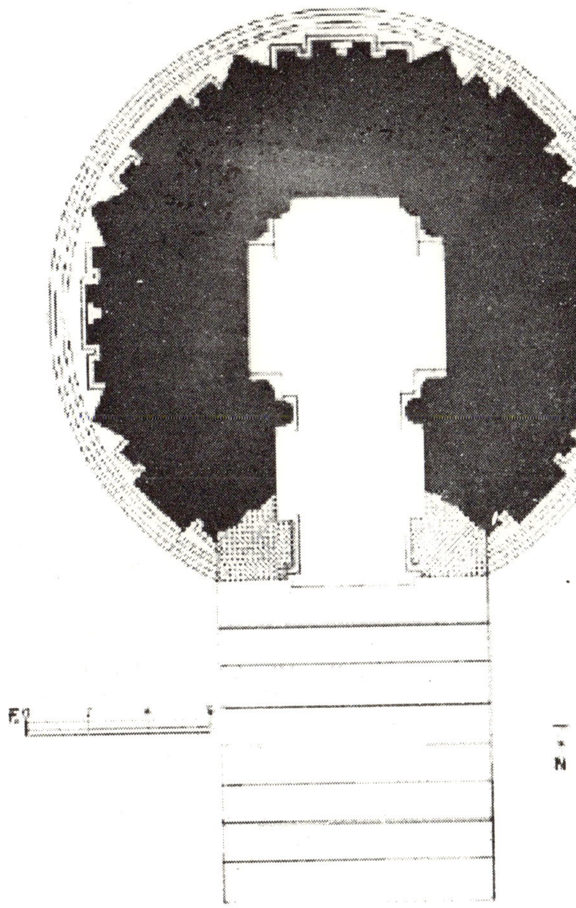

Fig. 7. Plan. Surya Temple, Tinduli

Rāmāyaṇa, Mahābhārata and Archaeology

K.N. DIKSHIT*

The Indian traditions and mythological stories are reflected in the Puranas and the Epics. Pargiter, Raychaudhry and Bhargava provided sequential history on Indian chronology. B.P. Sinha while writing on Indian tradition and archaeology mentioned that "often in sheer despair and confused by the inconsistencies, and mythical accounts in the ancient traditional literature, it was held by some like D.C. Sircar that the entire accounts are imaginary and certainly provide no base for sober history". (Sinha, 1985; 103-109). The historians and archaeologists while dealing with traditions have correlated many chalcolithic and historical cultures with one or other Pauranic dynasties but missed the identity of the authors (*Puratattva* 8; 83). The concern of B.P. Sinha about the impact of archaeology on the epics *viz.* the most popular and living traditions about Rama story and the Rāmāyan and about Krishna and the Mahābhārata was to know whether they are myths or are real. He concluded that 'the Mahābhārata and archaeology have very much concurred. Archaeology and traditions in case of the Rāmāyan, may not play hide and seek for long'. Serious attempts were also made earlier and data was compiled in 1973 by H.D. Sankalia in Rāmāyana: Myth and Reality and in 1976 in Mahābhārata: Myth and Reality by S.P. Gupta and K.S. Ramachandran (eds.).

Similar exercise was also done in the West specially in Lebanon, Palestine and Syria to corroborate the results of excavations with the Biblical cities (Albright, 1966).

B.B. Lal was the first in the Indian sub-continent to view the archaeological data against the background of literature and opined that a large number of sites associated with the Mahābhārata story contain the same ceramic industry, i.e., the Painted Grey Ware in their lower level (Lal, 1954-55, *AI*, 10&11). The excavation at Hastinapura, named after King Hastin of the Pauraṇic dynasty confirmed the stratigraphy of the Painted Grey Ware in the upper Ganga basin. He proposed a time bracket of c.1100-800 B.C. for PGW and associated these settlers with the early stock of Aryan in India.

While this was the picture of Mahābhārata from archaeological angle, B.B. Lal took up in 1975 a National Project called 'Archaeology of the Rāmāyana Sites'. Since 1977-78, this project was jointly directed by B.B. Lal and K.N. Dikshit on behalf of the Indian Institute of Advance Study, Shimla and Archaeological Survey of India respectively. The excavations carried out at places connected with Ṛama's story especially Ayodhya, the capital of Ikshavakus put forward a hypothesis that the Ṛāmāyana tradition is later than Mahābhārata which was against the accepted Indian tradition which placed Rāmāyana to *Tretāyuga* and Mahabharata to *Dwāparyu-*

*Indian Archaeological Society, New Delhi.

ga. In this papar, the earlier stand based on the comparative stratigraphy of the excavated sites associating the early NBPW times with Rāmāyana story has changed due to the recent excavations at Ayodhya by the Archaeological Survey of India, which has pushed back the antiquity of the site on the basis of C 14 dates to pre-NBPW horizon.

The Excavations

Under the Rāmāyana project, excavations were jointly directed at Ayodhya the capital of Rama: Sringaverapura, where Rama crossed the Ganga; Bhardvāja Ashram where he sojourned for a while; Nandigrāma, from where Bharata ruled the kingdom, Chitrakuṭa where Rama stayed for a pretty long period, and Pariar where Lakshmaṇa left Sita at the behest of his elder brother Rama (Lal & Dikshit, 1983).

Ayodhya

Situated on the right bank of the Saryu river in Faizabad District of Uttar Pradesh, the ancient mound of Ayodhya covers about a square kilometer of area. Over here excavations were carried out in 1975, 1976-77 and 1979-80, altogether at fourteen different spots (See *IAR*). These are located variously, along the river on the western and northern peripheries, in the heart of the settlement, as well as on the eastern and southern sides, and include many of the traditional spots, such as the Janma-Bhūmi area, Hanumāṇa-Garhī, Sīta-kī-Rasoī, Nala-Tīlā, Kauśilyā-Ghāta, etc. The Banaras Hindu University also did some work nearly a decade ago at this site.

The excavations revealed in the lowest levels the Northern Black Polished Ware period, a thin-sectioned pottery, very well fired, highly shining and having a variety of shades, viz. coal-black, steel-grey, indigo, golden, etc. There are some shapes which begin in the early phase but die out later. The same is the case with the associated red ware which shows changes from phase to phase.

Iron, which had already come into use in the Painted Grey Ware period, continued with greater vigour in the Northern Black Polished Ware period. A variety of agricultural tools were also found. This, in due course, resulted in agricultural surplus and an all-round rise in the economy. Thus trade and commerce began to flourish, as indicated by the coming into being of a system of weights-cylindrical pieces of various sizes, made of jasper, agate, chalcedony, etc. A little later in the same NBPW Period, coins, variously of silver and copper, either punched or cast, began to be used, showing very clearly another step forward towards urbanization. Within this very period there is also the evidence of town-planning, with houses of kiln-burnt bricks, though this feature does not belong to the early phase.

Terracotta art as well as jewellery showed an evolution and greater variety. The archaic-looking grey figurines of the Painted Grey Ware Period got partially modified and were given a shining slip, similar to that of the Northern Black Polished Ware. The beads and pendants included those of crystal, excellently faceted, and of other semi-precious stones, often produced to imitate birds and animals.

After the Northern Black Polished Ware Period towards the end of the third century B.C., the occupation at Ayodhya continued through the Śuṅga, Kushāna and Gupta periods to the medieval times. In fact, the site is under occupation even today, but with these periods we are not concerned at the moment (see Pl. 1).

Nandīgrāma

Right near the tank known as Bharata Kund, about 10-12 km. south of Ayodhyā, there is no ancient mound. However, a bit away, on the south of the Tamasa, there does exist a mound. It has no specific name and is just called 'Rahet' a word which is locally said to mean 'a habitation'. However, it is this mound that is generally thought to represent the ancient site of Nandīgrāma. Excavation revealed that the occupation over here too began with the Northern Black Polished Ware and not earlier.

Sriṅgaverapura

At Sriṅgaverapura, excavated since 1976-77, two periods of occupation, preceding the NBPW Period, were encountered. From bottom upwards, these are distinguished respectively by the Ochre Colour Ware, and the Black-slipped Ware. While the former occupation commenced in the eleventh century B.C., the latter began, after a break, only around the middle of the tenth century

B.C., as revealed by the thermoluminescence and carbon-14 dates. However, between the black-slipped ware and the NBPW periods there is no break and the latter would appear to have commenced around 700 B.C. a consistent occupation, the NBPW period came to an end some time in the third century B.C., thereafter there is evidence successively of the Śuṅga, Kushāṇa, Gupta, Rajput and medieval periods. Though not quite relevant in the context of the present discussion, a passing reference may be made to the discovery of a 2200 m long tank of kiln-burnt bricks constructed around the beginning of the Christian era. With its feeding channel, silting chambers, 'horizontal and vertical warpings', and a waste weir, the tank is indeed a unique example of hydraulic engineering in ancient days, of which India can rightly be proud (Lal & Dikshit, 1978).

Chitrakūṭa

Though a systematic excavation yet remains to be carried out at Chitrakūṭa, it may be mentioned that surface-exploration including trial trenching of the ancient habitation over which the old township of Chitrakūṭa is situated has revealed the presence of the NBP Ware, black-slipped ware and associated red ware in exposures in between the late medieval temples viz. Yajnavadi temple standing on the left bank of the Mandakini river at Ramaghāṭa. The clear pre-NBPW horizon could not be encountered (IAR, 1980-81, 70).

Bharadvāja Āshram

At Bharadvāja Āshram there was no Ochre Colour Ware occupation. However, in a matrix of sandy alluvium black-slipped Ware was found inter-mixed with the Northern Black Polished Ware, indicating that the site witnessed a late phase of the black-slipped ware together with the beginning of the Northern Black Polished Ware. The only other occupation met with the Bharadvāja Āshram was that of the Gupta Period, assignable to circa fourth-sixth centuries A.D., as evidenced by the typical pottery and terracotta seals and sealings (IAR, 1982-83, 90).

Pariār

The word Pariar is a distorted form of Parihār and Sītā was abandoned here by Lakshmaṇa at the instruction of Rāma. Five trenches were sunk and one of them was inside the courtyard of a house (IAR 78-79). The excavation revealed a mixed deposit of Ochre Coloured Ware, Black slipped ware, black burnished ware and black-and-red ware in the lowest levels, whereas only black-and-red ware and black slipped ware continued in next period. Period III was represented by the PGW and next Period IV with NBPW. It was finally capped by Suṅga-Kushāna deposit. As the lowest level has a sandy deposit, it appears that the wares of Period II having a deposit of 0.40 m. got mixed up from some nearby region. Amongst the antiquities mention may be made of terracotta beads and discs, bone points, copper and stone objects (Lal & Dikshit, 1979; 26-31).

Recent Excavations at Ayodhyā

The Archaeological Survey of India further excavated Ram Janmabhumi area under Hari Manjhi and B.R. Mani, though in different circumstances in 2002-2003. Eighty-two trenches were laid out adjoining to the earlier excavations carried out by B.B. Lal, K.V. Soundarajan and K.N. Dikshit from 1975 to 1980 (*IAR* 1975-76 to 1979-80 and see Pl. 1. These new trenches were also meant to verify the anomalies noticed in Ground Penetrating Radar Survey. The cultural sequence started from NBPW-Suṅga-Kushāṇa-Gupta-Post Gupta (Rajput)-Medieval-Sultanate level-Medieval-Mughal-late and Post-Mughal level. But 14C dates supplied by Birbal Sahani Institute of Palaeobotany, Lucknow gave a new interpretation to the chronology of lowest levels. (Hari Manjhi and B.R. Mani, 2003, Appendix I).

As revealed in earlier excavations the Northern Black Polished Ware was again noticed in the lowest levels alongwith grey ware, black slipped ware and associated red ware but instead of placing it between c.600-300 B.C., the present excavators on the basis of material evidence and Radiocarbon dates placed the beginning to c.1000 B.C. There was no structural activities in this level except pieces of burnt clay with reed impressions. Other minor objects to mention a few included broken weights, ear-studs, discs, broken animal figurine, iron knife, glass beads, bone points and a round signet with legend in Aśokan Brāhmī.

To mention in the words of the excavators "the site (Trench AYD-1 (G7) has also proved to be significant for taking back its antiquarian remains for the first time to the c.1300 B.C. (1250±130B.C.)". There are more C-14 dates corroborating the evidence of early dating from this phase viz. 910 ± 90 B.C, 880 ± 100 B.C. and successive levels of the same period also confirm the continuity (710 ± 90 B.C. 530 ± 70 B.C. and 320 ± 80B.C.). The discovery of these dates belied the earlier excavators of the site.

C-14 Carbon Dates, Supplied by BSIP, Lucknow

Sample No./BS No. Depth (m)	Age of the sample based on the Value of half life = 5570-30 yrs	Calibrated age range (yrs)
No.7 AYD-1 2152 G-7 (16), 9.15	2830 ± 100 BP (880 BC)	CAL BC 1190-840
No.8, AYD-1 2153 G-7 (19), 11.0	2860 ± 100 BP (910 BC)	CAL BC 1210-900
No.9, AYD-1 2154 G-7 (20), 11.53	3200 ± 130 BP (1250 BC)	CAL BC 1680-1320

Discussion

As the lowest levels were encountered only in a restricted area and it was not possible for the excavators to extend the digging in adjoining areas without removing the debris of the upper levels, the material evidence itself speaks that the lowest levels which were devoid of any structural activities belong to pre-NBP levels as is the case with the other excavated sites located in adjoining areas, viz. Sriṅgaverapura, Hulās Kherā, Sohgaurā, Narhan, Rajghaṭ, etc.

The excavations carried out at Lahurādeva also revealed early dates of pre-NBP horizon (Tiwari and Srivastava, *Puratattva*, 32). The acceptable time bracket of NBPW period has always been bracketed between c.600-300 B.C. since it was proposed at Hastinapur where it was separated for the first time from PGW, although PGW continued in western U.P. in the early levels of NBPW. The PGW users lived in huts and mud houses. In eastern U.P. and Bihar, the epicentre of NBPW, the wares of pre-NBPW period i.e. black slipped, grey ware, black-and-red ware and burnished grey ware, also continued in the early levels of NBPW. In both the pre-NBPW horizons, except the use of iron no burnt brick, coins, fortification, epigraphs, etc. were noticed and this material situation continued in the early levels of NBPW. It was only from mid NBPW levels say at the beginning of 4th century B.C., coins, fortification, etc. started appearing. It was infact this phase of NBPW which witnessed the evolved City States in Gangetic doab and in other adjoining regions.

Literary Tradition

When the early NBP was declared as the common denominator to all the Rāmayaṇa sites and was declared as the time of Rama's story, it was found contrary to all most all literary traditions. B.P. Sinha called 'it a big jolt to cherished belief' that the Rāmayaṇa story is later than that of the Mahābhārata. He pointed out that B.B. Lal in his reconstruction of Mahābhārata chronology leading to identification of PGW culture with the Mahābhārata times, relies on the Pauranic genealogical accounts from Udyana to Parikshit for even the flood of Hastinapur, he rejects completely the pre-Parikshit royal dynasties in the Purāṇas because it seems counter to his proposed thesis. His identification of Siradhvaja of Janaka with Janaka contemporary of Yājñavalkya is also not unchallenged. There have been many Janakas and more than one Yajnavalkya (Sinha, 1985, 106-107). To make the conclusion more acceptable, Sinha pleaded for more extensive excavation and exploration of the sites related with Ramayana. Renewed excavations at Ayodhya in 2003 confirmed his view.

Emergent Picture

The new archaeological evidence from Ayodhyā noticed in 2003 and the comparative stratigraphy of the excavated sites which revealed pre-NBPW deposit has strengthened the Hindu myths and belief that the story of Rāma and Ayodhyā is earlier than the story of Krishna and Mahābhārata and Hastinapur. The earlier analysis of correlating them with early Northern Black Polished Ware now stand altered and goes more in favour of placing the Ramayan episode to pre-NBPW horizon.

BIBLIOGRAPHY

Albright, W.F. 1966. *Archaeology and Historical Analogy and Early Biblical Tradition*, USA.

Gupta, S.P. and K.S. Ramachandran (Ed.) 1976. *Mahabharata: Myth and Reality*, Delhi.

Indian Archaeology-A Review. Published by Archaeological Survey of India.

Lal, B.B. 1954-55, Excavations at Hastinapur and other Explorations in the Upper Ganga and Sutlej Basin, *Ancient India*, 10-11, New Delhi.

Lal, B.B. and K.N. Dikshit, 1978. Sringaverapura: A Key-site for the Proto history and Early History of the Central Ganga Valley, *Puratattva* 10, 1-7.

———, 1979. Pariar—An Eastern Outpost of the Painted Grey Ware Culture, *Puratattva* 11, 26-31.

———, 1983. The *Ramayana and Archaeology*, Shri Rama in Indian Culture, (Ed. T.P. Verma) Ayodhya.

Manjhi, Hari and B.R. Mani, 2003. Ayodhya: 2002-2003. *Excavation at the "Disputed Site"*, Archaeological Survey of India, New Delhi (Photostat Copy).

Sankalia, H.D. 1973. *Ramayana: Myth and Reality*, Delhi.

Sinha, B.P., 1985. *Indian Tradition and Archaeology*, Archaeological Perspectives of India Since Independence, Delhi, 103-109.

Tiwari, Rakesh, *et al.* 2002. Excavation at Lahuradeva, District Sant Nagar, U.P., *Puratattva* 32, 54-62.

NOTES AND NEWS

Newly Discovered Rock Paintings from Nagargota in Maharashtra

Nagargota (20° 35' E., 79° 33' N.) in district Chandrapur, Maharashtra lies slightly over 102 km from Nagpur approachable via Nagpur-Nagbhir road leading to Kanpa. There is a regular bus service connecting this place besides rail link upto Kanpa, on the Nagpur-Nagbhir section. Towards west of Kanpa there is one village Shankarpur about 8 km on Kanpa-Chmur road. From Shankarpur towards 6 km from south there is a village named Dongargaon. Nagargota is 1.2 km from Dongargaon.

The rich and varied topography of the district is almost unparalleled anywhere else in the state. The geological variety of the rock formation played a very important role to attract the human settlement. This region is outside the Deccan trap area and falls geologically in the Gondwana formations. The rock paintings of Nagargota lies in Wughai hill locally known as Sitamai dongar. Principally these hillocks are one of rudaceous ferruginous sand stone, mineralogically these sandstones are composed mainly of quartz and some mica flakes. Stratigraphically this sand stone belongs to upper Permian to lower Triassic.

Papamiya Tekadi, which is 5km north-east of the Chandrapur town having early paleolithic tools i.e. bifacial choppers, handaxes and cleavers. In the same section from the upmost gravel, overlying a thick deposit of silt, were picked up blades, scrapers, burins and awls which are related to blade and burin industry. A similar succession of industries was noticed at Jhari Mangral on the Bhadga Nala in the Wainganga basin.

Survey of Indian Paintings

Rock paintings in India were first recorded by the pioneering discoveries made in 1867 by Archibald Carllyle in Mirzapur District, Uttar Pradesh. The first rock engravings of South India were brought to light by F. Fawcett and Kupgallu in 1892. Then onwards various scholars tried to study on the painted rock shelters in systematic approach.

Since then, more than 5000 painted rock-shelters have been reported from different parts of the Indian subcontinent but majority of them are in central region. V.S. Wakankar had mentioned about the rock-shelters in Vidarbha region of Maharashtra, but he did not speak on the rock shelter paintings.

Surprisingly no painted rock shelter was found in Maharashtra. Outside Maharashtra there are many painted rock-shelters i.e. the area of Nimar and Chindwara in Madhya Pradesh lying in the north of Vidarbha region, in the east Gupansar area in Chhatisgarh and Betamchela, Adoni, Balchaker, Hassan Patri area in the South in Andhra Pradesh. All painted rock shelters are far away from the Nagargota site. Considering this distance, the importance of Nagargota painted rock shelter is peculiar one. There is no mention of other painted rock shelter till date in Maharashtra.

Structure and Position of Painted Rock Shelters

The Nagargota painted rock shelters were discovered by the authors in 1998. These are situated between south and north region. The hillock, where the painted rock shelters are situated, is about 135 m above the ground level. There are four shelters running from south-west to north-east. The entire hill is covered with dense horny bushes, shrubs and grass. It is a very difficult approach to the rock shelters. Big sand stone boulders and deep grooves can be seen easily.

On the top of four shelters, there is a huge terrace at the height of about 15 m. measuring 50x10m. The roof of this terrace has collapsed. The terrace appear like a ship-dake. The north, south and west sides are open. The height of eastern wall is 20 m and forms cliff side and provides space for paintings. The cliff side panel height is about 7 m. Beneath this panel one small cell was observed, which is man made (measuring 1.65 m x 1.65 m x 1.65 m), having the architectural features of the Satvahana period. The rock shelters of Nagargota are situated on the watershed lines. The line of water divide is about 1/2 kilometres towards west.

The rock shelters at Nagargota reveal paintings on the roof, exterior side and clif side. The total number of paintings are 35. The animal figures are in 22 number, while human figures are 13. These are executed mostly in dark red and purple red colour. The paintings typically depict barasingha and deer. Human figures are not shown carrying any metal weapons. Most of the animal paintings depict cattle-both wild and domesticated ones.

The rock paintings can be categorised into two sequence. The earliest paintings are relatively larger and executed in dark red. In the second stage of paintings, the human figures, domesticated animals and horse are

The details of the painting are given below

Sr. No.	Subject	Colour
1)	Human figure	Dark red
2)	Row of four deer	Dark red
3)	Grazing deer	Dark red
4)	Tiger	Dark red
5)	Running deer	Dark red
6)	Two big barahsingha	Dark red
7)	Big deer and below small deer	Faint red
8)	Big animal figure superimposed by barasingha	Dark red
9)	Barasingha	Dark red, Outline yellowish wite colour
10)	Big animal below head of barasingha	Dark red
11)	Deer with small horses	Dard red
12)	Human figure performing dance	Dark red
13)	Cattle	Dark red
14)	Animal figure	Dark red
15)	Four animal figures and eight tiny figures (human figures joining hand in hand)	Dark blackish red
16)	Horse rider	Bright red colour

Remaining paintings are very disturbed and Subjects cannot be identified.

shown in yellowish white colour and bright red colour. In this stage the size of the paintings are different. Animals figures having maximum height is 30 cm and length 40 cm and minimum height is 7 cm and length 4 cm. Some animal figures are very small in size. Out of thirteen, seven human figures depicted in the rock shelter are tiny in size. Four human figure shows average size of 18 cm. In height. The human figures are in dark red black colour.

Chronology

The first group of paintings of Nagargota appear to belong to Mesolithic period (C. 10000-2500 years). The most significant evidence in the present context is however, that of the recovery of what have been termed as 'Microliths'. They have been reported during our explorations. The microliths have been classified into two main categories i.e. geometric design and non-geometric design. Mostly blades and points have been registered. These type of microliths were also recovered from the rock-shelters in Madhya Pradesh. The style, technique and colour depicted in the paintings are similar to Bhimbetka and Pachmarhi paintings.

The second stage of paintings are associated with megalithic culture. Near the rock shelters, on the two vertical surfaces of the huge boulders, quite interestings paintings were observed. In the crevices were painted a long row of human figures. There is another painting of a man riding the horse and one big circle is shown in front of the horse.

Around the vicinity of Nagargota are dolmens at Hirapur, stone circles at jodhali, megalithic habitational site at Kahali Ramtek, stone circles at Bondegaon, Megalithic Black- and red ware from Mayar, stone circle of Mayar and 13 menhirs at Nagbhir. Dolmens at Hirapur are very near to Nagargota. Iron Age Megaliths such as dolmen cist, stone circle and menhir as well as habitational sites are datable to C. 1800-200 B.C. The excavations of megaliths at Takalghat, Mahurjhari and Naikund in Vidarbha have revealed horse bones and horse bits suggesting that the megalithic builders were horse-riders. The depiction of the horse riding indicates the relation of megalithic culture. Rock paintings at Hire Benkal (Karnataka) show a large number of horse-riders carrying swords, bows and arrows used in hunting. These paintings, in view of their style, kind of figures painted belong to Neolithic-megalithic overlapping stage i.e. C. 700-500 B.C.

The Nagargota rock paintings belong to mesolithic and megalithic period. In Vidarbha region very few evidences of neolithic period have been recorded at Naikund and Nagalwadi excavations. The evidence of horse in the painting indicates the relation to the megalithic culture. At present, we put the Nagargota rock paintings in a time bracket that ranges, between 15000 B.C. and 800 B.C.

Conclusion

The rock-paintings flourishing exclusively in the prehistoric period continued to develop in the megalithic period. The subject matter applied by the Prehistoric man was the faunal world. The technique adopted was both in silhouette and outline. They were not professionals. For more detail study of paintings, excavation work should be done as early as possible.

BIBLIOGRAPHY

Pande S.K., "Problem of dating the Indian Rock Painting", *Madhya Bharati*, Journal of University of Sagar, 1965-67, Vol. 16, pp. 129-33.

Sundra, A, "Select Rock-Painting of Karnataka", *Rock Art of India*, Bhopal, 1984, p. 145.

Wakankar, V. S. "Bhimbetka and Dating of Indian Rock-paintings" *Rock Art of India*, Bhopal, 1984, pp. 44-56.

Lecturer, Smt. K.L. College, Amravati University, Amravati — **G.K. Mane**
Research Scholar — **Ganesh V. Halkare**
Research Scholar — **Purushotam Dahedar**

Lapis lazuli in Protohistoric and Historic Context

Introduction

According to Gordon Childe, 'Urban revolution is the end product of a slow accumulation of expanding food surpluses and increasingly specialized technical know-how' (Childe, 1979). In other words, the social surplus was useful for the exchange purposes, which gave way to long distance trade. This brought about demand for highly prized raw materials. Technological development favours an increase in work productivity and a corresponding in the demand for imported goods (Piperno, 1973).

Lapis lazuli was one of the luxurious commodities of demand for personal adornment, house decoration and book illumination in India from the earliest times. The name Lapis lazuli is said to be derived from 'Lazward' a Persian word meaning blue. Lazrite is an absolute synonym of azurite and hence the mineral is named after its colour and its resemblance to azurite. Lazurite is a rare mineral occurring usually in crystalline limestone as a product of contact metamorphism. It is a mineral of somewhat complex composition, containing silica, alumina, sodalime, iron, sulphuric acid, sulphur and chlorine (Watt, 1972). Features are characterized by its blue colour and the presence of associated pyrite. It is soluble in hydrochloric acid with slight evolution of hydrogen sulphide gas (Dana, 1997). The thick whitish parts in lapis lazuli account for the presence of calcite. The refractive index is about 1:50 on the refractive scale. The density of the common type is between 2.7 and 2.9 or higher if much iron pyrite is present. The hardness is five and a half on Moh's scale (Klein and Hurlburt, 1977).

Sources

Many scholars after carrying out elaborate researches on its sources came to the same conclusion. The oldest lapis lazuli objects so far reported in south western Asia comes from the site of Zaghe in the rgion of Qazrin in Iran dated to 4000 B.C. (Tosi and Vidale, 1990). The presence of earliest prehistoric mines of lapis lazuli, copper, turquoise and lead in Chagai district had been noted by M. U. Hasan in his research work (Hasan, 1986:5). According to Jarrige, the major sources could be isolated to very limited areas in the Chagai Hills of Southern Baluchistan and in the area of Badakshan, North Afghanistan (Jarrige, 1981). The Lapis Lazuli mines are located at B.B.Dick near Afghanistan-Pakistan border and the location of Shortugi, a Harrapan settlement close to the lapis mines of Badakshan is decidedly significant from the point of view of lapis trade (Lahiri, 1992). Lapis occurs in significant quantities in the Kerannas Munjas district of Badakshan (Asthana, 1982). Pliny dated to early centuries of the Christian era states that lapis lazuli was a costly imported item of India (Rockhem 1961). Thus lapis lazuli was coming from very limited sources in Badakshan, Afghanistan, Siberia and Lake Baikal.

The presence of lapis lazuli in the Nagpahar hills, 4.8 m to the west of Ajmer has been mentioned by R.H. Irvine (cited in Roy 1939:169), although this report was never subsequently confirmed (Lahiri, 1992). This could be possibly the sodalite, which resembles lapis to a great extent.

Lapis lazuli from Protohistoric and Historic sites

Protohistoric Period

In the Indian contest, the earliest data of lapis lazuli beads are found from the early protohistoric sites. At

Mehrgarh (III), a large number of flakes, unfinished beads and fragments of lapis lazuli and other semi precious stones along with flint drills and macro-drills are seen on the surface of M.R. 2 (Jarrige, 1981). Here the most common type found was the cylindrical beads, a few biconical beads, pendants of cross shape, heart shaped, W shape and drops were discovered from graves. Nal (southern Baluchistan), Kulli, Mehi, Shahi Tump, Q13, Saraikhola II, Jalilpur II, Amri I and Padni Wahi also yielded lapis objects. Nal yielded about 70 beads (Hargeaves, 1929). The types included cylindrical (main type) and discoid and flat ones. According to Hermman, the discoid beads were made out of cylindrical beads (Hermman, 1986). At Shahi Tump, 19 small beads were excavated (Sankalia, 1974). These sites can be corroborated to middle of the 4 millennium B.C. and earlier than 2nd millennium B.C.

Harappan sites of Saria Khola (near Rawalpindi), Gumla, Jalilpur (near Multan), Harappa, Amri, Pandi Wahi, Jhukar, Karchat, Mohenjo-daro, Chanhu-daro, Nagawada, Dholavira, Motipipli and Bagasara, reveal the occurrence of lapis lazuli objects/beads. In the period II of Saraikhola, six lapis beads were reported but without any detail (Pakistan Archaeology, 1970). Raw stones and beads occurs in Jalilpur (Mughal 1974). Truncated cone-shape bead (one) comes from Amri (Cassal 1961), Pandi Wahi (Majumdar, 1934) and Jhukar; Quetta valley (Q13) was found a barrel-shaped bead (Fairsrvis, 1956). Mackay has reported six barrel-shaped beads, one long thin glazed bead and a round-topped cone probably a gamesman from Mohenjodaro (Mackay, 1943). At Harappa, three elliptical barrel beads, one conical pendent and a flower pendent were reported. The flower pendent was excavated from Cemetery H (Vats, 1940). Three beads of cylindrical and one bicone had been unearthed from Lothal (Rao, 1973). Nagwada yielded fourteen lapis beads cylindrical shape. Kalibangan report (Chakravarti, 1978) speaks of lapis beads but details are missing. Motipipli and Bagasara (Exavation being carried on by the Department of Archaeology, M. S. University of Baroda) has so far yielded a few lapis beads having cylindrical shape.

The late Harappan sites such as Dadheri, Dher Majra, Mithathal and Zekhada (Gujarat) has yielded Lapis beads. More than eight beads of lapis have been reported from three of Chacolithic culture, Ahar (2500 B.C.), yielded one cylindrical bead (Sankalia, Deo and Ansari, 1969). Navdatoli yielded several cylindrical, barrel and disc beads (Sankalia, 1958). Somnath (Mehta, 1976) and Nevasa (Sankalia, 1960) reported one bead each of a very poor quality.

Historic Period

In the early Historic sites the number of lapis objects significantly increases. A solitary long square rectangular bead has been reported from Sardarghar in Bikaner district in the PGW level (Niharika, 1993). In the northwestern region, Shai Khan Dheri and Taxila yielded number of lapis objects. From Shai Khan Dheri, objects like one corner less cube, one bird shaped bead, one broken finger ring in the shape of a recumbent lion and one terminal oblate disc bead, occurs in the 1st - 2nd centuries of the Christian era (Chakravarti, 1978). Nineteen lapis objects were found in the Bhir mound of Taxila dated to 6th -2nd centuries, B.C. The main bead types were square cylinder, square bicones, hexagonal barrels and drop pendants (Marshall, 1951). Five sites of NBPW culture like Charsada in district Peshwar, yielded three beads, Nevasa (Sanklia, 1960) and Rajghat (Narain and Singh, 1976-78) yielded two beads each, Sravasti (Sinha, 1967) one and Taxila reported lapis beads. These beads have represented more than seven shapes and most of them were cylindrical. In Sirkap dated 1st century B.C., thirty objects of lapis occur. According to Beck the main types of beads were barrel, convex cones, vase bead, lion shaped and beetle shaped beads. Other objects were small spheres, cubes and a small *triratna* (Beck, 1941). A relic casket from the Stupa A-II of Jaulian was decorated and the inner casket contained some lapis paste. In Period V of Nevasa, dated 1st century B.C. to 3rd century A.D., only one barrel-shaped bead was found (Sankalia, 1960) Piklihal, in Karnataka, also yielded five lapis beads (Allchin, 1960) Maski yielded six lapis beads from its Megalithic levels dated to 200 B.C. to A.D. 100 and seven from early Historic levels (Thapar, 1957 AI No. 13 1957). A very important Megalithic site, Raigir dated to 2nd century A.D., yielded seventy-three beads and other lapis fragments and most common shapes were cylindrical (Beck, 1930). Nagara period III, in Gujarat, has yielded ten beads of cylindrical, circular and spheroid shape dated to early centuries of Christian era (Mehta, 1968). The Satavahana levels of Brahmapuri, (Maharashtra), dated 2nd century A.D. yielded six lapis beads mostly cylindrical and barrel-shaped and a seated human pendant. The quality of lapis is generally poor in this site (Sankalia and Dikshit, 1952). Kaundanyapur (Dikshit, 1968), Bhokardan (Deo, 1974), Nasik (Sankalia and Deo, 1955) and Adam also yielded three, two and two lapis beads of cylindrical, barrel and tablet shaped respectively. Two sites in the Gangetic plains like Prahladpur (Narain and Roy, 1968) and Pandu Rajar Dhibi have also yielded lapis beads and fragmentary pieces (Dasgupta, 1964).

Manufacturing Technology

The study carried out by Tosi and Vidale in 1968 on the technological features of a chalcolithic assemblage of industrial debris from the sites of Mehrgarh. It is one of the earliest sites with evidence of lapis processing so far identified in South Asia dated 4 millennium B.C. 470 fragments of lapis lazuli including flakes form the assemblage, semi finished defective elements and some unfinished beads. The manufacturing here was carried from a preliminary squared blocklet. They were then shaped by chipping of corners until they were made into elliptical faceted contour. The next stage was grinding, whose contour usually showed from 6 to 8 sides and the surface was convergent. The last stage was carried out by chert drills or blade for bipolar perfroation. Here the debitage of lapis lazuli while manufacturing beads were higher than of the finished products. The study suggested that the stones were brought in a semi-processed state (Tosi and Vidale, 1990).

Excavation at Tepe Hissar (1931-32) by E. Schmidt for the University Museum and by Soviet Academy of Sciences and excavation at Shahr-i-Sokta by the Institute ltalino permils Medio ed. Estremove Oriente revealed the existence of technologically advanced towns and villages on the Western slopes of Afganistan plateau. The strata corresponding to a 3000-2000 B.C. in the large settlements at these two sites yielded large quantity of chips rejects and finished objects of lapis lazuli as well as implements made of flint and jasper. These excavations revealed the whole process of lapis lazuli working and of the stone implements assigned to the individual phases of the process. Large number of lapis Lazuli rejects revealed the initial process when examined under microscope (Tosi and Piperno, 1973). To separate lapis from its limestone cortex (calcite), the block was first polished and incision of 1mm was made with the help of flint microblade. Separation was carried out by striking the block at the point of incision at an angle probably using the indirect striker method. To carry out this process the blocks were made softer probably by heating since at Sharh-i-sokta, signs of cracking and darker colour of the surface of several blocks has been unearthed. Thus a rough shape of desired bead was obtained. Drilling was the next stage which was a delicate process as the rate of debitage is much is much more high. Polishing was the last phase in the manufacturing process. From these sites, there is no direct evidence of polishing, as there is lack of any polishing implements. In some cases polishing proceeded drilling and drilling occurred before smoothening. Flotation of all earth from these sites revealed hundreds of tiny microliths borers for drilling, semi finished, broken and finished beads. The borers shower traces of wear and patches of lapis lazuli powder adhering when microscopic analysis of the borers were carried out (Tosi and Piperno, 1973).

Beads at Tepe Hissar were not made by flaking technique but mainly by burin blows. At Hissar the processing was scattered all over the site probably having several workshops each of a few artisans, whereas, at Shahr-i-Skta there was a single large production center and the presence of specialized artisans depending on centralized authority controlling the external and internal demand (Tosi, 1969).

Although the amount of lapis lazuli used during the Harappan those may be seen less found than that of Mohenjodaro or even Egypt, this material has been found in most of the excavated site/s and some process of manufacturing was definitely being conducted at Mohenjodaro (Mackey, 1938), Harrapa (Vats, 1940), Chanhu Daro (Mackey, 1943). In the early historic times, the sites like Taxila, Nevasa, Rajgir, and etc. has yielded lot many fragmentary pieces, unfinished and few finished beads. Thus a study of the manufacturing process need to be carried out in the early Historic times so as to know the technique of different periods.

General Observations

The sophisticated and elaborate complex shapes of ornaments from different sites found in different period shows that this material was the ultra societal-communication systems assuming probably very specific meaning in funerary rituals (Tosi and Vidale, 1976). The limited industrial evidence available defines a simple technique of reduction, a well-defined technological identity and the debitage shows a low degree of morphological variability. Being found from limited sources, the commercial transactions were characterized by one of more intermediaries. The exchange value of the commodity was a proof that they were no longer exchanged on a basis of a direct and strictly temporary evolution, but as a function of usefulness of the exchange ıtself. The merchants thus became a full time worker in lithic industry who in turn might stimulate new production and manufacturing activities in his community as a function of exchange of goods most of which might have in transit. Due to the increase of demand over supply, there was a rise of cost, speed of production, speed of transport, rise of technology and production. There was the elimination of worthless material to reduce deadweight and allowed the semi-precious product to be sold in the other sites at a higher rate. Thus if the cost is to be calculated, it would be the total of cost of extraction, the manufacturing cost, the middlemen's commission, transport, processing, taxes and profits.

While concluding this paper many queries arises. Firstly the quantities of debitage were more than that of the finished products from the manufacturing sites of different times. Secondly typology of the objects remained almost the same over the different periods. This brings about the question whether the manufacturing technique remained the same in early historic period and later times also or whether by manufacturing the beads the waste product was more than the beads? Thirdly there was an increase in the supply in early historic period; Is this because of the use of sodalite, which is similar in appearance and was abundantly used in the Indian sites? Thus a detailed study of the manufacturing process, microscopic analysis and ethno archaeological studies of lapis objects need to be carried out to answer some of the question raised here.

BIBLIOGRAPHY

Allchin, F.R., 1960, *Piklihal Excavations*, Hydrabad.

Asthana, S., 1982, *Harrapan trade in Metals and Minerals, A Regional Approach: Harappan Civilization*, (ed) B. L. Possehl, New Delhi.

Bhan, S., 1975, *Excavation at Mithathal and other explorations in the Sutlej Yamuna Divide*, Kurukshetra.

Beck, H.C., 1930, Notes on Sundry Asiatic Beads, *Man & Environment*, Vol: 30, Poona.

Bungarelli, M.G., 1974, Tepe Hissar: Prelimanary Report on the Surface Survey August 1972, *East & West*, Vol: 24, No 1&2, Rome.

Chakravarti, D. K., 1978, Lapis Lazuli in Early India, *Man & Environment*, Vol: II, (ed) V. N. Misra, Ahmedabad.

Child, B,. 1979, *The Urban Revolution: ancient Cities of the Indus*, (ed.), G. L. Posseshl, New Delhi.

Das Gupta, P.C., 1964 Excavation at Pandu Rajar Dhibi: *A Bulletin of the Directorate of Archaeology*, West Bengal No. 2, Calcutta.

Deo, S.B., 1974, *Excavation at Bhokardan*, Nagpur.

Fairservise, W.A., 1965, *Excavation in the Quetta Valley*, New York.

Hassan, M. U., 1989, *Recent Archaeological Finds in Baluchistan and their Implications*, S.A.A.Congress New Delhi.

Jarrige, J.F., 1981, *Economic and Society in the Early Chalcolithic Bronze Age of Baluchistan: New Perspective from Recent Excavation at Mehrgarh*, (ed.), H. Hartel, Berlin.

Klien, C., & C. S. Hulburt, Jr., 1977, *Manuals of Mineralogy* after J.D. Dana, 20th Edition, New York.

Lahiri, N., 1992, *The Archaeology of Indian Routes upto c. 200 B.C.*, New Delhi.

Mackey, E., 1938, *Further Excavations at Mohenjodaro*, Delhi.

Mackey, E., 1934, *Chanhudaro Excavations*, Delhi.

Majumdar, N.G., 1934, *Explorations in Sind*, Delhi.

Marshall, J., 1951, *Taxila*, Cambridge.

Mehta, R.N. & D. R. Shah, 1968, *Excavations at Nagara*, Baroda.

Moreshwar, G., & M. G. Dikshit, 1968, *Excavations at Kaundintapur*, Bombay.

Mudhal, R., 1974, New Evidences of the Early Harappan Culture from Jalilpur. *Pakistan Archaeology*, Vol. V & XXVII. Rawalpindi.

Nanavti, J. M., R. N. Mehta & S. N. Chaudhary, 1971, *Excavation-1956*, Baroda.

Narain, A.K., & T. N. Roy., 1986, *Excavations at Prahladpur*, Varanasi.

Narain, A.K. & P. Singh., 1976-78, *Excavations at Rajghat*, Part III, Small Finds, Varanasi.

Niharika, 1993, *A Study of Stone Beads in Ancient India*, Delhi.

Olf Prufer, 1952, Nalgarh 1951, *Interim Report on the Excavations carried out at Dher Majra*, Calcutta.

Sankali, H. D. et. al, 1958, *The Excavations at Maheshwar and Navdatoli* 1952-53, Poona.

————, 1960, *From History to Prehistory at Nevasa*, Poona.

————, 1969, *Excavations at Ahar*, Poona.

Sankali, H.D. M.G. Dikshit, 1952, *Excavations at Brahamapuri* (Kolahpur), 1954-56, Poona.

Sinha, K.K., 1967, *Excavations at Sravasti* 1959, Monograph of the Department of Ancient India history, Culture and Archaeology, No. 2, B. H. U., Varanasi.

Stien, A., 1931, *An Archaeological Tour in Gedrosia*, Calcutta.

Tosi, M., 1973, Sharh-I-Sokta & Tepe Hissar Tracts on the Earliest History on the Iranian Plateau, *East & West*, Vol. XXIII, Rome.

—— and M. Vidale, 1990, *Palaeorient* Vol. 16/2., Rome.

—— and M. Piperno., 1973, *Lithic Technology Behind the Ancient Lapiz Trade*, Vol. XVI, Rome.

Vats, M. S.1940, *Excavations at Harappa*, Delhi.

Watt, G., 1980, *A dictionary of the Economic Products of India*, Vol. IV, Calcutta.

Department of Archaeology,
Faculty of Arts,
M.S. University,
Baroda

Shushmita Sen

Unpublished Copper Hoard from Bhandar, District Pali

During the famine relief work being carried out in the month of June, Year 2001, an interesting find was hit upon by one of the labourers named Palaram Maghwal, S/o Phaulal at village Bhandar (73°20' N Latitude and 24°96' E Longitude, tehsil Bali, district Pali, Rajasthan). This place is at a distance of 102 km. towards south from district head-quarters Pali. The find under discussion is the copper hoard from Bhandar village comprising of 41 copper bar celts. These copper bar celts were found in a *nadi* or pond called *Deetheoda Ka Talab* (a pond of *Deethoda*) which is on the south-west of village Bhandar at a distance of 2.5 km. Nearby, to the east of this pond *Deethoda* is a rivulet which flows northwards and empties itself into the Jawai Dam. Topographically, this pond is in a natural depression and its filling capacity extends almost a kilometer in area. It is a government land for cattle grazing and comes under the revenue land records of village Bhandar. The copper bar celts under discussion were found in a square of ten by ten feet, while digging for famine relief programme and was situated on the southernmost end of this pond, close to a huge natural rock. From the mouth of the finder Palaram Meghwal—while digging with a pickaxe at the depth of about one foot, he hit upon something hard and metallic, lying loose and systematically arranged one atop the other, covered with dirt and totalling 42 in number. These celts were collected and distributed amongst the workers. By the time the officials at the police-station at Nana (4 km. south of Bhandar village) took notice of it, the localites did whatever they could, in their capacity i.e. acid wash, rubbing, scratching, breaking, deforming etc. to quench their curiosity and greed for it being something precious. Only 41 copper bar celts could be recovered through investigation by the police officials.

This copper hoard was acquired by the Curator, Bangar Government Museum, Pali on 17-01-2002 where it is currently preserved under the aegis of the State Department of Archaeology and Museums, Rajasthan. It is registered against the serial numbers 203 to 243 in the antiquity register of the museum[1]. The copper hoard from Bhandar is almost, 4,000 years old and is the second largest one of its kind (in terms of copper celts) next only to Ganeshwar where from 58 copper celts were found in 1977 (Agarwal 1979).

The find spot of copper hoard from village Bhandar was visited by the author. Extremely scarce ceramic with few rim and body sherds of red ware, present an unresolved mystery about habitation. It is interesting to note that this area is rich in stones of varied sizes.

Underneath is a detailed statistical tabulation of the 41 copper bar celts from Bhandar village. All the observations are preliminary to the chemical treatment.

As regards dimensions of these copper bar celts, the average length varies between 24 to 26 cm. Only two celts (bar celts no. 26 and no. 30) are 26 cm. long. The average thickness of the celts is approximately one centimeter and the minimum and maximum weight is 1204 and 1554 gms. respectively. The shape of these copper bar

[1]The Copper hoard was acquired by Mr. Syaeed Azam Hussain, Curator, Bangar Government Museum, Pali. I am thankful for the kind help and cooperation extended by him in studying the objects under reference. The author has provided plates of fourty one bar celts, but as most of the bar-celts are of common nature, only one plate consisting of six bar celts has been selected.

			Breadth of Bar Celt (in cm)			Breadth of Bar Celt (in cm)		
S.No.	Plates	Length (In. Cm.)	Bute End	Centre	Working End	Butt End	Centre	Weight (In Gm.)
1.	Pl. 1	25.15	5.8	7	7.4	0.42	1.05	1474
2.	"	25	6	6.8	7.7	0.44	1.04	1282
3.	"	25.15	6.5	7	7.8	0.54	1.11	1380
4.	"	25.1	5.7	6.8	7.5	0.69	1.19	1554
5.	"	24.8	6.2	6.7	7.9	0.58	1.12	1518
6.	"	25.1	5.9	6.9	7.7	0.44	0.84	1354
7.	Pl. 2	25.25	5.9	6.7	7.7	0.43	1.10	1418
8.	"	24.95	5.9	6.7	7.5	0.55	1.10	1412
9.	"	25	6	7.1	7.75	0.57	1.09	1550
10.	"	24.6	6	6.7	7.8	0.45	1.10	1330
11.	"	24.6	5.9	6.8	7.5	0.51	1.09	1318
12.	"	24.8	6	6.8	7.65	0.37	1.01	1250
13.	Pl. 3	24.7	6	7	7.6	0.37	0.94	1220
14.	"	24.7	6	6.8	7.7	0.43	1.04	1304
15.	"	25.05	6	7	7.9	0.53	1.09	1436
16.	"	25	5.5	6.7	7.6	0.45	1.00	1230
17.	"	24.55	6.1	6.7	7.5	0.47	0.92	1204
18.	"	25	6.1	6.9	7.8	0.52	1.07	1254
19.	Pl. 4	24.65	6	6	7	0.52	1.09	1310
20.	"	25.1	5.9	6.8	7.7	0.37	1.16	1342
21.	"	25.1	6.4	6.7	7.4	0.35	1.09	1284
22.	"	24.5	6	6.9	7.6	0.49	1.09	1396
23.	"	24.3	6.3	6.8	7.9	0.43	0.92	1364
24.	"	24.8	6.3	6.7	7.7	0.44	1.05	1368
25.	Pl. 5	25.2	6	6.7	7.7	0.55	0.96	1340
26.	"	26	6.5	6.6	7.7	0.45	0.91	1374
27.	"	25.4	6.2	6.8	8	0.58	1.05	1452
28.	"	25.8	6.	6.7	7.55	0.37	1.14	1506
29.	"	25.3	5.9	6.7	7.7	0.31	1.16	1486
30.	"	26	6.2	6.8	7.9	0.42	1.05	1402
31.	Pl.6	25.4	6.1	7	7.6	0.36	1.02	1282
32.	"	25.4	6.1	6.9	7.7	0.35	0.93	1290
33.	"	25.5	6.2	7	7.9	0.45	1.02	1430
34.	"	25.4	6.5	6.8	8.1	0.53	1.12	1428
35.	"	25.4	6.3	6.7	7.8	0.44	0.87	1334
36.	"	25.2	6	7	7.8	0.31	1.10	1490
37.	Pl.7	25.6	6	7	8	0.47	0.91	1394
38.	"	25.5	6.3	7	7.8	0.38	1.05	1472
39.	"	25.4	5.5	6.6	7.6	0.55	0.105	1324
40.	"	25.3	6.2	6.9	8.1	0.46	1.10	1368
41	"	25.35	6	6.9	7.7	0.47	0.99	1368

celts is long and rectangular with maximum thickness in the centre. The butt part and the working ends are comparatively thin while the section of these celts exhibits somewhat lenticular profile. The two faces of these celts converge into a sharp blade at the working end, as visible in the section.

In general, most of the working edges of celts are slightly convex in plan. These celts were probably cast in closed moulds of clay or stone which, on cooling, were dressed by forging. On physical examination, one finds immense nature activity on these celts in form of patina and heavy incrustation. The surface of the celts is irregular at places with holes which may be due to certain impurities or air bubble. Although, most of the copper bar celts are complete but some are fractionally distorted. A corner of the blade of bar celt no. 15 and no. 20; a corner of the butt part and the working edge of bar celt no. 21; both the corners of the working edge of celt no. 33 and a corner of the working edge of bar celt no. 38 and no. 39 are missing. The blade of copper bar celts no. 13 and no. 23 bears fresh notched marks. There appears to be a round indentation mark near the butt end of bar celt no. 20. Chemical cleansing shall pellucid the picture in this regard.

Quite a good number of copper finds from southern and south-western Rajasthan had been reported in the past. Six copper celts from Padaliya (Agarwal, 1979) in district Chittorgarh; five copper celts, one knife-blade, one sheet, a bangle and two rings from Ahar in distict Udaipur; copper objects from Mavli Dangiyan (Rajasthan Patricka 1995) in district Udaipur; a flat copper celt from Elana (Bulletin of Rajasthan Museum 1984-85) in district Jalore; a copper hoard of 25 copper celts, three bar celts, three swords, eight pieces of copper rings or bangles besides one complete bangle, 820 copper ingots of small, 21 of medium and five ingots of large size from Varman (Dhaka, 2002) in district Sirohi are some paradigms of finished copper objects in this region.

Studies in the past have revealed the richness of Aravalli region with regard to chalcopyrite copper ores deposits. The existence of large amount of copper slag at Rohira in district Sirohi on the border of Rajasthan and Gujrat; the evidence of extensive copper processing at Danta tehsil (Gujarat) lying north-west of Ambamata mines which itself were under use in the Mauryan period; copper mines near Pind at Bhadesar-Bhindar in district Chittorgarh and Rajpur Dariba in district Udaipur, Put before us ample proof for local copper ores processing. In fact, it seems that the inhabitants of this area were acquainted with the skills required for mining and metallurgy based on the locally available raw material. Technological expertise and methodology employed by these people need further probe by scientific laboratory analysis.

The copper bar celts from Bhandar village are quite different from those of Ganeshwar, Padaliya and Varman when compared with the six copper bar celts from village Nandalalpur, tehsil Chaksu, district Jaipur, which have rounded butt ends with splayed-out sides and convex working edges. We find that those from Bhandar are almost like bars with straight sides and slightly convex cutting edge. Also the butt ends are not so roundish. It is worth mentioning that bar celts from Bhandar are devoid of any indentation marks as found on the celts from Ganeshwar and Varman.

The recent discovery of copper hoard from Bhandar adds another chapter to the copper findings in northern India and Rajasthan in particular. Further investigation in this area shall be a welcome gesture for adding more to our existing knowledge.

BIBLIOGRAPHY

Agrawala, R.C., 1978, 'Copper Celts And An Indus Arrow-Head from Kulhade- Ka-Johad, District Sikar, Rajasthan', *Man and Environment*, vol. II, p.123 and plate.

Agrawala, R.C., 1979, 'More Copper Finds From Rajasthan', *Man and Environment*, vol. III, pp. 91-92 and plates.

Rajasthan Patrika- A Daily Hindi Newspaper, 1995, 24th December, Rajasthan Patrika Press, Kesargarh, J.L.N. Marg, Jaipur, p.16

The Researcher- A bulletin of Rajasthans Archaeology and Museums, Jaipur, 1984-85; 'Exploration, year 1977-78, Departmental Activities', vol. XIV-XV, p.195

Dhaka, Ambika, July-Dec. 2002, 'Unpublished Copper Hoard From Varman, District Sirohi', *Nucleus*, vol. II, No.2, pp. 121-128 and plates.

Kuppuram, G., 1989, 'Copper and Bronze Industry', *Ancient Indian Mining, Metallurgy and Metal Industries*, vol. I, Sundeep Prakashan, Delhi, pp. 25-141.

Agrawala, R.C. & Vijay Kumar, 1993, 'Ganeshwar-Jodhpura Culture: New Traits In Indian Archaeology', *Harappan Civilization*, Ed. By Gregory L. Possehl, Delhi, pp. 125-134 and plates.

Agrawala, R.C. 1984-85, 'Proto-Historic Copper Bowls From Rajasthan', *The Researcher*, vol. XIV-XV, Jaipur, pp. 1-3 and plates I-II

Agrawala, R.C. 1984, 'Aravalli- The Major Source of Copper For The Indus and Indusrelated Cultures', *Frontiers Of The Indus Civilization*, Ed. By B.B. Lal and S.P. Gupta, pp. 157-162 and plates.

Ambika Dhaka

Research Scholar
67, Bajrang Vihar, Near Durgapura Rly, Stn., Jaipur-302018

Indian Archaeology Today – A Mature and Scientific Discipline*

I was pondering over for long about writing the current status of Indian Archaeology, which is, I must state, based on sound footing and has attained a scientific status as a result of organized work by a number of institutions and individuals. I owe Supriya Varma for stimulating me to write this paper, which, otherwise, would not have seen the light so soon. This short paper is a reply to her immature and childish allegations and criticism about the current status of Indian Archaeology made in a review article entitled "Is Archaeology an Immature Discipline", published in the *Indian Historical Review,* Volume XXVIII, Number 1-2 (January 2001 and July 2001), pp. 151-159), without understanding or considering the fundamentals of archaeology and its limitations. Only those practicing archaeologists, actively involved in executing field oriented research works, and not armchair archaeologists, will understand these aspects and the subject in great depth.

We all must agree that the Archaeological Survey of India, one of the biggest Government organisations in India, whose network is spread all over the country, Deccan College, Post-Graduate and Research Institute, Deemed University, a premier Institute in South Asia imparting and undertaking quality teaching and research in the field of archaeology, Department of Archaeology, Universities of M.S. of Baroda, Allahabad, Banaras, Kurukshetra, etc., have contributed immensely to the development of Indian archaeology. These Institutions, especially the Archaeological Survey of India and Deccan College, were established and being run by dedicated and world-renowned scholars, who developed world-class infrastructure for undertaking field and laboratory oriented researches. The excavations of sites like Taxila, Harappa, Mohenjodaro, Hastinapur, Navdatoli, Inamgaon to name a few, have demonstrated sound methodology and excavation skill developed by Indian archaeologists and the reports of these excavations are not merely descriptive, but are analytical and interpretative, demonstrating sound theoretical knowledge of the excavators. The work of Subba Rao entitled *Personality of India* published in mid fifties is a classical work and is relevant even today as it incorporates some of the concepts of New Archaeology, propounded much later by Western and American Anthropologists. This demonstrates that Indian Archaeologists are not merely borrowing concepts and theories from outsides as is claimed by some, but have capability to develop them on their own. The success achieved by some archaeologists can be attributed to their positive thinking, receptive mind and endeavour to constantly improving methodology or recovery of data and application of scientific aids in this subject.

I very much appreciate the efforts of young scholars like Supriya Varma, who are taking deep interest in Indian Archaeology and thinking about various aspects. However, they should keep in mind that on archaeological theories developed elsewhere and relevant to that particular region or area can be applicative to other regions having different ecological and geographical/geological conditions. One should be aware that archaeology cannot provide answer for everything and there is a scope for a lot of guesswork. I have every reason to question credibility of Supriya Verma who finds it very easy to criticise well conceived and executed research work of others. Neither she is an archaeologist nor she has produced work

*This is a reply by Dr. Vasant Shinde to Ms. Supriya Verma's review article published in Indian Historical Review, New Delhi.

better or even equivalent to the one she criticises. Only people like M.K. Dhavilikar, V.N. Misra, V.H. Sonawane. R.S. Bhist or others of the same stature who have done pioneer work in this field are entitled to criticise such works. I will very much appreciate if Supriya Verma spent more time in the field and try to produce original work of high standard than wasting her valuable time in only finding faults with every other work. The language of archaeology can be read or interpreted by those who do not actually practice it.

While reviewing my book entitled *Early Settlements in the Central Tapi Basin*, published by Munishiram Manoharlal Publishers Pvt. Ltd in 1998, she has raised a number of queries on methodology and interpretation aspects. I feel it necessary to answer some of her quarried and criticism, which I will attempt one by one:

1. Supriya Verma writes "Vasant Shinde's study of the early settlements in the central Tapi basin is claimed by the author to be the first exhaustive work in the area of settlement archaeology undertaken in India". It is at least expected from the person criticising work of others to quota sentences correctly. The statement made by me is "The present study of the settlement pattern is the first of its kind for the central Tapi Basin. I stand by this statement as my work is the first exhaustive work of settlement pattern on the Chalcolithic community of Central Tapi Basin". The works on settlement patterns carried out by Dhavalikar, Makkhan Lal and I are of the same nature and therefore there is bound to be a lot of similarity in the fundamental methodology used. We have worked in different regions and on different cultural groups.

2. Had Supriya Verma read my book carefully, she would have noticed that I have discussed settlement pattern of different Chalcolithic cultures separately, sufficiently explaining changes in the location of sites during the different cultural periods. I have mentioned in the beginning a number of limitations for the collection of data for settlement pattern studies. In the light of large-scale destruction of the sites and loosing of vital data, I have done my best to record what is available and retrievable. In case Supriya Verma travels to some parts of the Deccan, she will realize that the locations of early farming communities is largely (not only) determined by these two factors, water and soil. This is also true in the case of Gujarat. There is bound to be similarity in the explanation of settlement patterns of the Chacolithic in this region and Gujarat studies by Gregory Possehl, and hence using identical terminology for certain headings. Herding units have been identified on the basis of location of sites near the grassland. Verma suggests there must be numerous other factors such as subsistence, technology, function, outside world, and so on which would have played a role. However, it should be made clear that the identification of site as a herding unit reflects its function and subsistence practiced by the people at this site.

3. The date on the site size is bound to be vague considering a number of limitation. There are only a couple of sites like Pompii where everything is buried *in situ* without any further disturbances and destructions. In the case of most of the sites, there is always a lot of displacement and disturbances caused by various natural and human agencies. Sites in the Tapi basin are no exception to this. However, if read carefully, it will bee seen that the data is carefully analysed and explained with the help of tables and charts. I am rather surprised to read the statement of Verma that there is no table indicating the exact site sizes during different cultural periods. This indicates her lack of perception of the subject. The factors like man, median, mode, range, standard deviation and coefficiency of variations can be considered, provided we have perfect data with us.

4. Supriya Verma suggests that the site typology reconstruction should have been based on differences in size, function and morphology. She is indeed not in a position to understand the concept of settlement pattern as these are the very factors that are considered for the reconstruction of site typology. She should keep in mind that by mere reading Flannery's writing without the sense of practical knowledge, it is not easy to understand this subject. How does she suggest that there is lack of evidence for the chiefdom society during the Malwa phase? Considering the evidence from sites like Inamgaon, Daimabad, Prakashe, Navdatoli, Eran, Nagda, for the craft specialization and the presence of public buildings, there

is hardly any doubt about the existence of a chiefdom society during the Malwa period. Verma needs to read excavation reports from other sites also along with the Inamgaon report and try to understand and interpret relevance of the hardcore data.

5. Verma is critical about my identification of Jorwe sites as Randomly Dispersed and suggests I should have used the nearest neighbour statistics. I will greatly appreciate if Verma can show to me that she has undertaken similar kinds of study by using a complex mathematical model she has mentioned in her review article (p. 155). I have already mentioned that the sites are found located where there are sufficient resources available and sites follow resources. There is indeed no need to use this mathematical model, which most archaeologists do not understand and they make no sense.

6. I have mentioned that a rough hexagonal pattern exists during the Late Harappan phase around the site of Kurkwade and the sites around are its satellite settlement. It is true that some of the sites identified as satellite are larger than even the parent settlement. Here there is a difference in the habitation deposit. Kurkwade has considerable thick habitation deposit implying its long occupation whereas habitation deposit of its satellite is thin suggesting their either seasonal or short occupation. Larger sites do not appear to have been occupied at one and the same time, but such a large area may have been brought under occupation by the people gradually. Verma herself agrees that there are serious limitations in the application of central place theory. I need not repeat these limitations here. I have also mentioned and agree with Verma that the problem of a relationship between population and size cannot be easily worked out.

The status of Indian archaeology today is indeed very robust and the subject is growing day by day. India is an open air ethnographic museum and this rich wealth is of great importance to us as it enables reconstruction of past lifeways. We need to blend properly the theoretical and practical aspects of archaeology and take help of other scientific discipline where it is required. We need to strengthen our data base and use various scientific methods to analyse. The new generation is really gearing up and is ready to accept new emerging challenges.

Vasant Shinde

Department of Archaeology
Deccan College
Post-Graduate and Research Institute
Pune

Buddhist Remains in District Visakhapatnam (Andhra Pradesh)

Visakhapatnam in Andhra Pradesh is called "Jewel on the East Coast" and it flourished during the reigns of the Mauryas, the Pallavas, the Cholas and the Gangas. It was later transformed into a port town by the British. Today it boasts of India's largest ship building yard, with a natural harbour, a beach stretching endlessly against a backdrop of low hills dotted with secluded covers and reeks. No other place in this state is as blessed as Visakhapatnam with its scenic surrounding, pollution-free environment and cleanliness to a large extent. Besides golden beaches, lush green vegetation, beautiful roads and ancient temples, it is a historian's delight. Excavations conducted on the north coast belt, reveal sites of Buddhist heritage between 3rd century BC and 7th century AD during the rule of the Mauryas, the Satavahanas, the Ikshavakus and the Vishnukundin kings. Buddhism soared to great heights in this land. It received great impetus due to king Ashoka's missionary zeal. Buddhism also kindled the creative genius of the people of Andhra Pradesh. In-fact the Andhra art influenced the art-forms of Sri Lanka and Suvarna Bhoomi i.e, S-E Asian countries.

Andhra Pradesh had close relations with Buddhism from the early Christian era which is evident from the fact that no where else in the entire South such a large number of Buddhist sites are coming to light day by day yielding information of the great religion. The innumerable sites that dot Andhra from Salihudam in the north of Peda-Ganjam in the south and from Gutti in the west to Battiprolu in the east are clear proof of the fact that Buddhism had popular appeal to the Andhras. Buddhism had its sway in the entire Kalinga-Andhra region. Writings of foreign travellers as well as discoveries of the remains of Buddhist shrines in this part form the sources to trace the magnificent growth of Buddhism in the past. From the period of Robert Sewell until the present day the discoveries and researches made by the State and Central Archaeology Department, as well as relevant Departments of various Universities brought a number of Buddhist monuments to light.

In this paper three such sites are considered. Interestingly, Andhra Pradesh witnessed 3 phases of Buddhism - *Hinayana, Mahayana and Vajrayana*. There are approximately 140 Buddhist sites as of now. This is the only State where 19 Buddhist relic caskets have been recovered. A general survey of the Buddhist sites in Andhra Pradesh reveal that the north coastal region played a dominant role in the propagation of *Hinayana* school of Buddhism.

Thotlakonda

The first site, Thotlakonda (17°15'N, 83°23'E) lies at about 15 km from Visakhapatnam on the Bheemilli beach road located on a hill at 128 m altitude over looking the sea. In Telgu *'Thotla'* means rock-cut troughs and *'konda'* means hill. This place was within the influence of ancient Kalinga region which was an important source of dissemination of Buddhist culture to Sri Lanka and various parts of S.E. Asia. It provides an insight into the process of Trans Oceanic diffusion of Indian culture, especially Buddhism. A hill on the sea coast with *Slubrious* climate was an ideal attraction for the Buddhist monks to build a monastery complex. The placid sea sheltered by the deeply incurved coastline, provided a safe haven for anchoring ships. How this place was discovered is very interesting. Thotlakonda came to light during an aerial survey by the Indian Navy for setting up a Naval

Base on the north-eastern sea coast. After its discovery major excavations were conducted by the State Archaeology Department during 1988-92. The excavations established the existence of a *Hinayana* Buddhist-complex which flourished between 200 BC and AD 200. The habitation area over the hill covers 350x250 m and is dotted with a number of stupas, viharas etc. The complex has an apsidal chaitya griha, stupas, chaitya and viharas on either side. Eleven rock-cut troughs for storing rain water, each having 4 to 8 steps to descend and draw water for drinking purposes. The situation of these troughs is in the N-E and S-W parts of the hillock, which suggest the selection of slopy parts of the summit for collection of maximum rain water. One can see the remains of a 64-pillared congregation hall meant for holding *Uposatha* assembly or religious discourse. A stone pathway runs along the complex representing high standard of civic life.

Considering the probable functions or utility of the structure, as well as their constructional details, the remains are classified into: A) Religious B) Secular C) Civil. Religious structure included the main stupa, chaityas, votive stupas and platforms. Secular structures are viharas, congregation halls, *bhandargaras*, refectory etc. Civil constructions are cisterns, drainage and stone pathways.

In the *Hinayana,* great stress was laid on the veneration of the stupa in which the mortal remains of Buddha were enshrined. The practice of erecting mounds (*stupa*) over the corporeal remains of the preachers has a pre-Buddhistic origin seen throughout the world. Around 5th century BC Buddhist stupas gained definite form and became universal. They may have been erected to commemorate the memory of four categories like Buddha, Pratyeka Buddhas, Arahats and Chakravartins or universal monarchs or deities. These enshrined the corporeal remains i.e., bones collected from the funeral pyres of the above said revered personalities. The early Brahmi inscriptions allude to chaityas and very rarely to stupas. *Chaitya* refers to a shrine or icon in a shrine. We find references of chaityas in the Ramayana and the Mahabharta. Krishna Murthy in his book *"Mirror of Indian Culture"* opines that chaityas were originally Brahmanical in origin, subsequently appropriated by the Buddhist and that it cannot be considered as exclusively of Buddhist origin (Krishna Murthy K. 1983). But in Buddhist theology it stood for a sacred edifice as well as a memorial. The stupas in the north coastal Andhra Pradesh have brick rims at the periphery while the inner space are filled with clay and rubble. The dome is raised over another smaller inner brick rim leaving vacant space for circumbulation while the inner space is filled with clay and rubble. In course of time, due to heavy weight the rublle fell on the inside drum and the dome bulged causing cracks resulting in irrepairable damage to the body of the stupa.

At Thotlakonda *'Harmika'* of the second variety can be noticed in the stupas i.e., a solid stone having a cushion-shaped base. It exhibits finely incised bands of acanthus and creeper motifs topped by an inverted pyramidal member with a socket at the top to carry a simple shafted parasole. It is indeed an excellent example of post-Satavahana plastic art.

One more interesting feature noticed at Thotlakonda is the provision of a square platform around the drum having a flight of steps leading to the path of circumambulations. Whether the main stupa at Thotlakonda contained relics of Buddha is not known as there is no epigrahical evidence of it. It is likely that the main stupa underwent renovations during later times after the original edifice became dilapidated. However, it might be presumed that the spot where the original stupa stood has not been changed as it is the only prominent and elevated spot situated at the north-eastern end of the complex overlooking the vast expanse of the sea towards east, with a chain of hills towards north and west.

A row of four stupas veneered with dressed stone slabs were noticed on the northern side of the main stupa. These might have been erected during different periods by different patrons. Few broken pieces of stone fragments of votive stupas were found in west direction. Few mutilated remains found in the southern side of the stupa can be seen in the museum. Mutilated *Buddhapadas*, a miniature figure of Muchilinda Naga can be seen in the museum.

Secular structures are the viharas which form an important group of buildings in the Buddhist complex. Based on the measurement of the brick used for each monastery and the levels on which they were raised, it is presumed that these monastries were built by different patrons. It is also noticed that as and when it became necessary to accommodate more visitors, the earlier units were extended by adding a series of cells without disturbing the original alignment. However, extreme care was taken to see that all the secular units were on the south where the ground takes a gradual slope and religious structures were erected on the north. The viharas were more or less square. It had a common verandah paved with lime concrete floor. A peculiar feature noted here was the doorways to the cell, which were provided at the sides, instead of in the middle, so that the inmates might have privacy.

Material used for construction was fine mud mortar and well levigated lime for plastering internal and external faces of the wall. Presence of numerous sea shells in the lime plaster, indicate the these were grounded and mixed with riverine gravel for preparing lime concrete mortar. This is a common practice even today in the villages of the coastal areas.

A large number of fragments of perforated tiles found in and around the viharas, suggest that the viharas were covered with tiled roofs, supported by rafters of palm wood. A number of fine stucco pieces of floral and lotus petal designs recovered outside the vihara, indicate that the exterior walls were ornamented with stucco work. An abraded Satvahana lead coin with an animal figure was found outside one of the cells on the verandah. An interesting find in the corner of the verandah was a Roman silver coin of Augustus Tiberius. Excavations here yielded broken red ware finials, fragments of storage jars, bowls of Black and Red Ware and few iron nails. The iron nails seem to suggest the existence of wooden door or wooden frames for the tiled roofs.

The viharas with seven cells and a common verandah facing the congregation hall appears to have undergone modification in three phases. During the earliest phase there appears to be an apsidal stupa-chaitya at this place with an apse in middle and two long arms on either side. When gradually the stupa-chaitya fell into disuse the two long arms of the chaitya were converted into a common running verandah of the proposed vihara and the hind space of one of the arms was utilized for a series of cells. During last and final phase, the alternate partition walls of the rooms of the second phase were reduced in height to make sleeping platforms inside the rooms. During the last phase the partition walls were strengthened by adding one more brick course besides the already existing ones. Thus, making it clear that there was no inhibition to convert a religious structure into a secular. Flight of steps were provided for entering the common verandah, one of them provided with a neatly dressed moon stone having a much abraded and illegible Brahmi label inscription. Each flight of steps of the vihara was connected to the congregation hall by means of pathways. All the seven cells were more or less square and equal in size provided with benches built in brick inside. Provision of benches or sleeping platforms built into the wall, is commonly seen in rock cut Buddhist caves (Nagaraju S. 1981) as at Nasik, Ajanta etc. Another important find in the vihara was a stone spherical ball with an approximate diametere of 6 inches and well ground, which might have been used as a weight measure for grain etc. Similar spherical weights of smaller sizes were also noticed at Peddabankur (Krishna Shastry, 1983). Remains of a 64 pillared Assembly Hall with each row having eight pillars stands in the middle part of the vihara complex which might have evidently been used for holding *Uposatha* assembly and to recite the *Pattimokkha*[1]. The Assembly Hall had entrances on all the four sides which is clear from traces of pathways to the hall. In the middle of the Hall there was a brick built platform which has a flight of steps paved with a moonstone. This was evidently used for seating the senior most *'Acharya'* to recite *Pathimokkha* to the assembly of monks.

Due to the heavy weight of the super structure and the fragile nature of the khondalite stone in which the pillars were carved, and also due to the inadequate foundations, most of the pillars were found crumbled and broken into bits. During excavation, a series of halls in a row came to light towards south-east of the stupa and a huge dump of pottery was discovered including bowls, conical and shallow vases, pots, lids, a pot holding coin of Satavahana period, a blue glass bead etc. Thus, it was presumed to be the kitchen complex. Moreover, according to ancient Indian Vastu, kitchen or *'Aggisala'* should be sit-

[1]Pattimokka is a collection of various monastic rules as contained in *Vinaya Pitaka*. It was prescribed by Buddha that this must be recited by all buddhists on the *Uposatha* day i.e. 14th, 15th and 8th day of a month. The recitation must be done collectively by Sangha. According to *Mahavagga* 11,3,4, p. 243vol.xiii. Pattimokkha is the beginning, it is the face [*Mukamutham*], it is supreme of all good.

uated on the south-east. The exterior and interior surface of the walls were plastered with fine stucco work, depicting floral and mythical animals. These pieces were collected from excavations. Among them, was, *'yali'* or mythical lion with short horns and broad grim face. They might have been fixed on either side of the doorway. This is an important evidence which helps to trace the origin of stucco at least to the 1st century AD. It also appears that decoration of structures with stucco figurines travelled together hand in hand with brick construction.

Lastly, the civil structure at Thotlakonda, a series of rock-cut cisterns of *'kupas'* were excavated for collection of rain water. There are indications to show that these were excavated in rock and provided with lids over each having an opening at one corner. Due to fragile nature of the rock, the lids crumbled into the cisterns. Channels were provided wherever necessary along the gradients for free flow of water from higher contrours, some cisterns were inter-connected by way of channels in order to collect the surplus water, flowing from those situated at higher contours to those at the lower. Altogether about eleven cisterns were found.

The stone pathway was yet another important feature of this Buddhist settlement which cannot be overlooked. The undulating surfaces of the hillock were conveniently exploited by providing flights of steps from one level of the pathways to the other. The whole arrangement stands as testimony to the bountiful patronage and high standard of civic life. This also reflects the contemporary urban scene in the early centuries of the Christian era.

Keeping in mind the finds of the excavation it may be presumed that the Buddhist settlement at Thotlakonda was established during 3rd century B.C. i.e., in Mauryan times. Thus it can be concluded that on close examination the sculptural remains reveal that Buddha was never represented in human form, but there are several symbolic representations like the *Buddhapadas* which were decorated with *Dharmachakra, Swastika*, the throne of Buddha etc. There are also a good number of miniature stupas, probably worshipped as independent units. Summing up the evidence, it may be presumed that the establishment finally wounded up during the last part of the 3rd century A.D.

Whatever prompted the Buddhists to establish a monastery at the top of this hill with its hazardous ascent and descent, the same reason might have led to its decline and decay. The lofty stupas shining during day time with their white lime plaster and with rows of wick lamps during night might have served as guiding landmark for the nautical commuters. Despite of the location of the stupas on the hill there was sufficient availability of water by rain fed rock-cut cisterns. Construction of permanent pathways, paved with dressed slabs and protected by side revetments, might have been necessary to avoid slush and slime caused by heavy rains. The mode of construction of these pathways throw an interesting light on the contemporary engineering techniques.

The monastery established for over three centuries, reached its prosperity by the second century of the Christian era, a period that brought in the embellishment of the drab brick structures with sculptural and stucco ornamentation. Though, material used for stone sculptures was khodalite which is locally available, yet the quality of art was as superior as that of Amaravati and Jaggayyapetra (both in Andhra Pradesh). Though the prosperity of this place was short lived as by the middle of the 3rd century A.D. it started to decline and gradually fell into disuse. One doesn't know the actual cause of its decline but one can derive conclusions. May be due to increasing popularity of *Mahayana* Buddhism or due to newly acquired dominance of Brahmanism or may be due to decline of foreign trade or shifting of the network of commercial activity that this monastery fell into isolation. Thus by the end of the 3rd century A.D. it was deserted.

Bavikonda

Another site is Bavikonda (17°14'N; 81°25'E) which is located about 15 km from Visakhapatnam on the beach road to Bhimli Town and 3 k.ms from Thotlakonda. In Telgu *'Bavi'* means a well and *'Konda'* means a hill. Thus it means a hill of wells. It too, like Thotlakonda is located on a hill at an altitude of 138 m. It lay along the ancient trade route which connected Andhra Pradesh with Northern India through Kalinga. Excavations in 1982-87 brought to light an extensive Buddhist establishment consisting of main stupa i.e. *Mahachaitya*, few votive stupas, a circular chaityagriha and two apsidal chaityagriha embedded with relic casket, a vihara complex, stone and brick built votive stupas, stone pillared halls, rectangular halls, congregation hall, stone path way, refractory, etc.

An analytical study reveals that the *Mahachaitya* at Bavikonda had a simple and superb architectural style, with a plain brick outer railing, devoid of any ornamentation, clockwise staircases leading to the ayaka platforms and the upper *pradakshapatha* (Pachauri, S.K., 1993). Three abandoned water tanks were also found which may be providing drinking water to the monastery. The adjoining cistern to the tank might be used for colouring of robes worn by monks. Like Thotlakonda here also two types of structures can be seen-religious and secular. From the Buddhapada slabs it is evident that *Hinayanism* was practiced here.

Sankaram

The most beautiful of all places was Bhojjannakonda and Lingalakonda (collectively called Sankaram), a small village located at 41 km. from Visakhapatnam on the banks of Sarada river. It got its name from Sangharma which meant monastery. The relics of a legendary past were unearthed by Alexander Rea in 1907. It is locally know as Bojjannakonda. Many monolithic votive stupas, rock cut caves, brick built structural edifices and Satavahana coins date it back to Ist century A.D. Excavation here yielded several clay tablets conical and square seal impressions bearing figures of seated Buddha, pagodas and Buddhist creed formulae. The main stupa consists of square platform approached by a flight of steps, a drum and a dome commanding a panoramic view of the fertile countryside. It has dominating myriads of carved rock and rarely brick built stupas one above the other. This eastern hillock bears a richer architecture of the two hills.

Lingalakonda, the second hillock is carved like *matsya* with innumerable rock-cut monolithic stupas. The conversion of an entire surface of the top of a hill under large number of stupas is a rare event. A beautiful figure of *'Harithi'* was found here. The vihara was active for about 1000 years, spanning the *Theravada Mahayana* and *Vajrayana* phases of Buddhism. A number of seals bear the inscription. *"He damma hethu prabhaya"*. It is the same as found in Kalinga script of the 5th century A.D. and proto Nagari script of 8th century A.D.

Alexander Rea who excavated the site asserts that the monoliths here may be ascribed to the time corresponding to that of the shrines erected by Ashoka. On the basis of the sculptures found here which are crude and primitive in design, Rea argues that crudeness points to the early period of undeveloped workmanship, but not to the late period of decadence because Buddhism did not survive sufficiently long after the Amaravati epoch. He also argues that the structures are themselves of very early date as is clear from the large size of bricks (17"x19"x3"). Such large bricks have never been found in the southern structures which date later than the 2nd century A.D. The extent of the remains and their character show that the Buddhist monuments of Sankaram have been an important one. There is no other ancient Buddhist monuments like Sankaram throughout South India. Scholars opined that Buddhist monument like Borobudur, in Java is modelled after this structure at Sankaram (Kolluro Suryanaryana).

All the three sites reveal that the political control of the region lay in the hands of the Satavahanas whose influence is concentrated around Dhanyakataka on the banks of Krishna river. Such great centres were abandoned due to various reasons. Perhaps the decline and decay of these settlements may be due to the lack of patronage as a result of shifting of trade centers, popularity of *Mahayanism* and finally the revial of *Brahmanical* faith. It was also the time when Buddhism was moving away from *Theravada Hinayanism to Chaityakavada Mahayanism* indicating an ascendancy of merchant guids. (Journal of Archaeology, 1990).

BIBLIOGRAPHY

Journal of Archaeology Vol. 3, No.1, 1990, p.59

Krishna Murty K, Mirror of Indian Culture, p.143 (Delhi, 1982); Also in Krishna Sastry V.V, *The Proto and Early Historical Cultures of Andhra Pradesh* Plate-90 (Govt. of a. p., 1983

Krishna Sastry, V.V, *The Proto and Early Historical Cultures of Andhra Pradesh*, pp 207-208 [Govt. of AP, 1983].

Kolluru Suryanaryana, *'Possibilities and Challenges in the development of Tourism in Buddhist heritage sites in Kalinga Andhra'* (Unpublished work)

Nagaarju, S, *Buddhist Architectures of Western India*, p 85 [Delhi, 1981].

Pachauri, S.K. ed, *Recent Buddhist Discoveries in Visakhapatnam District A.P.*, p.9[Govt. of A.P., 1993].

Jyoti Chandra

Lecturer
Arya Girls Collegs
Ambala Cantt (Haryana)

Pañchanna Gaṇēśa From British Museum–An Iconographical Study

In Hindu iconography icons of Brahma, Śiva, Agni and Vishnu generally show that multiple heads numbering two, three, four or five. But rarely, the images of Gaṇēśa who belongs to the family of Śiva are also shown with multiple heads. The extant images of Gaṇēśa reported from Varanasi reveal the manifestations of Gaṇēśa as *dvimukha, trimukha* and *pañchamukha.* Besides these, a few more images of Gaṇēśa having five heads are reported from Orissa (Puri and Konark), of which one is now exhibited in the British Museum, London. The pañchanana Gaṇēśa images, which are rare, pose complex problems in iconographical and religious studies as regards to its origins and development. Further, in the appreciation of the art and iconography of the images of Gaṇēśa and also for the better understanding its religious implications, meaning and significance, it is essential to focus on the strange physiognomical form of this God with five elephantine heads and an enormous belly, accompanied by the Goddess and mounts. In the present paper it is intended to highlight the composite nature of this deity and the diverse myths and religious motifs that came to be associated with his character in the Sanskrit texts including the Puranas that contributed to the iconogrphy of pañchanna Gaṇēśa with special reference to the five-faced image of Gaṇēśa of the British Museum, coming from Konark (Orissa).

Gaṇēśa with single head had been reported in early art forms as garland bearer (or as *yaksha*?) in Amaravati railing-sculptures (Burgess), as *dvārapāla* at the entrance to the Buddhist caves at Bojjannakonda, A.P. (Hanumantha D. Rao, 1993) that had fallen under the influence of *Mahāyāna* Buddhism or as *dvārapāla* at Bhumra (or 5th century A.D.) (Getty Alice, 1936) which was differently identified by Coomaraswamy as the *yaksha* form of Gaṇēśa. Images of Gaṇēśa in different stances that is standing, seated and dancing or independently or associated with his consort as cult God or as an attendant figure accompanying the figures of Śiva and Pārvati and Kārttikēya or with the other Gaṇas are known through the stone sculptures that spread over the different parts of India. They reveal the development of the iconography of Gaṇēśa through the historical times. Interestingly, the images of Gaṇēśa have assumed multiple heads and hands, which carry different weapons and attributes for certain specific reasons. Usually, Gaṇēśa is involved in the *dhyanas* as having one head, which, following the Tantras should be one fifth of the total length of the body; but there are forms with two, three, four or five heads. Alice Getty observed that Gaṇēśa with three heads was never represented in India and that the Hindus did not know him with four heads. But this is not true as P.K. Agrawala reports a few images of Gaṇēśa from Varanasi with multiple heads in the Indian context. (Agarwal P.K., 1997) Besides these, a row of five elephant headed figures seated in *lalita* posture close together in a row identified as *Pañch-Gaṇēśa* has also been brought to light from Varanasi. This unusual theme of *Pañch-Gaṇēśa* iconography has been corroborated by the further evidence of similar figures of Gaṇēśa known from Rajasthan through two sculptures. (Agarwal R.C., 1997) Five standing figures including four Ganapatis in dancing postures and an elephant, all poised on lotus flowers is noticed from a Śiva temple at Jamaroli near Jaipur. The mount of Gaṇēśa, a rat, occurs below the figures in each case. Like the four human bodied figures of Gaṇapati with elephant heads, the freestanding elephant in the group also has a halo similar to the other figures and thus represents the god Gaṇapati, beyond any doubt. Another relief from the Somesvara temple at Kiradu depicts all the five Gaṇapati in their usual elepahnt-faced human form. (Dhaky M.A., 1967) Unlike the wall panel reported from Jamaroli the figures of Gaṇēśa are seated in a row representing an identical icon type, but with a difference in the attributes held by their hands and also the direction in the turn of their proboscis. The two figures on left have their trunk turned to their right, a feature quite uncommon in Gaṇapati sculptures. From these two sculptures it is interesting to find the elephant without human body along the images of Gaṇēśa. Although there is no textual reference to the iconographic form of Gaṇēśa fully as an elephant, Gaṇēśa is referred to as *Gaja Vināyaka* in Kāsī Khaṇḍa of *Skanda Purāna*. It has been described in the *Narasiṁha Purāna* that Gaṇēśa had assumed the form of an elephant to cause serious troubles to the demons. (Narsimha purana) In the *Gaṇēśa Purāna* of Gaṇēśa Sahasranāma, Gaṇapati has been described as an elephant with its tail (*lāngūla*) tying ropes or tying post (*alana*), chains (*nigada*) and a pond for merry-making (*kēḷi sarōvara*) (Ganesha Sahasram).

The icon of five faced Gaṇēśa (*pañchānana Gaṇēśa*) probably hailing from Konark (40" high) is now being exhibited in the British Museum. Thomas E. Donaldson described it as Śakti Gaṇapati since Gaṇēśa is shown as seated in *lalitāsana* holding a small female figure on his left thigh and has ascribed to the 13th century A.D., which is under discussion. The five-faced and ten-handed image of Gaṇēśa is highly interesting because of its iconography. The front right hand of Gaṇēśa is extended in *varada hasta* holding a pomegranate while his left hand holds a broken tusk. The remaining right hands hold an *ankuśa*, arrow, trident and *chakra* while the corresponding left hands hold sugar cane, *nāga pāśa*, an ear of paddy and lotus flower. The crescent moon adorns the *jaṭas* and the hair is arranged in *jaṭā mukuṭa*. The central forehead is decorated with dropping festoons of pearl strings dropping from the head gear which is arranged in the pattern of *kīrtimukha* at its base. While the central head is dominating that is depicted frontally, the two heads on either sides with the proboscis of each flanking face being curled up and carved in profile. The trunk of the central head hangs straight down and curles to the right. It is observed by Alice Getty that in south India, practically the proboscis is never shown lifting the cakes when it is turned to the right, while it is common to lift the cakes when the turnk is turned to the left. Here it is interesting to note that the end of the turnk is coiled seemingly balancing a ball shaped cake (*mōdaka*). A trefoil shaped *tōrana* rimmed with beads frames the heads of the God. Behind the *tōrana* is found a tree with its branches spreading symmetrical to either side forming an ornate canopy with flowers and fruits being visible. Flying *vidyādharas* are carved on the two upper corners of the slab. Below the seated image of Gaṇēśa is his mount, beneath his left leg, while the elephant with its raised trunk is shown to the left side in smaller proportions. According to a south Indian legend, the presence of rat, that usually accompanies Gaṇēśa, is connected with the absence of one of the tusks of Gaṇēśa. It mentions that once there was a giant demon with the face of an elephant that was unconquerable either by God or by man. Being a demi-god, Gaṇēśa, fought with him with some possibility of success. During the course of his encounter with the giant demon, Gajamukhēśvara broke Gaṇēśa's right tusk, which was then caught by Gaṇēśa and thrown against the giant demon as a weapon. As a result of it the demon instantly turned into a rat and was taken into the service by Gaṇēśa as his vehicle.

Gaṇēśa according to some legends has two consorts called Buddhi and Siddhi, the personifications of wisdom and success. Although he is never shown in the accompaniment of these two consorts, he is carved with a dēvi seated by his side or on his lap; and is referred to as Lakshmi. In the image of the British Museum, the Goddess is shown as seated on his left lap with two hands, in smaller proportions holdig the lotus flower in her left hand by its long stalk, looking at the god in great adoration. The goddess is seated embracing Gaṇēśa with her right hand and she is decorated with *hāras*, armlets and bracelets. She wears *kirīṭa mukuṭa* on her head. The pedestal is decorated with stalks of foliage and on either side of the *āsana* are shown the attendant figures, the mounts of Gaṇēśa and the goddess. The legs of the *āsana* are decorated beautifully with a *gaṇa* supporting a *virala* motif with a stylised elephant in crouching position beneath the rampant lion. The carving of the female figure with Gaṇēśa is indicative of the Tantric influence in the ritual of worshipping Gaṇēśa and the popularity of Śākta worship. The followers of the cult of Śākti Gaṇapati worship him in association with his female counterpart. The seated figures of dēvi on the left lap of Gaṇēśa is sometimes called Lakshmī. Gaṇēśa's association with other deitis particularly with Lakshmī is known from a stone sculpture of 8th century A.D. now in the University

Museum of Philadelphia. In it Gaṇēśa is shown with a goddess to his right side. Interestingly it is a rare representation of *svābhishēkamūrti* aspect of Lakshmī as the Goddess is shown receiving the *abhishēka*, possibly because of the round shaped symbols, which she holds above her head with her upper arms.(Shivarudraswamy S.N., 1999) They may be taken for vases out of which water is pouring over her head. Generally, Lakshmī is bathed with sacred water poured over her by two elephants from either side in the Gajalakshmī group. The presence of the elephant below the Gaṇēśa image along with his own mount clearly suggest that the goddess is no other than Lakshmī. Lakshmī, the consort of Vishṇu is associated with elephants, rain and water and the religious myth of anointing the goddess at the time of churning of the ocean of milk has been described in *Mahābhārata* and *Matsya Purāṇa*. Although there appears to be no direct association in the classical texts between Lakshmī and her elephant and Gaṇēśa, the connection has not been lost in the Hindu religion as both of them are treated as the providers of well being. (Courtright B. Paul, 1985) Gaṇēśa and Lakshmī are linked by the common figures of the elephant, as they are the deities whom the devotees venerate in seeking the fulfillment of their wishes and goals.

By 10th century *Gaṇapati* became an important deity when the *Gāṇapatya* sect set up the cult of five *Śakti Gaṇapatis* with different iconographical features mostly reflecting in the number of arms and colour of the deity called: *Ucchiṣta Gaṇapati* four-armed, red in colour; *Mahā Gaṇapati*, ten-armed, red in colour, *Ūrdhva Gaṇapati-*, six-armed, yellow in colour, *Piṅgala Gaṇapati*, six-armed, yellow in colour; *Lakshmī Gaṇapti*, four or eight-armed, white in colour, while Śakti is yellow and carried a lotus flower in her hands. Gaṇēśa in the form of *Lakshmī Gaṇapati* or *Śakti Gaṇapati* was worshipped by the followers of the Śākta cult, who differed in the mode of worship of the God by adopting the unconventional means (*vāmāchāra*- "left-handed" tradition) to symbolise their belief that the liberation of the soul could be achieved by the routes other than the ordinary or traditional prayers and rites (*dakshiṇāchāra*- "right-handed" tradition) (Mahadevan T.M., 1960). The ritual practices followed in the *vamachara* worship which is also observed by the followers of *Gāṇapatyas* and other sects varied greatly from the use of symbols compatible with conservative Brahmanism to the excessive behaviour permitting the people of all castes to partake in the rituals and allowing the *pañcha makaras* (*madhya, māṁsa, matsya, mudra* and *maithuna*) in their cult practices. (Payne E.A., 1933) In this connection should it be viewed that the worship of Gaṇapati in an unconventional manner in which the proboscis of the central (frontal) head of Gaṇēśa is carved as turning towards right instead of the left side to facilitate the worship of the God with the left hand by the devotees. In this aspect it is comparable to the group of five elephant-faced forms of Gaṇēśa (datable to 11th century A.D.) of Sōmēśvara temple at Kiradu, wherein two figures on the left, have their turnks turned to their right.

Five-faced Gaṇēśa has been described in the iconographical texts like Śilparatna, Rūpamaṇḍana and Kriyākramadyōti as Hēraṁba Gaṇapati.(Rao T.A.G., 1914) Anantānandagiri's *Saṁkaravijaya* refers to a subsect of worhippers of Uccihiṣta Gaṇapati who worship the deity called Hēramba. (Samkara Vijaya) The Hēramba Upanishad eulogises the five-headed form of Gaṇapati. The five-headed form of Gaṇapati is frequently represented in Indian, Nepalese and Tibetan art. In the art forms of Hēramba of Pañchamukha Gaṇapati, their heads are arranged in different ways, they bear different atttributes, sit on different vehicles and are sometimes accompanied by a consort. In the Vidyāṇava Tantra there is no specific reference about the arrangement of the heads. On the other hand, it decribes the colours of the five heads as white, yellow, dark blue, white and saffron. (Buhnemann G. 1989) The colours of the five faces of Hēramba show close similarity to those of the five aspects of Śiva i.e., Īśāna, Tatpursha, Aghōra, Vāmadēva and Sadyōjat. Śritattvanidhi describes the five faces as being the colour of the pearls, yellow and dark blue, the colour of mother of pearl, and the colour of China rose (red). The similarity between the *dhyanas* of Sadāśiva and Hēraṁba is very much evident and has already been observed by the art historians. Although there is no textual description given for the arrangement of the five heads of Hēraṁba, different art traditions are observed from the extant images. Broadly these can be categorised into three types based on the arrangement of the heads as mentioned below:

1. the heads are arranged in one row (Bhattasali N., 1929)

2. four heads are arranged on either side of the central

head in two tiers – one above the other (profile) (Agarwal P.K.)

3. four of the heads face the cardinal points and the fifth is put centrally on the top

4. The heads are arranged in three tiers, all facing the front: three at the bottom, one in the second tier, and one in the third tier

The image of Gaṇēśa from the British Museum is very much similar to the five elepahnt faced Gaṇēśa reported by Alice Getty found in the Munshiganj district, Dacca, Bangladesh and an image of Gaṇēśa reported from the Śiddha Mahādeva temple at Puri described below, as the five heads are in the same tier, that is with two on either side of the central head which is much larger than the other four heads. Likewise, the five faced image of Gaṇēśa set up in a room over the image cell of Dhundirāja Gaṇēśa in the Visvanāth Gāli, Vāranāsi is also very much similar to Gaṇēśa image of the British Museum in the arrangement of the five heads.

The religious symbolism that lies behind the representation of Pañchamukha Gaṇēśa can be realised from the birth stories of Gaṇēśa contained in the Skanda Purāna. According to one myth about the origin of Gaṇēśa, the elephant headed demon Mālinī drinks Pārvatī's bath water mixed with the seed/dirt and produces a son with five elephant heads. (Jacobi J, 1914) Śiva reduced these five faces to one thus amputating the four heads of Gaṇēśa in the process of cutting away Gaṇēśa's demon portion to render him fully divine. Thus the mythological story reveals the origin of Gaṇēśa from Pārvatī, who androgynously provides the creative substance and one demon mother Malini who brings forth the five-headed Gaṇēśa.

An image of Śakti Ganapati (34" x 20"), which is much closer to that of the icon of Gaṇēśa of British Museum in its iconography has been noticed by T.E. Donaldson. The image datable to 13th century is inserted into a niche flanking the entrance of Siddha Mahādēva temple at Puri. It has been assumed by Donaldson that originally it hails from Konark and kept in the niche at a later period. The five elephant-headed god is shown seated in lalitāsana with Śakti seated on his left thigh. The front natural right hand holds a pomegranate, while the left front hand carryies bells (*ghanṭa*). The remaining right hands hold a broken tusk, small trident, arrow and chakra, while the corresponding left hands have a lotus, a small stringed bow and mace (*gada*). The proboscis is curled up to the left and holds an indistinct object. The head to the centre is shown in frontal position, while the other four heads-two on either side of the central one are depicted in profile. The hair has been arranged in a conical design ornamented with jeweled bands. *Sarpa yajñapavita* adorns the body and the lower garment is shown spreading on the *āsana*. The two-handed Śakti is shown seated in *lalitāsana* embracing the God with her right arm while she holds the lotus in her left hand. The lower part of the pedestal is missing and the vehicle of the God is not visible. Below the feet of Gaṇēśa is a large *ghaṭa* (vase) with stalks and leaves on either side. Excepting few varaitions in holding the weapons and attributes shown in the hands, the rest of the iconographical features generally tally with that of the image of Gaṇēśa from British Museum. Since the lower part of the pedestal of the Puri image is missing, the details of the mounts of the deities cannot be made out. The variations between these two images are in the manner of the curling up of the proboscis of the central head. While it turns to right in the case of the British Museum image, it is shown as curling towards the left side in the Gaṇēśa image of Puri. Further the weapons like small stringed bow, *gada* and bell are absent in the image of the British Museum while they are present in the Puri image. Likewise, it is observed that sugarcane, *nāga pāśa* and ears of paddy are present in the British Museum that are absent in the image reported from Puri. These variations in the iconographical features between the two images under study clearly indicate a different ritual tradition in worshipping Gaṇēśa that is different from that of the usual brahmanical tradition. It seems that the British Museum image has close association with the ideals of fertility and prosperity since it shows the *naga* in the manner of *pāśa* as well as the sugarcane and that the image addresses the religious needs of the devotees who were desirous of securing progeny, wealth and material prosperity.

Studies conducted earlier on the five-fold representations in India have revealed three definite stages in the development of its iconography on the basis of the extant images reported from Varanasi, Rajasthan and Madhya Pradesh. In the first stage, the images of four seated

Ganapatis and an elephant form the group of Pañch Gaṇēśa[1] while the next stage is that in which five Gaṇapatis occur in their common elephant-headed form without the presence of the elephant (animal form). To this stage can be assigned the five elephantheaded Gaṇapati images noticed at Puri and Konark (now placed in the British Museum). In the third stage of the development of the iconography, sometimes a sixth God was also added to accompany the group of five Gaṇapatis. Thus the iconograpic study of the five elephant faced Gaṇēśa from British Museum is quite interesting as it has revealed the worhship of Gaṇēśa influenced by the Sakta and Tantric ritual traditions giving rise to the creation of a new iconographic form such as the five elephant-headed god called Hēramba in association with Lakshmī as his Śakti with the turn of the gods' central probascis to his right which is unusual, suggestive of the *vāmāchara* traditions practiced in worshipping the god.

REFERENCE

1 The Carving of the elephant (purely in animal form) on the lotus seat along with four Gaṇapatis, vehicle rat repeated five times near their feet and the halos around all the images observed at Jamaroli (near Jaipur, Rajasthan) proves beyond doubt, the deity stutus of the elephant that constitute the Pañcha-Gaṇeśa theme.

BIBLIOGRAPHY

Anantanandagiri., *Samkaravijaya*, p. 87.

An image of Śiva as Svābhishēkamūrti has been reported very recently. See S.N. Shivarudraswamy., "Svābhishekamūrti. A Rare Image of Śiva" in *Proceedings of Indian Art History Congress*, Delhi, 1999, pp. 81–83.

Burgess., *Amarāvati*, Pl 30 No. 1.

Dvimukha, trimukha and five-faced Gaṇēśa forms of late medieval period are reported from Varanasi by P.K. Agrawala; See P.K. Agrawala., "Some Varanasi Images of Gaṇapati and Their Iconographical Problem" in *Artibus Asiae*, vol. XXXIX 1977/2, pp. 139–155.

E.A. Payne., *The Śāktas*, Calcutta, 1933 pp. 4–5 and Mahadevan *op.cit.*, p. 210–211; Sir J. Woodroffe., *Śakti* and *Śaīkta*, p. 89.

Gaṇēśa Purāṇa. Pūrvārdha, 46, 31–32, *Gaṇēśa Sahasram*; Also see, N.P. Joshi., "Puranas as Interpreters of Icons" in *Kala*, vol. VII, Delhi, 2001.

Getty, Alice, *Gaṇēśa*, Oxford, 1936, Pl. 3 (b).

Gudrun Buhnemann., *Forms of Gaṇēśa A Study Based on Vidyārṇavatantra*, Wichtrach, 1989, pp. 66–69.

J. Jacobi., "Brahmanism", *Encyclopaedia of Religion and Ethics*, 1914, p.807–808

M.A. Dhaky., "Kiradu and the Maru Gurjara Style of Temple Architecture" *Bulletin of American Academy of Benares*, vol. I, 1967, p. 42, fig. 68.

N. Bhattasali., *Iconography of Buddhist and Brahmanical Sculptures in the Dacca Museum*, Varanasi, 1929, pl LVIb; B. Bhattacharya.,*The Indian Buddhist Iconography Mainly Based on the Sādhanamāla and other Cognate Tantric Texts of Rituals*, (Reprint) 1980 fig. 5; Balasubrahmanyam., *Early Chōḷa Andhra*, *t* pt I Bombay, 1975, pl 311; alice getty., *op. cit.*, p. 15, pl 4 (b).

Narasimhapurāṇa, 25, 13, p. 73.

Paul B Courtright., *Gaṇēśa Lord of Obstacles, Lord of Beginning*, Oxford, 1985, p. 22.

Prithvi K Agrawal., *op. cit.*, fig. 18 (Varanasi image datable to 16th–17th centuries A.D.)

R.C. Agrawala., "Newly Discovered Pañcha Gaṇēśa from Jaipur, Rajasthan" *Jouranal of Oriental Institute*, Baroda vol. XXI, Nos. 1–2, 1997, p. 107, ps. I-II.

Rao., D. Hanumantha, "A Unique Sculpture of Gaṇapati from Sankaram" in *Sri Ramachandrika* (Prof. Oruganti Ramachandraiya Fesschrift) *Essays on Indian Archaeology, History, Epigraphy,*

Numismatics, Art and Religion ed. By A.V.N. Murty and I.K. Sarma, vol. II Delhi, 1993, pp. 347–350.

Skanda Purāṇa, Kasi Khanda, 57, 104, p. 398.

T.A.G. Rao., *Elements of Hindu Iconography.*, vol. I, Pt Ii, Madras, 1914, Appendix C p. 7.

T.M. Mahadevan., *Outlines of Hinduism*, Bombay, 2nd edition, 1960 pp. 203–211; C. Chakravarti., *Tantras, Studies on Their Religion and Literature*, Calcutta, 1972, p. 85.

Andhra University
Visakhapatnam

Prof. M. Krishna Kumari

Babour Temples of Jammu

Babour, a small village is situated about 38 km north-east of Jammu and nine km. north of Mansar lake. At this place there is a group of six stone temples of great antiquity. The ancient name of the site is Babbapura referred to twice in the *Rajatarangini*[1]. This ancient site is situated on a plateau, about square 4.8 km. square in extent in the Dansal Dun of the inner hills. According to the tradition current among the people of the area there were thirteen temples but now only six exist in various stages of decay. There are reasons to believe that Babbapura was the capital of the Duggar from about the tenth century to the middle of fourteenth century during which period Jammu had been forsaken as the seat of Government due to recurring Arab and Turk invasions (Hutchison & Vogel, 1994).

The largest of these six temples is situated to the east of the group. It is a double structure with a pillared *mandapa* (hall). The temple is built on a plinth 2.6 metres (8feet) high. It is approached by a flight of steps from the west side. The plinth or Jagati is a square platform, about 16.50 metres each side. Its doorway which about 2.20 metres high and 1.15 m wide, is profusely ornamented with carved human figures and floral reliefs. According to R.C. Kak, "the roof was supported on two rows of twenty four filleted columns (Kak R.C., 1972)". The columns are surmounted by capitals. The chief distinguishing features of these capital are extremely well carved with interesting large elephant heads and trunks. The roof of monolithic columns are about 2.75 metres in height.

The *mandapa* has approach to two main sanctums each 2.15 metres squares. These are intervened by a third sanctum. The two large sanctums have also a small *antarala* each. The *antarala* (porch) of all the three sanctums have twenty fluted columns surmounted by capitals. In addition to these sanctums there was a fourth one, smaller in size than others. Extermally the whole of the stone construction was elaborately carved.

Devi Bhagvati Temple

From architectural point of view the temple of Devi Bhagavati in the temple complex at Babour can be placed between 850 and 1050 A.D. (Sehgal). The shrine is a highly oriented structure built in stone. It comprises of a single chamber sanctuary with a *mandapa* in front. The *mandapa* is entered by an entrance in its west wall. The latter has flights of steps both inside and outside. The roof of the *mandapa* is supported on four round fluted columns, which stand on a plain base.

The temple walls were richly carved on the outside with divine figures and sacred motifs. These sculptured reliefs unfortunately are much mutilated. In the left jamb of the doorway is a figure of the river Goddess Ganga standing on a crocodile. On opposite panel is another figure, completely obliterated, must have been of Yamuna. The lintel bore the nava graha in relief.

The temple courtyard is littered with dressed and carved stones fallen from the temples. Two of these, almost as big as the one which carried the figures of

---

[1]First reference in the Rajatarangini is to Kirti, the ruler of Babbapura (i.e. Babbapura during the reign of King Kalsa of Kashmir 1063-1089 A.D.), Babbapura is again mentioned in the reign of King Sussla when Vajadhara, The Lord of Babbapura played a significant role in Kashmir affairs *Rajatarangini*, VII, 538.

Ganga, bear images of Ganesha and Bairava (Gupta Prashant). Figures of Vishnu, Lakshmi and Annapurna have also been discovered.

The inner sanctum contain two round shaped small *pindis* of brown colour emerging from the ground. Besides these, figures of Kali and Durga are also installed there. Kali is shown in standing posture, having four hands in which she is holding sword, damru and bowl respectively. A figure of lion is also depicted as standing behind her. The image is engraved on small stone slab black in colour. The figure of Durga is represented as riding a lion holding various weapons in her four hands. This image is of white marble.

The whole temple complex is under the control of Archaeological Department. Worship in the Devi Bhagavati temple is performed by local priest (Charak S.S.).

Babour Temple or Shivdivala

In the opinion of R.C. Kak, the temple situated in Babour proper and known to the people around as Sivadivala, is probably later in date than the other remains at this place. It had a *mandapa,* an *antarala* or vestibule and the sanctum or *garbhagriha.* The *mandap* in front has alltogether disappeared leaving behind only some traces of lower courses. The structure of the shrine which exists, contains only the *garbhagriha*, internally 2.20 m^2. and some 5.50 m. high ceiling in the form of concentric circles and an *antrala* measuring 2.1x1.40 m. The *Sikhara* is in the shape of stepped pyramids with a narrow flat which is surmounted by an egg-like dome, on top of which is placed a ribbed *amalaka* which has on top *kumbha* (pitcher) or kalsa on which is planted a *trisul* and *dhwaja*(Gauhar J.N.). It seems that the super structure has been reconstructed out of some old material and new design. The shrine is a living one and is visited daily by devotees from the nearby inhabitations. R.C. Kak observed that the temple was constructed over an older crumbled shrine, as some part of it e.g. the columns and the *amalaka,* are very different from other parts. The relief work on the external surface of the wall is much later than the columns and some sculptures in the temple. The most outstanding is the Siva-Parvati group of black marble, including the Ganesa and lance-bearing Karttikeya and Nandi.

Anand Babour Shrine

There is a ruined temple situated away from the village on the raised bank of a *nala.* It is locally known as 'Anand Babour' temple. On a rectangular plinth, which is almost buried under ground, is a block of three chambers with a separate vestibule for each of them and the pillared hall or *mandapa* in front of them. The entrance and some other parts of it are in such a ruined condition that it is much difficult to describe its architecture. Externally the temple is plain and sparsely decorated. The ornamentaion include human figures, animal effigies, floral reliefs and images of deities. Almost all of these are in decayed state.

Kalādhera Temple

Kalādhera or 'Black shrine' is now in a ruined condition and any useful description of its architecture is very difficult. It stands on a large rectangular (*jagati*) plinth about 23.25x16 metres in dimension and about 3 metres in height, approached from the east by a flight of steps. The existing structure shows that the temple was much plainer than the other temples. Like other temples it has a pillared hall which is at present roof less, and a cella with an *antarala* in their midst. The door jambs though chiseled finely, are plain. The lintel above has a niche ornamented with floral designs. According to R.C. Kak, the capitals are similar to the columns of the larger temples and adorned with projecting *makara* heads facing the centre, but have disappeared.

The base of the columns are plain, heavy and square. There are traces of pilasters also. The two free standing door jambs of the entrance to the sanctum have each two niches with ogee-arch carved tops. Each of the niche contains a mutilated figure. The low remains of the wall show that the temple was externally well decorated with human figures, niches and floral motifs.

Near the Kaladhera temple, there is another ruined temple, which stands on a high platform (*jagti*), it contains three conventional portions marked out by the remains of walls i.e. the *cella*, preceded by an *antarala* and the *mandapa*, the latter approached through the *mukhadvara* on top of the flight of steps. The gateway is nicely decorated. Externally, the temple seems to be *triratna* in style, with walls and offsets without much carved ornamentation. Only the outer surface of the structure of *cella* and *antarala* is a little ornamented.

In addition to the main shrine, there are traces of two more shrines in the same compound; one is in front of the temple and the other at the back of the temple to the right. All the temples of Babour are built up of sandstone, which was available locally. The stones used for the construction of these temples seems to be little softer; hence were chiseled carefully and then employed. It is also noticeable that no mortar has been used in the construction of these temples. The stones used for the construction are not of a good quality stone, the builders used stone slabs of very huge sizes to ensure stability.

BIBLIOGRAPHY

Charak, S.S., *History & Culture of Himalayan States*, Vol. VIII.

Ganhar, J.N., *Jammu Shrines and Pilgrimages*, Jammu, 1985, p.151

Gupta, Prashant, *Shakti Shrines of Jammu Region, A Study in religious Prospective*,Ph.D.thesis, p.57

Hutchison & Vogel, *History of Punjab Hill States*, Vol. II Delhi, 1994

Kak, R.C., *Antiquities of Basholi and Rammagar*, Delhi, 1972, p.21.

Sehgal, *Ancient Temples of Babour*, Jammu, pp.70-71.

Anita Billawaria

Senior Fellow
Centre for History & Culture of
Jammu & Ladakh Studies
Department of History,
University of Jammu, Jammu

Ganesa Images in Himachal Pradesh–An Iconographical study

With the sky-high snow clad mountains and the plains both, Himachal Pradesh has been known from time immemorial as the *Land of Gods,* who have their abodes in the entire state. On account of its ancient religious traditions and deities enshrined in this state, belonging to different cults and creeds, Hindu, the Buddhist and the Jaina pantheons, Himachal Pradesh has remained an integrated socio-cultural entity since the very early times.

Ganesa is one of the most popular gods of Hindu pantheon and occupies the main position among the major Hindu gods (Yadav Nirmala, 1977). He is worshipped before the commencement of every act, considered good for life. The devotee worship him as *'Vighnesa'* (the lord of removing obstacles), *Mangaldata* (the giver of welfare and of auspicious things), *Buddhividhata* (god of wisdom), *Siddhidata* (the bestower of success).

There are several stories of Ganesa's birth in puranic literature. He is said to be have been born either independently or by Parvati or Siva alone or by both. The Ganesa, the non Aryan deity of ancient time rose to the position of the great god in later Gupta period after his admittance into the Brahmanical pantheon. The most popular deity at the present time in the Hindu Pantheon has not been clearly referred to in the Rig-Veda. More over, Ganapati mentioned in the earliest literature refer to *Brihaspati* not to Ganesa. He is clearly mentioned first time in *Baudhayana Dharma-sutra* with Rudra and his consort. He is called Vinayaka in *Atharvasirash* upanishad. Ganesa has several epithets such as *Vakratunda, Ekdanta, Hastimukha, Lambodara* and *Vighna.*

The genesis of Ganesa may be traced in the Mahabharata where the *ganas* of Rudra are said to have had animal's faces. The *Matsya Purana* also records that Rudra *ganas* are *vyaghra-mukha* and *gaja-mukha.* This, earliest image of Ganesa possibly evolved from *yaksha* and *naga* figure and as such the elephantine face might have been borrowed from them. Coomaraswamy as well as Jouveau – Dubreuil traces the evolution of Ganesa sculpture from *Gajanana – Yakshamurti* from the Amaravati railings (Getty Alice, 1992) [now in collection of Madras Museum], said to be not later than the beginning of our era, as the transitional form of Ganesa. The *yaksha* is crouching under the weight of a long, serpent-shaped garland, upheld at interval by other *ganas.* Only a part of the body is left, but enough remain to show that the *gana* is short and of the usual *yaksha* corpulence. Another representation of this type is found on frieze of the stupa belonging to early centuries near Mihintale in Cylone, in which one of the *ganas* is elephant-headed and is represented with one tusk. The elephant-faced gana is seated with an attendant on either side facing him.

The earliest sculpture of Ganesa is exhibited in Mathura Museum of Kushana Period (3rd century AD). Another sculpture found from at Sankisa (5th century AD) is exhibited now in the Museum, Fur Volker-Kunde. The figure is disproportionate with heavy head and trunk and stumpy legs. He holds a bowl in his left hand and a tusk in the right hand. In the early Gupta period, we notice a further development of this type but it's affinity to the *yaksha* form still persists, but in the later stage Ganesa becomes an independent identity. A large number of images were made adorned with different attributes. He is popular throughout India and even certain other region adjoining the country. Himachal Pradesh, too, has, had quite a large share of the idols of the god. Stylistic and iconographic features of some of these are discussed below.

The earliest known stone sculpture of Ganesa in Himachal dates back to the early seventh century AD, now in the State Museum Shimla. It was found at village Dohgi, Una district. It retains some features of the Gupta style. The sculpture appears quite powerful and somewhat bulky. The partly eroded four-armed deity seated in *ardha-paryankasana* having *yajnopavita* visible on the belly. His association with this style of *asana* is because of his potbelly. Due to bad state of preservation, its iconographic details are totally defaced, it is difficult to describe the whole image correctly.

An almost life size brass image of seated Ganesa of the 8th century c.700-750 AD is under worship at Bharmour, district Chamba. An inscription on its pedestal depicts that it was the work of Gugga (Ohri V.C., 1991), an architect in the reign of Meruverman (early 8th century AD). Ganesa is seated on a *simhāsana* (lion throne), and is bedecked with jewels that are distinctive to Chamba and the modeling of the body is very similar to Kashmir work. The god is three-eyed and his trunk first turns towards left and then right, makes a 'U' shape curve. He is holding *svadanta* in the lower right hand and *akshamālā* in the upper right hand while a *paraśu* in the upper left and a *modak-pātra* (vessel of sweetmeat) in the lower left hand. A human figure with elephant's ears appears in front of the pedestal between the two lions. The composition of metal used for the sculpture and its casting technique also show the influence of southern Kashmir.

A fragment of another sculpture displayed in the State Museum Shimla depicts a pot-bellied Ganesa (*tundila*) seated with one leg bent and other in *maharaja-lilāsana* on a circular cushion placed on a *pañcharatha*-pedestal. The image is fragmentary and its part of torso and lower part are extant. A *mūṣhīka*, the *vahana* of the deity, is seated at the left of the pedestal. Behind the deity, a female devotee with folded hands appears. The snake-head visible on the belly of the image indicates that it served as *sarpa-yajñopavīta*. The modeling is smooth, natural and the proportions are classical. These are typical features of the early Pratihara style. The sculpture belongs to 8th century AD.

An image of Ganesa seated on Simhasna of early ninth century AD is seen on the door-lintel of the Siva temple at Jagatsukh, district Kullu. He wears a *dhoti*, the folds of which can be noticed between his legs. The two-armed Ganesa holds a *modaka- pātra* in the left hand and probably an *akshamālā* in the right hand. His trunk first hangs straight, then turns towards the left, and is placed on the *modak-pātra* where its tip makes a curl. The lion vahan of the god indicates the belief and its association with Kashmir.

An image of four-armed Ganesa is seen in Mahadeva temple at Bajaura, district Kullu, belongs to c.900 AD. He is seated in *lalitāsana* on a double-petalled lotus seat. His seat is supported by a human figure appearing in front of the pedestal between the two lions. Ganesa wears a necklace, a long garland and an under garment. The folds of his under garment can be noticed below his right foot. The attributes in his four hands are *svadanta* in the lower right, a *paraśu* in the upper right, a lotus with stalk in the upper left and a *modaka-pātra* in the lower left hand. The attributes in the hands of this image are according to the *Matsya Purana* but their order is different in the image. The right tusk is depicted and his ears are adorned with the lotus and bud shaped ornaments. His trunk first hangs straight, then turns towards the left, and is placed on the *modaka-pātra* where its tip makes a curl. The traces of a halo in the back, which is now broken, can be noticed.

A stone sculpture of four-armed Ganesa (Thakur L.S) is seen in a *gavaksha* (window) of the Durga temple at Hatkoti in district Shimla. He is wearing his usual ornaments and is shown seated on a double petalled lotus in the *ardha-paryankāsana*. He is holding a *mūlkanda* (radish) and a *paraśu* (battle-axe) heading downwards and is placed on pedestal in his left hand which is a rare representation while his right upper hand holds a lotus in an umbrella like form which is the peculiar feature of this area, and perhaps an emerging trait of the Kushan-Kashmir sculpture. The lower hand of the god rests on his thigh. The sculpture belongs to c.9th century AD.

A four-armed Ganesa sculpture is at Bachoonch, district Shimla carved with typical Pratihara style showing local elements in the form of a lotus and a long receptacle for *modaka* in his hand. He is seated on a raised seat in *lalitāsna* wearing ornamented conical crown, bell necklace and *sarpa-yajñopavīta*. The use of garland of bells is seen in yaksha figures of early 2nd century AD. These figures are the ancient prototype of the idols of the Ganesa. He is broad-shouldered, pot-bellied and has small-legs. The deity as usual with one tusk, *śūrpakarṇa,* an elephantine face with plain halo at the back. It has four hands and proboscis turned to the left and rising up to the shoulder. He holds a *paraśu* (battle-axe) in his right upper hand and his lower right-hand held in *tarjanī* pose holds a rosary. His upper left hand holds a lotus while the lower left hand rests on his thigh, holding the long receptacle of ambrosia-pot, touched by the proboscis. The image corresponds to the description of the *Aparājitaprichchha* and the *AgniPurāṇa.* The sculpture may be assigned to early 10th century AD. Another rare sculpture of Ganesa from the same place carved quite skillfully is seen seated in *bhadrāsana.* He is wearing his usual ornaments. The proboscis turned towards the right instead of the left holds *modaka* in it. His vahana mūṣhika appears at the right. His stout body appears attractive and the head is somewhat small, suggesting a later development.

A four-armed brass image of Ganesa seated on a raised pedestal in *ardhā- paryankāsna* from Sarahan, district Shimla (now in the State Museum) belongs to 10th century AD. He is wearing his usual ornaments. The deity is as usual with one tusk, *śūrpakarṇa,* pot-bellied, and a lotus-type halo of the Pratihara period. His proboscis turns towards left and tapering towards the end and touches the *modak- pātra.* He is holding a lotus bud in upper right hand and. the lower hand is shown in *tarjnī mudrā.* His upper left hand holds *paraśu* and a heaped modak-pātra in the lower left hand. His *vahana* (vehicle) *mūshika* is approaching the *modak- pātra* at the left.

Dancing form of Ganesa is also popular in sculptural representation. An eight-armed dancing Ganesa sculpture of 10th century AD is seen at Hatkoti in district Shimla. The deity is shown raising his right leg in the air and the left leg is slightly bent in a rhythmic pose. The deity wears a small crown, necklace, bracelets and a loincloth. A snake serving as the sacred thread has its loose flowing end indicating the vigorous action of the dance. He is shown as usual, pot-bellied *śūrpakarṇa* and has a single tusk with a proboscis turned to left. The eight-armed deity is holding a snake above his head in the two backhands in a whirling posture. The upper right hand shown in *tarjanī mudrā,* carries an *akshasutra* (rosary), while the lower right hand holds a lotus in an umbrella like form. The left upper hand holds *mūlkanda*(radish) and a *modaka- pātra* is shown in the lower left hand while the lower most hand is broken . Two attendants are shown on either side while *gandharva* figures are carved in relief at the upper part of the slab. The figure is full of grace and all the details are demonstrated in such a remarkable manner that shows how the artist of that remote area could convert an iconic grosteque into an elegant piece of sculpture.

A similar kind of Ganesa sculpture is also seen in the Surya temple at Nirath, district Shimla. This stone dancing Ganesa belongs to c.10th AD. based in Pratihara style,while body is typical, his rather thin head would later develop into a folk style (Postal M, 1985). The eight-armed god is dancing on a *tri-ratha* throne with his left foot raised up. His crown shows conical shape, a necklace of bells and a long *naga-yajnopavita.* His left tusk is broken off and the right one, intact visible. Starting from the lowest right hand, his first hand holds the handle of a *paraśu,* second hand is in *abhaya-mudrā* with an *akshamālā* in it, *svadanta* is kept in the third, fourth hand holds the serpent-hood and in the right hands the fifth hand holds its tail, a lotus flower with stalk in the sixth, a *modaka-pātra* near the shoulder is kept in the seventh hand and the eighth hand is hanging down in dancing attitude. The *modaka-pātra* is conical and is heaped up with *modakas* on which the curled trunk of the deity is placed. The serpent above the head is kept in such a way that it has made an arch above his head.

A rare sculpture of six-armed Ganesa i. ˈoı ɹ in Vaidyanatha Siva temple at Baijnath, district Kangra. He is dancing with his right foot slightly raised and the left foot resting on the pedestal. This dancing posture is known as the *chatūra.* His headdress is adorned with a triangle at its front and third eye is carved vertically at the centre of the forehead, which is a common feature seen in the sculpture of the Chamba and Kangra region. The god is shown with necklace, bracelets, anklets, a *sarpa-yajñopavīta* and a *vanamala.* His lower right hand hangs downwards, while his middle hand held in *abhyamudrā* also holds an *akshasutrā* and the upper left hand holds a *parśu.* He holds a lotus stalk in upper left hand, a *modaka- pātra* near the shoulder in the middle left hand and his lowermost hand is hanging down and is holding the hem of the garment. A lion on the right and an elephant on the left are seated facing outwards. Three *gandhrvas* beating the drum are carved beneath the seat. The image can be ascribed to c.14th century AD.

An interesting sculpture of four-armed standing Ganesa is under worship in Panchvakra temple at mandi. He is wearing a long garland passing through his shoulders and reaching down to the legs. He is shown with elongated face, wearing conical crown. He holds his usual attributes in his hands. The folds of *dhoti* appear between the legs. This kind of representation is commonly seen in the sculptures of the Beas valley. The deity has a curious protruding patch-like naval and the trunk is thick, while the treatment of eyes is also fish-like showing mannerism towards the folk type of work. The sculpture is contemporary to the temple, built in AD 1520 by a ruler of a Mandi State. A stone sculpture of four-armed Ganesa from the same place carved in folk style seated on a lotus pedestal is wearing a typical crown that is commonly seen in the Chamba area. His elongated face and high forehead have prominent eyebrows and has protruding fish-like eyes. He is wearing *dhoti* of which folds clearly appear between the legs. His trunk is small and stout. Lotus appears like a disk in his hand. Two *mūṣhikas* appear on either side at the base of pedestal.

Ganesa image is also noticed in the pedestal of Kamaksha Devi at Karsog, district Mandi. His trunk turned towards the right, he is holding a *modaka-pātra* and a *paraśu* (battle axe) in the right hands, while a *mūsala* and a *lotus* in left hands.

The figure of Ganesa is seen in association with *Saptamātrkās* at the *toraṇa* of the idol of *Mahishasurmardini* at Hatkoti and Shiva temple at Baijnath. A Ganesa sculpture of c17-18th century AD is displayed in State Museum, Shimla. *Shakti* is shown seated on his left side and not at his thigh as usual. The couple is seated on a circular cushion supported by two crouching lions serving the mount of Ganesa.

Ganesa is often seen in association of Siva, Parvati and Kartikeya in Pahari miniature painting. A Guler miniature painting of period c.1780 AD depicts Ganesa clapping with four hands and his trunk is raised upwards in the air in roaring position. The deity is wearing his usual ornaments and is shown in saffron colour.

Many examples of the images of Ganesa carved in wood are seen in the wooden temples of later medieval period in the valley of the *Satluj*, *Beas* and the tributaries of the *Jamuna* in H.P. These folkish works are quite interesting and suggestive of the great popularity of the god. Ganesa also found in the Chamba embroidery where the deity is embroiled in folk style with their usual garments and attributes indicating the common popularity of the god.

The plains of Haryana and Punjab lie roughly to the west of hills of Himachal Pradesh and in the east bounded by the high ranges of Himalaya Mountain bordering Tibet. Uttranchal and Uttar Pradesh are on its south side while the state of Jammu and Kashmir is on its north. The stylistic traits and ideas in plastic arts of Kashmir and Uttar Pradesh have influenced the art in Himachal Pradesh.

The stylistic traits and ideas in plastic arts of Kashmir appear strongly on the sculptures of Chamba & adjoining region of Himachal Pradesh. The crown showing conical edges and impression of third eye, which is the peculiar features of Kashmir art styles and composition of metal are also similar to the Kashmir region. While the sculptures of Shimla, Sirmour and Kullu regions shows the influence of Gangetic plain. A trade route leading from plains of Uttar Pradesh to Central Asia passing through these areas are responsible for spreading this style in these areas. The sculptures of the areas reveal that they posses the stylistic sophistication of Pratihara style. The figures have hypnotic expressions in their eyes with gentle arched eye brows, soft smile and dignified expressions by marvelously rounded faces.

Some sculptures of Mandi & Kullu shows the mix trait of both the styles i.e. Kashmir and Pratihara. These areas became the meeting place of both the styles and even some local traits appears on these sculptures. The fold of *dhoti* appearing between the legs and lotus like an umbrella are the some local features of the area. Hence having a different geographical condition no independent style developed in the area.

A comparative chart of ornamentations of Ganesa shows the gradual development of ornamentations in different period of Himachal Pradesh.

Some Evidences of Ganesa in Buddhist Monasteries of Western Trans-Himalayan Region in Himachal Pradesh

Perhaps no temple of any deity could be conceived without Ganesa in it. Besides the Brahmanical Hindu temples, the god Ganesa penetrated in Buddhism as well and his presence can be noticed in Buddhist monasteries of Himachal Pradesh as well as the Tibetan Thakas (Nagar Shantilal, 1990). But it is true that the evidences of presentation of Ganesa in Buddhism particularly in Himachal are found very limited.

For example, the presentation of Ganesa in Buddhist monastery could be seen. The best evidences of it are found in Tabo monastery situated in Spiti valley of Lahaul and Spiti district of Himachal Pradesh. The region belongs to Western trans-Himalaya and is bounded by Ladakh Region of Jammu and Kashmir on the north and on the west and south west, Lahaul sub-division of Lahaul and Spiti and Kullu tehsil of Kullu district. Kinnaur district is situated in south-east and Tibet (China) is on the eastern side of the region (Handa O.C, 1994)

The door-frame of *Byams-pa chenpo lha-khang* (dedicated to the very imposing image of Boddhisatva Maitreya) temple of Tabo monastery shows an example of a mixture of Hinduism and Buddhism. It has very fine carved wooden figures of the Buddha in different postures on the door lintel. It is very interesting that below the Buddha's postures a carved wooden figure in the centre of the door-frame (*lalatbimba*) has been identified to be of Ganesa by A.H. Francke. On the basis of iconographical study it can be noticed that the seated Ganesa has two hands but attributes of the both hands are not visible. His tusk first turns towards the left and then it is placed on the *modaka-pātra*. His crown reminiscent of a Kuluta-type.(Thakur L.S, 2001) Except these icons it is difficult to identify the whole image of Ganesa correctly.

Another worthwhile example of presentation in Buddhism is also can be noticed in Tabo monastery in the form of Stucco of Ganesa. The *Gtsug lha-khang* (literally means academy and also this term has frequently been used to mean temple) at Tabo is the most central and important temple of the Tabo monastery. The medium-sized stucco-image of Ganesa is seated on a raised platform on the entrance way to hall on the left of the door in meditative posture.(Handa O.C, 1994) The Ganesa statue has been placed on the left side of *Vajrapani*. The seated Ganesa has two hands, the first hand is in *abhaya-mudrā*, and the left hand holding *modaka-patrā*. He wears a long *yajnopavita*. Traces of a triple crescent-type crown, reminiscent of a *Kuluta*-type is visible.(Thakur L.S, 2001) His tusk first hangs straight with little towards left, then turns towards right. Mouth is completely open. There are some figure may be flower are visible in the front of the pedestal.

Due to confluence of faiths and association of both religion a number of cases can seen that the Buddhist deities are worshipped as Brahmanical deities and vice-versa. For example, one of the most famous temple of Kali or Durga at village Udaipur in Lahual popularly known as Markula Devi. According to A.H. Francke observation, the Buddhists of Lahaul worshipped the Goddess Markula as *Do-rje-phang-mo* (Sanskrit Vajra-varahi), who is indeed a Brahmanical deity and is revered by Hindus as *Mahishāsurmardini*. Other example can be noticed here that the depiction of scene of Mara's assault on Buddha, seated in *Bhumisparsa mudra*, together with the scenes from the *Ramayana* and the *Mahabharata* marvelously engraved over the wooden ceilings of the temple. The depiction of scenes shows again the confluence of faiths by both Hindus and Buddhism.

Another example of the association of faith can be seen in *Trilokinatha* temple at Tunde in Lahaul. The god is dedicated to Brahmanical deity Siva known as *Trilokinatha*, but in Tibetan it is popular as *Raspagastha* meaning all seeing god. Except it, two other temples of *Trilokinatha* and *Panchavaktra* situated in Mandi are also dedicated to Siva. The gods of both temples are also believed to be of Buddhist association because *Trilokinatha* in the valley of Trans-Himalayan region has been identified with *Bodhisattva Avalakitesvara*.

Against the above observation of Ganesa's presentation and acceptance in Buddhists pantheon, L. Austine Waddel observes that Ganesa is not revered in Buddhism (Waddel, L.A, 1979). According to him the Buddhist god of wealth, *Jambhala*, is a form of Kubera or Vaisravana and his form is partly like his relative or prototype, the Hindu Ganesa. He has identified the attributes of the god *Jambhala*, as in his right hand the god holds a bag of jewels, or money, or grain, symbolic of riches and in his left an ichneumon or mongoose, which is the conqueror of snakes, the mythical guardians of treasure. About the Buddhist god *Jambhala*, Nalini Kanta Bhattasali also observes the same veiw as observed by Waddel.(Bhattasali N.K., 2001)

On the other hand, on the basis of available evidences of confluence and association of faiths by the both Hindu and Buddhists, it may be stated that the evidences of Ganesa in the form of wood carving on the main door-frame and in the form of statue in the most important Buddhist monastery at Tabo are not a simple case. These evidences confirm the presentation and acceptance of Ganesa by Buddhism in Himachal Pradesh.

Dr. O.C. Handa has given records in his book titled Tabo Monastery and Buddhism in the Trans-Himalaya, (New Delhi, 1994) that in of construction of Tabo monastery thirty two crafts-men were engaged. The master craftsman was Bidhika and all were Hindu belonging to Kashmir, Kullu and Kinnaur region. If it is presumed that the presentation of Ganesa in Tabo monastry was due to the Hindu craftsmen, then a question arises as to why the Buddhist religion accepted carved figure of Ganesa on the door-frame and placing a statue of Ganesa in the most important place in Tabo monastry, patronised with great care by Rin-chen-bzang-po.

BIBLIOGRAPHY

Bhattasali, Nalini Kanta: *Iconography of Buddhist and Brahmanical Sculptures in the Dacca Museum*, New Delhi, 2001, pp.34-35.

Getty, Alice: *Ganesa, A Monograph on the Elephant-Faced God*, New Delhi, 1992, p. 25.

Handa, O.C.: *Tabo Monastery and Buddhism in the Trans-Himalaya*, New Delhi, 1994, p.21.

Nagar, Shantilal: *The Temples of Himachal Pradesh*, New Delhi, 1990, p.56.

Ohri, V.C.: *Sculpture of Western Himalayas*, Delhi, 1991 p. 78.

Postel, M. and others: *Antiquities of Himachal*, Vol.1, Bombay, 1985, p.64, Fig. 80.

Thakur, L.S.: Architectural and Sculptural Art of H.P. in Journal *East and West*, Vol. 36 No. 1-3 p 256.

Buddhism in the Western Himalaya, Oxford, 2001, p.121.

Waddel, L. Austine: *Buddhism and Lamaism of Tibet*, New Delhi, 1979, p.368.

Yadav, Nirmla: *Ganesa in Art and Literature*, Jaipur, 1997 p.1.

Arun Kumar Singh

Lecturer
Department of History
H.P. University, Shimla-171005

Cement and Mortar in the Ancient Structures:
Observation on Pyrotechnological Developments in the Ganga Plains

There is a direct connection between the advancement of pyrotechnology and development of construction techniques. Ceramic, terracotta, metal and cement/mortar are the important pyrotechnological expressions during the antiquity, which have influenced the course of human civilizations. Here, we propose to draw attention to the last named technology, i.e., cement/mortar in Ancient India. We wish to address ourselves to some problems which have not received due attention of scholars so far. When and why the need for cement/mortar was felt in India? What was its composition at specific cultural stages? Does the analytical analysis of cement/mortar speak of a proper understanding of nature and types of mortars/cement available or was it a random application of some paste? We propose to pick up samples from different cultural stages upto 18-19 century structures before the beginning of the so-called Portland cement and make a comparative assessment to answer the queries raised above.

Some work of this nature has been done earlier which is used here for making comparative assessment with the samples analysed by us. As in most of the cases, the Indus Civilization represents a distinct identity in comparison to the plastering and binding agents used in the subsequent cultures. Nevertheless, the comparison of the cement/mortar of the Indus Civilization with the ones used during the Early Historic times onwards in the Gangetic Plains is in order. We aim to throw light on the nature and techniques of structural activity at certain nodal points of Indian history. We come across two terms being used frequently, plaster and mortar. According to *Encyclopedia of Indian Archaeology* by A. Ghosh "Plaster is defined as a material used for coating walls and mortar may be defined as a plastic building material generally made by mixing lime with sand and water". Wesbster's Seventh New Collegiate Dictionary describes cement 'as a binding element or agent, a substance to make objects adhere to each other or 'a powder of alumina, silica, lime, iron oxide & magnesia burned together in a kiln and pulverised and used as an ingredient of mortar and concrete.'

The procedure involves expert control of temperature in preparation of proper cement/mortar. There is, therefore, direct connection between advancement in pyrotechnology and use of cement/mortar in a civilization.

Natural Cements (including hydraulic cement)

The first natural cement was made in small upright wood burning kilns that were fired for about a week, after which the clinker was ground between millstones by waterpower.

When CO_2 is removed from pure limestone (calcium carbonate) by prolonged heating, a process known as calcining takes place. This results in quick lime (calcium oxide) slakes rapidly reacting in water with the volution of considerable heat and the product (calcium hydroxide) forms putty that does not set under water. Its use as a plaster or mortar is dependent on its interaction with CO_2 in the air and the resulting formation of a moderately hard form of calcium carbonate. The calcined product of such a limestone, which has a high calcium content, is a natural cement called "fat lime". When the limestone contains upto 25% of an argillaieous (clay-containing) material, such as shale, the calcined product reacts slowly with water, there is then not a rapid evolution of heat but a slow one, and, therefore, a hard product is formed that does not disintegrate under water. The calcined product with a relatively low 10% to 20% silica and alumina content are usually called 'hydraulic limes', while those with a silica and alumina content of 20% to 35% are referred to simply as 'natural cements'. Magnesia may be present in both kinds materials in concentrations of 10% to 25%.

By the middle of 1st millenium BC, structures of more permanent nature started appearing in the Gangetic plains. It is closely linked with the 'second urbanization' and a true beginning of 'Iron Age' in this region. A regular use of baked bricks starts with certain amount of development of pyrotechnology at this stage with terracotta, cement/mortar and metallurgy. Such a concurrence is significant, indeed. One may wonder about the reason behind this simultaneous occurrence. Why is it that in an area where well developed potteries were being used for several centuries and which had a favourable soil or clay available in abundance the baked brick structures do not show up till much later? In an attempt to find answers to these questions, we decided to focus our attention to one of these items and to examine the cement/mortar which was being used in the early structural remains. Certain studies have already been taken up on the subject by scholars like Sanaullah, (1926-27, 1929-30), Dr. B.B. Lal, (1967), Prakash and Rawat (1965), H.C. Bharadwaj, R.N. Singh, K.K. Jain and others. These studies, however, are few and far between. We propose to make a comparison of the cementing and plastering material at different periods in the following lines.

The Harappans constructed permanent structures and used plasters/cement. The tradition discontinues for nearly thousand years. It appears in a changed form subsequently. What is the nature of this change? What are the compositions at later stages? Was the techniques learnt afresh again? Baked brick structures re-emerged from the Mauryan period onwards in different parts of India. It must have been at this stage that mortar and plastering were required, experimented with and rediscovered.

Dr. B.B. Lal, the Archaeological Chemist of India (ASI) analysed the plaster/cement from Mohejodaro (1967). His results show that there were two types of cement used in the Indus Civilization structures - gypsum and a lime cement. Gypsum cement was of light grey colour and was used in several buildings. Lime mortar was restricted to drains and floor. Gypsum, however, does not appear to have been used as an ingredient in the cement/mortar of the later times.

The plaster/cement analysed by us is from the Ashokan pillar area of the famous site of Sarnath. It shows that the plaster contains high percentage of $CaCO_3$ (56%). The details are given in the table below.

At a later period, plaster samples of Kausambi were analysed by Prakash and Rawat, (1965). They suggested that the plaster sample contains mainly lime. In mortar samples from Kausambi, sand and slaked lime are mixed in the ratios of 1:1 and 3:2.

The analysed samples of the plaster from Ajanta used as the base for paintings made of ferruginous earth reinforced with rock, grit or sand and fibrous vegetable materials, with no lime. But traces of a whitish layer on its surface just below the pigment layer indicate the presence of lime, kaolin or gypsum, (Paramasivam, 1937).

In the plaster from the Gupta buildings of Bhitari, high percentage (74%) of silica along with 14% of lime is present. Iron oxide and alumina contents measure upto 9%. Magnesia and alkalies are also present, while gypsum is completely absent. This analysis was done by H.C. Bhardwaj.

In Chola painted plasters, a pure and rich lime containing calcium oxide up to 66% is used for finished plaster with small quantities of gypsum associated with it.

In the Gangetic plains from Varanasi region, the mortar/plasters were analysed from old buildings constructed between Mauryan periods to 18-19 century A.D. The results are given in Table 2. The chemical analysis of these three samples of mortars shows that they contain maximum percentage of $CaCO_3$ thus indicating presence of lime. Sand (silica) was mixed with lime to prevent excessive shrinkage or drying. The hardening of lime is caused by the following chemical reaction.

$$Ca(OH)2 + CO2 \sim CaCO3 + H2O$$

Another fact that may be highlighted through this analysis is that the mortar/cement from the site of Ashokan pillar at Sarnath contains higher percentage of

$CaCO_3$ in comparison to other mortars from Chetsingh Quila and Ramnagar Fort of Varanasi, both belonging to pre-modern period. This shows that the mortar of Sarnath (belonging to a much earlier period) is harder than the mortar of Ramnagar Fort and Chetsingh Quila.

The cement/mortar appears to have undergone changes at different cultural stages, viz. Maurya, Sunga-Kushan and Gupta times. This surface on which the plaster was applied (i.e., brick, stone, mud, etc.) and purpose of the plaster also appear to have affected its basic composition. Our study of mortars/cement from different cultural stages as used in the Early Historic times, albeit on limited scale, and being still at an elementary level, helps us in arriving at the following conclusions -

1. Use of gypsum in the plastering and cementing material totally disappears after the Indus period.

2. Even at Mohenjo-daro, mortar used in drains, etc., shows complete absence of gypsum. This indicates that the Indus people had a good understanding of types and nature of plastering materials and their specific usages. Line was washed but on a limited scale.

3. In contrast, in the Gangetic plains, lime appears for the first time in 1st millennium B.C. at Kausambi. The composition of cement/mortar here is Al_2O_3 + Fe_2O_3. Another interesting point to be noted here is that iron oxide comes to be used in plastering materials. The inclusion of iron oxide gives the cement/mortar a comparatively higher strength.

4. The results of rough plaster analysis from the Ajanta caves show that the technique of making plaster was gradually reaching an advanced stage. Here a new kind of plaster for the walls appears to have been devised which was specially made for a smooth surface required for executing the paintings. It is different from other plasters in its composition. The mud plaster contains very low percentage of $CaCO_3$ while having a very high amount of sand and clay. The percentage of Al_2O_3 + Fe_2O_3 is very high which is noteworthy and important from the point of view of understanding of the behaviour of material by the artisans of the period.

5. The results show that the $MgCO_3$ in Indus mortar is very rich in comparison to others. This indicates that the Indus people knew the technique of protecting walls from water, because $MgCO_3$ is a material which makes the cement/mortar water resistant.

6. The analysis undertaken by us at B.H.U. from the ancient monuments of Varanasi region reveals an important feature. A fairly good percentage of organic matter (8-9% in the four samples) has been found to be present in these samples (Table I). Originally, this must have been much higher which has oxidized and lost over a prolonged exposure to elements. It may be deducted on this basis that for adding strength to the plaster, plant material and several organic substances must have been used, as still known to be in use by the traditional masons in different parts of India. Unfortunately, the analysis of other sites does not provide adequate information on this subject. The exact composition and the way of processing are significant to understanding the building art of the ancient times.

If we refer back to the question raised in the beginning of this discussion, we may suggest that after the decline of the Indus Civilization, the pyrotechnology also shows a marked decline. After a long span of time, with development in firing-kilning technology, structural activities show a spurt of growth.

The present note aims to highlight the significance of studies in mortars and plasters. Preparation of mortar and cement discussed above leads to a better understanding of behaviour of fire and heat control, raising the temperature at least upto 900∞-1000∞C in the kiln for such cements. This may be linked with a more advanced pyrotechnology during the Iron Age. The use of iron oxides as an strengthening agent in cement/mortar as evidenced at Kausambi strongly suggests an inter-relationship between the use of iron and other pyrotechnological activities, including the present one. This could possibly be one of the important causes for the absence of permanent structures in a period earlier than this.

Table - 1

Sites	Cement/ Mortar	$CaSO_4$ CH_2O	$CaCO_3$	Sand + Clay	Gypsum: sand	Lime: Clay	$MlgCO_3$	Al_2O3+ Fe_2O_3	Lime:
Mohenjodaro	Gypsum mortar from wall	63.25	1.64	3.52	2:1	–	–	–	–
Mohenjodaro	Lime mortar from drain		39.96	47.48		1:1	8.83		
Harappa	Lime mortar		35.02	51.39			10.62		2:3
Kausambi	Plaster		49.17	38.09			2.72	9.67	2:3
Kausambi	Mortar		49.97	29.95		2:1	2.72	4.78	
Ajanta Mud Plaster	Rough Plaster		1.78	60.00			2.00	17.00	
Bhitari	Plaster		13.80	73.50			5.42	8.64	1:1
Chola	Rough Plaster		49.76	49.97			1.07	1.59	1:1
Chola	Finished Plaster		90.72	7.02			0.77	1.06	12:1

Table - 2

	Silica insert matter clay	Organic matter	Moisture	$CaCo_3$	CO_2
Sarnath Mortar 3rd Century BC	0.289 gm	8.84%	0.61%	56%	0.31%
Chetsingh Quila Mortar 19 Cent.	27.4%	6.98%	0.64%	53%	0.32%
Ramnagar Quila Mortar 17 Cent.	29.4%	9.12%	0.58%	49%	0.38%

REFERENCES

1. Lal. B.B. in Ghosh, A. ed. (1967) *Ajanta Murals*, New Delhi, 53

2. Prakash, S. & Rawat, N.S., (1965) in *Chemical Studies of Some Indian Archaeological Antiquites*. *Bombay*.

3. Paramasivam, S. (1937) *Technical studies in the Field of Fine Arts*, 5, 228-31.

Vibha Tripathi
Devendra Mohan

Department of AIHC & Arch.
Department of Civil Engg. I.T.
Banaras Hindu University
Varanasi - 221 005

Brief Report on a Few Recent Excavations*

Excavation at Panda, District Samastipur, North Bihar.

The work in this region is being conducted under the supervision of Bijoy Kumar Chouwdhary, Director K.P. Jaiswal Research Institute, Patna. Three years of excavation in this region revealed a rich N.B.P.W. layer followed by Kushana township. Last year a trench measuring 10m x 5m was laid down on the top of the mound behind a Govt. Middle School. A sequence of four cultural periods was in the occupational thickness of 6.88 m deposit.

Period I belonging to the Chalcolithic Phase is characterised by the ceramic industry, which includes black and red ware, blacked slipped ware , red ware, and grey ware. Among antiquities stone hammer and axe pestles, copper hook, bone arrowheads, micro beads, etc. were found. An important find was an earthen oven mixed with husk. Period II belong to the N.B.P.W phase,which also revealed N.B.P.Ware, blacked slipped ware, grey ware, black ware and red ware. All the pots are made of well-levigated clay. The shades of N.B.P.W. bear silver, golden, steel blue, jet black and chocolate colours. Common types of the N.B.P.W are bowls of different sizes dishes with in curved rim, etc. Antiquities found include knife, sickle, daggers, spearheads made of iron, etc. beads of semiprecious stone and bone arrow heads are note worthy.

Period III includes a solitary Kushana copper coin, and one sealing inscribed on Kushana Brahmi. Vigorous structural activity can be seen in this phase. Four ring wells were recovered from this phase having 13, 15,16 and 24 courses respectively. A brick wall running from north-east to south-east was unearthed in the Kushana horizon. In the same horizon was found ceramics of early Christian centuries, having various shapes like bowls, incurved rims, dishes, etc. The notable antiquities noticed are terracotta beads, pendants, crude animal and human figurines, copper earrings, iron knifes, antimony rings, ivory objects, etc. Period IV is marked by structures made of broken bricks , robbed from earlier phase. Other finding of this phase include knife edged rim of bowls, in red ware, typical of Gupta period. However no other such findings typical of Gupta period were found.

Excavation at Viratpur, District Saharsa, Bihar

The exploration /excavation at Viratpur was undertaken by Sri Ajoy Kumar Sinha, exploration and excavation officer, Directorate of Archaeology, Govt. of Bihar.

Last year's excavation work revealed four major strata. Layer 1 is about 20 cm thick only and potsherds of red ware variety were found. Layer 2 is about 35 cm thick. It is disturbed by a number of pits. A 3 cm thick-rammed floor was found covered by reused bricks of single course. The red ware potsherds of various types like vases, earthen lamps, etc., were found in large numbers.

Layer 3 is about 80 cm thick consisting of compact blackish soil. This layer has yielded a few pits along with a few antiquities, such as terracotta balls, iron objects,

*Courtesy Archaeological Survey of India.

stone beads, animal figurines etc. Potsherds were found in abundance, they include vases, carinated handies, long and narrow necked jars etc. A few potsherds show Kushan influence being micacious in appearance and some belong to the pre-Kushan period. Layer 4 is 1.25m thick consisting of only medium grained yellowish sand. This layer is completely free from antiquities and potsherds.

Further excavation at Sirpur, District Mahasamund, Chhattisgarh.

Excavation of the site on the southwest of the Buddhist nunnery was undertaken by Sh. Jagat Pati Joshi and Sh.A.K.Sharma (Retd. S.A.; Project Director A.S.I.). The mound on the northern end of the site was numbered SRP-4 and the adjoining one was numbered SRP-5.

The mound SRP-4 revealed a Buddha Vihara built in an area of 425 sq. metres, datable to 7th–8th century A.D.during the time of Mahasiva-gupta Balarjuna.It faces the Mahanadi on the west and is built on similar lines as the earlier excavated Siva temple and nunnery. The entrance to the vihara i.e. ardhamandapa, projects forward from the main western wall. The gateway is made of cist and latritic blocks with sandstone images of Ganga and Yamuna, the bottom portions have been exquisitely carved with serpents chasing rats, sleeping cows and dogs and dancing peacocks and *kirtimukhas*. There are two monolithic octagonal pillars decorated with ghata pallava carvings and flanked on either side by bhara-vahakas. Between the entrance and the mandapa there is a 6.0 m wide six pillared antarala. The mandapa is a central twelve monolithic pillared complex with only ghata pallavas on the top portion and the rest of the pillar being simple squares. The mandapa is surrounded uniformly by 2.70 m wide and 17.0 m long corridors on all the four sides. On the north and the south side are five and four monk cells respectively. The cells are of the size of 2.40 x 2.25m except the central ones, which measure 3.20m x 2.25m. All the cells can be approached from the corridor through a 50 cm wide door. The garbhagriha is on the eastern side and is projected back by 1.0 m from the main wall and measures 1.40x 1.30 m. there is a high pedestal on the eastern wall and semi-circular pedestal made of bricks on the north and south side. Three images of Buddha in *bhumisparsha* mudra made of chalkstone and soapstone were recovered from the garbhagriha. The gateway of the garbhagriha has been impressively decorated with naga-purusha and naga-kanyas. The walls of the garbhagriha are made of bricks measuring 40 x 20 x 7 cms, 41 x 24 x 7cms, 40 x 20 x 6.5 cms and 37 x 20 x 7 cms., they have been coated with lime plaster and faint traces of fresco on the internal side can be seen.

To the south of SRP-4 is another long mound, oriented towards the north-south, which has revealed the largest Buddha Vihara of Sirpur. Two construction periods for the same structure have been cited. The original complex was a west facing structure built on an area of 450 sq metres. The foundation of the entire complex was made of black schist stone, and the super structure was made of bricks with stone uprights and lintels for the doors. The structure is double storied and has a staircase 1.0m wide made of stone. The ardha-mandapa is tri-ratna in plan and rests on highly decorated monolithic octagonal pillars, depicting Buddha in *bhumisparsha* mudra. The entrance doors on both the sides have been decorated with beautifully carved mithuna figures, animals, birds, honeybees, snakes, frogs, dancing rats etc. The garbhagriha houses two lion pedestals and a monolithic Buddha in bhumisparsha mudra. This image is flanked by two pedestals, one on each side perhaps for Bodhisattva images. Surrounding this are ten cells for monks generally measuring 2.40 x 2.0 mts.

Along side these structural remains were found four fragmentary inscriptions engraved on red sand stone in very fragile condition. One of them reads 'Teevardeva' and the other 'Harshgupta'. It appears that this vihara came during the time of these two personalities around A.D. 560, and continued up till the time of his son Harshgupta, whose inscription appears for the first time. Apart form this, another inscription of 5th-6th century A.D. in Brahmi script and sanskrit language on a baked clay seal was found with the emblem of Chief Architect Taradatta. The fourth inscription is a typical Buddhist Beej-mantra seal.

In the second stage of construction all the rooms were blocked by brick walls upto the height of 1.50 metres and the doors wee converted into niches. The partition walls and the back wall of the central three rooms on the southern side and one room on the eastern side were demolished to make way for construction of another mandapa measuring 12.50 x 9.0 metres. To approach this mandapa a separate entrance was created on the west side, just abutting the decorated brick wall of earlier structure.

Alongside the structural discoveries many artefacts were also recovered from the viharas, such as iron nails, clamps, doorjambs, pestles and grinders, lead weights etc. Most of the iron objects, were screw type of locks found in licked condition to show that the owner must have left in a hurry due to some impending calamity. Evidences show that the calamity had occurred in the form of massive flood.

Excavation/Exploration of Sanganakallu, Karnataka

The Karnataka, Telegu, London and Cambridge Universities jointly undertook a research project, to study the Neolithic and Iron Age remains of southern Deccan. The main focus of the study was the prehistoric site of Sangankallu - Kupgal complex of Bellary dist. The aim of the project was to explore and excavate the archaeological and landscape features of the area so that an insight may be gained towards the indigenous processes of neolithisation and the rise of megaliths and further transition to early history. The work included surface exploration and study of various temporary and permanent habitation sites. Stone quarrying areas, tool production area, rock art sites, ash mounds, and megalithic burials, along with small-scale excavations of the same. During the systematic field walking small rock art sites and rock shelters rich in microlithic industry were discovered containing partially exposed human burials. Also exploration was done to investigate the relationship between the archaeological and geographical features (landscape consisted of naturally sculpted granitic tor-inselburg formations), which exposed the fact that the ash-mound sites were influenced by the patterns of visibility.

Micro-morphological and bulk geo-archaeological sampling was done of the exposed ash mounds (burnt cattle dung mounds) at three different sites to reveal the process of ash mound formation. Also five trial trenches were dug at the dolerite dyke area, which revealed 1m thick debitage of dolerite material. These debitage included several thousand flakes and chips spread over an area of one hectare. Further flake tools of exotic chert material were also found. The nearest known source of 'chert' is in Kurnool limestone formations in Kurnool district of Andhra Pradesh. The limestone caves in Kurnool district of Andhra Pradesh were first cited by Sir Robert Bruce Foote, since then this area is famous as an important source of raw material for upper Palaeolithic to Neolithic-Chalcolithic communities.

Rock art motifs found are predominantly pictographic, dominated by the depictions of long horned, humped domesticated cattle. They are found abundantly in the Sangankallu - Kupgal area. These motifs include ithyphallic and dancing figures, hunting, bull capturing and sexual scenes, etc. Also in the same area can be found 'musical stones' (dolerite boulders which contain multiple grooves made when struck by granite stones to make music) which have been noticed for the first time in the same vicinity as the art motifs. Considering the fact that most of the motifs are to be found in high rocky area accessible to only the physically able, these 'musical stones' suggest that rock art production or the viewing of them was a part of a ritualised sensory experience available to only a part of the society.

Excavation at Barakur, District Udipi, Karnataka.

Barakur is a historical metropolis on the west coast of Karnataka.The work in this area is being done under the direction of S. Nargaraju, B. Narasimhaiah, S.V.P. Halakatti, of M.H. Krishna Institute of Indology, a body of Mythic Society, Bangalore. The site belongs to a early historical site. Two forts, eighteen temples and many remains of an ancient town including over 50 inscriptions were found. The site was the ancient capital of the Alupas of Tulunad and later a provincial capital of Vijayanagara and Keladi rulers, and also of Haider Ali of Mysore. The excavation intends to bring to light the cultural sequence of the area and trace the development from the ancient and medieval periods.

Last years' work exposed structural remains to represent three constructional phases, it also revealed a sprawling residential complex, made of laterite bricks, comparable to the noble man's quarters at Hampi. This structure built in two-phase shows continuity in occupation with the second phase consisting mostly of repairs and additions. The plan shows a central area with a hall on the north and stepped platforms on the other three sides probably for seating dignitaries. On the south eastern corner is the utility section, and the throne room is on the west side with a passage way leading in to the audience hall. The area of the living rooms and the utilities were located on the west of the audience hall. The whole area is surrounded with a enclosure wall which is roughly about 80 cms thick. A large number of tiles were found in the form of debris indicating to the type of roofs that were in practice in that period. Apart from these not many pottery pieces were found. Some crude featureless sherds of red ware were discovered of medieval period. About 15 sherd of Chinese ware were found datable to 15th--16th century A.D.

The remains of the third phase was scanty as they had been haphazardly made of reused bricks and debris of the previous phases. Some of the other artefacts found like the pestle, pottery, mud ovens, indicate a later date perhaps of the 17th–18th century A.D. Apart from these other antiquities found included some lead ingots, goldsmith's hammer of copper, fragmentary soapstone images, glass bangle pieces, etc.

Excavation of a Sailboat at Thaikkal (Kadakkarapally), District Alleppey and Exploration of Kerala coast.

Excavation of a sailboat has been carried under Dr M.V. Nair - Director General, with the assistance of Ms. Jenee Peter and Dr Selvakumar - co-coordinators, State Institute of Archaeology, Museology and Conservation, Govt. of Kerala,Cochin.

In the previous years, the main trench KPY1 was excavated exposing an ancient boat, specially the north and the central parts. In the last year's work (2002-2003) apart from exposing the southern part (bow) of the boat, another trench KPY II, west of the main trench, was excavated to reveal more information about the site.

In the main trench KPY I, the bow (southern) part of the boat was excavated intact. The orientation of the boat is about 48? west of the true North with the bow side tilting towards south west. On the south side the walls of the boat are better preserved than the north end,(stern side) which has damaged. The boat is divided into 12 compartments. Wooden and iron nails have been used. The floor of the boat has two layers of wooden plank; the upper plank is twice as thick as the lower plank, which is 4cm thick.Along side the boat on the southern side was found a dressed lime (kankar) stone. Also in the same area was found a wooden lever, probably used to steer the boat. Among other findings potsherds, wooden fragments, shells, etc were also found.

Trench KPY II has not yielded much information, however a few pot sherds, shell fragments have been found. Beach sand with various types of shells has been found at a depth of 150cm below the surface level. C-14 dating of a wooden piece from the boat carried out by Birbal Sahani Laboratory (Lucknow) has given a date range from 920 ñ 1060± bp. The wood has been identified as Atrocarpus Hirsuta Lamk (Aanjali in Malyalam) by B.S.L. and Kerala Forest Research Institute. This is the first time that a boat /ship is being excavated in India dating to almost a 1000 years before present. Work for the year 2003-2004 has been approved. The site however is not protected centrally or otherwise.

Excavation at Bhon and Exploration in Pruna basin, District Buldhana, Maharashtra.

The work in this area is being conducted under the supervision of Dr. B.C. Deotare, Reader, Department of Ancient Indian History, Culture and Archaeology, Deccan College Post-Graduate and Research Institute, Pune. In the last season a trench of 2 x 2m in the central part of the mound was dug out exposing a habitational deposit of 2.5 metres. Ceramic findings revealed potsherds of fine black and red ware, red ware having engraved lines on the inner side. These sherds are common types found in the other regions of Pruna basin especially at Kholapur, Bhongaon, Bhatkuli etc. Other antiquities found on the site include terracotta beads, pendants, shell bangles, broken iron rods, and bone stylus, etc. Most importantly a lot of rice grains along with husks and pulses and cereals were recovered. The dominance of rice indicates rainfall and trade. Alongside such discoveries two floors levels with postholes were also exposed indicating structural activity.

At mound IV the exposed brick structure shows different shapes and sizes of well-fired bricks ranging from rectangular, square, and tapering at one end. On the lower side sun backed bricks were also exposed. These findings can be dated to the Satvahana period, but further excavations are necessary.

Excavation at Boxanagar, District West Tripura, Tripura

The site was excavated by R.D. Singh, Archaeological Survey of India, Guahati Circle. The site Boxanagar which is centrally protected is about 40 km west of Agartala. It is almost on the edge of Bangladesh border. The landform is a vast alluvium plain with elevated land-masses locally called *tila.* A rivulet named Aurimangal, flows one km east of the mound. It is now almost filled with silt deposits. Clear evidences of a paleochannel can be seen in this area. The mound is approximately three acre in area. The chronology of the site has been fixed to 7th- 8th century, A.D. on the basis of the textual findings on the clay seals.

In the first season's excavation a massive brick built stupa of *triratha* plan (15.40 m x 15.40m) has been exposed. The structure consists of a large basement with eight tapering mouldings and a beautifully carved *medhi.* On the western side the damaged portion has been identified as a harmica measuring (2.30m x 2.30m x 1.50m). The cause of damage has been attributed to natural factors. Different brick sizes have been used namely 30x 23 x 6 cm, 31x 24x 5 cm, 31x 24x 5 cm and 31 x 25 x 6 cm. Mud mortar has been used.

In the second season's excavation, a chaityagriha has been discovered on the eastern side of the stupa. The exposed plan is rectangular in shape, measuring 18.10 x 10.65 m externally, and is aligned to the east-west direction. The superstructure except the sidewalls, which stand approximately 1.65m vertically from the foundation level, has been damaged. On the stupa side both the walls of the chaityagriha and the stupa are joined. The walls are upto 1.25m thick .On the eastern side a small staircase has also been discovered used to enter the chaityagriha.

Various antiquities have also been found. The central chamber of the stupa has yielded 150 pieces of clay sealings of Buddhist creed. A number of clay votive stupas have also been found coated with a red slip. From the chaityagriha terracotta carved bricks with kumuda motifs, one terracotta spindle whorl, hopscotch, etc, has been found. A notable discovery was made in the form of a Buddhist deity with four hands seated in padmasana.

The pottery found is red in colour and made of finely levigated clay; and is mostly wheel turned. The various shapes found are shallows dishes, handis, medium sized pots etc. A few sherds with external impressions of the back of tortoise have also been found.

Excavation/ Exploration of Moghalmari, District West Midnapur, West Bengal.

The excavation of the site was undertaken by Dr. Asok Datta, with the assistance of Dr. R.K. Chattopadhyay, Dr. Bishnupriya Basak, University of Calcutta, Archaeology Deptt. West Bengal. The excavation was conducted as a compulsory academic feature for the final year M.A. students, in order that they may become acclimatized to the practical aspects of excavation.

The Moghalmari,(Maghalmari) in West Midnapur district in West Bengal is a early historical site. Last years exploration revealed a distinct mound circular in shape measuring 80 x 80m with a early medieval period structure. The site has also yielded some structural remains of Gupta period along with various inscribed Brahmi terracotta plaques, inscribed stone sculptures representing both Hindu and Buddhist iconography. The site of the excavation Dantan (Dantan police station) might be similar to Dantabhukti referred to in the Jataka stories.

Compiled by
Gency Chaudhury

Indian Archaeological Society

Major Projects

Atlas of the Indus-Saraswati Civilization

In the year 2000 the Indian Council of Historical Research cleared proposal of Indian Archaeological Society for preparing an Atlas of the Indus-Saraswati Civilization under its scheme of major projects for a period of three years. The project is now over and we are preparing the manuscript for the press.

There are as many as 191 site-distribution maps and 400 page text covering practically all excavated sites and the areas where the cultural remains of the Indus-Saraswati Civilization have been found, particularly in India and Pakistan. However, Afghanistan, Turkimenistan, Iran, Mesopotamia, Baharain and Oman have also been included in this Atlas showing sites with the Indus-Saraswati or Harappan antiquities. The maps covering India and Pakistan have been prepared according to the present-day District boundaries, State boundaries and Country boundaries to help researchers at various levels of their work. The maps show the location of each site according to their latitude and longitude.

The sites are mentioned in the maps by their names so that there is no confusion, which sometimes occurs if the sites are mentioned by numbers. This we have done even in the case of Bahawalpur sites in Pakistan where they are in large numbers and located very close to each other. (Pl. 1).

The sites have been grouped broadly under three groups: the Early Indus-Saraswati, the Mature Indus-Saraswati and the Late Indus-Saraswati. (Pl. 2). The Early Indus-Saraswati includes Hakra as well Kot Diji-Sothi sites.

The dates are broad brackets for each one of them which are now accepted all over the world since these are based upon caliberated radiocarbon dates. Richard Meadow and J.M. Kenoyer (2003) have used these brackets for the periodisation of Harappa. There are, of course, at least two phases in the Early Indus-Saraswati and three phases in the Mature Indus-Saraswati at Harappa but that is not only a matter of detail but also site-specific.

There is also a list of all the sites with their longitudes and latitudes. Gregory Possehl had listed them in his book *The Indus Age*. However, in quite a few of them the coordinates had to be corrected. We have used GPS, an instrument which was not available to the old field-workers for recording exact coordinates; Survey of India maps alone were available to them. For maping and plotting we have used a software named Geo-Media Prof. 4 for greater accuracy than what we get when manually produced.

The geo-physical maps are primarily based upon satellite imageries and field-work put together and published in recent years. The rivers, the mountains, the deserts, the seas, etc. are also based upon satellite imagery as adopted by the internationally recognised atlas published by Oxford.

The Atlas also includes the West Asian sites, the

coordinates of many of which are not available to us. Moreover, the political situation in Iraq, Kuwait, etc. is presently in termoil to make attempts to obtain data required by us. We had, therefore, to depend on the old available data.

The *Atlas of the Indus-Saraswati Civilization* is, however, much more than mere site-distribution maps since the underlying concept was cultural. It is a cultural Atlas. It embodies the data on the material remains unearthed at the excavated sites. The remains include major architectural remains such as the Great Bath at Mohanjodaro as well as the movable antiquities such as the seals and sealings. There are also the animal bones, human remains, burials, botanical remains, etc. which find place in the Atlas.

The data on each cultural item from excavated sites have been tabulated along with the references of publications where they appeared. This method has been adopted to present the innumerable of data in a restricted space with quick and exact referencing. This, it is hoped, will help the researchers in locating his material in practically no time.

There are a few subjects which are basic to our understanding of the dynamics of the Indus-Saraswati Civilization. For example, the rationale behind the changed nomenclature—from the Indus Valley Civilization to the Indus-Saraswati Civilization.

India is a country where traditions are still in to practise and where literary traditions go back in time to thousands of years. The Rigveda is still considered to be the oldest literary text available to us even though it is not easy to date it exactly. We all are aware of the fact that all ancient texts, including epics, could not be totally based upon imagination. With this premise the Holyland Archaeology had started and new light was thrown on the problems of correlating literature and archaeology. Some success was always achieved though not complete success. Hence, the flow of the Saraswati and the question of drying up of the Saraswati plus the archaeology of the Harappan Civilization can not be completely brushed aside even though we can never be sure about many inferences drawn by scholars unless the script is deciphered and the language is identified.

There are many other aspects and dimensions of the Indus-Saraswati Civilization, including metals, metallurgy, technology, urban planning, water management, etc. which are covered in the *Atlas of the Indus-Saraswati Civilization* to make it as much comprehensive as possible and not making it another mega volume.

S.P. Gupta

Growth of Cities in Ancient India

The project "Growth of cities during the second urbanization in India (1000 B.C. -100 A.D)" – a three year project - was undertaken as a project sponsored by the Indian Council for Historical Research by the Indian Archaeological Society, New Delhi. The project commenced in January 2001 and will end in December 2003. This is a project sponsored by the Indian Council of Historical Research, the amount disbursed so far is Rs. 10,98,527/- of which an amount of Rs. 10,23,533/- has been spent. This is an ongoing project. Second urbanization in India is considered to have commenced after the introduction of iron in India sometime during the close of the second millennium BC. However, growth and flowering of cities seems to have happened around 600 BC when the sixteen mahajanapadas were well established. Considering the ceramic evidence it appears that post-Painted Grey Ware period marked the beginning of cities with the appearance of Black slipped and the Northern Black Polished wares. Formation of cities -urbanism - or urbanization happened primarily in the Ganga plains to be followed later in other regions i.e. in the Deccan and south India. The process of urbanization culminated after the reign of the Mauryan emperor Asoka and thereafter the formation of cities and urbanism spread to other parts of India and by the time of the Kushanas completely developed forms of cities can be seen. In the formation of cities (read urbanism) not only trade but also political and religious factors seem to have played a active role. Thus Jainism and Buddhism exerted their influence in this process. The Sunga and Satavahana periods witnessed unprecedented economic and long distance trade activities in manufactured goods giving a fillip to urbanism in India.

Urbanism from the embryonic stage to the fully developed creature i.e. the emergence, growth, flowering, and decay of the cities did not, as is believed by some scholars, culminate in the first century AD but continued till the 5th-6th century AD and beyond the first millennium AD as witnessed by the temple cities, like Tanjavur and Sriranagm to name a few, the former dating in the times of the Imperial Chola monarch Raja Raja the Great.

This project does not envisage much theoretical discussion and proposition conducive for the development of cities. However, previous studies of several scholars will perhaps be collated to see how far the norms and conditionalities laid by them could be gainfully utilized in justifying our conception of a city, whose material culture conforms to the pre-conditions laid down by them.

Before embarking upon the collection of data on the material culture of the prospective sites that could be termed as a city, it is proposed to make use of our vast written literature, albeit late in compilation, to understand how a city is described *viz.* late vedic literature, the Upanishads, Puranas, the epics – Mahabharata and the Ramayana, Buddhist literature viz. the pitakas, jatakas and the Tamil Sangam works and the two famous epics in Tamil the Silappadikaram and the Manimekhalai.

In this effort the study had been regional as well

zonal following the river basins. Thus the river valleys/basins followed are the Ganga-Yamuna doab, Middle Ganga, Lower Ganga, Narmada and Tapti, Krishna, Godavari, Kaveri, and its tributaries, Manimukta, Mahanadi etc. For our purposes, cities will be classified as power centres (fortified cities viz. Pataliputra , Kausambi, etc.), trade and economic centres with "high consumer potential (port cities like Kaveripattinam, Bharuch as well as towns showing trends of urbanism — Sengamedu, Dhatava etc.) cultural and religious centres (Rajghat, Thanjavur) and centres of learning (Kanchi), (Map).

Considering the vastness of our country our study has been confined only to a few representative cities.

It has been our aim to locate and study hinterland towns with urban trends of prominent regional city centres and a to a great extent we are successful in this regard. The study of Arikamedu an entrepot on the eastern coast revealed that besides it being an Indo-Roman trading centre it was also a pivot for regional exchange system. This aspect came to light during our study of Sengamedu, on the Manimukta river, a town with urban trends.

Our evidence shows that in peninsular India, especially in the southern states habitation began with the megalithic culture with its predominant Black-and-Red ware. Yet we find no trend of urbanism at this level. It seems that urbanization of southern India was a late phenomenon.

The picture in western Deccan is a little different. Many urban centres flourished along the main trade routes close to Buddhist establishment. Trade, particularly Indo-Roman trade, Buddhism and the political patronage of the Satavahana rulers accelerated urbanism in this region.

Likewise Vidharba and its adjoining region exhibited urban trends. Here the origin of urban centres was closely connected with the pre-existing megalithic settlements. Religion, also played an important role in the process of urbanization during the early centuries of the Christian era. It also appears that the region was not much influenced by the Indo-Roman trade. Alternatively domestic trade played an important role

The following is the break up of the sites studied river-basin wise:

Mahanadi delta (Sisuaplgarh, Dhauli, Tapanga, Aragarh, Manikapatna and Radhanagar); Krishan (Dharanikotta, Amaravati, Verapuram and Nagarjunakond); Bhima (Sannaathi); Tungasbhadara (Sataniokotta); Hagari (Braghmagiri and Chandravalli); Palar basin (Kanchi, Mamallapuram and Vasavasamudram); Kaveri and its tributaries (Uraiyur, Kaveripattinam, Karur and Kodumanal); Ariynkuppam (Arikamedu); Manimukta river (Sengamedu); Vaigai basin (Madurai an Alagankulam); Tamraparani (Korkai); Wardha and Wainganga (Adam and Pauni and Kaundinyapura) Betwa and Bes (Besnagar); Shipra (Ujjain); Tapi (Dhatva); Hiran (Somnath); Vadi (Amreli); Narmada (Bharuch), Banas (Rairh), Upper Ganga (Hastinapur, Kampilya, Sankisa, Ahichchhattra, Kausambi and Mathura); Middle Ganga valley (Rajghat, Saket, Pataliputra, Rajgir) and Lower Ganga (Mahasthangarh, Tamluk, Chandraketugarh and Mangalkot); Sutlej (Sanghol and Ropar); Yamuna(Sugh); In this list sites are with hinterland towns/villages showing some urban trends.

Coming to the theoretical part, the parameters laid down by Gordon Childe seem to cover the entire gamut. Of the ten parameters some of them are considered not valid by many scholars. Now we will consider these parameters as also the reasons for rejecting some of them by a few scholars and see what conditions are essential for the growth of urbanism in India.

Till now four interim reports have been submitted to the ICHR consisting of 418 pages with 196 pages of illustrations.

K.S. Ramachandran

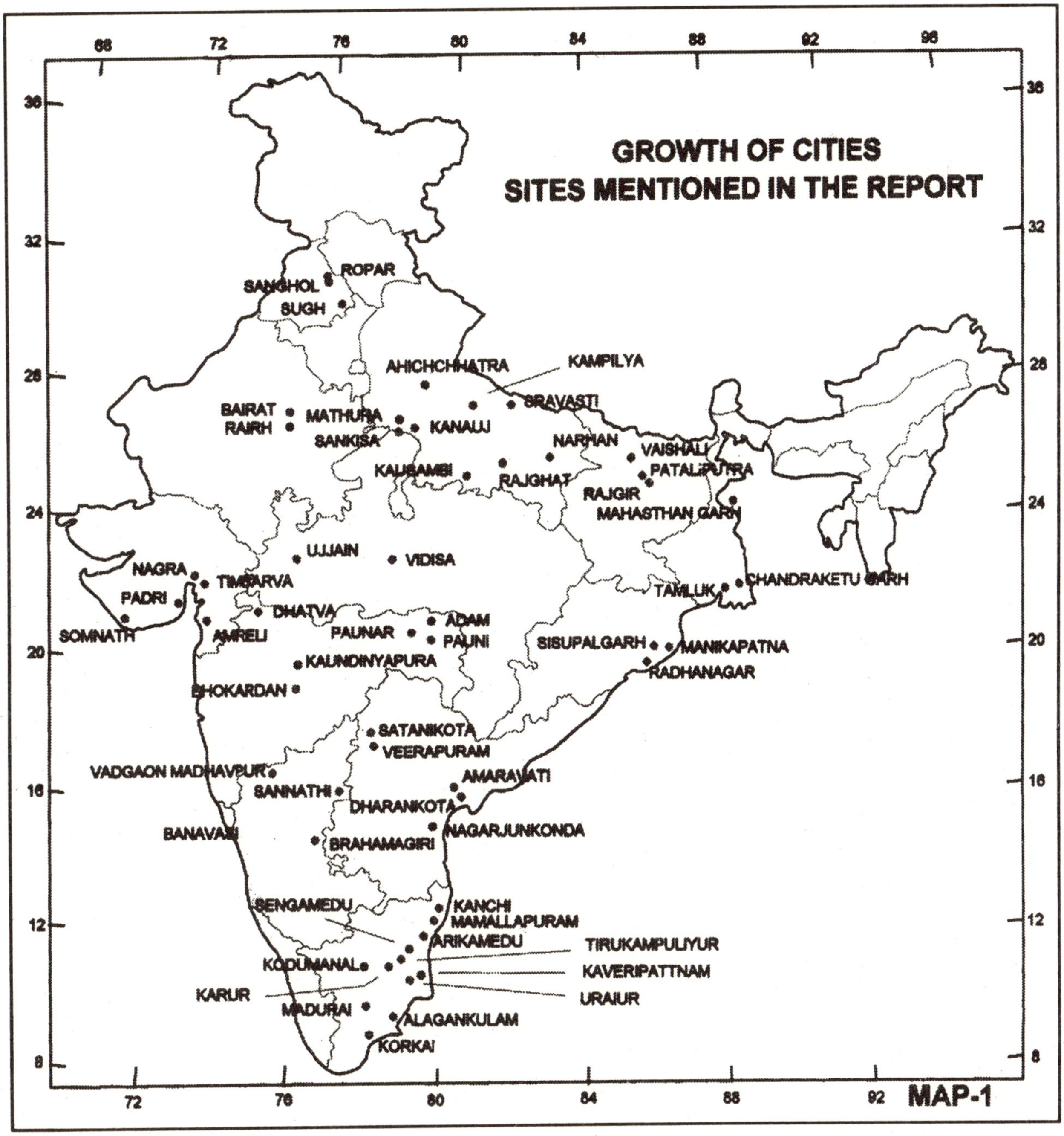
GROWTH OF CITIES
SITES MENTIONED IN THE REPORT
ROPAR
SUGH
AHICHCHHATRA
KAMPILYA
BAIRAT
RAIRH
KANAUJ
NARHAN
VAISHALI
RAJGHAT
RAJGIR
UJJAIN
VIDISA
NAGRA
PADRI
SOMNATH
DHATVA
PAUNAR
ADAM
KAUNDINYAPURA
SISUPALGARH
MANIKAPATNA
RADHANAGAR
SATANIKOTA
VEERAPURAM
SANNATHI
NAGARJUNKONDA
BRAHAMAGIRI
KANCHI
MAMALLAPURAM
ARIKAMEDU
TIRUKAMPULIYUR
KAVERIPATTNAM
KARUR
URAIUR
ALAGANKULAM
KORKAI
MAP-1

Select Earthquake Affected Monuments of Gujarat

INTRODUCTION

This report contains a survey of the status of some of the most important monuments of Gujarat especially in the region of Kutch, Saurashtra and Surendranagar. These structures protected and unprotected by the state government suffered due tothe severe earthquake of 26 January, 2001. The focus of the report is not limited to damage caused due to the earthquake but attempts to examine the issues involved in their restoration and conservation.

The Indian Archaeological Society sent a team of country's leading historians and archaeologists comprising Prof. B.B. Lal, Shri M.N. Deshpande, Dr. S.P. Gupta, Shri D. Krishnani and myself to Gujarat from 9th to 14th February, 2001 to examine the damage caused to the cultural properties.

A project proposal by the Indian Archaeological Society was prepared on 'Salvaging and conserving the damaged source material of History and Archaeology in Gujarat' and sent to the Indian Council of Historical Research (I.C.H.R.) in national interest, for preparing a status report. I.C.H.R. sympathetically considered the project and sanctioned a grant for the survey of the affected monuments.

Background

The magnitude 7. 72 earthquake that struck Gujarat, India at 8:46 AM on January 26, 2001 devastated a large number of villages and towns over a wide area of Gujarat. The damage was particularly severe in the Kutch Region. The records show that the strong motion lasted for 85 seconds while the lighter shaking lasted longer than that. The region was hit by a similar earthquake in 1819 which had brought massive destruction in the region. This earthquake had a profound effect on structures of all types, from traditional masonry to contemporary reinforced concrete, on the whole, the damaging historic buildings and sites including city walls, forts, palaces, temples, 'havelis', and civic structures. For those buildings that have survived, the level of damage is often extensive enough to make them particularly vulnerable to

1. being hastily dismantled or cleared up on the grounds that they pose life safety risks, or are a "useless" heap of rubble (without a methodical documentation for future reconstruction or research)], especially the unprotected structures, or

2. being subject to further damage from monsoon rains (when the annual monsoon comes), which is usually in late June. Fortunately (for the monuments) it has hardly rained for the last two years after the 26th January earthquake of 2001.

Objectives

This report is an effort to bring to light the importance to conserve the several structures of great historical importance in the earthquake-affected region of Gujarat. The report examines the present status of the structures including structural damage and specific problem areas (weathering, encroachment and need for government protection) with recommendations for their conservation.

Methodology

The report covers basic documentation, restoration needs and observations for feasibility of regional conservation. The previous available/published drawings and photographs were also compared with the existing condition of the structures. The recorded observations are presented through drawings, photographs and in a tabular form. The documentation was done through measured drawings and photography.

Scope and limitation

The region of Gujarat consists of innumerable ancient sites of historical content. This report does not attempt to cover any large portion of the sites, rather focuses on the more important sites in the earthquake affected regions of Kutch and Saurashtra. Further, the sites that fall under the purview of ASI were not taken up. The selection of the sites is based on region and relative importance as per the priority list of department of Archaeology, Gujarat. The time and resources required to extensively document and assess all the sites would fall beyond the limitations of the present report. Therefore, some sites which were considered less important were not documented through measured drawings, instead, sketches and photographic documentation were done to record the present status of the monument. The preliminary conservation estimates pertaining to the monuments could not be worked out because of many hidden factors.

The damage assessment of monuments/heritage buildings have been done in detail. However, two examples from the status report are mentioned here.

1. LAKHESVARA TEMPLE

Location: Kera (Kerakot), Kutch

Age of the Structure: circa 930-940 AD

Type: 'Sandhara' Temple facing east.

Special Features

- The 'prasada' has an exquisite 'simhakarna'.
- The 'bhadravalokana' consist of stone screens and carved 'vedika'
- Constructed in yellow and red stone, hard in nature with carving on most 'sikhara' members sharp till date.

General condition

DAMAGE: Severe shaking of the entire structure has made it unstable and structurally precarious.

Parts have collapsed and dislodged; majority of structure is out of plumb.

PROTECTED: Dept. of archaeology, Gujarat.

BOARD: Present.

SITE BOUNDARY: Defined and the inside is partly landscaped.

ENCROACHMENT: None.

LIGHTING: The huge installations block the view and stand out prominently.

ENCROACHMENT: There is no recent encroachment within the temple complex, but the fort wall of Kerakot which was built over the plinth of the temple and composed of temple parts indicates that it was itself an encroachment on the temple ruins. The plinth has now been cleared and restored by the Deptt. of State Archaeology. There is a temple attached to the fort-wall of Kerakot in the east.

Problem Situations

Structurally unstable, precariously standing stone members with life safety risks. The structure is unstable and needs immediate work to dismantle the standing structure, before further damage occurs.

Damage Assessment

Location	Material & construction	Damage type	Recommendation
'Bhadravalokana' of the north wall of 'mandapa'	stone	Has collapsed in the earthquake. The collapsed debris lies untouched even after two years. The smallest of pieces lie in the exact position of their fall; amazingly no one has touched or overturned them. Some part of the wall and the 'kapili' still stand.	Fortunately the pieces lie untouched; it is possible to reconstruct the ornamental parts with a high degree of exactness. The debris needs to be attended carefully along with documentation. The pieces need to be identified, numbered and then removed. The standing parts need to be dismantled before reconstruction.
'Kapili' on the north	Stone	Shaken state. The upper parts are severely dislodged.	
The plinth	Stone	Has been restored by the Dept. of State Archaeology and is in a good condition.	At many occasions the ornnamental pattern had not been reproduced. A consistent approach for reproduction of detail needs to be followed either a reproduction of detail or no reproduction of detail.
'Simhakarna' on the north, west and south	Stone	Has survived the earthquake, but severely dislodged; the veneer is held in a precarious condition. Some pieces have fallen.	Needs to be carefully dismantled and erected again. Being the most splendid example of a 'simhakarna', it needs urgent and high priority restoration efforts.
The 'sikhara'	stone	Mostly missing Some parts have collapsed, especially on the south-west corner. The fallen parts lie on the plinth below.	Needs to be carefully dismantled and erected again.
Main 'amalaka'	Stone	Fallen (not in the recent earthquake) and lies in the north.	Should be restored after the entire 'sikhara' is reset.
'Dvara' and 'garbhgrha' of the temple 'Garbhagrha'	Stone	The articulated 'dvarasakha' of the 'mandapa' has survived at the site. The previous records of the 'garbhagrha' reveal a loss of articulated architectural members including 'chandrashila'. The walls of the 'garbhagrha' have been partly restored.	The restoration must utilize the existing members on site. The members are accessible and usable but requir identification. All restoration must identify such members at the site.
North 'bhadravalokana' of 'mulaprasada'	Stone	Structurally disturbed and out of plumb.	Needs to be carefully dismantled and erected again.
West 'bhadravalokana'	Stone	Part missing, weathered and structurally disturbed.	
South 'bhadravalokana'	Stone	Severely damaged; mostly collapsed	

2. NAVALAKHA TEMPLE

Location: Ghumli, Jamnagar.

Age of the Structures: 12th - 13th cent. AD

Type: 'sandhara' type with a pillared 'gudh mandapa' facing east.

Special Features

One of the most exquisitely carved temples in Gujarat. Similar to Navalakha temple at Sejakpur and the Sun temple at Modhera.

General condition

DAMAGE: Dilapidated condition. Extensive damage has occurred due to the earthquake to the structural members. All structures are "shaken" and members are dislodged. Parts have collapsed and most members are cracked, including columns, slabs and walls. There is intense weathering at many locations. Most affected are the 'mandapa' (in the north), the 'sikhara' (collapsed inside). The 'garbhagrha' suffers with very severe weathering.

PROTECTION: Dept. of Archaeology, Gujarat.

GUARD: Permanent guard stationed at site.

BOARD: Present.

SITE BOUNDARY: Two gates and a barbed wire fence are present around the site.

Damage Assessment

Location	Material & Construction	Damage type (after earthquake)	Recommendation
'Sikhara'	Stone	Many parts have collapsed.	The entire structure is in such a severely damaged and dangerous condition after the earthquake, that it can only be dismantled and re-erected.
Walls of the 'mulaprasada'	Stone	Badly affected due to shaking- the insides have bulged due the thrust of the core under excessive force. Almost all veneer stones have cracked and split.	As most structural stones have cracked and split, even temporary struts cannot be of much help.
'mandapa'	Stone	The existing 'mandapa' on the east and north sides has collapsed including the upper structures. The south side stands with most slabs (ceilings) split and columns cracked. The collapsed and broken members of the 'sikhara' and 'mandapa' lie in the region of the 'antarala'. Some of the previous steel suports have been crushed under the debris.	Any restoration work needs to identify the long lying stone members at the site, which need to be restored to their positions in the reconstruction process. (Unlike the earlier restoration of the plinth which did not utilize the members lying at site).
Plinth of the temple	Stone	The northern part had been restored earlier. The southern part is intact but damaged due to the falling members and weathering.	
'Jagati'	Stone	It had been partly restored and is in an intact condition.	
'Garbhagrha'	Stone	The ceiling had been provided with steel post & beam supports as the stones of the walls have considerably reduced in dimension due to intense weathering. There are open gaps in the wall at the masonry joints.	

SUMMARY OF SURVEYED SITES

	Name and location	Place	Type	Protected	Reported by Burgess	Damage	Conservation need
KUTCH REGION							
1	Lakhesvara temple	Kera, Kutch	Temple	State Arch.	M	Partly collpsed. Structurally unstable	IMPORTANT: The entire structure of great value needs to be dismantled and reset in position.
2.	Rani Rajai's temple, Ruan-Ra'no-gadh	Manjal, Kutch	Temple	State Arch.	AKK	Partly collapsed Structurally unstable	URGENT:The collapsed portion needs to be methodically dismantled any further damage occurs.
3	Vadimedi, Puan-Ra no-gadh	Manjal, Kutch	5-celled Structure	State Arch.	AKK	Partly collapsed Srtucturally unstable	IMPORTANT: The collapsed members need to be identified; The precariouslystanding members need to be dismantled.
4	Jain temple	Kanthkot, Kutch	Temple	State Arch.		Completely Collapsed	
5	Gate	Kanthkot, Kutch	Gate	State Arch.		Severe Structural damage	
6	Old structures and Pavilion	Bharudia, Kutch	Small Temples	Not listed		Pavilion members are dislodged and scattered	URGENT: The sites must be procured by State Archaeology dept. and the members salvaged.
7	Old temple & Kund	Chaubari, Kutch	Temple & Kund			Completely collapsed and restored by villagers	
8	Jakhs talav	Jakhs, Kutch	Lake with Approach steps	Not listed		Some members dislodged and and have fallen	URGENT: The fallen parts need to be salvaged.
SAURASHTRA REGION							
9	Menal Vav	Virpur, Rajkot	Step-well	State Arch.		Structurally unstable	URGENT: A column and beam location requires immediate work.
10	Khambhalida Rock-cut caves	Khambhalida, Rajkot	Rock-cut Structures	State Arch.		Partly collapsed Severe weathering	URGENT: Water drainage system requires urgent reconditioning to prevent damage in rains.
11	Navalakha temple	Ghumli, Jamnagar	Temple	State Arch.	AKK	Partly collapsed Rest structurally unstable	MOST IMPORTANT: A well planned restoration work at a large scale.
12	Ganesha temple	Ghumli, Jamnagar	Temple	State Arch.	AKK	Weathering	
13	Navalakha Kund	Ghumli, Jamnagar	Kund	State Arch.	AKK	Dislodgement	

	Name and location	Place	Type	Protected	Reported by Burgess	Damage	Conservation need
14	Jetha vav	Ghumli, Jamnagar	Step-well	Not listed	AKK	Partly collapsed Vegetation	
15	Vania temple	Ghumli, Jamnagar	Temple	Not listed	AKK	Ruins	
16	Bhrigu-kund and temple structures	Ghumli, Jamnagar	Kund & temples	State Arch.	AKK	Encroachment	
17	Chaileshwar temple	Ghumli, Jamnagar	Temple	State Arch.	AKK	Partly collapsed Structurally unstable	URGENT: In the absence of the collapsed wall the existing part needs struts to support the surviving superstructure.
18	Ramapol (gate)	Ghumli, Jamnagar	5-arched gate	State Arch.	AKK	Partly collapsed Structurally unstable	URGENT: The surviving bracket and shaft need struts.
19	Palia stones	Ghumli, Jamnagar	Palia	Not listed	AKK	Some missing and trampled	URGENT: Valuable direct records (Sources) of history, need documentation
20	Derani-Jethani stepwells	Ghumli, Jamnagar	Step-well	Not listed	AKK	Partly collapsed Structurally unstable	
21	Sonkansari group of temples	Ghumli, Jamnagar	Group of 20 temples	State Arch.	AKK	A temple is missing; dislodgement	URGENT: Temple no. 4 should be dismantled before its collapse. Stapling of lintel of temple no.3.
22	Vekia vav	Bhuvaneshwar, Jamnagar	Step-well	State Arch.	AKK	Encroachment	IMPORTANT: The cracked beams need staples.
23	Bhuvaneshwar temples	Bhuvaneshwar, Jamnagar	Small temples	State Arch.		Dislodgement	
24	Pachtar temples	Panchyatna	State Arch.		AKK	Sinking of foundations Dislodgement Encroachment	
25	Ranpur fort	Ranpur, Jamnagar	Fort	Not listed		Partly collapsed Structurally unstable	URGENT: The exquisite gate is threatened by a damaged corner, which needs immediate repair.
26	Dhingeshwar and other rock-cut caves	Ranpur, Jamnagar	Rock-cut structures	State Arch.		Encroachment	
27	Shani-kund and old temple	Hathla, Jamnagar	Kund & temple	State Arch.		Encroachment Severe weathering	
28	Modhpar fort	Modhpar, Jamnagar	Fort	State Arch.		Partly collapsed	IMPORTANT: The water tank and royal quarters need restoration.
29	Bileshwar	Bileshwar, Jamnagar	Cop-type temple			Under restoration	

	Name and location	Place	Type	Protected	Reported by Burgess	Damage	Conservation need
SURENDRANAGAR REGION							
30	Mauni Bava temple	Than, Surendranagar	Temple	State Arch.		Partly collapsed	
31	Sun temple	Than, Surendranagar	Tample	ASI		Under restoration	
32	Old Jain shrine	Than, Surendranagar	Small temple	ASI		Severe weathering	
33	Fort wall	Than, Surendranagar	Fort wall			Structural damage	
34	Dak Bungalow	Navasudamda, Surendranagar		Privately owned		Partly restored.	IMPORTANT: The only surviving Dak Bungalow in Gujarat.
35	Madapola (Gate)	Jhinjuvada, Patan	6-arched gate	State Arch.	M	Partly collapsed Structurally unstable	IMPORTANT: Traffic should be restricted. The collapsed members should be salvaged.
36	Nadwada (Gate)	Jhinjuvada, Patan	6-arched gate	State Arch.	M	Severe weathering	
37	Dhamapola (Gate)	Jhinjuvada, Patan	6-arched gate	State Arch.	M	Dislodgement Severe weathering	
38	Rakshasapola (Gate)	Jhiniuvada, Patan	6-arched gate	State Arch.	M	Severe Structural damage Structurally unstable	URGENT: The structure is precariously standing and needs immediate structural supports.
39	Small gate 1 ("Junipost")	Jhiniuvada, Patan	gate	State Arch.		Severe Structural damage	URGENT: The structure is precariously standing and needs immediate structural supports.
40	Small gate & bastion, near step-well	Jhiniuvada, Patan	Gate & circular bastion	Not listed	M	Severe Structural damage Structurally unstable	URGENT: The structure is precariously standing and needs immediate structural support.
						Structurally unstable	The structure must be listed as protected site.
41	Main talav	Jhinjuvada, Patan	Ghats	State Arch.	M	Weathering	
42	Jhilkeshwar talav and old shrine	Jhinjuvada, Patan	Ghats and temple	State Arch.		Sinking of 'ghats'	
43	Fortwall	Jhinjuvada, Patan	fortwall	Not listed	M	Partly collapsed	URGENT: The structure made of destroyed temple parts need to be salvaged, and the wall *must* be listed as a protected site.

AKK: Report on the antiquities of Kathiawad and Kutch, James Burgess (1875)

M: Memoirs on the remains of Ghumli, Gop and in Kutch, James Burgess (1875)

The Status Report has 51 text pages, 26 pages of line-drawings and 79 coloured plates. In the Introduction: background, objective, methodology, scope and limitation are given, whereas table 1 gives the list of survey sites. In next chapter detailed survey of select structures and monuments protected by the State Department of Archaeology, region-wise namely Kutch, Saurashtra (Rajkot and Barda) and Surendra Nagar have been given. After this, heritage restoration and conservation issues have been taken up which is followed by recommendations for restoration and conservation. In the end in Table 2 Summary of survey sites has been given. This is a detail and exhaustive survey work not carried out before in any part of the country.

The report has already been handed over to the Chairman, Indian Council of Historical Research in July, 2003 and a copy to the Director, Department of Archaeology, Govt. of Gujarat, Ahmedabad for his information.

K.N. Dikshit

BOOK REVIEWS

Ashok Vardhan Shetty, *Excavations at Mangudi,* Deptt. of Archaeology, Government of Tamil Nadu, 2003, iv + 75, 27 plates, 13 figures. Price 78/-

This is a small brochure containing the results of a small excavation conducted by the Department of Archaeology at Mangudi in the district of Tirunelveli. The results does not vary much from other historical sites in the state excepting that at Mangudi. According to the excavator, a Microlithic level (mesolithic/Teri site culture) has been observed followed by the historical level. The brochure contains history of Mangudi and sites in and around Mangudi. The usual historical period ceramics are found besides the Rouletted ware and Russet coated pottery. What is significant is the preponderance of variety of graffiti marks and Tamil Brahmi inscriptions on the sherds. Several black and white plates and line drawings illustrate the brochure.

K.S. Ramachandran

Ashok Vardhan Shetty, *Excavations at Perur,* Deptt. of Archaeology, Govt. of Tamil Nadu, 2003 iv + 59. Plate. Price 60/-

Kongunadu encompassing the modern districts Comibatore, Erode, Salam, Namakkal, Karur, Nilgiris and some portions of Dindugal and Dharmapuri is replete with ancient remains. It is one such region rich in mineral wealth (the beryl from this region was very much sought after by the Romans and western world). Several ancient historical sites have been often excavated here which give us a fair knowledge of the early historical period of this region. Mention may be made of a few important excavated sites like Kodumanal, Perur and Karur; the last one has been identified with Vanchi, the Chera capital.

The present book embodies the outcome of the limited excavation at Perur, in Coimbattore district, on the Noyyal, a tributary of the Amaravati, which joins the sea near Karur.

The book is divided into nine chapters, the first being introduction giving brief history of the region and a summary of some sites excavated here viz. Kodumanal, Vellalur, Boluvampatti, Sulur, Sundakamuthur. The second chapter tells us the aims to be achieved by the excavation succeeded by the sequence of cultures. The deposit is divided into four cultural periods. Period I represented by black-and-red ware, Russet coated painted pottery, black and red ware. The pottery had post- firing graffiti marks. Ceramics of Period II consisted of all the ceramics of the earlier period besides a brown slipped ware. Beads comprised of semi-precious stones, glass coral, terracotta, etc, as also terracotta human and animal figurine. Periods III and IV yielded red ware and black wares and a few terracotta grooved tiles. A terracotta circular seal "with a bow flanked by two lamps and the cresent at the top" was an important find. In period IV one encounters burnt bricks, grooved tiles etc.

The chronology is as follows: Period I: 300 BC, Period II: 1st century BC- 3rd century AD, Period III: 3rd-6th century AD and Period IV: 6th to 9th century AD.

The book carries a brief description of the antiquities recovered from the excavations and a description of the ceramic shapes. Several plates and figures illustrate the book.

K.S. Ramachandran

B.B. Lal, B.K. Thapar, J.P. Joshi & Madhu Bala, *Excavations at Kalibangan:* The Early Harappan (1961-1969), 2003, (Archaeological Survey of India, New Delhi. pp.340+xvi, 58 plates, 75 figures and 35 charts. Price Rs.1000/-.

This is for the first time that we have gained an insight into the formative period of the Indus-Saraswati Civilization through the publication of this long-awaited excavation report on one of the major Harappan sites in India, Kalibangan, located on the dried-up course of the Saraswati in District Hanumangarh, northern Rajasthan. It is divided into thirteen chapters and is supplemented by four scientific and technical reports, making it a comprehensively treated subject. The major chapters deal with subjects like Geomorphology, Environment and Climate, Chronology, Culture-complex, Stratigraphy, Structures, Pottery and other antiquities. Technical reports are on pottery, metals, animal remains and plants and seeds.

The Report, however, is confined to the lower levels of Kalibangan, designated as 'Early Harappan'; the Mature Harappan levels, it is hoped, will be dealt with in the next volume, on which, we gather, the work is in progress. It may, however, be mentioned that the present publication is also a full treatise on the Early Harappan Civilization.

The analysis of the material presented by the authors has shown the following facts.

That, the Indus-Saraswati Civilization, as represented by what is now generally called 'Mature' phase, was preceded by a culture-complex now generally called 'Early Harappan' although in the past it was also called 'Pre-Harappan'. The Early Harappan was, however, a stage in the development of first urban cycle in India. Its story starts from what is called 'Hakra Phase', the remains of which are found mostly in the Saraswati basin sites. It is also called 'Ravi Phase', but only in the context of the stratigraphy worked out at the site of Harappa. Its remains are also found in the lower levels (Period I) of Jalilpur, a site located near Harappa. The general opinion is that 'Ravi' and 'Hakra' may be, by and large, one and the same cultural-complex with only a little variation because of local factors. However, the things may not be as simple as that since the Ravi phase dates at Harappa go back to 3300 B.C. at least, while the beginning of the Hakra Phase in the Saraswati basin goes back to 3100-3000 B.C. as is clear from the Radiocarbon dates obtained from Kalibangan and Kunal. The Early Harappan culture-complex includes yet another culture called "Kot-Diji-Sothi Culture". The authors have pointed out that each one of these cultures-Ravi, Hakra, Kot-Diji-Sothi and Kunal is marked by certain characteristic features which distinguish them from each other and yet they together created the Formative Period of the Mature Harappan Civilization since they do share several common features. For example, Kunal has given the evidence of primitive pit-dwellings while all other sites have given the evidence of square of rectangular houses of mud-bricks, with the occasional use of burnt bricks. The pottery in each case exhibits some characteristics, which are only occasionally shared by other sites. For example, pipal leaf motif with white fillings and black outline are more commonly found at Kunal than at Kot Diji. Gold and silver ornaments are more numerous at Kunal than at other places. Then, there appears to be a short-lived break in occupation at Kalibangan before Mature Phase starts, but this is just not there at Banawali where the third or upper-most phase (Ic) of the Early Harappan starts exhibiting most of the Mature Harappan characteristics. Kunal, of course, appears to be a single culture site; rarely do we find Mature Harappan pot-sherds on the surface. The seals of steatite and shell, square in shape and perforated knob at the back have been found at Kunal but without any writing on them, only some geometric motifs are there. However, graffiti on potteries are found everywhere, some of which resemble the signs used in the Mature Phase writing. At Harappa, in fact, at least in one example, three such signs are found engraved on the rim of an earthen pot.

Copper and bronze were used for making artefacts.

That there did appear at a very early point of time during the Early Harappan what is generally called "fortification" at all these sites, except Kunal, is significant. Houses were small but generally oriented along cardinal directions. Thus, urban characteristics had definitely appeared during the Early Harappan times.

Kalibangan is, however, also known for yielding the evidence of a ploughed field during the Early Harappan period.

And finally, it may be noted, that 'Ravi-Hakra-Kot-Diji' complex of the Early Harappan was having its concentration in the Saraswati basin not in the Indus basin.

The Report is, a very much welcome addition to our knowledge.

The photographs, the line drawings and the pottery-plates, both colour and black-and-white, are excellent. It is a very well produced Report and everyone interested in Indian archaeology and history must possess this book.

S.P. Gupta

Durga Dutta Sharma, *Kampilya Mahatmaya in verse (Sanskrit). Translated into English prose by Corredo Puchetti, Venetian Academy of Indian Studies Series No. 3, Venice, Italy.* D.K. Printworld (P) Ltd. pp. xxii, 1-208, 2003, New Delhi.

The book has an excellent forward by Gian Giuseppe in which Panchalas from Rigvedic times have been highlighted through the archaeological discoveries in the area.

The work includes original Sanskrit text, comprising 1363 couplets (slokas). At the end of every verse is given a literal translation in English, The text is appended with a forward, preface, and a introduction, from the original manuscript, besides a glossary and bibliography.

Durga Dutta Sharma was invited by Goswami Bhariongiri to compile the *Kampilya-mahatmaya,* or the glory of Kampliya, which had earlier been attempted by excellent poets like Sukrasanidhiji and Durganath Misraji, who attempted to compile it on the basis of the Puranas.

Sharma has utilized Mahabharata, and the Puranas and the pattern of the description of Mahatmaya.

Following the tradition of Mahabharata at the end of each chapter name and number of the chapter is mentioned. The translator here has ignored the name of the chapter. For example at the end of the first chapter it mentions, *"Iti Sri Kampillmahatmye Siva-Nandi Samvad Kalyotopatino Nam Prathmodhyaya"*. He translates as, "Here ends the first chapter of Kampilya Mahatmya". However the translation narration has uninterrupted flow.

The narration of the Mahatmya starts from the Dwapara and beginning of the Kaliyug. The narration states that the name Kampila is made of three syllables namely Kam, Pila. Kam is, Kan-jansu, pi is pinak (bow) of Siva and la is from Lakshmipati. The first five chapters discuss origin of kala, the importance and creation of Mantra and Diksha, Trymkesvara-lingam and the greatness of Rameswara temple. The next five chapters deal with the battle between Dronacharya and Drupada. The Pandavas fought on behalf of their preceptor Dronacharya. Panchala was captured by the Pandavas, later south Panchala was given to Drupada. Initially north Panchala was retained by Kurus. As relations between Kaurvas and Pancalas developed, north Pancala was also given to Draupada. The next fifteen chapters are devoted to the *svayamvara* of Draupadi, and, her marriage with five Pandavas. It is followed by the genealogy of the kings of Kampliya, monuments and sacred places around, and, other religious issues related to the *tirthas* in and around Kampila. The translator has appended notes relating to the places mentioned in the chapter number 38 with the names of the modern villages and places around. It is indeed an addition to our knowledge.

On the whole this is an excellent attempt not only to publish an old work with translation but also to contribute its historical data towards writing up of the regional history of the central Ganga-Yamuna Doab.

R.P. Sharma

Usha Agarwal, 2003. *Directory of Museums in India, 2003,* Sandeep Prakashan, New Delhi. pp- i ñ xii + 370. Rs 1270/- . Hardbound.

The author, currently the Director of Museum Development cell of INTACH is a widely experienced officer in the administration of museums in India. Her work is a project report supported by INTACH and Indian Council of Conservation Institute and Museums Association of India. The first 12 pages of the book are marked in Roman numbers from I to XII, containing the title of the book, printers information, contents, preface to the second and first editions, and the details of information format. The next 370 pages are marked in Arabic numbers from 1 to 370.

The information in the Directory is supplied according to the name of states, numbering 1 to 32. The format of the description of the museum includes name of the city, name of the museums with name of the district, pin number, working timings, weekly holidays, entrance fees for adult and child, ownership, date of foundation, designation of the authority who is the controlling head, details of the collection, publications of the museum, library, and information regarding permission to photograph the exhibits. The text is supplemented with, a). index of cities, b). Index of types of museums, c). controlling authority of museums, d). number of types of museums, and, e). number of museums in a particular state.

The book nearly gives all the relevant useful information for the museologists, tourists, visitors, scholars and libraries. The nature of the work is encyclopaedic and is a positive contribution to the museum sciences.

R.P. Sharma

D.P Tewari, *Excavations at Charda,* Tarun Prakashan, Lucknow, 2002, pp. i -viii + 195, figures 28, plates 55, Price: Rs. 500/-

The excavations at the mound of Charda, Jamogh north east of Lucknow were undertaken under the Research Project of the 'Archaeology of North Koshal Region'. The author gives a detailed introduction of the site, its environment, geomorphology and previous work done in the area. Chapters dealing with cuttings, stratigraphy, floors, structures besides description of ceramic and other finds, are given along with drawings and coloured photographs.

In conclusion it seems that the author has been able to establish a complete cultural sequence of the Tarai region.

Sonali Gupta

Edwin Bryant, *The Quest for the Origins of Vedic Culture. Indo Aryan Migration Debate.* OUP, 2002.

This book is primarily a historiographical study of how various scholars, over a course of a century or more, have rejected the idea of the external origin of the Indo-Aryans by questioning much of the logic, assumptions, and methods upon which the theory is based. Bryant uses the term Aryan to denote the Vedic speaking people. Since the term is Sanskrit, the author has adopted this denomination miniature in the context of his descriptive label *Indigenous Aryanism,* which refers to the speakers of Vedic and related dialects.

Western scholars have generally been unaware, or dismissive of voices from India that have been critical over the years of this European reconstruction of their country's History. The author has very appropriately quoted Dilip Chakrabarti, who in his book *Colonial Ideology: The Socio-Politics of Ancient Indian Past* (Delhi, 1997), has said, however well meaning such scholars and their publications are, they have taken it upon themselves the task of interpreting the past heritage of a very large number of people who belong to various nation states and may like to formulate their ideas of the past.

In the first chapter *Myth of Origin, Europe and the Aryan Homeland Quest* the author has outlined the most prominent features of history that are most directly connected with the problems of Indo-Aryan origins. The mainstream of western academic circle, Bryant discusses blatant ideological and religious attitude of the eighteenth and nineteenth centuries in the west that co-opted Aryan discourse in some form of fashion. The author has quoted Lucien Fevre, Paliakov, linguist F.Bopp and others who consider India the cradle of civilization. On the other hand opinions of western scholars differ.

In the second chapter, the author has pointed out the early Indian responses i.e. nationalist response to colonial construction of early Indian history. They were quick to incorporate the orient list view of ancient India into their political agenda. From religious perspective, the brahmanical viewpoints are linguistic evidences produced by different linguists in support or against the theory of 'Indigenous Aryanism'. The 'Indigenous Aryan' position is by now far too widespread to be ignored.

Ancient Indian pre-history and proto-history is an extremely rich and fascinating area of study, but unfortunately, the origin of Indo-Aryans has become inextricably enmeshed with the politics of representation.

The author recognizes the extent to which both sides of debate have been driven by political, racial, religious and nationalistic agenda. His intention is to present the interpretation of evidence from all rational perspectives and point out various assumptions underlying them. Though the author has tried to present the both side of theories but the book is titled towards Indo-Aryan side of family compared to Indo-European problems. He has quoted primary voices to substantiate the theories to suggest that how a historical construct that is taken very much for granted by most of us—the Aryan invasion/migration theory-is-viewed when seen through different cultural religious and political perspectives.

This book has focused mostly on scholars who have actively argued for the indigenous origin of the Aryans. The author also points out the obvious lack of communication, and often interest, between many Indian and western scholars on this subject. The author states that no informed western scholar speaks of invasions anymore.

This book is voluminous and encyclopedic. The 367 page book contains original views of the authors of the various theories. Though the author has expressed his opinion on the value of some arguments being contested and inability to reach to any conclusion regarding the original home of the Aryans, he is forthcoming with the analysis of the western as well as with the endogenous Aryanism. It is a brilliant Survey of the study of the Vedic Aryans.

Vijay Laxmi Singh

K. Paddayya 2002, *Recent Studies in Indian Archaeology*, Munshiram Manoharlal Publishers Pvt. Ltd. and Indian Council of Historical Research, New Delhi, pp.1-454. Price. 950/-.

This book on recent studies in Indian archaeology is a collection of seventeenth articles giving an adequate idea about the development of Indian Archaeology starting from palaeolithic times since independence to medieval times. It also includes physical dating methods used in determining the chronology of Indian archaeology. Under Stone Age the articles on lower palaeolithic and mesolithic phase of a limited area of the country and the problem of ashmounds of southern Deccan have found place.

The chalcolithic phase has been dealt in details taking into account the articles of all the aspects of Harappa Culture, chalcolithic phase in Western India and other proto-historic cultures of Ganga valley including the early users of iron in India. The articles on 'Historical archaeology' and 'Medieval archaeology' have also been included.

There is an article on 'Rock-art of India'. The contribution of 'Science in Indian Archaeology' and the "Role of monsoon in evolution of pre-historic cultures" are also there. The Harappan technology and Human skeletal biology are other issues included in the book. The authors have used the latest archaeological data for information and interpretation.

The radio carbon dates including other related disciplines used in understanding Indian archaeology have also found place. But at the same time there are also a few gaps that remaines uncovered which were required to be filled up by inviting a few more articles.

The book is useful for the scholars and to the students, as it is upto data on the topics dealt but also have a good selected bibliography.

K.N. Dikshit

Mani Kamerkar and Soonu Dhunjishah, 2002. *From the Iranian Plateau to the Shores of Gujarat.* The story of Parsi Settlements and absorption in India, K.R. Cama Oriental Institute, Allied Publishers Private Limited, Mumbai, pp.220, 38 photographs including coloured ones. Price 390/-. Hard bound.

The authors engaged in historical research for the last fifty years have studied original sources, such as *farmans,* legal agreements, property sale deeds, diaries of the early Jain monks showing that the Parsees, though a minority community, having attained a significant position in the eco-political fabric of the western India. It is a protracted struggle to trace the migration of the Parsees in western India, and their consequential absorption into the Indian social system, retaining at the same time individualistic, and original socio-religious traits.

The book is divided into ten chapters. The chapter 1 deals with the Parsees in their homeland Iran and Indo-Iranian cultural interaction. The chapter 2 deals with the location of Iran mid-way between Near East, and South-East Asia that helped to make them much at home with Mesopotamia on one hand, and, South-east Asian civilizations on the other and Bacteria, and the Margiana oasis, south of the river Sazartes (Sya Darya river). The excavations conducted there revealed a Bronze Age habitation. Fire pits and signs of liquid oblatious *(hoam)* were found in excavations. Between 2000-1500 BC these people moved towards south-east and south-west. It was during this period that Gathas of Ahur Mazda in the west, and, hymns of Rigveda were composed.

The second influx of the Parsees occurred from onwards of 7th and 8th centuries AD. A large number of Parsees took refuge in Kohistan, and mountainous region of Khorasan and followed the route along the western coast from Rann of Kutch, Daman, Dun, Gulf of Khambhat, Bharuch, Surat, and Bombay. The centre of the settlements of the Parsees is located between Khambhat in the north and Surat in the south.

Chapters 3,4,5,6,7 deal with the development of the towns namely Navsri, Surat, Bharuch, Khambat, and Bilimora. These towns saw their development from a tiny village to a prosperous town. Every one of these towns is discussed in a separate chapter individually. The chapters 8 and 9 deal with social and, religious customs and traditions, and, role of the Parasees in the struggle for Indian freedom.

The last but not the least, important is chapter 10, which deals with the making of Mumbai from seven islands to an economic and financial capital of India, also simultaneously highlighting the role of Parsees as catalytic agents of the glorious change.

There is an index at the end of the book and the exhaustive notes appended at the end of each chapter are important additions to the book. The book is important for the scholar, as it is interesting to a lay reader, who will certainly enrich his knowledge.

R.P. Sharma

Noboru Karashima (ed) 2002, *Ancient and Medieval Commercial Testimony of Inscriptions and Ceramic-sherds.* Alamu Printers, Chennai, pp.i-xii + 307, 5 maps, 32 figures, price is not mentioned.

Karashima's book is the outcome of the International project entitled 'Medieval Commercial Activities in the Indian Ocean as Revealed from Inscriptions and Chinese Ceramic-sherds' organized by Taisho University, Japan. During the last two decades much attention has been paid to the merchant activities in the Indian Ocean. Yet, so far published books deal mostly with the times after the advent of the Europeans.

The present volume embodies many articles by eminent scholars working in the field of medieval trade. Abraham's book *(Two Medieval Merchant Guilds of*

South India), deals with south Indian merchant guilds Manigramam and Ainurruvar which is, certainly an important contribution to our understanding of Indian Ocean trade in medieval times. Further, since the publication of her book there have been several new dates that have come up, relating to these merchant guilds. The present book has fulfilled this lacuna. Besides, the book also includes Chinese ceramics discovered in Southeast Asia, South Asia and West Asia, which are obviously important indicators of the vigorous mercantile activities of their respective times.

This book is divided into three parts: Part I dealing with the inscriptions of the merchant guilds, Part II with Chinese ceramics, and Part III with historical relations between two regions. All the three parts consist of several chapters, including a general survey of the topic and studies of some particular inscription or site, or of a problem. Apart from these main three parts, there are appendices as well giving the texts and translations of some important inscriptions, and also a list of merchant-guild inscriptions.

The book is well illustrated with photographs, maps and Tables, and it will be useful for students and scholars for those in researches of Indian ocean merchant activities.

T. Arun Raj

O.P. Agrawal and Nanda Amara Wickramasinghe, 2002. *Materials and Techniques of Ancient Wall Paintings of Sri Lanka,* published by INTACH, Lucknow and Sandeep Prakashan, New Delhi, pp.1-175, Price 2000/-.

The book is divided into 5 chapters with an appendix on methodology of analysis, a bibliography and also an index. The wall paintings of Sri Lanka were systematically studied in the past by R.H. De Silva who described the paintings as oil emulsion gum tempera. The chapter one deals with the introduction to the problem, whereas the chapter two traces the history of wall paintings in Sri Lanka. Chapter three devotes to various techniques and materials used for production of paintings and chapter four which is the main contribution of book, gives the results of the scientific analysis of the paintings by using the methods such as micro-chemical analysis, optical microscopy, X-ray diffraction analysis and FT-IR spectroscopy for the identification of pigments and binding medium.

The author have also analyzed the plaster by preparing the Cross-Section of the plaster. This have helped them in to get a real insight into a fabrication technique of Sri Lanka.

The details of the material used at each site have been mentioned. The scientific studies have established that the wall paintings of the early period in Sri Lanka especially at Sigiriya, Tivanka Image House and Mahiyangana Relic chamber was neither fresco nor tempera. O.P. Agrawal the first author has even named this technique as 'Rajasthani technique' or fresco lustro. It has the characteristic of both fresco as well as lustro, the reason being that the paintings were executed on wet-lime plaster but a binding medium was mixed with the pigment. However, as mentioned by the author the tempera technique also continued in Sri Lanka as noticed at Vessagiriya, Situlpahuwa and Pulligoda.

A work of this nature is also needed to study the wall paintings in India.

The book is a welcome study in understanding the scientific studies of wall paintings in the world.

K.N. Dikshit

Yasuda, Yoshinori, 2002 (Ed.). *The Origin of Pottery and Agriculture*, International Research Centre for Japanese Studies, Japan. pp.1-400, List of Contributors, Index. Price (not quoted).

This book is divided into five parts having 22 chapters, a brief introduction on the significance of agriculture in human history and a conclusion emphasizing the shift from the monastic to pluralistic view of civilization. It is copiously illustrated with photographs, line-drawings, maps besides several tables.

Prof. Yasuda, the editor of this volume, is one of the

leading scholars in the field of Environmental Archaeology in Japan. He has emphasized that the history of human civilization was always viewed through the western perspective and the eastern world particularly the Far East was overlooked, while it is well a known fact that Japanese and Chinese scholars have broughtforth traces of earlier human civilization based on rice cultivation and fishery. The established notion that West was the earliest region of agriculture and pottery stands challenged and now it has been shown that the East preceded the West. Prof. Yasuda, who is a major contributor of this volume postulated five periods of revolution corresponding with the period of drastic global climatic changes, which were largely responsible for significant epochs in the development of human history because the beginning of agricultural led to surplus food production and also served as a platform for the development of urbanization. The monistic concept of Childe for the development of urbanization was replaced by Ito's agriculture revolution model known as 'Environmental Revolution' that has been identified in five different regions of the world. In fact it is this model which was kept in the mind while the beginning of agriculture and domestication of plants was discussed and reported by different authors in their papers. Prof. Yasuda has cautioned that significance of different ecological conditions and various other factors were responsible for independent domestication of plants and the East Asian region will have to be treated different from the Western region.

The conclusion drawn in this book pointed out that two fertile crescents, namely Eastern Asian fertile crescent of rice and West Asian fertile crescent of wheat existed and the origin of pottery and agriculture can be better understood in this broader framework.

This book which is very well printed is most welcome in understanding the human history specially origin of pottery and agriculture in global context.

K.N. Dikshit

Anuradha V. Kumar, ed.2001, *Conservation of Building Stones,* INTACH, Indian Council of Conservation Institute, Lucknow and Sundeep Prakashan, New Delhi,.pp.i-xv+ 229,price Rs. 1600/-.

The author is an established scholar in the field of conservation of historic buildings and their preservation. She has extensive exposure to all types of historic structures having different building materials from India and abroad. However, the book deals with the different types of building materials used in India since 232 B.C., along with their problems and remedies of preservation and conservation of historic buildings.

It is a comprehensive book written in lucid style, following a straight narrative writing. It is divided into three sections. The section one reviews the nature of building stones, their relevant properties and construction technology used in buildings. The second section deals with the diagnosis of stone deterioration with various mechanisms of deterioration namely physical, chemical and also biological. The last one talks of the treatment of building stones, the methodology and the various consolidants used at the sites.

All these chapter are extensively detailed ones and well explained with diagrams, tables wherever necessary. It is also supported by a select bibliography. The book has been printed in good quality and is a must for beginners in the field of building conservation.

Gency Chaudhuri

S. Raja Gopal. (ed.) 2001, *Kaveri- Studies in Epigraphy, Archaeology, and History- in Prof. Y. Subbaraylu Felicitation Volume.* Chennai Panpattu Publishers (P.) Ltd.,I-xxx + 714, Price Rs. 450/- (Student Edition) & Rs. 1000/- (Library Edition).

The volume 'Kaveri' felicitates Professor Y. Subbaraylu, doyen of the Tamil University, Thanjavur. Beginning with a brief tribute to the professor popularly known as YS to his students and colleagues, this volume contains sixty-five well-researched papers, authored by eminent scholars; majority of whom have in someway or other worked with Prof. Subbaraylu.

This festschrift containing fifty-three articles in English and Tamil Language by the Scholars of the respective field is divided into four parts. The first part has twelve of the Professor's papers, mostly relating to the Chola period which was his major field of research; the remaining three parts deal with Epigraphy and Archaeology, History and Art, Religion, Language and Culture.

Among the articles of importance mention may made of Iravatham Mahadevan's 'A Unique Chola seal from Orissa', Kesavan Veluthat's 'The Mauryan Presence in South India', K. Rajan's 'Recent Advances in Early Historic Archaeology of Tamil Nadu', T. Satyamurthy's 'Identification of Bandar – A Sangam age Port', R. Poongundran's 'Vel in Sri Lanka Brahmi inscriptions', A. Ekambaranathan's 'Jainism under the Early Pandyas', P.D. Balaji's 'Ganesa in Cave Architecture' and D. Dayalan's 'Behati'- 'New Light on Gupta Architecture in Madya Pradesh'.

In the article 'The Mauryan Presence in South India' Veluthat argues that, earlier scholars exaggerated the political presence of the Mauryas in Karnataka. He also says that the considerable influence of the Mauryan state in Karnataka was due to trade contacts and spread of religious movements, and not because of political organization. K. Rajan has attempted micro area graffiti, Tamil Brahmi and ethno archaeological analysis of early phase of Tamil Nadu with the help of archaeological, epigraphical and numismatic findings. Nambirajan in his article 'Recent explorations in Gingee Taluk, Tamil Nadu' has documented the occurrence of Mesolithic and Neolithic sites in Gingee region, which will help us to understand more about succeeding cultures i.e. Iron age and early historical people. Satyamurthy in his article gives importance to the unknown but one the famous pearl-port called Bandar besides Korkai and Mantai.

This volume is undoubtedly a significant contribution to ancient and medieval south Indian study in particular, and other areas in general. It is printed in good quality paper, with black-and white plates and maps and illustrations.

T. Arun Raj

D.P Tewari, *Antiquarian Remains from Kalli Pachchhim Excavations,* Archaeological Museum, Department of A.I.H & Archaeology, University of Lucknow, 1999, pp.i- xiv +136, figures 27, plates 51, Price: Rs. 200/-

The book by Dr. Tiwari deals with the excavation of a site "Kalli Pachchhim" primarily to understand the archaeology of North Kosala region. This report is divided into five chapters. The first chapter being the introduction gives a general outline of the site and its environs as per the previous work done here. Rest of the chapters two and three deal with stratigraphy and chronology. The deposits has been divided into four periods 1st dating to 7th century BC – 1st century AD, the 2nd period dating to 1st – 4th century AD the third dating to 4th – 8th century AD and the last dating to 8th – 12th century AD. The fourth chapter is the most important and deals with ceramics found in the several periods which are similar to the ones usually found in the Indo-Gangetic plain. Some coins have been found which are under treatment.

The book carries several photographs and plates and is printed on art paper.

Gency Chaudhury

K. Rajan, *Archaeology, Principles and Methods,* pp.274 inclusisssve of phot graphs and line drawing, bibliography and index, Manoo Pathippakam, Thanjavur. Price: Hard bound Rs. 450 and paper back 200/-

A number of books on archaeology, archaeological methods, field archaeology i.e. excavation and exploration techniques have been published. Most of them are highly technical or the ones dealing with abstract theories which sometimes are beyond the comprehension of students and lay men. Rajan's book overcomes this. Written in simple understandable language this is not only a text book for students of archaeology but also a guide for those who are interested in the culture and heritage of ours.

The book is in seventeen chapters covering besides introduction, topics like history of archaeology, theories, field methods dealing with archaeological exploration and excavation, archaeological stratigraphy, recording of field data, archaeological photography, conservation of the find in the field, analysis of data, methods of archaeological dating, surveying and preparation of maps besides newly introduced (in India) marine archaeology. For carrying out the archaeological work it is obvious that the organization should have enough technical staff.

Having carried out archaeological works it becomes useless if it is not published in a proper manner. Rajan offers enough guidance how an archaeological publication should and what are the essential parts an archaeological report should be divided into.

In this book the most interesting chapters are archaeological theories where culture, functionalism, New Archaeology, Processual theory, contextual archaeology, behavioural, archaeology and gender and archaeology today, etc.

The chapter on dating methods is comprehensive including latest methods using physics, chemistry, botany viz. radiocarbon, thermoluminescence, fission tract, dendrochronology, geochronology etc.

In short this is a book that one interested in archaeology should posses.

K.S. Ramachandran

REPORT OF THE XXXVI ANNUAL CONFERENCE

Report of the XXXVI Annual Conference of Indian Archaeological Society held at State Institute of Archaeology, Art History, Conservation & Museology, Hill Palace, Thripunithura, Kerala from 19th-22nd December, 2002.

The Annual Conference of the three Societies namely Indian Archaeological Society, Indian Society for Prehistoric and Quaternary Studies and Indian History and Culture Society, was inaugurated by Shri Sikandar Bakht, His Excellency, the Governor of Kerala on the 19th December, 2002 at SIAACM, Hill Palace, Thripunithura, Kerala. He highlighted the activities of the State of Kerala in the field of history and archaeology and also spoke about the long tradition of research and publication in Kerala started earlier by Maharaja of Cochin and Travancore. Prof. K.V. Thomas, Hon'ble Minister for Tourism and Fisheries, Govt. of Kerala delivered the Presidential address to the delegates of the three Societies. Shri T.M.Jacob, Hon'ble Minister for Water Resources, Archaeology, Archives and Museum, Govt. of Kerala inaugurated the seminar on "Maritime Heritage of India". Prof. M.G.S. Narayanan, Chairman, ICHR, New Delhi gave a special lecture on 'Muziris in Archaeology and Early literature of South India'.

After the inaugural function, Prof. Purushottam Singh gave the Presidential Address of the Indian Society for Prehistoric and Quaternary Studies followed by Prof. R.Nath who delivered the first B.R.Grover Memorial lecture of Indian History and Culture Society. Prof. A.Sundara delivered the Presidential Address of the Indian Archaeological Society.

After the end of inaugural function, deliberations on the seminar 'Maritime Heritage of India', organized by the Govt. of Kerala commenced at Hill Palace campus. The western coast of India had played an important role in maritime activities during the period c.200 B.C. to A.D.1200. The period marked flourishing maritime trade and cultural interaction with the west Arabian and Persian Gulf and eastern coasts of Africa. Dawood Dalvi outlined the maritime heritage of western coast of India in relation to Konkan. Whereas Suman Pandya discussed the locational significance and the trade relations of the Gulf of Khambhat within India and outside world. Sila Tripathi presented a paper on exploration and excavation of ship wrecks in Indian waters specially at Sunchi Reef and St. George Reef, both in Goa waters, datable to 17th-19th century A.D. M.V. Nair, P.K. Gopi and P. Sreedharan spoke on the excavation of a sail boat at Kadakkarappally, in district Alappuzha, Kerala. The excavation confirmed the shape and size of the ship. It appears that

Kadakkarappally was a habitational site during the 17th century.

Friday, 20.12.02

Morning Session:

SEMINAR ON MEGALITHS OF KERALA AND BEYOND

The theme of the seminar of the Indian Archaeological Society was introduced by Prof. A. Sundara and a number of scholars from Kerala, Tamil Nadu, Karnataka, Maharashtra etc. participated in the discussion. The recent archaeological discoveries and their impact on the archeology of megaliths in Kerala was presented by Dr. Hari Shankar. Shri N.S. Rangarajan presented a paper on "Recent excavations of Megalithic sites in Karnataka". Shri P.S. Joshi in his paper on "The Megalithis of Kerala and Beyond" emphasized a need to "shift" in orientation of methodology for understanding the megalithic culture of early Iron Age in India. K.M. Suresh presented a paper on anthropomorphic figures from Kumati and Hulikunte from Kudligi Taluk, District Bellary. Many of the enigmatic stone figures of anthropomorphs resembling those of the copper hoards sites have come to light in several places in Karnataka and Tamilnadu; the importance and meaning of the presence of these in the megalithic archaeology is attracting the attention of scholars. Shri K.N.Dikshit drew a parallel with the existing menhir-statues from Indonesia and Polynesian countries.

Afternoon Session:

ART

Anand, Kumar
Budhist Stupa at Kesariya in Bihar

Balaji, P.D.
Ear-Ornaments in Ancient Tamilagam

Margabandhu, C
Group of Temples at Village Garh

Singh, A.K.
Some observations on the Shikharas of the Kalachuri period Temples in the Eastern Vindhyas

Dr. Samak, S.G. and Jagdish
Aratalaqwadde Copper Plate of Kadamba King Priyavrata Varma

Kumar, Ajit
The vessel excavated at Thykkal, District Alappuzha – An Appraisal.

TRADE

Gupta, Sunil
Ptolemy's Pirate Coast: Early Historical Ports on the Kānara, South India.

Suman, Pandya
The Gulf of Khambat- A centre of marine Trade and Inter-action.

Raj, Arun and Rajesh, M
Sengamedu: A Hinterland Trade Centre of Arikamedu - Some Observations

Marwah, Jyoti
Mapping India's past from Spice Age to the Age of Spice Oils

Dalal, Kurush, Gupta, S.P., Dandekar, A.R., Mitra, R, Nanji, R and Pande, R
A Preliminary Analysis of the Excavations at Sanjan, district Valsad, Gurjarat.

Dandekar, Abhijit and Nanji, Rukshana
Pottery at Sanjan: Preliminary Observations

Saturday, 21.12.02

Morning Session:

Singh, A.K. and Singh, P.
Third Field season at Agiabir: 2000-1

Rajendran, P.
Studies on Geo-archaeology and Hominid find from Odai in Bommayarpalayam of Villupuram District in Tamil Nadu, South India.

Suresh, K.M.
Anthropomorphic Figures from Kumuti and Hulikunte

from Kudligi Taluk, Bellary District.

Sharma, R.P.
Archaeological Reconnaissance of the Sahibi Basin in North eastern Rajasthan and South Haryana.

Manuel, J.
Why Deny Evidence of Horse?

Afternoon Session:

Bhatt R.C., Nautiyal K.P. & Nautiyal M.K.
Himalayan Expeditions of the Maukharis and Huna Invasion

Irani Atusha,
Urbanization in Early historic Gujarat during the 1st BC – 5th AD

Jha, Satyendra Kumar
A Dvadasaditya from Baruar

Marcato Lucio and Dallaporta Annamaria.
Proposal for Creation of the Archaeological Map of U.P.

Pal, J.N.
Excavations at Jhusi.

Sethi, Vinod
Decipherment of the Indus Script.

Saturday, 21.12.02

Afternoon Session:

Mane, G.K.
Socio-Economic Status of Megalithic People of Vidarbha

Rangaraju, N.S.
Recent Explorations of Megalithic Sites in Karnataka

Misra, O.P., M.K. Maheshwari, B.K. Lohande, Ahmed Ali Jakir Hussain, L.P. Kadam
Kalyanpura Excavations-Sardar Sarovar Project

Ramjit and Abid Mohammad
Keshavpur – A unique OCP site in Aligarh District.

Sunday, 22.12.02

Morning Session:

Singh, A.K.
Dakshineshwar Mahadeva Temple at Nirmand: An Orientation and Architectural study.

Thanki Mugatlal, J.
Acupuncture Therapy in the History of India.

Tyagi, A.K.
The Antiquity of *Ramakatha* in Historical Perspective.

Mani, B.R.
Excavations at Sarnath: Some Reflections regarding Early phase, Stratigraphy and Architecture.

Sundra, A.
Samudra Manthana panel of a medieval temple, Hosagunda

Kannan, R.
Kumari Continent and Under water Archaeology.

The closing function was held on the 22nd December, 2002 and Prof. N. Unnikrishnan Nair, Vice Chancellor, CUSAT gave valedictory Address. Dr. P.K. Gopi, Organizing Secretary of the conference gave vote of thanks to the collegues and delegates.

K. N. Dikshit
General Secretary
Indian Archaeological Society

B-17, Qutab Institutional Area,
New Delhi-110 016

THE INDIAN ARCHAEOLOGICAL SOCIETY

BALANCE SHEET AS ON 31.03.2003

LIABILITIES		AMOUNTS (RS.)	ASSETS		AMOUNTS (RS.)
CAPITAL FUND			FIXED ASSETS		
Op. Balance	2,937,649.57		(As per Annexure 'A' attached)		13,801,564.00
Add:L.M.Fees	46,960.00				
Add:Income Over Expenditure	232,341.00	3,216,950.57	CURRENT ASSETS & INVESTMENTS		
CORPUS FUND		1,600,000.00	Fixed Deposits	2,777,290.00	
			Accured interest	211,346.00	2,988,636.00
BUILDING FUND		8,858,263.00			
Donation For Lectur Y.D.Sharma		100,000.00	Delhi Vidyut Board		86,886.00
Dr. A.K.Narain (Award)Fund		50,000.00			
Donation for Cupboards			Indian Council of Hist. Research		5,000.00
Op. Balance	20,000.00		SUNDRY DEBTORS & ADVANCES		
Less: Spent during the year	3,920.00	16,080.00	(As per Annexure'D' attached)		400,598.67
Donation for Podium		25,000.00			
Donation for Books			CASH & BANK BALANCE		
Op. Balance	19,000.00		S.B.I -45062		315,681.10
Add:Received during the year	4,000.00		S.B.I -45082		35,625.07
Less:Spent during the year	7,172.00	15,828.00	Indian Bank-460017		278,990.15
			Cash in Hand		8,755.65
Sri Gurudeva Ranade Award Fund		80,000.00			
PROJECT FUNDS					
(As per Annexure 'B' attached)		795,028.73			
SECURITIES					
India Infrastrucute Pub.Pvt.Ltd.		270,675.00			
LOANS & ADVANCES					
Dr.S.P.Gupta-Loan		623,000.00			
Akhil Bhartiya Itihas Sankalan Yojna		450,000.00			
Bharatiya Sanskrit Parishad		1,500,000.00			
SUNDRY CREDITORS					
(As per Annexure 'C' attached)		320,910.44			
		17,921,735.74			17,921,736.64

Sd/	Sd/	Sd/
Chairman	Treasurer	For Rajan Sharma & Co., Chartered Accountant

Place: New Delhi
Daed: 18.10.2003

(Rajan Kumar Sharma)
Prop.

THE INDIAN ARCHAEOLOGICAL SOCIETY

INCOME EXPENDITURE ACCOUNT FOR THE YEAR ENDED 31.03.2003

PARTICULARS	AMOUNTS(RS.)	PARTICULARS	AMOUNTS(RS.)
To Honorarium	258,750.00	By Delegation Fees	300.00
To Municipal Taxes	500,000.00	By Diesel Charges	8,672.00
To News Paper &Periodicals	1,625.00	By Electricity Charges	24,699.00
To Telephone Expenses	44,880.00	By Grant for Conference	90,000.00
To Conveyance & Travelling	84,988.00	By Grant for Puratattva-31-ASI	25,000.00
To Printing &Stationery	14,096.00	By Grant for Puratattva-32-ASI	25,000.00
To Electricity Charges	47,037.00	By Insurance Claim	16,853.00
To Establishment Expenses	32,870.00	By Interest	341,017.14
To Conference Expenses	100,470.00	By Rent	1,607,018.00
To Computer Repair & Maintenance	18,834.00	By Sale of Publication	98,902.00
To Repairs & Maintenance	377,336.00		
To Car Running & Maintenance	21,908.00		
To Hospitality Charges	5,131.00		
To Postage & Stamps	27,790.00		
To Internet Charges	11,670.00		
To Generator Running & Maintenance	26,524.00		
To Bank Charges	2,115.00		
To Centre for Research & Training in Hist, Arch and Palaeo-Envt.	2,000.00		
To Consultancy Charges	31,000.00		
To V.S.Wakankar Award	21,000.00		
To Ground Rent-D.D.A.	23,000.00		
To Professional Charges	21,000.00		
To Medical Expenses(Sundry)	18.00		
To Workshop on Fatehpur Sikri	5,000.00		
To Publication Expenses	131,708.00		
To Audit Fees	21,000.00		
To Advertisement Expenses	1,108.00		
To Depreciation	172,260.00		
To Excess of Income over Expenditure	232,341.90		
	2,237,459.90		2,237,461.14

Sd/
General Secretary

S/-
Treasure

Sd/
For Rajan Sharma & Co.,
Chartered Accountant

(Rajan Kumar Sharma)
Prop.

Place: New Delhi
Dated: 18.10.2003

OFFICE BEARERS OF THE INDIAN ARCHAEOLOGICAL SOCIETY

Patrons
Prof. B.B. Lal
F-7, Hauz Khas Enclave
New Delhi

Chairman
Dr. S.P. Gupta
B-17, Qutab Institutional Area
New Delhi 110016

Vice Chairman
Shri K.M. Srivastava
142, Venus Apartments
Inder Enclave, Rohtak Road
New Delhi - 110087

General Secretary
Shri K.N. Dikshit
B-322, Sarita Vihar
New Delhi 110044

Hon. Tresurer
Shri K.S. Ramachandran
C-139, Sarita Vihar
New Delhi 110044

Secretaries
Prof. V.N. Misra
Former Director
Deccan College, Pune

Shri R.S. Bisht
Director
Archaeological Survey of India
New Delhi

Dr. R.C. Aggrwal
Director
Archaeoloical Survey of India
New Delhi

Dr. R.D. Chaudhary
Director General
National Museum, New Delhi

Members of the Executive Committee
Prof. Vibha Tripathi
Banaras Hindu University
Varanasi

Prof. V.D. Mishra,
Allahabad University
Allahabad

Prof. V.H. Sonawane
M.S. University Baroda
Vadodra

Prof. K.V. Raman
Madras University
Chennai

Dr. V.S. Shinde
Deccan College
Pune

Shri J.P. Joshi
Fomer Director General
Archaeological Survey of India
New Delhi

Asst. Secretary:
Shri R.P. Sharma
New Dehi

Editor: Monographs/Newsletter
Sh. K.S. Ramachandran
New Delhi

Headquarter:

INDIAN ARCHAEOLOGICAL SOCIETY
B-17, Qutab Institutional Area, New Delhi - 110 016
Tel.: 26523728, 26852635 Tele-Fax:011-26960654
E-mail: ias_newdelhi@yahoo.co.uk
K.N. Dikshit: 26948971
K.S. Ramachandran: 26955209

INDIAN ARCHAEOLOGICAL SOCEITY
BOARD OF MANAGEMENT

Chairman

Dr. S.P. Gupta
Former Director
Allahabad Museum, Allahabad
B-17, Qutab Institutional Area,
New Delhi

Vice-Chairman

Shri K.M. Srivastava
Former Director
Archaeological Survey of India
New Delhi

General Secretary

Shri K.N. Dikshit
Former Joint Director General
Archaeological Survey of India
New Delhi

Treasurer

Shri K.S. Ramachandran
Former Registering Officer
Archaeological Survey of India
New Delhi

Members

Prof. B.B. Lal
Former Director General
Archaeological survey of India
New Delhi

Dr. R.C. Aggarwal
Director
Archaeological Survey of India
New Delhi

Dr. T.P. Verma
Former Reader
Deptt. of A.I.H.C. & Archaeology
Banaras Hidnu University
Varanasi

Prof. K. Paddayya
Joint Director
Deccan College,
Pune

Shiri O.P. Tandon
Former Director
Bharat Kala Bhawan, Varanasi
Media Centre
Gurgaon

Headquarter:

B-17, Qutab Institutional Area, New Delhi - 110016
(O) 26960654, 26562438 Fax:011-26960654
E-mail: ias_newdelhi@yahoo.co.uk
K.N. Dikshit: 26948971
K.S. Ramachandran: 26955209

Bindra, Plate-1. **Lothal:** General view of the dock. Inlet (second stage) is indicated by the seated figure and the spill-way by the standing figure.

Bindra, Plate-2. **Lothal:** Inner vertical face of the western embankment wall of the dock. The rebuilt portion is indicated by the standing figure.

Bindra, Plate-3. **Lothal:** Weep-holes in the flanking wall of the spill-way.

Bindra, Plate-4. **Lothal:** Vertical grooves for sliding the door shutter of the spill-way.

Bindra, Plate-5. **Lothal:** Inlet (first stage) in the northern embankment wall. Note the bowl-like depression in the section beyond the scale.

Bindra, Plate-6. **Lothal:** Anchor-stone in situ near the wall of the dock.

Bindra, Plate-7. **Lothal:** Eastern embankment wall of the dock.

Bindra, Plate-8. **Lothal:** Sill of the second stage inlet with remnants of the southern retaining wall (left-hand corner behind the scale).

Bindra, Plate-9. **Lothal:** The spill-way with horizontal grooves for wooden logs.

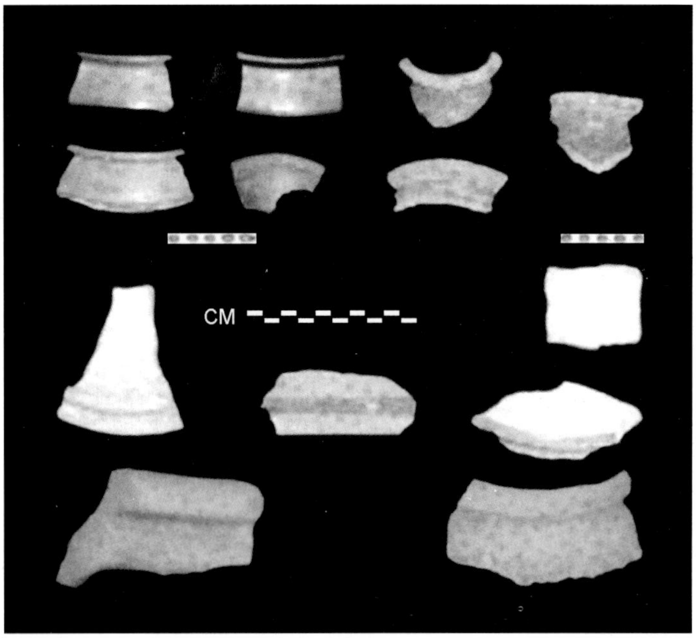

Shinde *et al.***,** Plate-1. **Pune:** Slipped and unslipped Red ware sherds.

Shinde *et al.***,** Plate-2. **Pune:** Grey ware.

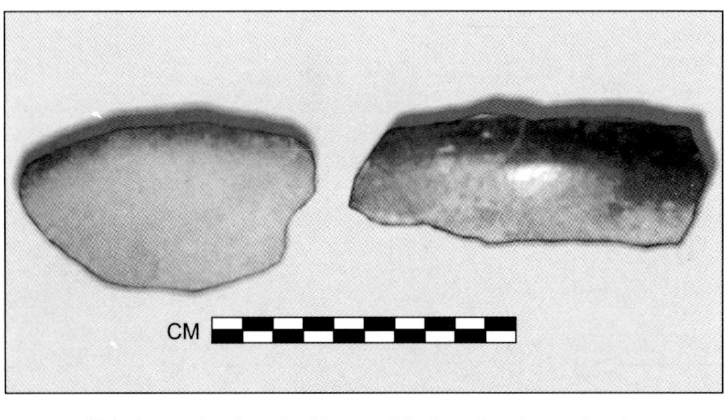

Shinde *et al.***,** Plate-3. **Pune:** Black-and-red ware bowls.

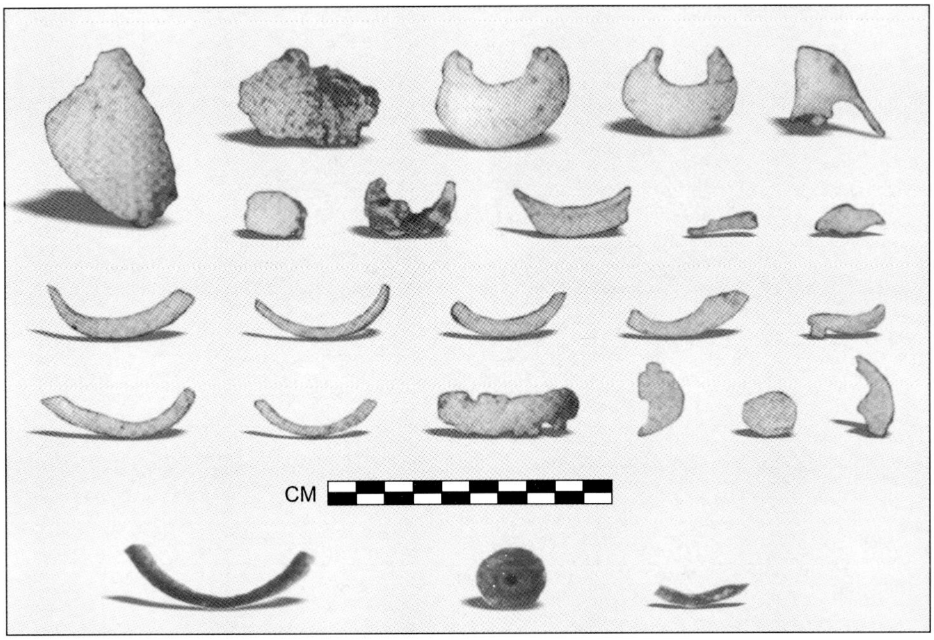

Shinde *et al.*, Plate-4. **Pune:** Shell debitage and objects. Arecanut terracotta bead flanked by glass bangle fragments are seen in the lower portion.

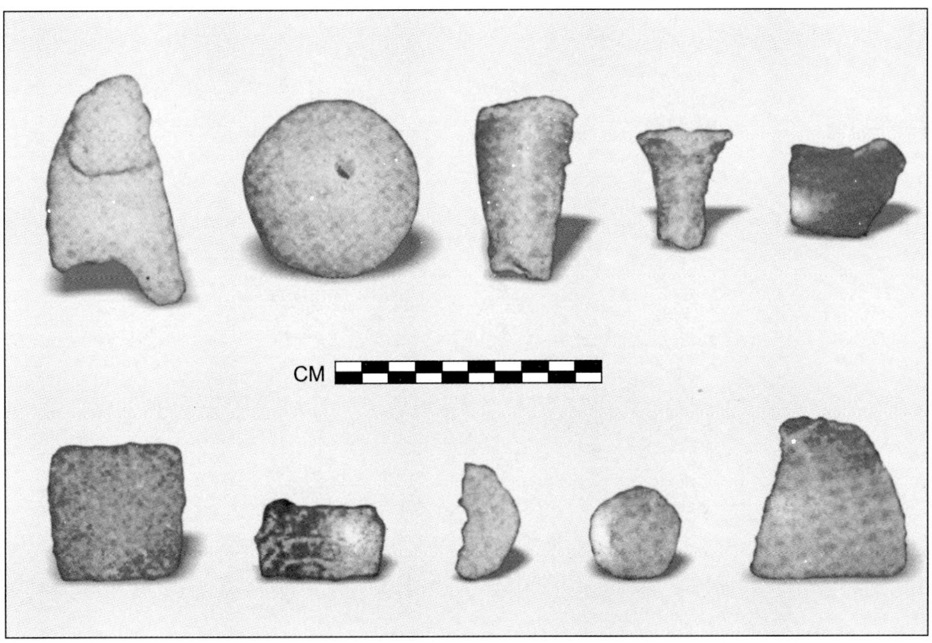

Shinde *et al.*, Plate-5. **Pune:** Terracotta/pottery objects: 1. Animal Figurine; 2. Head scratcher; 3, 4, and 5. Red Polished ware sherds; 6. Skin rubber; 7. Graffiti marks on a Grey ware sherds; 8. Fragment of a perforated disk; 9. A disk (Hopscotch?); 10. Brahmi letter Ma. Engraved on a potsherd.

Shinde *et al.***,** Plate-6. **Pune:** Rotary Quern.

Shinde *et al.***,** Plate-7. **Pune:** Vishnu image.

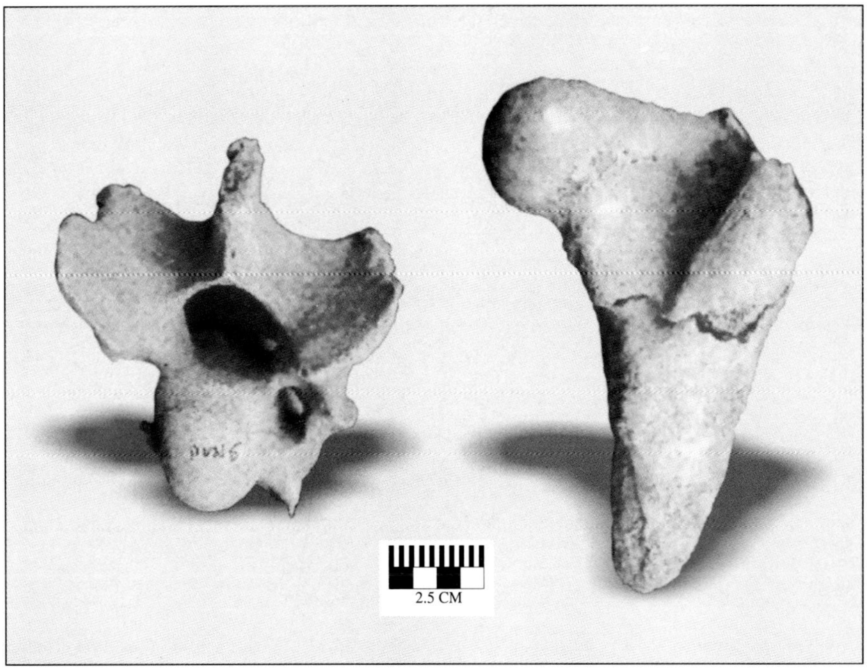

Shinde *et al.*, Plate-8. **Pune:** Cervical vertebra (left) and femur (right) of Bos indicus.

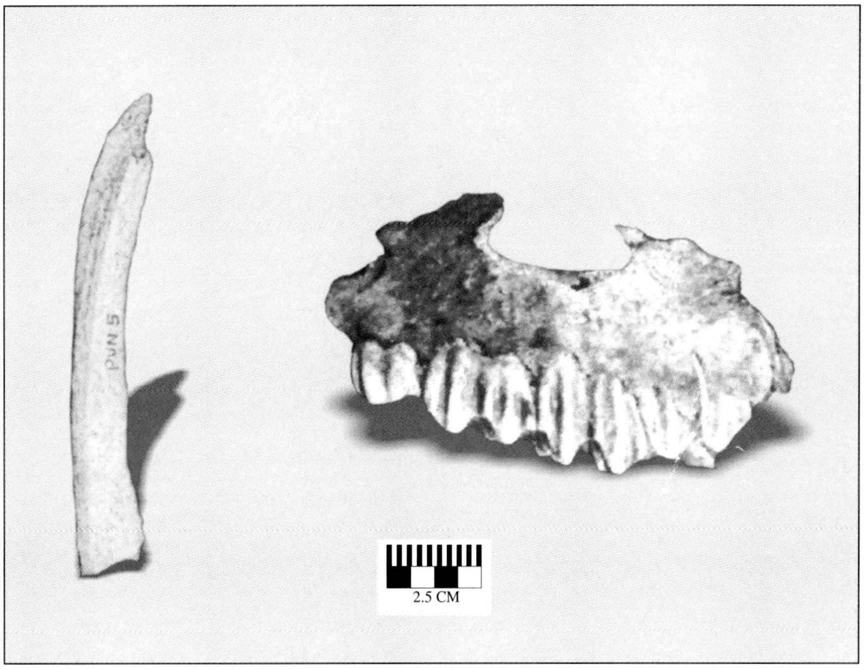

Shinde *et al.*, Plate-9. **Pune:** Bone tool made on rib of Bos indicus (left) and maxilla of Boselaphus tragocamelus (right).

Kanungo, Plate-1. **Karakambadi:** The site of Karakambadi.

Kanungo, Plate-2. **Karakambadi:** Trench 2 before opening.

Kanungo, Plate-3. **Karakambadi:** Alignment of broken crucibles in Trench 2.

Kanungo, Plate-4. **Karakambadi:** Broken crucible pieces and glass slags from Trench 2.

Kanungo, Plate-5. **Karakambadi:** Trench 2 with a test pit in one corner.

Kanungo, Plate-7. **Karakambadi:** Scraping at Trench 3.

Kanungo, Plate-6. **Karakambadi:** In Situ crucibles.

Kanungo, Plate-8. **Karakambadi:** Broken crucibles, frit and tuyere.

Kanungo, Plate-9. **Karakambadi:** In-situ frit.

Kanungo, Plate-10. **Karakambadi:** Potsherds found in the trenches.

Kanungo, Plate-11. **Karakambadi:** Potsherd with rims found in the trenches. Five broken crucible pieces and glass slags from Trench 2.

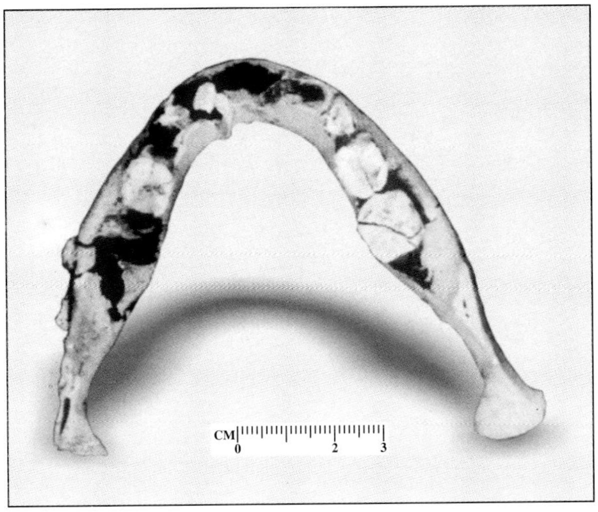

Mushrif *et al.*, Plate-1. **Kudatini:** Mandible.

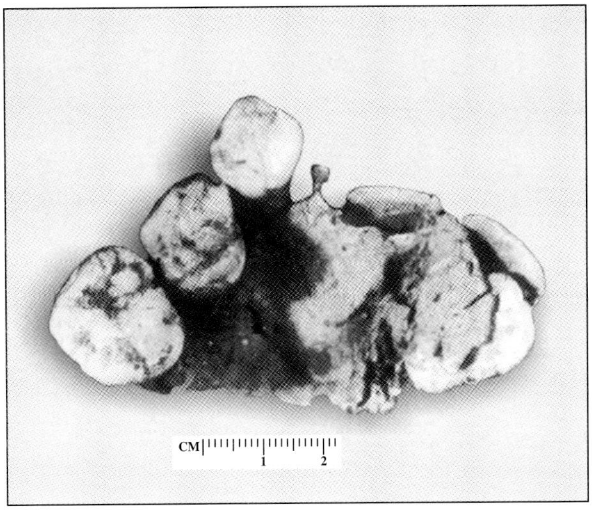

Mushrif *et al.*, Plate-2. **Kudatini:** Maxilla.

Mushrif *et al.*, Plate-3. **Kudatini:** Maxillary left canine.

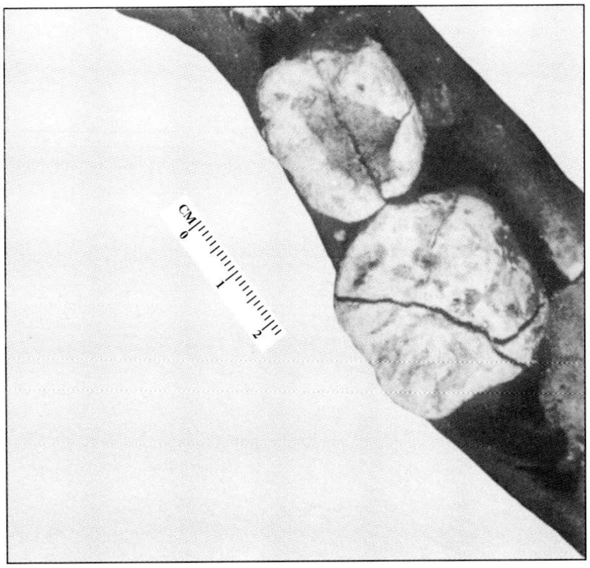

Mushrif *et al.*, Plate-4. **Kudatini:** Mandibular molars.

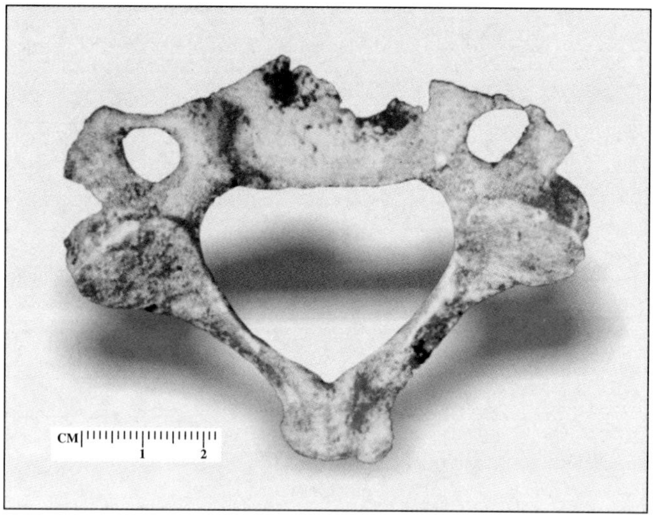

Mushrif *et al.*, Plate-5. **Kudatini:** Third Cervical vertebra: superior view.

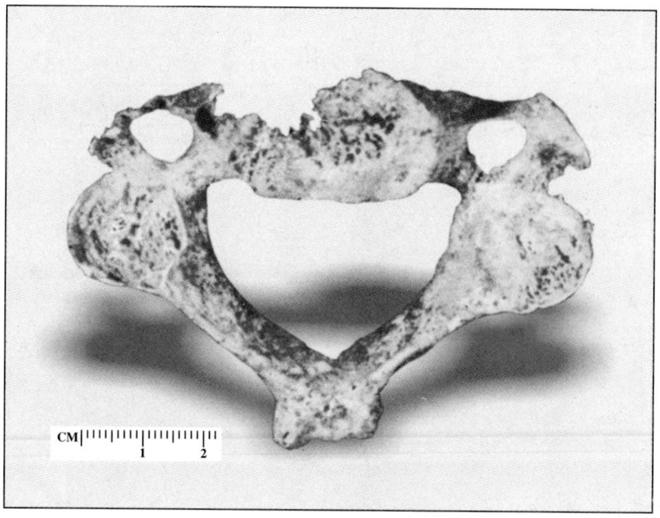

Mushrif *et al.*, Plate-6. **Kudatini:** Third Cervical vertebra: inferior view.

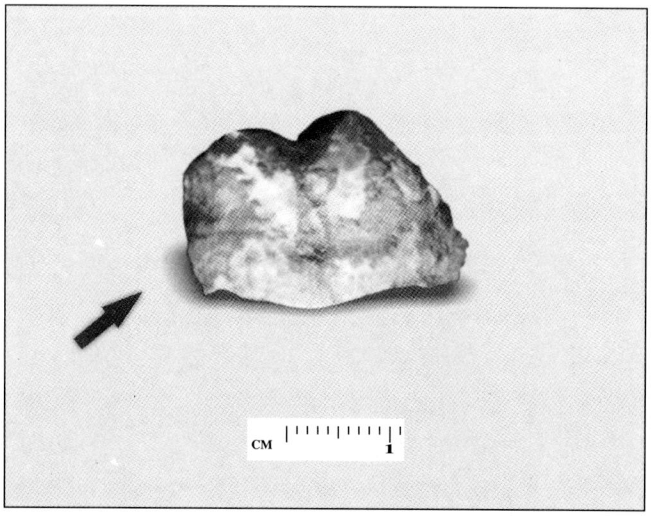

Mushrif *et al.*, Plate-7. **Kudatini:** Enamel hypoplasia: maxillary RM2.

Dikshit, Plate-1. **Ayodhya:** View of excavated trench, Janmabhumi site (IAR 1976-77). Recent excavations in 2003 by ASI was conducted on this mound.

‘Prasada’(north)

‘Bhadravalokana’ of mandapa (north).

The ‘kapili’(north)

Dikshit *et al.*, Plate-1. Lakheshvara Temple.

Southeast

Southeast

East view of the collapsed
'Bhadravalokana' of 'mandapa'

The collapsed part of the 'mandapa' 'Bhadravalokana' in the north untouched even after two years of the earthquake *(a fortunate situation for the reconctruction and restoration)*

Dikshit *et al.*, Plate-2. **Kera:** Lakheshvara Temple.

East

West

Northeast

Dikshit *et al.*, Plate-3. **Ghumli:** Navalakha Temple.

Heap of collapsed members of the 'shikhar' and 'mandapa' (from north-above; from northeast-left)

NE part of the 'mandapa'

Dikshit *et al.*, Plate-4. **Ghumli:** Navalakha Temple.

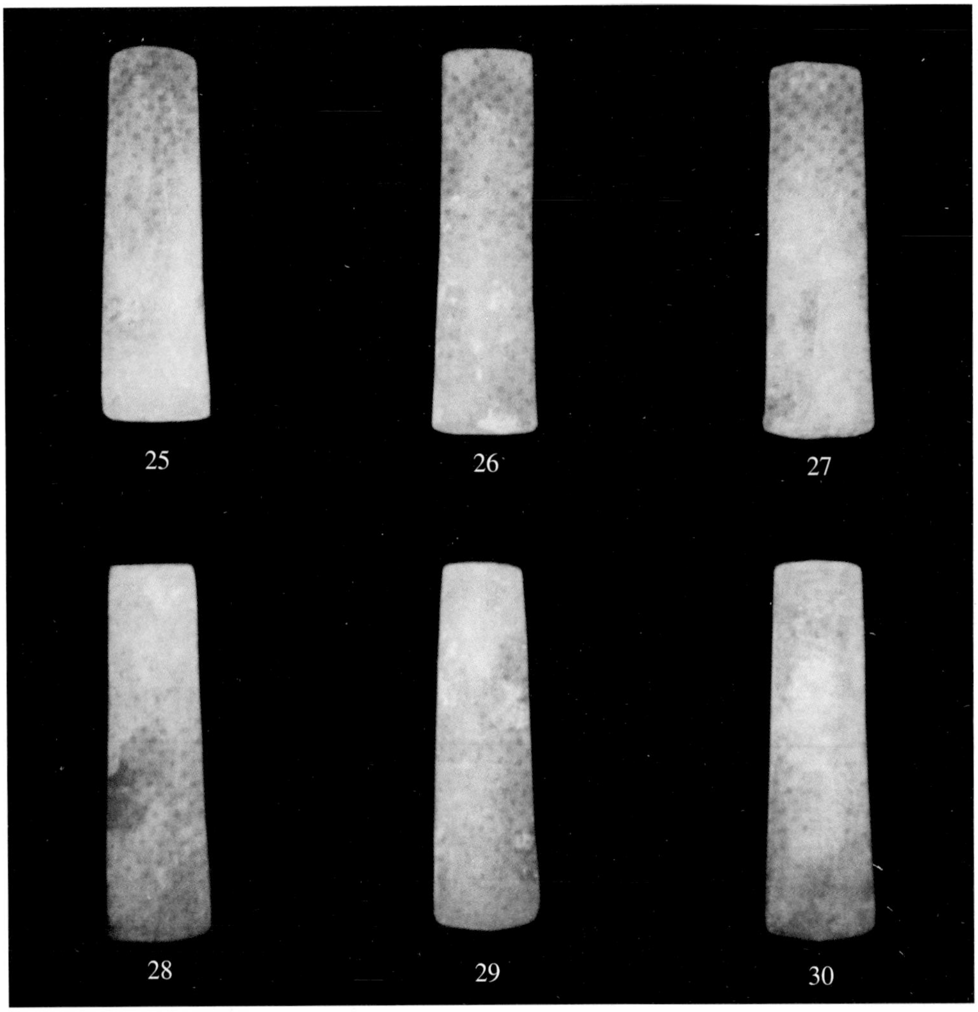

Ambika, Plate-1. **Bhandar:** Copper Celts.

Mane, Plate-1. **Nagargota:** Rock painting of cattle.

Mane, Plate-2. **Nagargota:** Rock painting of a human figurine riding a horse.

DISTRICT JIND, HARYANA
SITES OF EARLY INDUS-SARASWATI CIVILIZATION

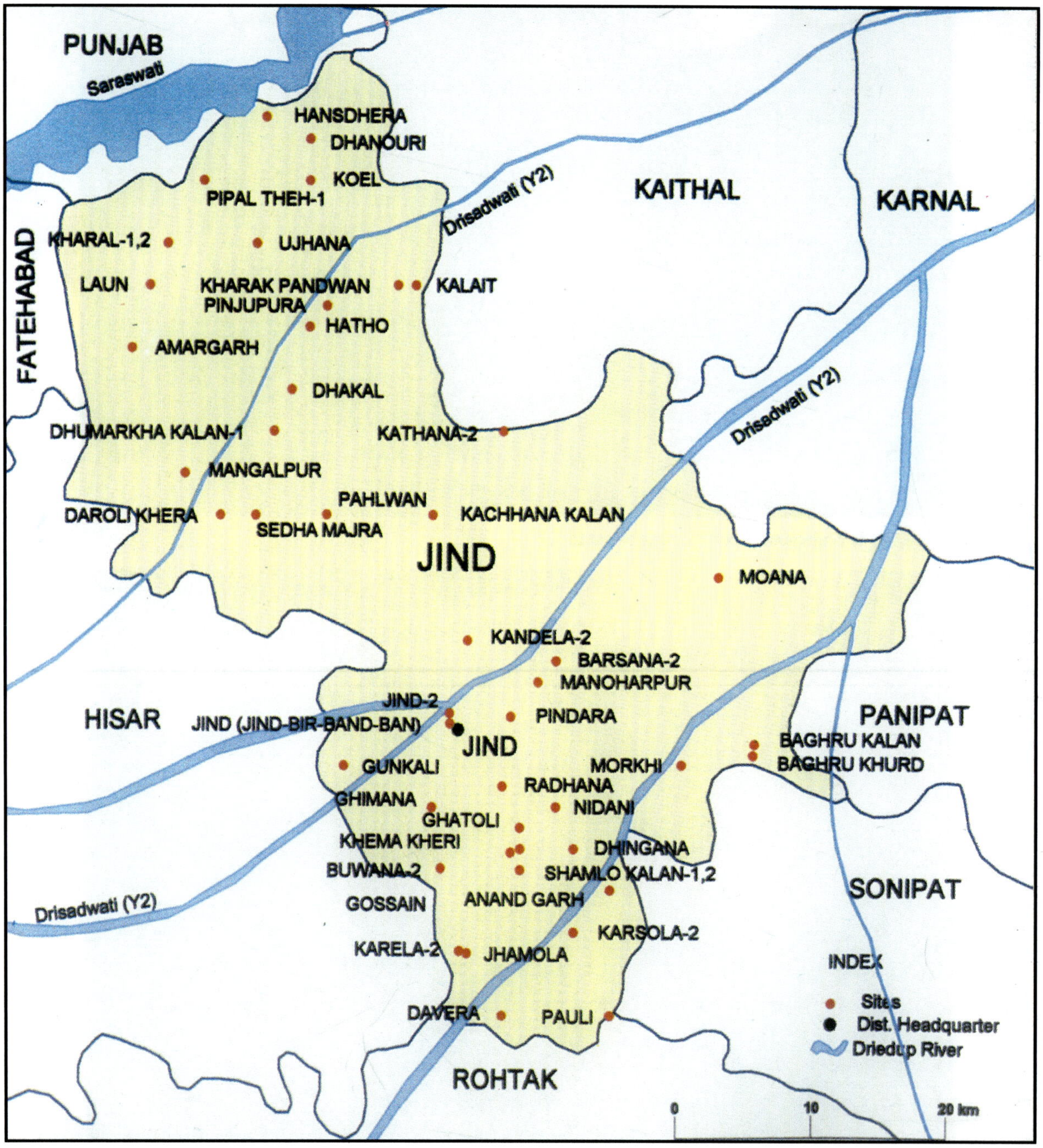

INDIAN ARCHAEOLOGICAL SOCIETY, NEW DELHI 2003

Gupta, Plate-1. Atlas of Indus Saraswati.

DISTRICT BAHAWALPUR, PUNJAB (Pakistan)
SITES OF THE MATURE INDUS-SARASWATI CIVILIZATION

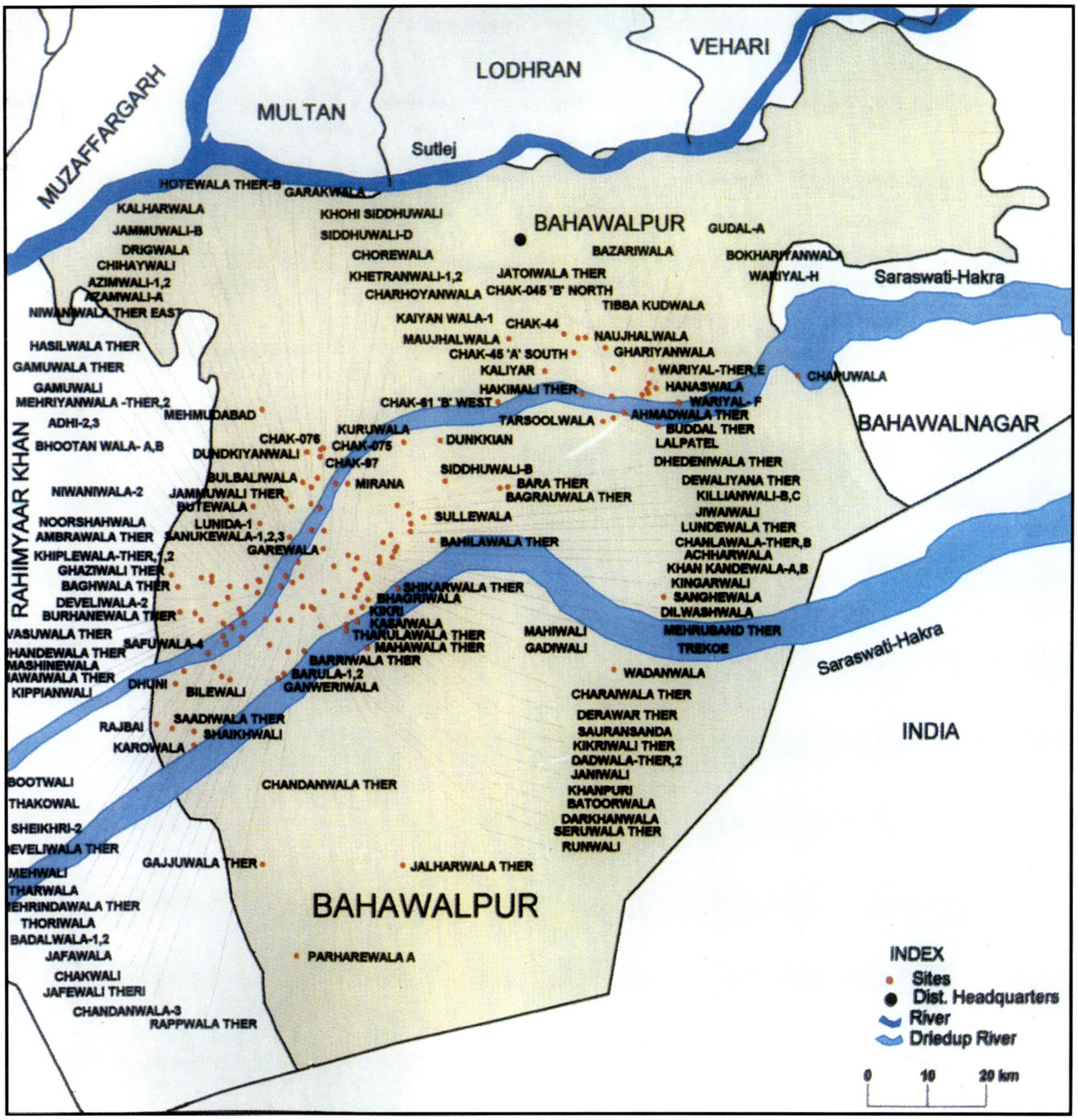

INDIAN ARCHAEOLOGICAL SOCIETY, NEW DELHI 2003

Gupta, Plate-2. Atlas of Indus Saraswati.

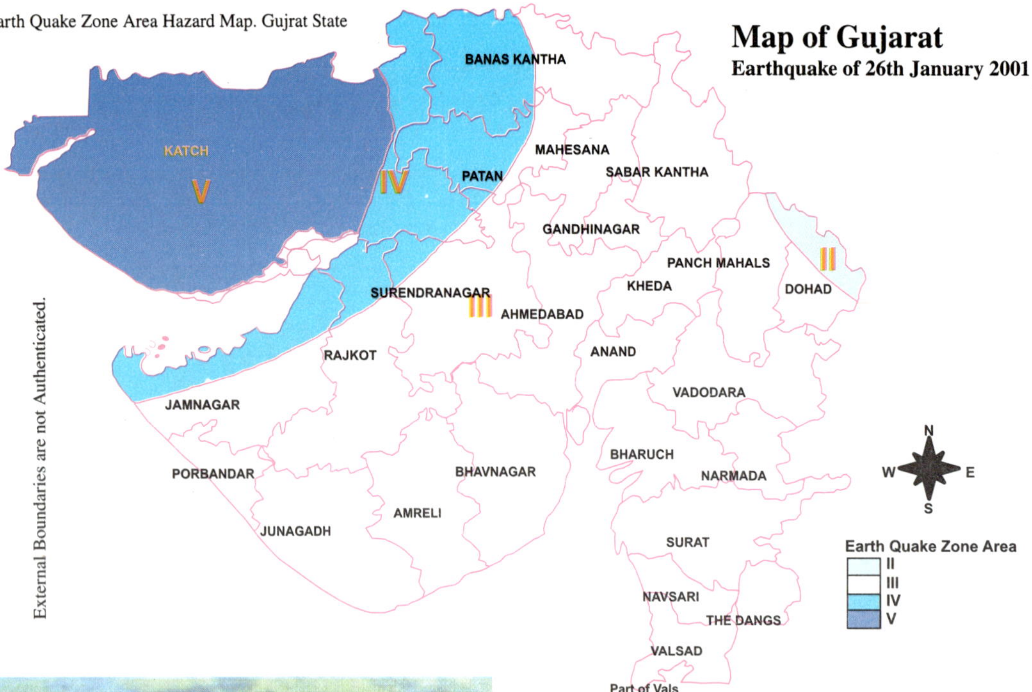

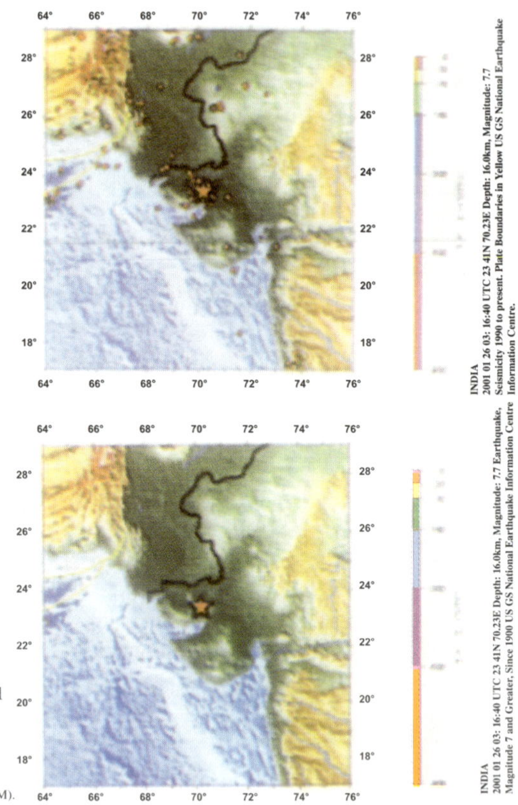

List of major earthquakes affecting the region of Kutch in recent past.

Year	1819	1820	1820	1828	1856	1882	1882	1903	1940	1956	1962	2001
Month	June	Jan.	Nov.	July	Nov.	June	June	Jan.	Oct.	July	March	Jan.
Magnitude	8.3	3.7	3.7	4.3	—	—	—	6.0	6.0	7.0	—	7.9

Source : Joint Report of the Indian Institute of Technology (IIT) Bombay and the Earthquake Disaster Mitigation Research Institute (EDM).

Dikshit, Plate-1. Earthquake affected Monuments of Gujarat.